TAKING SIDES

Clashing Views on Controversial

Issues in Family and Personal Relationships

FIFTH EDITION

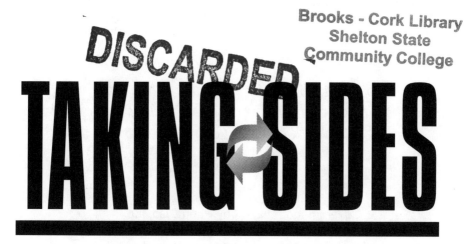

DISCARDED

TAKING SIDES

Clashing Views on Controversial

Issues in Family and Personal Relationships

FIFTH EDITION

Selected, Edited, and with Introductions by

Elizabeth Schroeder, MSW

McGraw-Hill/Dushkin
A Division of The McGraw-Hill Companies

To A. M. Towe, for unfailing love and support—and the constant reassurance that somehow the work always gets done

Photo Acknowledgment
Cover image: © 2003 by PhotoDisc, Inc.

Cover Art Acknowledgment
Charles Vitelli

Copyright © 2003 by McGraw-Hill/Dushkin,
A Division of The McGraw-Hill Companies, Inc., Guilford, Connecticut 06437

Copyright law prohibits the reproduction, storage, or transmission in any form by any means of any portion of this publication without the express written permission of McGraw-Hill/Dushkin and of the copyright holder (if different) of the part of the publication to be reproduced. The Guidelines for Classroom Copying endorsed by Congress explicitly state that unauthorized copying may not be used to create, to replace, or to substitute for anthologies, compilations, or collective works.

Taking Sides ® is a registered trademark of McGraw-Hill/Dushkin

Manufactured in the United States of America

Fifth Edition

123456789BAHBAH6543

Library of Congress Cataloging-in-Publication Data
Main entry under title:
Taking sides: clashing views on controversial issues in family and personal relationships/selected, edited, and with introductions by Elizabeth Schroeder, MSW.—5th ed.
Includes bibliographical references and index.
1. Family—United States. 2. Interpersonal relationships. I. Schroeder, Elizabeth, *comp.*
306.85'973
0-07-243568-2
ISSN: 96-85806

Printed on Recycled Paper

Preface

As human beings, we relate to each other on a range of levels. We are acquaintances and friends, colleagues and supervisors—partners, spouses, and family members. The issues that affect us in our lives, regardless of the roles we are playing at any given time, are as diverse as they are complex. These are issues that affect us on the personal level, as well as on the political and public policy levels. We receive messages from peers, family members, religious institutions, and the media about how we should and can act within the contexts of our family and interpersonal relationships, and we experience very specific repercussions for going with or against these messages.

Taking Sides: Clashing Views on Controversial Issues in Family and Personal Relationships will push you to look at a variety of relationships and how human beings interact in new and different ways. You will be asked to think about the extent to which parents have the right to make decisions for their children. You will be pressed to reflect on whether you think that lesbian, gay, and bisexual individuals have the right to marry or adopt children. You will be forced to examine your beliefs on the effects that various public policies have on families and individuals seeking to start families, and on the extent to which the government has the right to legislate parental and caregiver decision making.

Plan of the book This entirely new, fifth edition of *Taking Sides: Clashing Views on Controversial Issues in Family and Personal Relationships* contains 38 dynamic points of view separated into 19 challenging, often contentious questions, none of which have been debated within the pages of *Taking Sides: Clashing Views on Controversial Issues in Family and Personal Relationships* before. Each issue features an *introduction*, which provides the context in which each debate is waged. At the end of each issue is a *postscript*, designed to encourage ongoing thought and discussion about the topic. The suggested readings offer additional resources that you can consult for further information about each issue, and the *On the Internet* pages list relevant Web site addresses (URLs) that can continue to enhance your knowledge and challenge your values and beliefs on any and all of these topics.

A word to the instructor An *Instructor's Manual With Test Questions* (multiple-choice and essay) is available through the publisher for the instructor using Taking Sides in the classroom. A general guidebook, called *Using Taking Sides in the Classroom*, which discusses methods and techniques for integrating the pro-con approach into any classroom setting, is also available. An online version of *Using Taking Sides in the Classroom* and a correspondence service for Taking Sides adopters can be found at http://www.dushkin.com/usingts/.

Taking Sides: Clashing Views on Controversial Issues in Family and Personal Relationships is only one of many titles in the Taking Sides series. If you are interested in seeing the table of contents for any of the other titles, please visit the Taking Sides Web site at `http://www.dushkin.com/takingsides/`.

Acknowledgments   The first individuals I need to thank are Ted Knight and Juliana Gribbins from McGraw-Hill/Dushkin. Ted's optimism from day one and desire to push the proverbial envelope with the suggested topics were most welcome. Julie's professionalism, encouragement, and insightful feedback were beyond helpful. Their guidance and unfailing collegiality were invaluable to this entire process.

I also wish to thank:

William J. Taverner, director of education for Planned Parenthood of Greater Northern New Jersey, for being such a generous colleague. I would not have had the pleasure of working on this resource had it not been for Bill.

Giokazta Molina and Jeremy Schneider, for their excellent research assistance.

The Advanced Sexuality Educators and Trainers listserv, through which countless ideas are generated and exchanged. This listserv includes many of the leaders in the sexuality field, who are always willing to share their ideas and resources.

The authors of the articles listed in this book, some with whom I had the pleasure of communicating via e-mail throughout this process. Their writings enable us to discuss and debate vital issues relating to our lives and our entire society.

Joanna Rybak for her invaluable work on the instructor's manual.

As you read, do your best to remain open to different points of view. Avoid reading only the side with which you agree; be sure to review carefully the side with which you disagree. Understanding the viewpoint of a person with whom you disagree can serve to strengthen your own argument—and then again, it may just change your mind.

Elizabeth Schroeder, MSW

Contents In Brief

Contents

Den A. Trumbull and S. DuBose Ravenel, both pediatricians in private
practice, contend that spanking can serve as a valuable disciplinary
method and play a significant role in a child's development. They maintain
that well-planned-out spankings, those that the child is told about in advance and that are delivered without anger, can be useful, effective, and
appropriate deterrents to inappropriate behavior. Irwin A. Hyman, director
of the National Center for Study of Corporal Punishment and Alternatives,
argues that there is never any reason to hit a child. Focusing on the emotional effects of spanking, he asserts that spanking is much more likely
to teach children to tolerate and perpetuate violence than it is to correct
disobedience.

Greg D. Erken, executive director for Of the People, a nonprofit, parental-
rights organization, challenges the concept that anyone other than a
parent knows what is best for children. As the First Amendment exemplifies the principles on which Americans base discussions and debates
around free speech, he maintains that the parental-rights amendment
should do the same for parents' rights. Jack C. Westman, professor
of psychiatry at the University of Wisconsin–Madison, asserts that a
parental-rights amendment sets the government and parents up as enemies. He argues that many government policies, such as child neglect,
labor, and mandatory education laws, have served children and families
well. He contends that the amendment is unnecessary.

Patrick Fagan, a resident scholar in family culture at the Heritage Foundation, cites the increased stress, lower production, and higher social risks that follow children who are born to single-parent families. These negative factors, he asserts, lead to other social ills later in life, such as unhealthy behaviors for managing stress and relationships that are based more on sexual attraction than on emotional connection and therefore are unlikely to last. He acknowledges the perseverance of many single-parent households but argues that all things being equal, "the intact married family beats the single-parent family in every other measurable dimension." Stephanie Coontz, a family historian at The Evergreen State College in Olympia, Washington, counters that identifying a particular family type as the source of certain social ills is not only inaccurate but can also lead to ineffective public policies. The challenges facing many people, such as poverty, school delinquency, and work benefits, she contends are there whether a person is single or married. Coontz maintains that encouraging marriage as a panacea to these social ills is not the answer.

Issue 4.   Can We Raise "Gender-Neutral" Children?   42

Psychologist Sandra Lipsitz Bem uses her own children as examples that raising gender-neutral children is not only possible but also can result in positive self-esteem. She states that by discussing differences in genders without attaching a value to these differences, children who are raised with gender-neutral expectations will have a more open, positive view of the world in general. Sociologists Denise A. Segura and Jennifer L. Pierce contend that gender and gender role expectations are tied very closely to familial and cultural expectations. Referring to the Chicana/o culture of Mexico, they demonstrate that gender-specific role fulfillment is vital to certain cultures, ensuring the survival of important cultural traditions.

Issue 5.   Does Divorce Create Long-Term Negative Effects for Children?   66

Karl Zinsmeister, editor in chief of *The American Enterprise*, points to research and surveys showing that not only is divorce much more harmful to children but also that children themselves say they would rather remain in a household where parents argue and fight than to have their parents break up. Educators David Gately and Andrew I. Schwebel highlight literature that demonstrates how going through a divorce can actually strengthen a child, helping to build her or his self-efficacy and level of self-esteem.

Barbara Loe Fisher, cofounder and president of the National Vaccine Information Center, argues that the risks involved with vaccinating children need to be weighed by their parents. She asserts that in some states government policies relating to vaccinations for children discount the parents' rights to choose what is best for their children and that parents should be allowed to decide whether or not to have their children vaccinated. Steven P. Shelov, chairman of the Department of Pediatrics at the Maimonides Medical Center in New York City, points to the vast number of diseases, disorders, and deaths that are preventable thanks to vaccines early in life. He maintains that parents should trust in science and the extensive research that has been done on these vaccines and make every effort to ensure that their children are vaccinated.

The Alexander Graham Bell Association for the Deaf and Hard of Hearing, an international membership organization and resource center on hearing loss and spoken language, maintains that a cochlear device can lead to greater hearing and speech capability throughout a person's life. The National Association of the Deaf, the oldest and largest constituency organization focusing on accessibility and civil rights of Americans who are deaf or hard of hearing, argues that the cochlear implant treats deafness as a disability and ignores the historical and cultural aspects of deaf life.

Amicur Farkas, B. Chertin, and Irith Hadas-Halpren, faculty of the Ben-Gurion University in Jerusalem, Israel, see ambiguous genitalia as a true emergency. They assert that feminizing surgery should be done on an infant with congenital adrenal hyperplasia to ensure that as an adult woman she will have sexual functioning and be able to give birth. Alice Domurat Dreger, assistant professor in the Lyman Briggs School at Michigan State University, explores the ethics in recommending to parents that they should have their children's genitals altered surgically. With so little education available about the true meaning and options relating to children born with ambiguous genitalia, she wonders if any parents who decide that their child should have the surgery are truly giving informed consent.

PART 3   CHILDREN'S RIGHTS   147

The United States Fund for UNICEF, a United Nations agency working for the protection of children's rights, points to the successes that governments around the world have had in using the Convention on the Rights of the Child to promote children's rights and improve children's lives in general. UNICEF contends that the Convention reinforces parental rights and promotes values and norms with which no one could take issue, such as freedom from discrimination, access to adequate health care, and protection from physical harm and abduction. Catherina Hurlburt, a writer for Concerned Women for America (CWFA), maintains that the Convention on the Rights of the Child gives government more power over children's rights than parents would have. In giving children the right to "express their views freely in all matters," the Convention would, she argues, usurp parental authority and give children too much independence.

Teresa Stanton Collett, professor at South Texas College of Law, testifies in front of the U.S. House of Representatives in support of the federal Child Custody Protection Act. She advocates parental involvement in a minor's pregnancy, regardless of the girl's intention to carry or terminate the pregnancy. Parental involvement, Collett maintains, is not punitive; rather, it offers the girl herself additional protection against injury and sexual assault. Minors tend to have less access to information and education than adults; without this information and education, they are not able to provide truly "informed" consent, concludes Collett. Planned Parenthood Federation of America, Inc., the oldest and largest reproductive health organization in the United States, argues that parental notification and consent laws keep girls from exercising their legal right to access abortion. Notifying parents of their daughter's intent to terminate a pregnancy puts many girls at risk for severe punishment, expulsion from the home, or even physical violence. Planned Parenthood contends that, just as minors have the power to give their consent for other surgical procedures, they should be able to give their own consent to terminate a pregnancy.

PART 4   LESBIAN AND GAY FAMILIES   181

Issue 11.   Should Same-Sex Couples Be Allowed to Marry Legally?   182

The Lambda Legal Defense and Education Fund, a national civil rights organization for lesbian, gay, bisexual, and transgender individuals, as well as people living with HIV or AIDS, supports the right of two individuals to marry legally, regardless of the genders of the two people involved. The organization states that same-sex couples deserve the same social, legal, and financial benefits that heterosexual couples have. Princeton University professor Robert P. George asserts that marriage has historically been, and ever should be, between a man and a woman. He argues that recognizing a same-sex union as a legal marriage would destroy the institution of marriage as it has always been known, taking with it the moral values supporting marriage. A constitutional amendment is, in George's opinion, the only sure way of protecting the institution of heterosexual marriage.

Issue 12.   Should Lesbian and Gay Couples Be Allowed to Adopt?   194

The American Civil Liberties Union (ACLU), an organization that works to preserve the individual rights and liberties of all Americans, points to a growing area of scientific literature that maintains that children who are raised by one or two lesbian or gay parents are just as well off as children who are raised by heterosexual parents. Findings demonstrate, they say, that parents' sexual orientation has no bearing on their ability to raise a child, or on a child's own sexual orientation or gender identity—nor does it affect children's emotional development or educational abilities. Timothy J. Dailey, senior writer/analyst for cultural studies for the Family Research Council, points to studies showing that children do much better in family settings that include both a mother and a father and that the sexual behaviors same-sex parents engage in make them, by definition, inappropriate role models for children. He maintains that the purpose of a marriage is to create children biologically and that since a gay or lesbian couple cannot do this without outside assistance, they do not make suitable parents.

PART 5   MISCELLANEOUS RELATIONSHIP ISSUES   211

Issue 13.   Should People Not Cohabit Before Getting Married?   212

David Popenoe and Barbara Dafoe Whitehead, codirectors of the National Marriage Project, assert that living together before marriage can contribute to a higher chance of divorce down the line, leads to less satisfying relationships, and is contributing to a deterioration in society's regard for the institution of marriage. Dorian Solot and Marshall Miller, cofounders of the Alternatives to Marriage Project, maintain that our society overemphasizes marriage, discriminating against people who wish to commit to another person and remain unmarried.

Issue 14.   Do Women and Men Communicate Differently?   238

Philip Yancey, editor at large of *Christianity Today,* asserts that communication styles are different between men and women. He argues that in heterosexual relationships, partners are likely to fulfill stereotypical expectations of how men and women are supposed to communicate due to their upbringing and culture. Mary Crawford, director of the Women's Studies Program at the University of Connecticut, also states that communication styles are learned. However, she discusses the idea that young people are aware of these lessons and that fulfilling the expected communication stereotypes within heterosexual couples can lead to unsatisfying relationships, for women in particular.

PART 6   PUBLIC POLICY ISSUES   257

Issue 15.   Should Prostitution Be Legal?   258

YES: **James Bovard,** from "Safeguard Public Health: Legalize Contractual Sex," *Insight on the News* (February 27, 1995)   *260*

NO: **Anastasia Volkonsky,** from "Legalizing the 'Profession' Would Sanction the Abuse," *Insight on the News* (February 27, 1995)   *264*

Author James Bovard writes about the potential benefits of legalizing prostitution, such as increased human rights protections and health precautions. He argues that legalizing prostitution would decriminalize it, thereby reducing the criminal practices of rape and other abuses. Author and researcher Anastasia Volkonsky writes that prostitution itself is a human rights violation for every person who sells her or his body and sexual behaviors for money. She does not believe that legalization will reduce the incidences of abuse or other illegal activities, nor will it guarantee that either prostitute or customer would comply with laws pertaining to commercial sex work.

Issue 16.   Is Court-Ordered Child Support Doing More Harm Than Good?   270

YES: **Stephen Baskerville,** from "This Engine of the Divorce Industry Is Destroying Families and the Constitution," *Insight on the News* (August 2, 1999)   *272*

NO: **Geraldine Jensen,** from "Child Support Fights Poverty for Millions of Kids and Helps Families Get Off Welfare," *Insight on the News* (August 2, 1999)   *276*

Stephen Baskerville, teacher and spokesperson for Men, Fathers, and Children International, contends that the current state of the divorce "industry" discriminates against fathers, punishing those who have done nothing wrong along with those who have abused their children or broken other laws. He argues that the system relating to child support enforcement is corrupt and that it is fueled by individuals who make money by the fees they charge for their services. Geraldine Jensen, president of the Association for Children for Enforcement of Support, maintains that without court-ordered child support, children and families would remain dependent on welfare payments. She asserts that fathers deserve support as well but that collection of child support belongs with the federal government through the IRS to avoid overburdening child welfare agencies and the judicial system.

ethnicity, or culture but that social service agencies are actively inhibiting the process from taking place. Institutional biases, she argues, as well as personal preconceptions by some social service professionals about race, ethnicity, culture, and parenting issues, impede parents of color from adopting the children they seek.

Introduction

The Different Voices of Debate

Elizabeth Schroeder, MSW

The Taking Sides series asks readers to evaluate opposing viewpoints on specific topics. In some settings, readers will be asked to respond either verbally or in writing to a particular viewpoint. In other settings, readers will simply evaluate an issue on their own, examining their own values and beliefs as they pertain to each topic. Regardless of how you will be using this volume, it is important to reflect on the ways in which we can express our opinions effectively. It is also important to be aware of how language is used to express these views, at times clearly revealing the politics behind an argument and at other times cleverly obscuring the political agenda. Finally, it is vital to reflect on how differences of opinion affect our lives—in particular, when these differences involve issues relating to family and personal relationships.

Negotiation Versus Debate: Finding a Place on the Continuum

The most successful negotiations are between people of opposing viewpoints who are able to be flexible, compromising to the extent that they believe they can while still remaining true to the goals of the particular negotiation process. We see this in the workplace when an employee is requesting a higher salary. We see this in educational settings when a student disagrees with an instructor's assessment of a paper or project. We see this globally in the international peace process. A supervisor may say, "I can't give you a 10 percent raise, but I can give you 5 percent." An instructor may not be able to raise a student's grade, but may be willing to offer the student an extra-credit assignment. A leader of one country may not be able to offer as much land to the leader of another country, but may be able to offer an increase in import/export relations. Both sides in any negotiation know how much power it has to leverage. If both sides have done their homework, they know how much the other has to leverage, as well.

Progress cannot be made, and a conclusion cannot be reached, without both sides giving in at least a little. When either side interprets "a little" to be "too much," the tendency is to shut down—to retreat to a less flexible vantage point in order to protect whatever advances may have already been made. In addition, as in a poker game, there is often an amount of forcing one's hand that goes on from either side. The same employee may say that she has a job offer from another company that can pay the 10 percent increase, thereby forcing her current employer to decide whether to meet her demands. A student may have a comparable assignment written by a classmate that received a higher grade, thereby revealing instructor bias against the student. A leader of one country can issue an ultimatum to a leader of another country. All of these are examples of negotiations.

A debate, however, is quite different. The most successful debates are between people who have diametrically opposing views on a given subject. An absolutist view, with no room for questioning one's tenets or beliefs, may be judged as inflexible in social circles, yet is quite effective when one is involved in a debate. Political candidates, for example, emphasize this quite well during a campaign. A candidate who is clear and consistent in her viewpoints will be likely to be seen as a clear and consistent policymaker. A candidate who changes his mind on one or more issues is often accused of "waffling." As a society we want to hear that another person has made up her or his mind and intends to stay true to her or his word. Otherwise, we do not feel that we can trust that person.

It can be helpful to think of how people express their views in terms of a continuum. At one end of this continuum are staunchly conservative views, at the other are steadfast liberal views. In the center are what can be considered to be moderate views. It is important to note a few things about this continuum concept. First, there are many lines between liberal and moderate, and there are many between moderate and conservative. This means, for example, that not all people who identify themselves as liberal agree with everything that might be outlined in a liberal agenda. Second, how we label our own views may be different from how others label us. It is important to note the difference between a person's views and a person's identity. A person may identify with a particular political ideology or party, yet hold views that may not match those of that ideology or party. For example, a person can have moderate views about social policies, liberal views about government involvement, and conservative views about financial issues. Third, everything is relative. One person may be seen as moderate until someone more conservative comes along. The first person may then be seen as liberal rather than moderate. Finally, expressing views from a particular ideology can have both positive and negative consequences, depending on the audience in front of which one airs these views.

Desire and Reality: The "Should Be" Versus the "Is"

In debate, there is an inherent concept about which we are often not even aware —the "should be" versus the "is." Simply put, the "should be" is what we would like the outcome to be in a particular situation. The "is" refers to what the current state of that situation truly is.

We express our views in terms of what we think is, or would be, best. When this reflects the reality of a given situation, it is thought to be congruent with the "is"—or what is actually happening. However, "congruent" is not synonymous with "right." For example, if a person were to say, "I think that only men should be president of the United States," his opinion would be congruent with the current reality. A viewpoint can often carry additional weight because the opposing viewpoint, that a woman should be president, has never happened and may not happen for some time. As a result, the "underdog" opinion is often seen as less valid or lacking in strength. Do not fall into this trap! Compelling arguments that are based in sound logic can gain widespread support and can have the power to change society. A little over 80 years ago women could not vote. Forty years ago an interracial couple would never have considered holding hands in public. Thirty years ago (and for some, still today) a same-sex couple risked losing family, friends, and their lives by publicly sharing their relationship status with others. People arguing for the "should be" overthrew the people supporting the "is"—much to some people's delight, and to others' chagrin.

Basically, the "is" should not trump the "should be"—nor should it trump the "was." You may have heard someone argue a point, explaining that if something "has always been this way," it should not change. Many of us have had the experience of parents or grandparents beginning a statement with, "In my day, we . . ." It is tempting to discount these statements as outdated or otherwise inapplicable—yet it is important to remember that our values and beliefs are based very strongly and solidly in how we were raised. Our "was," as it were.

An example of the whole "should be" versus "is" debate centers around abstinence-only sexuality education and comprehensive sexuality education. Each side of the argument has a vehement "should be" that must be measured against the common "is" of our society. Consider the "should be" beliefs and expectations within each viewpoint as expressed in Table 1.

Table 1

Comprehensive Sexuality Education	Abstinence-Only Sexuality Education
• Young people should have access to age-appropriate information about sexuality in order to make well-informed decisions.	• Information about sexuality should focus exclusively on postponing sexual behaviors until a person is married.
• Young people should postpone sex until they are older, but information about contraception should be provided in case they do not.	• Providing information about contraception is the same thing as telling young people that it is okay to have sex.
• Sexual information should include information on a range of behaviors, experiences, and orientations.	• Heterosexuality is the norm and lessons should not be provided that have information on lesbian, gay, and bisexual individuals.

The interesting thing is, the two sides agree on a number of things:

- Young people should be able to avoid sexually transmitted infections.
- Young people should avoid too-early pregnancy.
- Young people should be able to feel good about themselves, including feeling good about their bodies.
- Young people should be able to say "no" to anything that they do not feel comfortable doing when it comes to sexuality.

Aside from these points, there is much less common ground between the two sides. Each side believes itself to be in the right and the other to be wrong.

Regardless of the viewpoint, here is a sample of the "is" against which both sides need to be measured:

- Approximately three million teenagers contract a new Sexually Transmitted Infection (STI) every year in the United States.
- There are still approximately one million teen pregnancies every year in the United States.
- The average age of first intercourse in the United States is 16.

As you can see, the beliefs of neither side, both those on which they may agree and those on which they may disagree, reflect the true reality of the world today. This introduces a third and vital concept when debating an argument—the "because."

The "because" is the justification for an argument or viewpoint and is at times regardless of the justification for the opponents' views. This is a fascinating aspect of debate. Quite simply, even though a person may have a strong justification, a listener can choose whether or not to believe that person. For example, comprehensive sexuality education supporters have peer-reviewed studies showing that abstinence-only programs, in their current formats, are ineffective. Their "because" is research—something one might consider to be a persuasive argument. Yet the U.S. government found this research irrelevant and instead has provided hundreds of millions of dollars in funding for the past six years to programs that teach abstinence-only-until-marriage as the expected norm for all young people. This is because the conservative supporters of the abstinence-only movement and many in the government believe that young people *should be* abstinent until marriage because that is the morally "right" thing to do. Thus, a factual "because" does not always carry the weight that a religious or moral "should be" does. Nowhere is this seen more clearly than when debating issues of family and personal relationships.

Recognizing the Language of Political Viewpoints

Oftentimes, we will read or listen to a debate that we may believe to be mainstream, but that is actually coming from either conservative or liberal ideology.

How do we sort through the language to know whose viewpoint we are actually reading? If we are reading a piece on the Internet that is written by a particular organization, selecting the "who we are" or "about us" link will often reveal conservative ideology that is based on religious teachings. When this language talks explicitly about God or Christianity, the bias of the group is clear. However, there is more subtle language that also tends to express a conservative ideology. For example, a group whose mission operates around "concern for the American family," who "champions marriage and family as the foundation of civilization," who talks about being "pro-family" and its opponents as being "pro-abortion," who discusses "traditional American values," and who identifies itself as "pro-life" is most likely going to represent conservative viewpoints.

A group whose ideology is more liberal will use language reflecting its views, as well. If the group's mission uses language that consists of having the "right to choose," protecting people's "civil rights," helping people "make informed and responsible decisions," and if it identifies itself as "pro-choice" and its opponents as "anti-choice," chances are it is more mainstream to liberal. Organizations that talk about "empowering women" and "religious freedom" will also be more likely to be seen as liberal.

This is important to note. Being identified as a particular ideology, regardless of whether that person identifies that way, can pigeonhole a person. Just as an actor who plays a particular role over and over again can become typecast, a person who uses certain language may be labeled as liberal or conservative and can have certain opinions attributed to her or him. A good example of this is the nonprofit organization, People for the American Way. Based on the descriptions and language examples discussed earlier, one might hear or read this organization's name and assume that it is conservative. However, it is much more liberal, focusing on freedom and democracy for all people living in the United States. This is why it is vital to separate the message from the person unless that person identifies her or himself in a particular way.

The Language of Debate Around Family and Personal Relationships

Discussing family and personal relationships, and the issues surrounding each, is much different from talking about one's favorite sports player, preferred political candidate, or any other topic. The word *family* itself is loaded, meaning different things to different people. "Personal" relationships involve people. Discussing family and personal relationships, therefore, is by definition more personal. As a result, people often debate topics from a visceral rather than an intellectual viewpoint, with the lines between the two occasionally being blurred. Inherent in debates about family and personal relationships are morals and values, which make any debate more challenging than one that is based on facts. Morals and values are rooted for many people in spiritual and religious beliefs. Once a higher being or entity enters the picture, ideologies shift. An argument that begins with "I think" will carry different weight from one that begins with "the church says," or "Buddha teaches us," or "according to the Torah," or anything else that is faith-based.

When you read the word *family*, what image comes to your mind? Some will see their own family, whether that is their family of origin or their current family system. Others will see a family as it may have been or as it is currently being portrayed in the media. Still others will see a family within the context of how it is defined in their religious settings. The definition of the word *family* is quite clear to some and much more diverse to others. In fact, if you were to ask different individuals what the word *family* means to them, you would very likely receive a number of different answers. However, when you are watching the news or listening to a political debate and the word *family* is tossed around, it is almost certain that the definition of family is quite clear: It is a man and a woman, legally married, with one or more children, living together in the same household. Some newscasters and politicians may have the parenthetical concept in their head about the religion of the ideal family, as well as the family's cultural or ethnic makeup.

For other people, those who were raised by a single parent, by an adult or adults who were other members of their family but not their own parents, by adoptive parents, by lesbian or gay parents, or by any other significant adult or adults, the use of the word *family* means something altogether different. Therefore, it is interesting to note that even with so much diversity of individuals, experience, and family systems, we still have a societal assumption in the United States that when someone in public discourse uses the word *family*, it is still within the context of a two-parent, one-or-more-child context—again, the "should be" versus the "is."

Among the ways in which Merriam-Webster's Collegiate Dictionary defines a family are:

a group of individuals living under one roof and usually under one head

a group of persons of common ancestry

a group of people united by certain convictions or a common affiliation

the basic unit in society traditionally consisting of two parents rearing their own or adopted children; *also* : any of various social units differing from but regarded as equivalent to the traditional family, [such as] a single-parent family

These definitions are similar, yet make interesting distinctions within each variation. Clearly, each of these definitions conveys values. Yet it is up to the reader to determine what that value is. For example, in the first definition it is implied that there is one leader in a family. However, although the gender of that person is not specified, our society makes the assumption in most cases that this is a male since the accompanying assumption is that the ideal home (the "should be" home) would have a mother and a father as parents. Yet later, an additional definition refers to "two parents" raising children. Once again, the gender or genders of the parents are not specified, yet we still make assumptions based on experience, values, and ideals. How interesting that one word can be defined in so many ways that can simultaneously reflect such different values within each!

Similarly, when someone refers to a relationship, what comes to mind for you? Is this a romantic relationship? If so, who are the people involved?

Merriam-Webster's offers these definitions of relationship:

> the relation connecting or binding participants in a relationship; kinship; a romantic or passionate attachment

For some people, a relationship equals marriage, or a courtship that has marriage as its eventual outcome. For others, a relationship does not include marriage because the couple chooses not to marry. For others, a relationship does not include marriage because marriage is not legally available to them. As with the word *family*, the word *relationship* can conjure up different values for different individuals.

Conclusion

Regardless of the ideology we espouse or the language we use in expressing this ideology, our arguments must have reason behind them. Many people can recall the most infuriating response from parents while we were growing up as, "Because I said so." This response worked solely because of the power differential between parent and child. However, two people who are closer in age and debating a topic should much more thoroughly explore their reasons.

For some, "I think" or "I believe" will suffice. Others will justify their arguments from an experiential standpoint, as in, "I have learned from my 15 years as a public school teacher that . . ." Some people need simply to identify themselves within a category; for example, as a father of two or as a bisexual woman. Still others will use religion and religious doctrine, as mentioned earlier. For some, the New Testament, Qu'ran, Torah, or other religious text is brought out to "trump" any other argument, challenging one's opponents to argue with God—or, at least, with the debater's definition of God. A Christian will be more likely to discount an argument that is based on the teachings of the Qu'ran than one that is based on the teachings of the New Testament because it is not congruent with her or his beliefs. Still others do not take religious texts literally, instead they interpret them within the context of daily life.

No matter what we believe, we must listen to people whose views are different from our own. We need to think before expressing ourselves. We need to do so confidently, yet respectfully.

Mother Teresa was quoted as saying, "Peace and war begin at home. If we truly want peace in the world, let us begin by loving one another in our own families. If we want to spread joy, we need for every family to have joy." She did not define family, nor did she define joy. Yet each person who reads this quote will have a different picture in her or his mind of exactly what a family is and what kind of joy would create peace. As you read this volume, you will see that the issues that relate to family and personal relationships are farreaching and diverse. Family and interpersonal relationships are not exclusively about what goes on at home—they are about what happens in the legislature, in court rooms, in our communities, in the bedroom, in the United Nations, and beyond. Emotions run high when discussing family and personal relationships. Watch carefully, and you will see how often emotion rather than intellect dictates arguments.

Project NoSpank

Project NoSpank is a resource for students, parents, educators, health care professionals, policymakers, and everyone who believes that children's optimal development occurs in nurturing, violence-free environments and that every child has the right to grow and learn in such an environment.

http://www.nospank.net

The National Parent Information Network (NPIN)

The mission of the National Parent Information Network (NPIN) is to provide access to research-based information about the process of parenting and about family involvement in education.

http://npin.org

The National Fatherhood Initiative (NFI)

The National Fatherhood Initiative (NFI) was founded in 1994 to lead a society-wide movement to confront the problem of father absence.

http://www.fatherhood.org

Children Now

Children Now is a research and action organization dedicated to assuring that children grow up in economically secure families, where parents go to work confident that their children are supported by quality health coverage, a positive media environment, a good early education, and safe, enriching activities to do after school.

http://www.childrennow.org

The Children's Defense Fund

The Children's Defense Fund provides a strong, effective voice for all the children of America who cannot vote, lobby, or speak for themselves. They pay particular attention to the needs of poor and minority children and those with disabilities.

http://www.childrensdefense.org

PART 1

Parenting Issues

*U*se of the oft-quoted expression "It takes a village to raise a child" is still met with understanding, thoughtful nods as we appreciate the concept that many people beyond the family structure play key roles in raising children. There are, however, numerous factors that contribute to, interfere with, detract from, and otherwise affect how parents raise their children. Parenting styles vary. The so-called "village" includes the government, which is met with open arms by some, and skepticism and mistrust by others. This part examines five questions that society often asks relating to parenting issues.

- Is It Ever Appropriate to Spank a Child?

- Does the U.S. Need a Parental-Rights Amendment?

- Are Single-Parent Families a Major Cause of Social Dysfunction?

- Can We Raise "Gender-Neutral" Children?

- Does Divorce Create Long-Term Negative Effects for Children?

ISSUE 1

Is It Ever Appropriate to Spank a Child?

YES: Den A. Trumbull and S. DuBose Ravenel, from "Spare the Rod?" *Family Policy* (September–October 1996)

NO: Irwin A. Hyman, from *The Case Against Spanking: How to Discipline Your Child Without Hitting* (Jossey-Bass, 1997)

ISSUE SUMMARY

YES: Den A. Trumbull and S. DuBose Ravenel, both pediatricians in private practice, contend that spanking can serve as a valuable disciplinary method and play a significant role in a child's development. They maintain that well-planned-out spankings, those that the child is told about in advance and that are delivered without anger, can be useful, effective, and appropriate deterrents to inappropriate behavior.

NO: Irwin A. Hyman, director of the National Center for Study of Corporal Punishment and Alternatives, argues that there is never any reason to hit a child. Focusing on the emotional effects of spanking, he asserts that spanking is much more likely to teach children to tolerate and perpetuate violence than it is to correct disobedience.

W hile a number of European countries have completely outlawed corporal punishment at home and at school, spanking one's child is legal in the United States. A recent national survey found that over 90 percent of parents in the United States spank their child at least once over the course of a given year. One might think that this would indicate overwhelming support for spanking children under certain circumstances. Yet public opinion about spanking is pretty equally divided, and it is a topic that continues to be debated hotly by parents, young people, teachers, and policymakers alike.

Antispanking proponents call spanking child abuse—even child sexual abuse, based on the fact that spankings tend to be delivered to the buttocks. Murray Straus, codirector of the Family Research Laboratory at the University of New Hampshire in Durham, explains that whether or not spanking is child abuse under the law tends to be determined by the extent of the physical damage done. Therefore, an open-handed swat to the buttocks would be considered on an equal level as a crack on the knuckles with a wooden hairbrush—as long as neither caused the child to require medical attention.

When it comes to legislating the rights of parents, the country is also divided. *The Christian Science Monitor* reported on a 1999 Massachusetts case where a man felt he had biblical justification for hitting his son with a belt. While doing so did not break Massachusetts state law, social services removed the child from his home because they believed that his father's disciplinary actions could place him at risk for future injury. The man appealed this decision, saying that this removal violated his right to raise his son according to his religious beliefs.

Opponents to spanking cite research demonstrating that children who are punished physically are more likely to be aggressive to others, including their own children once they have become parents themselves. Concerns have been raised about the effects spanking can have on a child's emotional development and on his or her future ability to relate to others in intimate relationships.

Other experts believe that the antispanking research and equating spanking to child abuse blow the issue completely out of proportion. They maintain that there is a difference between spanking and child abuse—between a disciplinary measure that is controlled, delivered with love, and clearly explained to a child as the consequence of disobedient behavior—and beating a child out of anger or frustration. Prospanking advocates also cite research in order to show that spanking can be an effective disciplinary tactic without negatively affecting a child's emotional development or creating a greater tolerance for aggression. They explain that whether a parent actually spanks a child is less important than whether the parent has a close relationship with the child. If the parent and child are close, and the child knows and understands that she or he is loved, then the negative effects of spanking are minimized.

As you read these selections, think about how each author presents his viewpoint. Do you believe that each has sufficiently refuted the other? On what are you basing your feelings? Think about your own experience of growing up. If you were spanked yourself, how does that affect how you respond to each viewpoint? If you were not, does that have any bearing on your opinion? If you are strongly opposed to spanking, are there any circumstances under which you believe that a spanking is ever justified? What would those include? If you believe that spanking is an effective disciplinary tactic, are there any conditions you would want to place on the type of spanking or how it is delivered?

In the following selections, Den A. Trumbull and S. DuBose Ravenel respond to the common assertions of spanking opponents with alternate research findings. They stress the importance of differentiating between disciplinary spanking and what they believe to be more clearly abusive forms of discipline. They state that "spanking is supported by history, research, and a majority of primary care physicians." Irwin A. Hyman provides bullet-point summaries of the more than 30 years of research highlighting the harmful effects of spanking. He explains that, in addition to the physical and emotional harm to the individual child, spanking also perpetuates racism, classism, and sexism on a societal level.

**Den A. Trumbull and
S. DuBose Ravenel**

 **YES**

Spare the Rod?

Opposition to parents spanking their children has been growing signifi-cantly in elite circles over the past 15 years.[1] No doubt much of this opposition springs from a sincere concern for the well-being of children. Child abuse is a reality, and stories of child abuse are horrifying. But while loving and effective discipline is quite definitely *not* harsh and abusive, neither is it weak and in-effectual. Indeed, disciplinary spanking can fall well within the boundaries of loving discipline and need not be labeled abusive violence.[2]

Or so most Americans seem to think. According to a recent Voter/Consumer Research poll commissioned by the Family Research Council, 76 percent of the more than 1,000 Americans surveyed said that spanking was an effective form of discipline in their home when they were children.[3] These re-sults are made all the more impressive by the fact that nearly half of those who answered otherwise grew up in homes in which they were never spanked. Taken together, more than four out of five Americans who were actually spanked by their parents as children say that it was an effective form of discipline.

In addition, Americans perceive lack of discipline to be the biggest prob-lem in public education today, according to a recent Gallup poll.[4] Several stud-ies show strong public support for corporal punishment by parents.[5]

Critics claim that spanking a child is abusive and contributes to adult dysfunction. These allegations arise from studies that fail to distinguish appro-priate spanking from other forms of punishment. Abusive forms of physical punishment such as kicking, punching, and beating are commonly grouped with mild spanking. Furthermore, the studies usually include, and even em-phasize, corporal punishment of adolescents, rather than focusing on preschool children, where spanking is more effective. This blurring of distinctions be-tween spanking and physical abuse, and between children of different ages, gives critics the illusion of having data condemning all disciplinary spanking.

There are several arguments commonly leveled against disciplinary spank-ing. Interestingly, most of these arguments can be used against other forms of discipline. Any form of discipline (time-out, restriction, etc.), when used inap-propriately and in anger, can result in distorting a child's perception of justice and harming his emotional development. In light of this, let us examine some of the unfounded arguments promoted by spanking opponents.

Argument #1: Many psychological studies show that spanking is an improper form of discipline.

Counterpoint: Researchers John Lyons, Rachel Anderson and David Larson of the National Institute of Healthcare Research recently conducted a systematic review of the research literature on corporal punishment.[6] They found that 83 percent of the 132 identified articles published in clinical and psychosocial journals were merely opinion-driven editorials, reviews or commentaries, devoid of new empirical findings. Moreover, most of the empirical studies were methodologically flawed by grouping the impact of abuse with spanking. The best studies demonstrated beneficial, not detrimental, effects of spanking in certain situations. Clearly, there is insufficient evidence to condemn parental spanking and adequate evidence to justify its proper use.

Argument #2: Physical punishment establishes the moral righteousness of hitting other persons who do something which is regarded as wrong.

Counterpoint: The "spanking teaches hitting" belief has gained in popularity over the past decade, but is not supported by objective evidence. A distinction must be made between abusive hitting and nonabusive spanking. A child's ability to discriminate hitting from disciplinary spanking depends largely upon the parents' attitude with spanking and the parents' procedure for spanking. There is no evidence in the medical literature that a mild spank to the buttocks of a disobedient child by a loving parent teaches the child aggressive behavior.

The critical issue is *how* spanking (or, in fact, any punishment) is used more so than *whether* it is used. Physical abuse by an angry, uncontrolled parent will leave lasting emotional wounds and cultivate bitterness and resentment within a child. The balanced, prudent use of disciplinary spanking, however, is an effective deterrent to aggressive behavior with some children.

Researchers at the Center for Family Research at Iowa State University studied 332 families to examine both the impact of corporal punishment and the quality of parental involvement on three adolescent outcomes—aggressiveness, delinquency, and psychological well-being. The researchers found a strong association between the quality of parenting and each of these three outcomes. Corporal punishment, however, was *not* adversely related to any of these outcomes. This study proves the point that quality of parenting is the chief determinant of favorable or unfavorable outcomes.[7] Remarkably, childhood aggressiveness has been more closely linked to maternal permissiveness and negative criticism than to even abusive physical discipline.[8]

It is unrealistic to expect that children would never hit others if their parents would only exclude spanking from their discipline options. Most children in their toddler years (long before they are ever spanked) naturally attempt to hit others when conflict or frustration arises. The continuation of this behavior is largely determined by how the parent or caregiver responds. If correctly disciplined, the hitting will become less frequent. If ignored or ineffectively disciplined, the hitting will likely persist and even escalate. Thus, instead of contributing to greater violence, spanking can be a useful component in an overall plan to effectively teach a child to stop aggressive hitting.

> *Argument #3: Since parents often refrain from hitting until the anger or frustration reaches a certain point, the child learns that anger and frustration justify the use of physical force.*

Counterpoint: A study published in *Pediatrics* indicates that most parents who spank do not spank on impulse, but purposefully spank their children with a belief in its effectiveness.[9] Furthermore, the study revealed no significant correlation between the frequency of spanking and the anger reported by mothers. Actually, the mothers who reported being angry were not the same parents who spanked.

Reactive, impulsive hitting after losing control due to anger is unquestionably the wrong way for a parent to use corporal punishment. Eliminating all physical punishment in the home, however, would not remedy such explosive scenarios. It could even increase the problem. When effective spanking is removed from a parent's disciplinary repertoire, he or she is left with nagging, begging, belittling, and yelling, once the primary disciplinary measures—such as time-out and logical consequences—have failed. By contrast, if proper spanking is proactively used in conjunction with other disciplinary measures, better control of the particularly defiant child can be achieved, and moments of exasperation are less likely to occur.

> *Argument #4: Physical punishment is harmful to a child.*

Counterpoint: Any disciplinary measure, physical, verbal or emotional, carried to an extreme can harm a child. Excessive scolding and berating of a child by a parent is emotionally harmful. Excessive use of isolation (time-out) for unreasonable periods of time can humiliate a child and ruin the measure's effectiveness. Obviously, excessive or indiscriminate physical punishment is harmful and abusive. However, an appropriately administered spanking of a forewarned disobedient child is not harmful when administered in a loving, controlled manner. Without the prudent use of spanking for the particularly defiant child, a parent runs the risk of being inconsistent and rationalizing the child's behavior. This inconsistent manner of parenting is confusing and harmful to the child and is damaging to the parent-child relationship. There is no evidence that proper disciplinary spanking is harmful to the child.

> *Argument #5: Physical punishment makes the child angry at the parent.*

Counterpoint: All forms of punishment initially elicit a frustrated, angry response from a child. Progression of this anger is dependent primarily upon the parent's attitude during and after the disciplinary event, and the manner of its application. Any form of punishment administered angrily for purposes of retribution, rather than calmly for purposes of correction, can create anger and resentment in a child. Actually, a spanking can break the escalating rage of a rebellious child and more quickly restore the relationship between parent and child.

> *Argument #6: Spanking teaches a child that "might makes right," that power and strength are most important and that the biggest can force their will upon the smallest.*

Counterpoint: Parental power is commonly exerted in routine child rearing and spanking is only one example. Other situations where power and restraint are exercised by the average parent include:

- The young child who insists on running from his parent in a busy mall or parking lot.
- The toddler who refuses to sit in his car seat.
- The young patient who refuses to hold still as a vaccination is administered, or as a laceration is repaired.

Power and control over the child are necessary at times to ensure safety, health and proper behavior. Classic child rearing studies have shown that some degree of power, assertion,[10] and firm control[11] is essential for optimal child rearing. When power is exerted in the context of love and for the child's benefit, the child will not perceive it as bullying or demeaning.

A Closer Look

Distinguishing Spanking From Abuse

Corporal punishment is often defined broadly as *bodily punishment of any kind.* Since this definition includes spanking as well as obviously abusive acts such as kicking, punching, beating, face slapping, and even starvation, more specific definitions must be used to separate appropriate versus inappropriate corporal punishment.

Spanking is one of many disciplinary responses available to parents intended to shape appropriate behavior in the developing toddler and child. It is an adjunctive corrective measure, to be used in combination with primary responses such as restraint, natural and logical consequences, time-out, and restriction of privileges.

Child development experts believe spanking should be used mainly as a back-up to primary measures, and then independently to correct deliberate and persistent problem behavior that is not remedied with milder measures. It is most useful with toddlers and preschoolers from 18 months to 6 years of age, when reasoning is less persuasive.

Moreover, child development experts say that spanking should always be a planned action by a parent, not an impulsive reaction to misbehavior. The

child should be forewarned of the spanking consequence for each of the designated problem behaviors. Spanking should always be administered in private. It
should consist of one or two spanks to the child's buttocks, followed by a calm
review of the offense and the desired behavior.

Table 1

	Spanking	Physical Abuse
The Act	Spanking: One or two spanks to the buttocks	Beating: To strike repeatedly (also kick, punch, choke)
The Intent	Training: To correct problem behavior	Violence: Physical force intended to injure or abuse
The Attitude	With love and concern	With anger and malice
The Effects	Behavioral correction	Emotional and physical injury

Argument #7: Spanking is violence.

Counterpoint: Spanking, as recommended by most primary care physicians,[12]
is not violence by definition ("exertion of physical force so as to injure or
abuse").[13] Parents who properly spank do not injure or abuse their child.

The use of this term "violence" in the spanking debate only serves to
deepen the confusion. Why do anti-spanking authors repeatedly fail to distinguish between abusive violence and mild spanking? The distinction is so
fundamental and obvious that its omission suggests that these authors use such
terminology for its propaganda value, not to clarify issues.

Argument #8: Spanking is an ineffective solution to misbehavior.

Counterpoint: Though the specific use of appropriate spanking has rarely been
studied, there is evidence of its short-term and long-term effectiveness. When
combined with reasoning, the use of negative consequences (including spanking) does effectively decrease the frequency of misbehavior recurrences with
preschool children.[14] In clinical field trials where parental spanking has been
studied, it has consistently been found to reduce the subsequent frequency of
noncompliance with time-out.[15] Spanking, as an effective enforcer of time-
out, is a component of several well-researched parent training programs[16] and
popular parenting texts.[17]

Dr. Diana Baumrind of the Institute for Human Development at the University of California-Berkeley, conducted a decade-long study of families with children 3 to 9 years old.[18] Baumrind found that parents employing a balanced disciplinary style of firm control (including spanking) and positive encouragement experienced the most favorable outcome in their children. Parents taking extreme approaches to discipline (authoritarian-types using excessive punishment with less encouragement or permissive-types using little punishment and no spanking) were less successful.

Baumrind concluded that evidence from this study "did not indicate that negative reinforcement or corporal punishment per se were harmful or ineffective procedures, but rather the total patterns of parental control determined the effects on the child of these procedures."

This approach of balanced parenting, employing the occasional use of spanking, is advocated by several child rearing experts.[19] In the hands of loving parents, a spanking to the buttocks of a defiant toddler in appropriate settings is a powerful motivator to correct behavior and an effective deterrent to disobedience.

Argument #9: Adults who were spanked as children are at risk for using violence as a means of resolving conflicts as adults.

Counterpoint: This theory comes from work done by Murray Straus of the Family Research Lab at the University of New Hampshire. Straus' conclusions are based upon theoretical models and survey results of adults recalling spankings as teenagers. His work is not clinical research, and many experts believe that his conclusions go far beyond his data. As with most of Straus' survey research, teenage spanking is the focus, not the selective use of spanking of young children by reasonable parents. The evidence for his conclusion disappears when parental spanking is measured between the ages of 2 and 8 years, and when childhood aggression is measured at a later age.

In a 1994 review article on corporal punishment, Dr. Robert E. Larzelere, a director of research at Boys Town, Nebraska, presents evidence supporting a parent's selective use of spanking of children, particularly those 2 to 6 years old.[20] After thoroughly reviewing the literature, Larzelere concludes that any association between spanking and antisocial aggressiveness in children is insignificant and artifactual.

After a decade of longitudinal study of children beginning in third grade, Dr. Leonard Eron found no association between punishment (including spanking) and later aggression. Eron, a clinical psychologist at the Univeristy of Michigan's Institute for Social Research, concluded, "Upon follow-up 10 years after the original data collection, we found that punishment of aggressive acts at the earlier age was no longer related to current aggression, and instead, other variables like parental nurturance and children's identification with their parents were more important in predicting later aggression."[21]

Again, it is the total pattern of parenting that determines the outcome of a parent's efforts.

Argument #10: Spanking leads a parent to use harmful forms of corporal punishment which lead to physical child abuse.

Counterpoint: The abuse potential when loving parents use appropriate disciplinary spanking is very low. Since parents have a natural affection for their children, they are more prone to underutilize spanking than to overutilize it. Both empirical data and professional opinion oppose the concept of a causal relationship between spanking and child abuse.

Surveys indicate that 70 to 90 percent of parents of preschoolers use spanking,[22] yet the incidence of physical child abuse in America is only about 5 percent. Statistically, the two practices are far apart. Furthermore, over the past decade reports of child abuse have steadily risen while approval for parental spanking has steadily declined.[23]

More than 70 percent of primary care pediatricians reject the idea that spanking sets the stage for parents to engage in forms of physical abuse.[24]

Teaching parents appropriate spanking may actually reduce child abuse, according to Larzelere, in his 1994 review article on corporal punishment.[25] Parents who are ill-equipped to control their child's behavior, or who take a more permissive approach (refusing to use spanking), may be more prone to anger[26] and explosive attacks on their child.[27]

Parental child abuse is an interactive process involving parental competence, parental and child temperaments, and situational demands.[28] Abusive parents are more angry, depressed and impulsive, and emphasize punishment as the predominant means of discipline. Abused children are more aggressive and less compliant than children from nonabusive families. There is less interaction between family members in abusive families and abusive mothers display more negative than positive behavior. The etiology of abusive parenting is multifactorial with emphasis on the personalities involved, and cannot be simply explained by a parent's use of spanking.

In a letter to the editor in a 1995 issue of Pediatrics, Drs. Lawrence S. Wissow and Debra Roter of Johns Hopkins University's pediatrics department acknowledge that a definitive link between spanking and child abuse has yet to be established.[29]

Finally, the Swedish experiment to reduce child abuse by banning spanking seems to be failing. In 1980, one year after this ban was adopted, the rate of child beatings was twice that of the United States.[30] According to a 1995 report from the government organization Statistics Sweden, police reports of child abuse by family members rose four-fold from 1984 to 1994, while reports of teen violence increased nearly six-fold.[31]

Most experts agree that spanking and child abuse are not on the same continuum, but are very different entities. With parenting, it is the "user" and how a measure is used much more than the measure used that determines the outcome of the disciplinary effort. Clearly, spanking can be safely used in the discipline of young children with an excellent outcome. The proper use of spanking may actually reduce a parent's risk of abusing the child.

Argument #11: Spanking is never necessary.

Counterpoint: All children need a combination of encouragement and correction as they are disciplined to become socially responsible individuals. In order for correction to deter disobedient behavior, the consequence imposed upon the child must outweigh the pleasure of the disobedient act. For very compliant children, milder forms of correction will suffice and spanking may never be necessary. For more defiant children who refuse to comply with or be persuaded by milder consequences such as time-out, spanking is useful, effective, and appropriate.

Conclusion

The subject of disciplinary spanking should be evaluated from a factual and philosophical perspective. It must be distinguished from abusive, harmful forms of corporal punishment. Appropriate disciplinary spanking can play an important role in optimal child development, and has been found in prospective studies to be a part of the parenting style associated with the best outcomes. There is no evidence that mild spanking is harmful. Indeed, spanking is supported by history, research, and a majority of primary care physicians.

ET CETERA, ET CETERA: GUIDELINES FOR DISCIPLINARY SPANKING

The following are guidelines that Dr. Den Trumbull has used to advise the parents he serves in disciplining children. These guidelines should help policymakers appreciate the legitimacy of disciplinary spanking.

1. Spanking should be used selectively for clear, deliberate misbehavior, particularly that which arises from a child's persistent defiance of a parent's instruction. It should be used only when the child receives at least as much encouragement and praise for good behavior as correction for problem behavior.
2. Milder forms of discipline, such as verbal correction, time-out, and logical consequences, should be used initially, followed by spanking when noncompliance persists. Spanking has shown to be an effective method of enforcing time-out with the child who refuses to comply.
3. Only a parent (or in exceptional situations, someone else who has an intimate relationship of authority with the child) should administer a spanking.
4. Spanking should not be administered on impulse or when a parent is out of control. A spanking should always be motivated by love for the purpose of teaching and correcting, never for revenge.

5. Spanking is inappropriate before 15 months of age and is usually not necessary until after 18 months. It should be less necessary after 6 years, and rarely, if ever, used after 10 years of age.
6. After 10 months of age, one slap to the hand of a stubborn crawler or toddler may be necessary to stop serious misbehavior when distraction and removal have failed. This is particularly the case when the forbidden object is immovable and dangerous, such as a hot oven door or an electrical outlet.
7. Spanking should always be a planned action, not a reaction, by the parent and should follow a deliberate procedure.

   - The child should be forewarned of the spanking consequence for designated problem behaviors.
   - Spanking should always be administered in private (bedroom or restroom) to avoid public humiliation or embarassment.
   - One or two spanks should be administered to the buttocks. This is followed by embracing the child and calmly reviewing the offense and the desired behavior in an effort to reestablish a warm relationship.

8. Spanking should leave only transient redness of the skin and should never cause physical injury.
9. If properly administered spankings are ineffective, other appropriate disciplinary responses should be tried, or the parent should seek professional help. Parents should never increase the intensity of spankings.

Notes

1. Fathman, Dr. Robert E. "Corporal Punishment Fact Sheet." July 1994.
2. Lyons, Dr. John S., Anderson, Rachel L., and Larson, Dr. David B., memo.
3. Voter/Consumer Research Poll, National Values. Commissioned by the Family Research Council, 1994.
4. "School Poll." *The Washington Times.* Aug. 28, 1995, p. A-2.
5. Flynn, Clifton P. "Regional Differences in Attitudes Toward Corporal Punishment." *Journal of Marriage and the Family.* 56 (May 1994): 314–324.
6. Lyons, Dr. John S., Anderson, Rachel L., and Larson, Dr. David B. "The Use and Effects of Physical Punishment in the Home: A Systematic Review." Presentation to the Section on Bio-Ethics of the American Academy of Pediatrics at annual meeting, Nov. 2, 1993.
7. Simons, Ronald L., Johnson, Christine, and Conger, Rand D. "Harsh Corporal Punishment versus Quality of Parental Involvement as an Explanation of Adolescent Maladjustment." *Journal of Marriage and Family.* 1994; 56:591–607.
8. Olweus, Dan. "Familial and Tempermental Determinants of Aggressive Behavior in Adolescent Boys: A Causal Analysis." *Developmental Psychology.* 1980; 16:644–660.
9. Socolar, Rebecca R. S., M.D. and Stein, Ruth E.K., M.D. "Spanking Infants and Toddlers: Maternal Belief and Practice." *Pediatrics.* 1995; 95:105–111.
10. Hoffman, Martin. "Parental Discipline and Child's Moral Development." *Journal of Personal Social Psychology.* 1967; 5:45–57.
11. Baumrind, Diana, Ph.D. "Rearing Competent Children." Damon, W. (Ed.) *Child Development Today and Tomorrow.* 1989; pp. 349–378. San Francisco, Calif.: Jossey-Bass.

12. McCormick, Kenelm F., M.D. "Attitudes of Primary Care Physicians Toward Corporal Punishment." *Journal of the American Medical Association.* 1992; 267:3161–3165.

13. *Webster's Ninth New Collegiate Dictionary.* 1987; p. 1316. Massachusetts: Merriam-Webster, Inc.

14. Larzelere, Dr. Robert E. and Merenda, Dr. J.A. "The Effectiveness of Parental Discipline for Toddler Misbehavior at Different Levels of Child Distress." *Family Relations.* 1994; 43 (4).

15. Roberts, Mark W. and Powers, Scott W. "Adjusting Chair Time-out Enforcement Procedures for Oppositional Children." *Behavioral Therapy.* 1990; 21:257–271, and Bean, Arthur W. and Roberts, Mark W. "The Effect of Time-out Release Contingencies on Changes in Child Noncompliance." *Journal of Abnormal Child Psychology.* 1981; 9:95–105.

16. Forehand, R.L. and McMahon, R.J. *Helping the Noncompliant Child.* 1981; pp. 79–80. New York: Guilford Press.

17. Clark, Lynn C. *SOS! Help for Parents.* 1985; pp. 181–185. Kentucky: Parents Press.

18. Baumrind, Dr. Diana. "The Development of Instrumental Competence Through Socialization. *Minnesota Symposia on Child Psychology.* 1973; 7:3–46.

19. Austin, Glenn. *Love and Power: How to Raise Competent, Confident Children.* 1988. California: Robert Erdmann Publishing. Also, Dobson, Dr. James. *The Strong-Willed Child.* 1985. Illinois: Tyndale House Publishers, and Coopersmith, Stanley. *The Antecedents of Self-Esteem.* 1967. New York: W.H. Freeman & Co. Reprinted 1981. California: Consulting Psychologists Press, Inc.

20. Larzelere, Dr. Robert E. "Should the Use of Corporal Punishment by Parents be Considered Child Abuse?" Mason, M., Gambrill, E. (Eds.) *Debating Children's Lives.* 1994; pp. 204–209. California: SAGE Publications.

21. Eron, Dr. Leonard D. "Theories of Aggression: From Drives to Cognitions." Huesmann, L.R. (Ed.) *Aggressive Behavior, Current Perspectives.* 1994; pp. 3–11. New York: Plenum Press.

22. Straus, Murray A. "Discipline and Deviance: Physical Punishment of Children and Violence and Other Crime in Adulthood." *Social Problems.* 1991; 38:133–152.

23. National Committee to Prevent Child Abuse. *Memorandum.* May 1995; 2(5).

24. White, Kristin. "Where Pediatricians Stand on Spanking." *Pediatric Management.* September 1993: 11–15.

25. Larzelere, Dr. Robert E., *op. cit.*

26. Socolar, Rebecca R.S., M.D. and Stein, Ruth E.K., M.D., *op. cit.*

27. Baumrind, Dr. Diana, *op. cit.*

28. Wolfe, David A. "Child-Abusive Parents: An Empirical Review and Analysis." *Psychological Bulletin.* 1985; 97(3): 462–482.

29. Wissow, Dr. Lawrence S. and Roter, Dr. Debra. Letter to the editor, in reply to corporal punishment letter. *Pediatrics.* 1995; 96(4): 794–795.

30. Larzelere, Dr. Robert E., *op. cit.*

31. Statistics Sweden. *K R Info.* May 1995; pp. 1–6. Stockholm, Sweden.

Irwin A. Hyman

↩ **NO**

Why We Hit and What It Does to Kids

There is much debate about the actual effects of corporal punishment. These debates center on issues of age at the time of hitting, the force with which children are hit, and the effects on long-term behavior and personality development. Rather than bore you with numerous statistics, arguments about the validity of various studies, and the fine points of each debate, I will summarize what I believe are the major effects of corporal punishment on children. But first let me share with you the results of a recent and very important scientific conference on spanking.

In February 1996, I was fortunate to be a part of a panel of experts convened by the American Academy of Pediatrics, with support from New York's Montefiore Medical Center and the U. S. Maternal and Child Health Bureau, to develop a consensus statement about the short- and long-term consequences of corporal punishment. Sharing the panel with me were distinguished social scientists and physicians representing both sides of the spanking issue. Despite heated debate and some slippage into rhetoric reflecting personal biases, we were able to produce a final statement of compromise with which we could all live. The individual papers and the consensus statement are published in a supplement to *Pediatrics*. Despite our care in crafting an objective statement of our findings, the results will most likely be distorted in the media.

In essence, the thirteen-point statement released by the group refers to spanking as defined as the use of an opened hand on the extremities or buttocks that is physically noninjurious. I believe force which causes redness, soreness or bruising is injurious and would not be acceptable to most members of the group. While the group admitted that there was little pro or con scientific evidence on the spanking of two- to five-year-olds, there was agreement that surveys and studies of older children suggest that spanking is not advisable. Even the researchers in favor of spanking admitted that noncorporal methods of discipline have been shown to be effective with children of all ages, that prevention of misbehavior should be stressed, that excessive spanking is one of many risk factors for poor outcomes in the lives of children, and that parents should never spank in anger. This may be an oxymoron, since studies of spankers and spankees indicate that some level of anger is almost always associated with spankings. Finally, the group rejected spanking and paddling in schools.

While the prospankers interpret the lack of research on the harmful effects of spanking with preschoolers as proof that it is OK, I disagree and maintain that there is no reason to ever hit a child. My summary of the research and clinical experience over 30 years follows:

- Corporal punishment should not be used in schools, since there is convincing evidence that it is a significant contributing factor to emotional, legal, and social problems.
- Frequent and harsh spanking is consistently found to be present in the lives of boys who are aggressive and disobedient, who lie, cheat, are destructive with their own and others' belongings, and who associate with friends prone to delinquency.
- Frequent and harsh spanking can cause young children to bottle up their feelings of fear, anger, and hostility. In later life these children are unusually prone to suicidal thoughts, suicide, and depression.
- Despite the age or gender of the child, the family's social class or ethnicity, whether the child was hit frequently or rarely, severely or mildly, whether there were high or low levels of interaction and affection in the home, and regardless of the degree to which specific situational variables may have mitigated the effects of the punishment, spanking consistently contributes to lowered self-esteem.
- In toddlers, many punitive approaches, including spanking, do not result in compliance, but end simply with the administration of punishment. (Studies show that preschoolers who are hit are more likely to be more impulsive and aggressive than those who are not spanked. Furthermore, toddlers can be taught, using behavioral techniques such as associating their word for pain with the street or electrical outlets, to avoid those dangerous situations. Childproofing the house and monitoring toddlers will avoid the so-called necessity of spanking to teach children to avoid danger.)
- Children who are physically punished are more likely to grow up approving of it and using it to settle interpersonal conflicts. Even children who have experienced "normal" spankings are almost three times as likely to have seriously assaulted a sibling, compared to children who were not physically disciplined.
- Contrary to popular belief, studies of corporal punishment in schools indicate that it is not used as a last resort. In fact, it is too often the first punishment for nonviolent and minor misbehaviors. Beatings for minor misbehaviors can cause many stress symptoms in children.
- Younger children are hit most often; spanking slowly decreases until late adolescence. This contributes to feelings of helplessness, humiliation, and resentment that may lead to withdrawal or aggression toward caregivers.

- Boys are hit much more frequently than girls, thereby sustaining sexual stereotypes.
- In schools, minority and poor white children receive "lickings" four to five times more frequently than middle- and upper-class white children. This contributes to racism and classism in our society.
- Regional comparisons show that the highest proportion of corporal punishment in America occurs in states in the South and Southwest. Florida, Texas, Arkansas, and Alabama have consistently been among the leaders in the frequency of hitting schoolchildren. It is unreasonable and unfair that children's location should determine the degree to which they may be legally victimized.
- Corporally punished schoolchildren, especially those with emotional and academic disabilities, have suffered all types of injuries including welts, hematomas, damage to almost all external and many internal body parts, and death.
- Studies demonstrate that eliminating corporal punishment does not increase misbehavior in home or school. Systematic use of positive alternatives, however, has been shown to decrease misbehavior significantly.

POSTSCRIPT

Is It Ever Appropriate to Spank a Child?

The expression "spare the rod, spoil the child" has been used throughout history to justify corporal punishment of children. In the 1960s and 1970s, spanking was not only widely practiced, it could be delivered by any adult with authority over a child—whether the adult was the child's family member, teacher, housekeeper, babysitter, or the parent of a child's friend. The assumption was that adults, across the board, knew what was inappropriate behavior and had the right to intervene as necessary.

There are many rules children must live by as they negotiate through childhood. However, problems arise when children receive conflicting messages about these rules. A child may overhear a parent using profanity, then be confused when he is punished for using it himself. A child might watch her parent smoke and ask why she cannot. And a child may not understand a spanking as punishment for hitting another child. Many argue that parents must provide consistent lessons, including explaining why a rule is being enforced; they should acknowledge that, indeed, some rules may not feel fair, but they must be adhered to all the same. Providing explanations does not rule out appropriate strictness in parenting. However, rules are much more effective when delivered by parents who model these rules themselves.

Trumbull and Ravenel appeal to their readers to evaluate spanking from a "factual and philosophical perspective," although doing so may ignore the fact that this issue is a highly personal one. A great deal of this debate centers around one's own experiences. While the frequency of corporal punishment has been decreasing over the years, there are many more discussions that need to take place about this highly sensitive topic.

Suggested Readings

James C. Dobson, *The New Dare to Discipline* (Tyndale House Publishing, 1996).

Elizabeth Kandel, "Physical Punishment and the Development of Aggressive and Violent Behavior: A Review," University of New Hampshire Family Research Laboratory (June 1992).

Robert E. Larzelere, "Should the Use of Corporal Punishment by Parents Be Considered Child Abuse?" in M. Mason and E. Gambrill, eds., *Debating Children's Lives* (Sage Publications, 1994).

Rebecca R. Socolar and Ruth Stein, "Spanking Infants and Toddlers: Maternal Belief and Practice," *Pediatrics* (vol. 95, 1995).

ISSUE 2

Does the U.S. Need a Parental-Rights Amendment?

YES: Greg D. Erken, from "Halt Social Engineering of the Nation's Families," *Insight on the News* (May 15, 1995)

NO: Jack C. Westman, from "License Parents to Ensure Children's Welfare," *Insight on the News* (May 15, 1995)

ISSUE SUMMARY

YES: Greg D. Erken, executive director for Of the People, a non-profit, parental-rights organization, challenges the concept that anyone other than a parent knows what is best for children. As the First Amendment exemplifies the principles on which Americans base discussions and debates around free speech, he maintains that the parental-rights amendment should do the same for parents' rights.

NO: Jack C. Westman, professor of psychiatry at the University of Wisconsin–Madison, asserts that a parental-rights amendment sets the government and parents up as enemies. He argues that many government policies, such as child neglect, labor, and mandatory education laws, have served children and families well. He contends that the amendment is unnecessary.

Questions around government involvement in family decisions have been raising controversy for years. More recently, we have seen the issue raised within the educational and medical settings. For example, some parents or other adult caregivers want to ensure their right to opt their children out of any school course they deem to be inappropriate for their child. Some support laws that would require their minor daughters to either obtain their permission or notify them before obtaining an abortion.

On June 28, 1995, the Parental Rights and Responsibilities Act (PRRA) was introduced in the House and Senate. It read, "The rights of parents to direct the upbringing and education of their children shall not be infringed." Proponents of the measure believed that the amendment would give parents additional legal support. Specifically, they mentioned parents' rights to control, without government interference, how their children would be educated and disciplined as well as the types of values their children would receive. The measure was not passed on the federal level.

Since then, some form of parental-rights legislation, including state constitutional amendments, has been introduced in at least 29 states. Some of the largest organizations in the country have expressed their support of the parental-rights amendment and continue to mobilize support for its passage in state legislatures. These organizations include the Family Research Council, Focus on the Family, the Christian Coalition, Concerned Women for America, and Of the People, among others. More often than not, they are defeated. However, they are usually rewritten and introduced anew. In states where new legislation is not written, proponents may attempt to incorporate parental-rights language into other proposed measures. The hope of parental-rights legislation is two-fold: first, that as the power balance in state legislatures change, more conservative policymakers will approve these measures; and second, that some type of parental-rights language will make its way onto the books by being attached to more mainstream proposals.

Mainstream opponents to the PRRA believe that parental authority is supreme; therefore, a constitutional amendment or other type of legislation is unnecessary. More liberal critics believe that this type of legislation is significantly more sinister. Their concern is that parental-rights initiatives would give parents *too* much power. Conservative parents, they believe, would have the legal backing they would need to challenge public school curricula. One organization supporting this viewpoint is People for the American Way (PFAW), a national advocacy organization located in Washington, D.C. PFAW maintains that parental-rights initiatives like the PRRA would "wreak havoc on public school curricula by providing the means for individuals to block sexuality and AIDS education programs and other curricula they find objectionable not simply for their own children, but for other parents' children as well." They also fear that giving parents constitutional rights would make investigating allegations of child abuse significantly more difficult for social service professionals.

In the following selections, Greg D. Erken advocates a federal parental-rights amendment. Jack C. Westman finds it ironic that individuals need a license to drive a car, but there are no requirements for becoming a parent. He argues that parental licensing would be a more effective way of ensuring more effective parental involvement in childrearing.

Greg D. Erken

 **YES**

Halt Social Engineering of the Nation's Families

Item: New York City, 1992. A broad, multiracial coalition of public-school parents stages an open revolt in reaction to the controversial "Children of the Rainbow" curriculum. Eventually, the "Rainbow" curriculum (including its condom instructions for fourth-graders) is thrown out, and its leading proponent, school chancellor Joseph Fernandez, is forced to resign.

Item: Sacramento, 1994. A statewide controversy erupts over the California Learning Assessment System, or CLAS, test, which solicits students' "feelings" about private family matters. After being denied permission to see the test their kids were compelled to take, angry parents flood Gov. Pete Wilson's office with phone calls. Wilson subsequently vetoes the CLAS test funding bill.

Item: Fairfax County, Va., 1995. A standing-room-only crowd of parents jams a local school-board meeting to influence the board's vote on sex education. "You can see why parents shouldn't be involved in family-life education," complains Dr. Robert Spillane, superintendent of Fairfax County Public Schools.

These incidents demonstrate why the national parental-rights movement has become a force in the public-policy debate of the 1990s. Parents increasingly sense that their most precious prerogative—the ability to teach their values to their children—is threatened. As government has taken on the responsibility for duties traditionally carried out by the family, parental rights have been eroded and the family has been weakened. Spillane's comment evinces a "we know what's best for your children" mentality that parents often encounter when challenging government bureaucracies. These skirmishes all beg the fundamental question: *Who decides* what's in the best interests of children—parents or the government?

The commonsense answer is found in a proposed parental-rights amendment to state constitutions: "The right of parents to direct the upbringing and education of their children shall not be infringed." The amendment has been or will be introduced in 25 state legislatures this year, often with bipartisan support.

The amendment is a direct transfer of authority from government bureaucrats back to families—where it belongs. It's a simple way to limit government and, at the same time, strengthen the family. The legislation is drawn from two Supreme Court cases from the 1920s, *Meyer vs. Nebraska* and *Pierce vs. Society of Sisters*, in which the court first recognized a constitutional basis for parental rights. In *Pierce*, the court held that parents have a right "to direct the upbringing and education" of their children. The *Meyer-Pierce* parental-rights doctrine formed the basis of the 1993 decision in *Alfonso vs. Fernandez*, in which a New York state appellate court overturned New York City's condom distribution program. The court held that distributing condoms in public schools without parental consent violated *Meyer-Pierce*.

While the *Alfonso* case was a victory for parents, some judges ignore the *Meyer-Pierce* doctrine (*Alfonso* itself was a narrow 3-2 decision). According to public-interest litigators on the front lines of the struggle for parental rights, *Meyer-Pierce* is effectively a dead letter. In Falmouth, Mass., parents filed suit in 1992 against a condom program similar to the one challenged in *Alfonso*. The county superior court refused to apply *Meyer-Pierce* and ruled against the parents. The case is on appeal before the Massachusetts Supreme Court. Likewise, in a California case stemming from the CLAS test controversy, a judge refused to grant parents access to the test, saying their concerns about intrusive questions were "too vague to have any viability."

Clearly, the violation of parental rights has become a systemic problem. By codifying *Meyer-Pierce*, the parental-rights amendment will revitalize and clarify the rights of parents. Parents deserve an explicit right grounded in their state constitution—not a court-interpreted right.

The amendment will give parents greater legal standing in three key areas.

Education.   Parents trying to become more involved in their children's education often are made to feel unwelcome by the education bureaucracy. Education Secretary Richard Riley laments the "significant obstacles" to parental involvement, the "disconnection between educators and parents" and the fact that parents' rights are "ignored, frustrated and sometimes even denied." Public education is facing a crisis of confidence among parents. The parental-rights amendment can help resolve this crisis by making schools more accountable to parents, whether they are concerned, for example, with the "dumbing down" of academic standards or with values taught at school that may conflict with values taught at home.

Health.   Parental approval should be obtained before schools distribute condoms to minors, or before an abortion is performed on a minor.

Family autonomy.   The U.N. Convention on the Rights of the Child, pending in the Senate, implies a fundamental restructuring of the relationship of parent to child and family to state. Barbara Bennett Woodhouse of the University of Pennsylvania views the child as "having a direct relationship with government . . . as public resource and public ward, entitled both to make claims upon the community and to be claimed by the community," while Jack Westman of the University of Wisconsin-Madison and others call for government "licensing" of parents. In light of these and other radical proposals, now is the time to clarify and codify our traditional notions of parental sovereignty.

While the parental-rights amendment provides a general right to raise one's child, this right is not absolute. The rights to free speech and religious freedom set forth in the Bill of Rights have their limits. So do parental rights. The Supreme Court has recognized that parental rights must be balanced with the state's interest in ensuring the welfare of children. In *Prince vs. Massachusetts* (1944) the court made it clear that, *Meyer-Pierce* notwithstanding, " ... neither the right of religion nor the rights of parents are beyond limitation." Under *Prince*, states may enact such regulations as compulsory education, vaccination laws and prohibitions on child labor. In cases such as *In re Phillip B.* (1979) and *Commonwealth vs. Barnhart* (1985), lower courts have explicitly ruled that "upbringing and education" provide no cover for abusive or neglectful parents.

Because the parental-rights amendment is a codification of *Meyer-Pierce,* the well-established limits to this doctrine—as well as common sense—will apply to the amendment. According to Michael J. Bowers, the attorney general of Georgia, "This right is not absolute nor should it be. Specifically, a parent cannot deprive or abuse his or her child, and I cannot imagine courts ever permitting such under the amendment."

Critics who cite tragic cases of abuse as grounds for opposing the parental-rights amendment ignore the fact that a child's most important right is to have an actively involved, loving parent to protect that child's interests. But parents are getting a mixed message: While leaders from the left and the right call for more parental responsibility, our laws continue to ignore parental rights.

The parental-rights amendment makes explicit the fact that parents are irreplaceable. It sends a message to public officials that parental rights must be honored and a message to parents that parental responsibilities must be fulfilled. When their rights are respected, parents naturally will become more involved and more confident in exercising their responsibility.

The parental-rights amendment does not give the answer to every question that may arise. Constitutional amendments provide a destination; they can't be expected to serve as detailed maps. But if we can agree on the amendment's underlying principle, we will be better equipped to deal with specific policy questions as they arise. Just as the First Amendment guides our debate on free speech issues, the parental-rights amendment can serve as our yardstick with which to measure the impact all policies and proposals have on parental rights.

Amending a state constitution is more difficult than passing a simple statute. But a statewide vote of the people for the parental-rights amendment will make it crystal clear to legislators, judges and bureaucrats that parental rights must be respected.

In little more than one year, the parental-rights amendment has moved from an idea to a bill introduced in half of the state legislatures. It has been hotly debated in Kansas, Missouri, Nebraska, North Dakota and Washington. Though it was recently defeated by narrow margins on the floor in Kansas and North Dakota, these early skirmishes have been very heartening to grassroots activists, who have vowed to continue fighting for the amendment—through petition drives if necessary. Grassroots parental-rights groups have launched an underfunded effort staunchly opposed by entrenched special interests such as teachers unions and the National Abortion and Reproductive Rights Action League. But by opposing this simple statement of principle, the elitists' profound distrust of parents has been exposed.

Our Founding Fathers spoke of certain "self-evident" truths upon which our nation was founded. Surely the notion that parents ought to have the primary responsibility for raising children was just such a "self-evident" truth. But now perhaps some of these truths no longer are so "self-evident."

In February 1994, home-schoolers discovered a certification requirement in a pending congressional bill that could have forced 99 percent of all home-schoolers out of business. Reaction was swift. Home-schoolers mounted an offensive that resulted in Congress receiving more constituent calls against the bill than were generated by gays in the military, NAFTA and the 1990 congressional pay raise combined. The House responded to this display of parental muscle by voting 412-1 to eliminate the certification provision. This is precisely the kind of grassroots campaign necessary to amend every state constitution—and eventually the U.S. Constitution—with the parental-rights amendment, to guarantee that parents retain the right to carry out the most important task they face—directing the upbringing and education of their children.

Jack C. Westman

License Parents to Ensure Children's Welfare

Of the People, the parental-rights organization, correctly faults local school policies that exaggerate the rights of children and minimize the rights of parents on such issues as sex education, condom distribution and health care. But the parental-rights movement mistakenly assumes that the schools or the government are trying to take over parental responsibilities. Of the People implies that child rearing is strictly a family responsibility.

As the National Commission on Children reported to then-President George Bush and Congress in 1991, "It is a tragic irony that the most prosperous nation on Earth is failing so many of its children. Solutions will depend upon strong leadership and the concerted efforts of every sector of society—individuals, employers, schools, civic, community and religious organizations, and government at every level."

In recent years schools and protective services for children have become involved in family affairs because too many parents are unable—or unwilling—to direct the upbringing and education of their children. For example, the Center for Children of Incarcerated Parents reports that 1.5 million children have an imprisoned parent. The Carnegie Corp. of New York concludes that "millions of infants and toddlers are so deprived of loving supervision, intellectual stimulation and medical care that their growth into healthy and responsible adults is threatened."

A growing number of incompetent parents are unable to handle responsibilities for their own lives, much less for their children's lives. They neglect and abuse their children physically, emotionally and sexually, as defined by state child neglect and abuse statutes. According to data collected from the 50 states by the National Center on Child Abuse Prevention and Research, annually substantiated cases of child maltreatment rose from 690,840 in 1985 to 1,016,000 in 1993, an increase of 47 percent. My analysis of this data reveals that some 2.7 million incompetent parents have both neglected and abused 3.6 million children.

Some social theorists have blamed this behavior on the stresses of poverty, racial discrimination and unemployment. But most parents who live in poverty, experience racial discrimination and are unemployed do not neglect and abuse their children. The direct cause of child neglect and abuse is incompetent parenting.

Incompetent parents contribute to the deterioration in the quality of public education and public safety throughout our nation, forcing the government to intervene in family life. Because that intervention often is ineffective, one in three neglected and abused children grow up to be violent, habitual criminals and welfare-dependent members of our society.

Our society clearly has a stake in competent parents who care about what happens to their children and who can restrain themselves from harming them. The financial benefit of competent parenting can be estimated by calculating the average contribution of productive citizens to our economy and the cost of incompetent parenting tallied by calculating the average loss of productive income and direct expenditures on habitual criminals. I estimate that competent parents contribute $1 million to our economy for each child they rear. Incompetent parents cost society $2 million for each child they neglect and abuse. The best social program for any child is a competent parent.

Parental rights and children's rights can be reconciled. The parental-rights amendment reinforces the expectation that the responsibility falls on parents to protect their children from our hostile and exploitative society. But nonparenting adults and community organizations also have a responsibility to model positive social values for children. The National Task Force for Children's Constitutional Rights, based in Litchfield, Conn., seeks an amendment to the Constitution that assures that every child shall "enjoy the right to a safe and healthy home, the right to adequate health care, the right to an education, and the right to the care of a loving family." If enacted, the amendment would reduce the pressure on all of us to create a benevolent society that protects and nurtures our young.

The rhetoric of the parental-rights movement suggests that government is the enemy of parents. Far from it: Government can and should do more to support competent parents by controlling inflation, giving families income-tax credits and the aggressive pursuit of child support. Competent parenting is a legal right in the sense that incompetent parenting, as shown by child neglect and abuse, is a cause for state intervention and the possible termination of parental rights. Child-labor laws, mandatory education laws and child abuse and neglect laws reflect the principle that children have rights and are not owned as property by their parents.

Government can prevent incompetent parenting by pursuing antiaddiction measures that reduce demand for illegal drugs and by aggressive law enforcement to make neighborhoods secure. In the educational realm, courses that discourage teenage pregnancy, reinforce abstinence and teach contraception will make better parents and stronger families.

Our government also should protect the civil rights of children to competent parenting, according to numerous bills of children's rights and a series of White House conferences on children. As efforts to overcome racism and sexism have shown, the implementation of any civil right requires regulation; not everyone is influenced by persuasion and education. A clear statement of each child's right to competent parenting with enforcement capacities is needed to signify that competent parenting is valued by our society.

Still, as it is now in the United States, any male or female at any age can assert comprehensive parental rights over a child they conceive, without the expectation that they should be competent to parent that child. They are free to neglect and abuse the child until the child demonstrates sufficient evidence of damage to warrant state intervention. Then the state attempts to prove that the parents are unfit—and also may be obliged to defend parents who are eligible for public defenders.

A parental-rights amendment does nothing to ensure that all children are competently parented. If enacted, it would make it more difficult to enact laws that protect children before neglect and abuse occur, and it would impede efforts to make parents more accountable for the care of their children. For example, in 1989 California enacted a law requiring parents of children with behavior problems to attend parent-teacher conferences at public schools. This is an instance of the helpful hand of government that the amendment would tie.

The amendment also would preclude setting standards for parenting. A proactive approach to the problem of dysfunctional families is for states to set legal standards for parenting. This would place the primary responsibility for child rearing with parents rather than with the state by default. Just as individual responsibility for driving a car is certified by a driver's license, the individual responsibility of a parent for child rearing would be certified by a parenting license. Then all parents, at least in principle, would be capable of directing the upbringing and education of their children.

Public and private agencies carefully screen adoptive and foster parents. State governments license every activity that affects other persons, and children are persons. Yet licensing parents unnecessarily evokes fears of governmental control of child rearing and of undue restriction of individual freedom. It requires a paradigm shift to seeing parenting through the eyes of children, not just the parents.

With a licensing process the question of parental competence would be faced before, rather than after, a child is damaged by neglect or abuse. Licensing would hold a parent responsible for competency rather than leaving children to endure incompetent parenting until they publicly exhibit signs of injury or neglect.

The initial requirement for a parental license would be the capacity to assume full responsibility for one's own life. Eighteen would be a reasonable age based on physical, social and emotional maturation and the likelihood of completion of high school. Parental or parental-surrogate assumption of responsibility for a minor and a minor's child would be required.

The next requirement would be the parent's pledge to care for and nurture the child and to refrain from abusing and neglecting the child. If this pledge was broken at a later time, the intervention upon a parent's rights would be based upon the failure of that parent to fulfill a contractual commitment to the child. The license would be revoked, rather than subjecting the parent and child to a quasi-criminal proceeding for termination of parental rights, as now is the case.

The third requirement would be completion of a parenting course or its equivalent. Family-life education already is provided in many communities and schools. Every high school in the country would require courses that prepare young people for the responsibilities of parenthood.

When vulnerable parents are identified by failing to meet these criteria, they would receive help. If they are unable or unwilling to adequately parent their children, existing child abuse and neglect laws would be enforced with timely termination of parental rights and adoption of the children.

However, the licensing of parents would entail little more administrative structure than currently is involved in marriage licensing, birth registration and existing protective services for children.

Licensing parents has little chance of gaining popular support—unless all of the organizations who speak for children and parents envision what life would be like in the United States if every child had competent parenting. If they all share that vision as an ultimate goal, they will find common ground.

Of the People and the National Task Force for Children's Constitutional Rights should unite in formulating a constitutional amendment that affirms that all children have the right to competent parents who direct their upbringing and education. Such a commitment would profoundly benefit all of our lives and future generations.

POSTSCRIPT

Does the U.S. Need a Parental-Rights Amendment?

Parents have a history in the United States of advocating for their rights successfully. In the 1920s, the state of Oregon passed a law mandating public school attendance for children ages eight to sixteen. This law restricted all children in this age group from accessing private or home education. Parents protested, the law was questioned, and the Supreme Court overturned it, finding, "The fundamental theory of liberty upon which all governments in this Union repose excludes any general power of the State to standardize its children by forcing them to accept instruction from public teachers only."

Clearly, this was an important distinction. Government should not dictate where a parent can send her or his child for education. However, at what point should government and parental power remain separate?

Ideally, all children would be raised by a parent, parents, or caregivers who are ready to be parents. Caregivers who are prepared to parent have some knowledge of child development. They are financially and emotionally prepared for the arduous challenges that accompany the potential joys of parenthood. However, this is an ideal scenario. The reality is, too many people have children without forethought. Some do well, and others do not. According to the National Clearinghouse on Child Abuse and Neglect Information, child abuse and neglect have been steadily increasing over the last 20 years. The most recent national data estimate that over a million and a half children are abused or neglected in the United States every year. Children from families with annual incomes below $15,000 are more than 22 times more likely to experience some form of maltreatment. Children from the lowest-income families were 18 times more likely to be sexually abused, almost 56 times more likely to be educationally neglected, and over 22 times more likely to be seriously injured from maltreatment.

We must remember that a federal constitutional amendment would guarantee the rights of all parents and caregivers—not just the loving, caring, prepared ones. With that in mind, what do you think should be done to ensure parents' rights and children's rights? How much is too much when it comes to guaranteeing legal rights of parents? Do you think the government has the right to dictate how people can or should raise their children? Where would you draw the line?

Suggested Readings

Arthur G. Christean, "Are Parents' Rights in Jeopardy?" *Education Reporter* (vol. 189, 2001). Available online at http://www.eagleforum.org/educate/2001/oct01/parents-rights.shtml.

Patrick Fagan and Wade Horn, "How Congress Can Protect the Rights of Parents to Raise Their Children," *The Heritage Foundation's Issues Bulletin No. 227* (1996). Available online at http://www.heritage.org/library/categories/family/ib227.html.

Christopher J. Klicka, *The Right to Home School: A Guide to the Law on Parents' Rights in Education* (Carolina Academic Press, 2002).

Geoffrey Scarre, ed., *Children, Parents, and Politics* (Cambridge University Press, 1989).

Mark Walsh, "Court Affirms Rights of Parents to Control Children's Upbringing," *Education Week on the Web* (June 14, 2000). Available online at http://www.edweek.org/ew/ewstory.cfm?slug=40scotus.h19.

Jack Westman, *Licensing Parents: Can We Prevent Child Abuse and Neglect?* (Perseus Press, 1997).

John W. Whitehead, *State vs. Parents: Threats to Raising Your Children (Faith and Freedom Series)* (Moody Press, 1995).

Title IV of H.R. 11, the Family Reinforcement Act: Hearing Before the Subcommittee on Government Management, Information, and Technology of the Committee on Government Reform and Oversight, House of Representatives, One Hundred Fourth Congress, first session, on H.R. 11, to strengthen the rights of parents, March 16, 1995. (A copy can be obtained from the University of Rochester's Rush Rhees Library. Contact: Thomas E. Hickman, 716-275-9320 or thickman@rcl.lib.rochester.edu.)

ISSUE 3

Are Single-Parent Families a Major Cause of Social Dysfunction?

YES: Patrick Fagan, from "Broken Families Strongly Correlate With a Range of Social Pathologies," *Insight on the News* (December 8, 1997)

NO: Stephanie Coontz, from "Social Problems Correlate More Closely With Poverty Than Family Background," *Insight on the News* (December 8, 1997)

ISSUE SUMMARY

YES: Patrick Fagan, a resident scholar in family culture at the Heritage Foundation, cites the increased stress, lower production, and higher social risks that follow children who are born to single-parent families. These negative factors, he asserts, lead to other social ills later in life, such as unhealthy behaviors for managing stress and relationships that are based more on sexual attraction than on emotional connection and therefore are unlikely to last. He acknowledges the perseverance of many single-parent households but argues that all things being equal, "the intact married family beats the single-parent family in every other measurable dimension."

NO: Stephanie Coontz, a family historian at The Evergreen State College in Olympia, Washington, counters that identifying a particular family type as the source of certain social ills is not only inaccurate but can also lead to ineffective public policies. The challenges facing many people, such as poverty, school delinquency, and work benefits, she contends are there whether a person is single or married. Coontz maintains that encouraging marriage as a panacea to these social ills is not the answer.

Discussions of the family structure are rooted deeply in moral values. Opinions are touted from religious institutions to political arenas to the media. What makes a family? What are the implications if a child is born into a single-parent family versus being raised by one parent as a result of divorce, the death of a parent, or because the couple never married? What about a same-sex couple that cannot legally marry or a family in which children are raised by a grandparent, aunt, uncle, or other adult caregiver(s)?

Conservatives maintain a hard line that a child should be raised by a married, heterosexual couple. In 1988, then-Vice President Dan Quayle stated, "Everybody knows the definition of the family. A child. A mother. A father." Four years later, Quayle criticized the then-popular television show *Murphy Brown*, saying, "It doesn't help matters when... Murphy Brown—a character who supposedly epitomizes today's intelligent, highly paid, professional woman—mock[s] the importance of fathers by bearing a child alone and call[s] it just another 'lifestyle choice.'" The implication in this and other arguments is that women who raise a child alone do so insufficiently, that the presence of a male figure is vital to ensure a healthy balance in the child's life.

On the other side of the argument are those who are not convinced that marriage is the answer. Looking at the problems children face exclusively in terms of parental union ignores the very real role that educational and income levels play in determining a person's social health and well-being. There are highly successful individuals who were raised by single parents or caregivers. Would those who think single parenthood is the root of social dysfunction encourage a woman to stay with an abusive husband if the couple had a child rather than choose to raise her child alone?

As you read the following selections, keep in mind the way in which the question is posed. Do single-parent families cause social dysfunction, or are they caused by social dysfunction? Does a single-parent family in itself imply some kind of dysfunction—and if so, what are your thoughts on those individuals who are not married or in a long-term, committed relationship and who choose to start a family? Also keep in mind that the arguments presented focus on heterosexual marriages. Since the issue is focused on single-parent families, do you think the authors would change their viewpoints if the two-parent family had two mothers or two fathers? Finally, consider the information shared about people of different racial and ethnic groups. What, if anything, do you think race and ethnicity have to do with the ability of a single-parent family to succeed today in the United States?

In the following selections, Patrick Fagan highlights a number of studies that point to the negative consequences of raising children in single-parent families. These consequences, he argues, negatively affect the greater society. Stephanie Coontz believes that single-parent homes are often the product of society's greatest challenges, including poverty. She does not think that the number of parents predicts how children will do in this setting, particularly since some single-parent households may have more supports available to them than some two-parent families.

Patrick Fagan  **YES**

Broken Families Strongly Correlate With a Range of Social Pathologies

Is the single-parent family a symptom or a cause of social disintegration in the United States? Paradoxical as it may sound, it is both. Obviously, people living in single-parent families do not have bad intentions, but they are trapped by their own or their parents' actions in a form of community that harms children. The evidence is all around us: dangerous, failing schools in America's inner cities, crime-plagued neighborhoods, crowded prisons and high rates of drug addiction.

Different family forms are the end result of two major kinds of rejection among adult parents: either out-of-wedlock birth or divorce. In 1950, for every 100 children born, 12 children entered a broken family. In 1992, for every 100 children born, 58 entered a broken family. With proportions this high it is more difficult for the nation to have a consensus on family life. But, even as the consensus decreases, the case for the intact married family becomes more compelling, as does the evidence that the single-parent family is a much riskier place for a child. Of course some single-parent families do a better—sometimes a much better—job of raising their children than some married parents do. But, all other things being equal, the intact married family beats the single-parent family in every measurable dimension.

That does not mean that single-parent families are to be blamed in any way—quite the opposite. Because of the difficulty of raising children, of forming the next nation, single parents need all the help they can get. But neither the nation nor single parents need to hear that their family form is just as good for their children as any other one. This will shortchange their grandchildren, doubly so, because behind every single-parent family is a serious and hurtful rejection between the adults. The rejection between the adults has myriad consequences for the physical, intellectual, emotional, economic and social development of the child and of society. No one can be indifferent to this rejection or say it does not have serious consequences. Claiming that all family forms should be equally esteemed is to insist—against all evidence—that there is no difference between the love of father and mother and the love of only one parent. We cannot afford to hide the truth just to be nice. Much more than feelings are at stake as the following summary of the broad directions of the social-science research data show.

Right from birth the health of the newborn is at risk. Controlling for education, income and health of the mother, being born out of wedlock increases the risk of infant mortality and of ill health in early infancy, according to the National Health Interview survey of 1989. Nicholas Eberstadt, a visiting scholar at Harvard University's Center for Population Studies, has written that the health of a child born to a college-educated single mother is at greater risk than the health of a child born to married grade-school dropouts.

The verbal IQ of children in single-parent families also is at risk. As Hillary Rodham Clinton has made popularly known, the verbal IQ of the child is intimately linked to the amount of verbal stimulation the child gets. The single parent has a hard time giving the same amount of stimulation as two married parents can give, all other things being equal. That is common sense.

The verbal IQ is the building block of education, and at all levels of family income the child from a single-parent family will perform at lower levels all through grade school, high school and college. This translates into lower job attainment and salary upon joining the workforce. This means that, overall, children of single-parent families are less productive in the marketplace as a group, produce less and therefore contribute less to the common tax base. At the other end of the job spectrum—welfare dependence—the risk is much higher for children from single-parent families.

Consider the correlation of personal psychological problems—the ability of children of broken families to control their impulses, particularly sex and aggression—and single-parent families. They will have more out-of-wedlock births and contract more sexually transmitted diseases. Crime rates also will be higher. Crime rates are low for children of married intact families, black or white, and high for children of broken families, regardless of race.

Alcohol and drug-addiction problems similarly are different for married and single-parent families, when all other things are equal. The same holds for teenage suicide and child abuse, where the rates of abuse are dramatically different across family structures. A recent British study found that the rate of child abuse is lowest in intact families, six times higher in blended families, 13 times higher in single-mother families and 20 times higher in single-father families. By far the most dangerous place for a mother or her child is in a family structure where the mother's boyfriend is cohabiting. Ample scientific data show that as a group children in broken families will not reach the same level of human capacity as children from intact married families. One of their parents will have shortchanged them despite the subsequent best efforts of the other parent or even of both parents.

The effects on parents themselves are different but similarly disruptive. David Larson, a psychiatrist and president of the National Institute for Healthcare Research in Rockville, Md., has noted that the emotional stress of divorce has the same effects on a husband's health as if he smoked two packs of cigarettes a day for the rest of his life; for the wife the effect compares to the impact of her smoking one pack a day for the same period.

The likely impact on the family life of the next generation is not a happy story either. A Princeton University study has found that compared to young women growing up in two-parent families, girls who are in single-parent families at age 16 are 72 percent more likely to become single mothers, too. While many children of broken families are determined and succeed in having a better marriage than their parents, all other things being equal, children from intact married families will be more likely to pull if off. Children of divorced parents are more likely to be anxious about marriage and more tentative in their commitment. Though understandable, this is not best for the marriages they enter.

These changes are having dramatic effects at the community level. Among our very poor families, those with incomes less than $15,000 per year, marriage has all but disappeared, and among working-class families with incomes between $15,000 to $30,000 a year, married parents don't exist for 45 percent of the children. As social scientist Charles Murray has observed, when the rate of single-parent families reaches 30 percent in a neighborhood, the quality of life dramatically collapses. Adolescent boys run wild and form gangs; crime rates soar and drug abuse increases.

In all likelihood many of these children will not marry as adults because they have not experienced marriage in their families or seen it around them. As time goes on, these communities have more and more second-, third- and even fourth-generation single-parent families. Judging from statistics released in the federal National Longitudinal Survey of Youth, this appears to be happening: The second generation is affected even more than the first. One may conclude from the survey that, as family ties progressively are frayed with each succeeding generation of single parenthood, the fabric of neighborhood communities unravels and, rather than being a source of support for families, the community becomes a hindrance to parents' ability to raise their children well. Increasingly, America's lower-income communities are becoming dangerous *anticommunities*—where social cooperation is less and less possible. This is most apparent in the public schools in poverty-stricken areas. But the same drift exists in middle-class neighborhoods.

It may be argued that the fundamental cause of our changing family forms is the change in relationships between men and women. Sexual mores have changed radically in the last three generations, and adult men and women find it less and less within their abilities to select, commit and follow through on lifelong marriage. The capacity to move from sexual attraction to emotional attraction to courtship to marriage to lifelong fidelity has diminished immensely. The ability of the sexes to love each other has been seriously eroded, and their children suffer, for if there is one thing that a child needs more than anything else from his parents it is their love for each other. Because love between the parents is the greatest nourishment for a child, with it the effects of poverty, lack of education and ill health all can be overcome. Without it the child spends much of life trying to make up for it, frequently being drawn down blind alleys of experimentation with sex, drugs and alcohol as substitutes for what he or she wants: the love that lasts through all the challenges and disappointments of life.

Alienation between men and women explains more about America's troubles than anything else. While those who have suffered this type of pain need the support and love of all the rest of us—and need it more than those of us blessed with married, loving parents—it does not help them to say that this pain is nothing and makes no difference. To do that is to deny the human heart finding its need and capacity for love, the biggest task of our existence. That this debate be flushed out is good and also critical for the nation. If we do not correct course on this one the United States will crumble and disintegrate. It already is well on the way there. The question is: Can we turn around in time to prevent national disintegration, and can we discover how the single parents of today can live to see their grandchildren with happily married parents?

Stephanie Coontz

↰ **NO**

Social Problems Correlate More Closely With Poverty Than Family Background

Family breakdown is behind all our problems."

"Marriage is the solution to poverty and social alienation."

Political pundits love one-ingredient recipes, whether for disasters or success. That may be understandable for people who live in 13-second sound bites, but it's hard on everyday Americans trying to sort through the complex challenges facing their families.

The idea that single-parent families are a major cause of the social dysfunctions in contemporary America glosses over the stresses facing two-parent families while telling one-parent families they essentially are out of luck. This isn't helpful to either family type. Worse, it leads to bad social policy, such as attempts to abolish no-fault divorce or pressure single mothers into getting married.

Let's start with a reality check. Three-fourths of married mothers with children work outside the home, earning on average 41 percent of family income. In 23 percent of couples, the wife makes more than the husband. Increasingly, women have the option to leave a bad marriage or refuse a shotgun one. At the same time, marriage organizes a smaller part of our lives than ever. The age of marriage for women is at a historic high, while for men it has tied its previous high in 1890. At the other end of life, the average 60-year-old has another 20 years to live. For both young and old, there are more opportunities for a satisfying life outside of marriage than ever before. Combined with women's new economic independence, this limits how many people feel compelled to get or stay married. Even if states repeal no-fault divorce, the partner with the most resources and least scruples simply can desert, fabricate evidence or move to a more permissive state.

Divorce, then, is probably here to stay. How big a cause of social dysfunction is that? It is true that children of divorced parents are more likely to have problems than children of always-married parents. But the average differences are not large and often stem from factors other than single parenthood per se.

Sometimes the "increased risk" associated with divorce, for example, sounds dramatic when expressed in percentages, but still remains quite small.

A parental divorce, for instance, triples the chance that a woman will have a premarital birth—but this raises the probability of such a birth from .05 percent to .17 percent. As Princeton University researcher Sara McLanahan points out: "Outlawing divorce would raise the national high-school graduation rate from about 86 percent to 88 percent. . . . It would reduce the risk of a premarital birth among young black women from about 45 percent to 39 percent."

What about the psychological effects of divorce? Obviously, kids raised by two involved, cooperating parents have a big advantage. But involved, co-operating parents are not always what kids get. It often is a bad marriage, rather than subsequent divorce, that accounts for children's problems.

About 20 percent of children of divorced parents have emotional and behavioral problems, compared with about 10 percent of children in married families. This finding certainly should concern us. But the difference is not always a result of divorce itself. Researchers studying children who do poorly after divorce have found that behavior problems often already were evident 8 to 12 years before the divorce took place, suggesting that both the child's maladjustment and the divorce were symptoms of more deep-rooted family and parenting dysfunctions.

Certainly, divorce can trigger new difficulties connected with loss of income, school relocation and constriction of extended-family ties. While some divorces improve the situation for kids by decreasing conflict, others lead to escalating hostility about custody and finances. Intense conflict after a divorce can be especially damaging to children. But rolling back divorce rights will not reverse the effects of bad marriages and may exacerbate the parental hostility associated with the worst outcomes for kids.

Individuals should know the risks of single parenthood, and parents who simply are bored with their marriages certainly should consider sticking it out. But life is too complicated to let some local judge veto whatever decision people end up making. A man who is discontented with his wife, for example, often treats his daughter with contempt, threatening the girls' self-confidence and academic achievement. An unhappy married woman may have trouble dealing with a teenage son's behavior that reminds her of her spouse. One recent study of teens found no overall difference in self-image by family form. But the lowest self-esteem of all was found in adolescents in intact families where the father, though not hostile, showed little interest in the youth.

Never-married single parenthood often is more problematic than divorce because it so frequently occurs in the context of income deprivation. But non-marriage is not the major cause of poverty in America and, since most low-income mothers were impregnated by low-income men, marriage is seldom the answer.

Correlations, contrary to sound-bite specialists, are not causes. Yes, kids in one-parent families are more likely to be poor, but there's a chicken-and-egg question here. Poor parents are twice as likely to divorce, unemployed men are three to four times less likely to marry in the first place and girls with poor life prospects are five to seven times more likely to become unwed teen mothers than more fortunate girls. According to Census Bureau figures, even if you reunited every single child in America with both biological parents, two-thirds of the kids who are poor today still would be poor. For never-married mothers who are not poor, factors such as maternal education and parenting skills have more effect on their children's outcomes than their marital status.

Marriage is not a psychological cure-all any more than it is an economic one. One study of teens who had a nonmarital birth found that the reading scores of their children were higher when the mothers remained single than when they married the father of their child, probably because such marriages tended to be especially conflict-prone. Similarly, single African-American teens have a lower infant mortality rate than those who marry. This is likely due to the fact that marriage to a man with poor job prospects or low wages provides less social support than maternal kin networks.

Parental conflict, in or out of marriage, is the worst psychological risk for kids. Poverty, income loss, residential insecurity and the social alienation caused by widening income disparities and mean-spirited finger-pointing are the worst social risks.

Poverty during the first five years of life leads to an average IQ deficit of 9 points, regardless of family form. Kids with elevated levels of lead in their bloodstreams or bones—a frequent outcome of living in run-down neighborhoods where the pipes and paint haven't been changed since 1975—are six times more likely to engage in violence and seven times more likely to drop out of school than other kids, again regardless of family form. Poverty also frequently produces bad parenting. Low-income mothers, whether single or married, are 60 percent more likely than other moms to inflict severe violence on their children.

It is true that our prisons contain disproportionate numbers of people who were raised in single-parent families. That's partly because most crimes occur in neighborhoods where desperation breeds both broken families and youthful violence, as well as depriving children of mentors beyond the family. It's partly because kids of single parents are more likely to have been exposed to adult conflict during the course of a marriage or a series of transitory relationships. The Rand Corp. reports that parental conflict has a stronger relation with youth delinquency and aggression than parental absence, per se.

When researchers have asked young people themselves how much delinquency they engage in, "family structure was unrelated to the seriousness of the offense." But school officials, juvenile authorities and police are more likely to record and penalize behaviors committed by children from single-parent families. Such children are more likely to be prosecuted, less likely to get probation and more likely to spend time in jail than kids of two-parent families who've committed similar offenses. Walter Bien, head of the preeminent German family research institute, reports he has found exactly the same pattern in Germany.

All this is not to deny that there are serious problems associated with many divorces and single-parent situations. Putting them in perspective, however, helps us avoid panic responses that create bad social policy and blind us to the many other forces that threaten effective parenting and child well-being.

Every family needs help raising children in today's fast-paced culture. Working parents, married or unmarried, need quality child care, medical insurance and livable-wage jobs. We must adjust our attitudes toward marriage, our work policies and our school hours to the reality that women are in the workforce to stay. We should provide marital and parental counseling before and during marriage, teaching individuals how to manage personal conflict. But we must pay equal attention to helping people minimize the acrimony of divorce when it cannot healthfully be headed off. Child-support enforcement should be strengthened and, if a spouse sacrificed earnings potential during the marriage to raise the children, the other spouse should provide a maintenance allowance for some period after the divorce.

Finally, we should tell the truth about the fact that almost any family that is not overwhelmed with other risks can learn to function effectively. For married parents, the key to successful parenting is mutual respect and good problem-solving. Divorced parents should minimize conflict, establish economic security for the custodial parent and keep the noncustodial parent acting like a parent rather than a rival or indulgent grandparent. Single parents must resist being seduced by the special intimacy such parents have with their children; they need clear limits and rules to deal with the inevitable separation issues of the teenage years. Stepfamilies require flexibility about gender roles and household boundaries, because there are four parents and four sets of grandparents involved in their kids' lives.

Every family is at risk when we pretend we can go it alone; we're almost all resilient when we get social support. The search for easy answers and quick-fix solutions deprives families of the support and information we all need.

POSTSCRIPT

Are Single-Parent Families a Major Cause of Social Dysfunction?

The current White House administration, under President George W. Bush, is emphatically pushing marriage as a feature in welfare reform. They, and other conservative groups, are pushing for a return to "promarriage" values. Opponents think that holding marriage up as the panacea to social ills is unrealistic. They believe that government programs need to focus more on eradicating the causes of poverty and less on providing financial incentives for those who decide to marry. They contend that even with two-parent heterosexual couples that have children, three-quarters of the female partners work outside of the home and are responsible for over 40 percent of the family's income.

John DeFrain, Ph.D., a family therapist and professor at the University of Nebraska in Lincoln, believes that we should focus less on external family structure and more on internal family functioning. He emphasizes that all families possess strength, regardless of structure. He believes that looking for problems in family structure will yield problems, while seeking strengths will reveal strengths. According to DeFrain, there are strong single-parent families, strong stepfamilies, strong nuclear families, strong extended families, strong families with gay and lesbian members, and strong two-parent families. He reminds us that every ethnic or cultural group has strong families—and every ethnic or cultural group has families that are not doing well financially or socially.

As with many controversial issues, the passion behind this topic is rooted in the language used by those expressing their opinions. Families of divorce are labeled "broken," a term that implies failure because the union was terminated. Even the term "social dysfunction" begs the age-old "chicken and egg" question—was social dysfunction present before single-parent families became more common, or did single-parent families appear only to be followed by social dysfunction? There is an adage that translates roughly to "whenever you point a finger at someone, you are pointing three back at yourself." With this in mind, one wonders if it is more important to determine whether or not single-parent families are the cause of social dysfunction or to look toward how our society can best support those who are in need, regardless of family structure.

Suggested Readings

David Blankenhorn, *Fatherless America: Confronting Our Most Urgent Social Problem* (Basic Books, 1995).

Nancy E. Dowd, *In Defense of Single-Parent Families* (New York University Press, 1999).

Sara McLanahan and Gary Sandefur, *Growing Up With a Single Parent: What Hurts, What Helps* (Harvard University Press, 2001).

Elizabeth A. Mulroy, *The New Uprooted: Single Mothers in Urban Life* (Auburn House Publishing, 1995).

David Popenoe, *Life Without Father: Compelling New Evidence That Fatherhood and Marriage Are Indispensable for the Good of Children and Society* (Harvard University Press, 1999).

Trudi J. Renwick, *Poverty and Single Parent Families: A Study of Minimal Subsistence Household Budgets* (Garland Publishing, 1998).

Caroline Wright and Gill Jagger, *Changing Family Values: Feminist Perspectives* (Routledge, 1999).

ISSUE 4

Can We Raise "Gender-Neutral" Children?

YES: Sandra Lipsitz Bem, from *An Unconventional Family* (Yale University Press, 1998)

NO: Denise A. Segura and Jennifer L. Pierce, from "Chicana/o Family Structure and Gender Personality: Chodorow, Familism, and Psychoanalytic Sociology Revisited," *Signs* (Autumn 1993)

ISSUE SUMMARY

YES: Psychologist Sandra Lipsitz Bem uses her own children as examples that raising gender-neutral children is not only possible but also can result in positive self-esteem. She states that by discussing differences in genders without attaching a value to these differences, children who are raised with gender-neutral expectations will have a more open, positive view of the world in general.

NO: Sociologists Denise A. Segura and Jennifer L. Pierce contend that gender and gender role expectations are tied very closely to familial and cultural expectations. Referring to the Chicana/o culture of Mexico, they demonstrate that gender-specific role fulfillment is vital to certain cultures, ensuring the survival of important cultural traditions.

When a baby is born, the first question most people ask is, "Is it a boy or a girl?" We need to know the baby's biological sex so that we know how to respond; we need to know whether to buy the pink "onesie" or the blue one, the doll or the football. Studies show that, in general, people tend to treat boys and girls differently from infancy. A boy is handled more roughly from infancy, a girl much more gently. When a male toddler falls down and begins to cry, we tend to tell him to get up and brush himself off. When a female child does the same, we are much more likely to scoop her up, talk to her gently, and reassure her of her safety.

When we are born, we have a biological sex. Our biological sex is determined by a combination of our genitalia and chromosomal structure. If we have a penis, testicles, and an XY chromosomal combination, we are male. If we have a vulva, ovaries, and an XX chromosomal makeup, we are female. If we have combined genitalia and/or chromosomal structure, we are intersex.

Gender, however, is a social construct that is communicated in gender identity and gender role expectations and expressions. Gender *identity* is who we know to be inside—male, female, or transgender—regardless of what our physical package may look like. Our gender *role* involves the ways in which we let people know what our gender is. Gender role expectations in most societies are based on a heterosexual relationship structure, looking at how males and females behave in relation to each other. One example of stereotypical gender role fulfillment would be a woman who wears only dresses, wears makeup, does not play any sports, and does not work outside of the home. She might be married to a stereotypical male, who is the sole income earner, goes out with the guys for recreation, and doesn't miss football or basketball games on Sunday afternoons. Then again, many males and females fulfill nontraditional gender roles. More and more women are seeking employment in what have traditionally been considered "male" jobs. We are also beginning to see an increase in the number of men who stay home to raise their children while their wives earn the family income.

Some people look at the increasing fluidity between the genders and think it is very positive. They believe that opportunities should be open to everyone, including opportunities for financial advancement, social recognition, and a range of emotional expression. Others believe the lines should remain clear. There are certain things that women cannot and should not do, and certain ways in which men should and should not act. The more we blur the lines, they argue, the more confused and conflicted a society becomes.

As you read the following selections, think about the advantages there are to being male in this society. What are the advantages to being female? In what ways do you think our expectations of people based on their gender benefit individuals? In what ways do they hurt?

In the following selections, Sandra Lipsitz Bem describes the extensive efforts she made to ensure that her children would recognize differences between people without correlating these differences to a person's biological sex. Bem argues that children who understand this concept are more open-minded and less likely to be either sexist or homophobic. Denise A. Segura and Jennifer L. Pierce, writing specifically about Chicana/o culture, argue that gender cannot be addressed in a vacuum. They argue that in Chicana/o culture, as in other cultures, the roles men and women/boys and girls fulfill are tied closely to what it means to be a member of that culture. Gender role fulfillment that some might view as stereotypical, such as having females be responsible for cooking and childrearing, is actually valued greatly and tied to maintaining cultural traditions and veracity.

Sandra Lipsitz Bem

 **YES**

Feminist Child-Rearing

Shortly before Emily was born, in 1974, I put an end to our public lecturing on egalitarianism and to interviews about our lives because I didn't want our children to become local celebrities, as we had become. Daryl and I did continue lecturing on egalitarianism in my undergraduate course on gender, however, and within a few years, I developed a second lecture for that course based on our lives, this one on the feminist child-rearing practices we had developed.

Until the 1990s, I rarely gave this lecture outside my class. As early as the mid-1980s, however, I did incorporate parts of it into my scholarly writing, and Daryl also wrote about it in his textbook on introductory psychology. As much as I may have once intended to protect my children's privacy, by the mid-1990s, the story Daryl and I told most often—about what happened to Jeremy the day he wore barrettes to nursery school—had become so well known that a feminist legal scholar used it (with my permission) as both the title and the prologue of a law review article on gender-specific dress requirements in the workplace.

I'll tell the barrettes story a little later. I mention it now only to highlight the fact that, although we were much less public about our feminist child-rearing than about our egalitarianism, here too we quickly transformed our private feminist practice into public feminist discourse. Hence I remember more about how I analyzed my life in public than how I lived my life on a daily basis.

I began thinking about feminist child-rearing in the late 1960s, when I read an influential article by the developmental psychologist Lawrence Kohlberg, in which he suggested that young children are rigidly gender-stereotyped in their thinking and acting not because of the way they are raised but because of their "cognitive-developmental stage." It is not our gender-stereotyped culture, in other words, that convinces our children (and especially our boys) to eschew anything and everything associated with the other sex, including toys, clothes, colors, and even people. No, this idea emerges naturally and inevitably from the child's own immature mind. No need to worry, though. With age and maturity will come a more advanced cognitive-developmental stage and hence a more flexible way of seeing both the self and the world.

"I don't believe this for a second," I thought to myself. It may be difficult to raise a gender-liberated child, but it is surely not impossible. And even the reason it's difficult is not primarily because of any cognitive limitation on the part of the child. It's because the child is situated in a culture that distinguishes ubiquitously on the basis of sex from the moment of birth. Given that social reality, moreover, it ought to be possible for even young children to be gender-liberated if we can inoculate them early enough and effectively enough against the culture....

How are children to be protected against the culture's sex-and-gender system? I always describe inoculating our own children in two distinct phases.

During the first phase, our goal was to enable Emily and Jeremy to learn about both male-female difference and the body without simultaneously learning any cultural stereotypes about males and females or any cultural stigmas about the body. Put somewhat differently, our goal was to retard their gender education while simultaneously advancing their sex education.

To retard their gender education, Daryl and I did everything we could for as long as we could to eliminate any and all correlations between a person's sex and other aspects of life. For example, we took turns cooking the meals, driving the car, bathing the baby, and so on, so that our own parental example would not teach a correlation between sex and behavior. This was easy for us because we already had such well-developed habits of egalitarian turn-taking. In addition, we tried to arrange for both our children to have traditionally male and traditionally female experiences—including, for example, playing with both dolls and trucks, wearing both pink and blue clothing, and having both male and female playmates. This turned out to be easy, too, perhaps because of our kids' temperaments. Insofar as possible, we also arranged for them to see nontraditional gender models outside the home.

I remember telling my class I was so determined to expose our children to nontraditional models that when Emily was very young, I drove her past a particular construction site every day because a female construction worker was a member of the crew there. I never let on that it was always the same site and the same woman we were seeing because I wanted there to be a time in her life when Emily didn't even think of such women as unusual. More important, we never allowed there to be a time in our children's lives when they didn't know that some people had partners of their own sex and other people had partners of the other sex. This was both extremely easy and extremely important in our family because so many of our closest relatives were either lesbians or gay men....

Another way we retarded our children's gender education was to monitor—even to censor—books and television. I had no qualms about limiting television to three hours a week because, in addition to being filled with gender stereotypes, it also kills children's brain cells (metaphorically speaking) by addicting them (again, metaphorically speaking) to a state of passivity. Books, in contrast, I hated even the thought of monitoring because I love books and wanted our children to love them, too. The problem is that if young children are allowed to sample freely from the world of children's literature, they will almost certainly be indoctrinated with the idea that girls and boys are not only different from each other but, even worse, that boys are more important. What else can one conclude, after all, when there are approximately ten boys in these stories for every girl and almost a hundred "boy" animals for every "girl" animal? (I'm not exaggerating.) Or when the few females who are in these books almost always stay indoors and at home—no matter what their age or species—while the males go outdoors and have adventures. Or, perhaps worst of all, when the females are so unable to affect their own environments that when good things happen to them, those things just fall out of the sky, whereas when good things happen to males, their own efforts have usually played a part in making them occur.

Not only did we censor books with traditional messages like these. For a time, we restricted our children's access even to feminist books like *William's Doll.* After all, for a child who doesn't yet know about the American cultural taboo with respect to boys and dolls, even a book that argues that it's all right for boys to have dolls is teaching a gender stereotype in the very process of trying to counter it.

To compensate for all this censorship, I worked hard to locate as many books as I could that were free of gender stereotypes. Ironically, this may have been easier in the 1970s than it is today because of the many small feminist collectives that specialized in producing such books then. And although I have no artistic talent, I was handy with my whiteout and magic markers, which I used liberally to transform one main character after another from male to female by changing the character's name, by changing the pronouns, and even by drawing long hair (and, if age-appropriate, the outline of breasts) onto the character's picture. Nor did I limit my doctoring to the main characters. I frequently changed even background characters who appeared in the illustrations from male to female because, if I didn't, the main character would be living in a world disproportionately populated by males.

The only time I remember this getting me into trouble was when I bought my children a Curious George book and decided to change the tall man in a yellow hat into a tall woman in a yellow hat. Never having heard of Curious George, I didn't know it was a series, and I also didn't know how very, very often the tall man would reappear. So, after making him a woman in the first book, I let her revert to a man in the rest of the books, thereby giving our children their first encounter with an implicit sex-change operation. They, bless their gender-liberated hearts, never seemed to notice.

When reading books aloud to our children, we also chose our pronouns carefully in order not to imply that all characters not wearing a dress or a pink hair ribbon must necessarily be male: "And what is this little piggy doing? Why, he or she seems to be building a bridge." Jeremy, in particular, seemed to hear this pronoun phrase as a single word because, for many years, he used the he-or-she form exclusively in almost all third-person contexts. If I asked Jeremy to tell me what Emily or Dad or some character in a book was doing, Jeremy would typically say that "heorshe" was doing whatever he or she was doing. I had thus unwittingly introduced a gender-nonspecific (but not neuter) third-person pronoun into the English language.

So much for retarding our children's gender education. To advance their sex education, we taught them about the body as early as we could. That is, we provided a clear and unambiguous bodily definition of what sex is. A boy, we said again and again, is someone with a penis and testicles; a girl is someone with a vagina, a clitoris, and a uterus; and whether you're a boy or a girl, a man or a woman, shouldn't matter unless and until you want to make a baby. Consistent with this premise, I also refused to provide a simple answer when the kids asked me in the supermarket or the park or wherever whether someone was a boy or a girl, a man or a lady. Instead I said (quietly, so as not to draw attention to myself) that I couldn't really tell without seeing under the person's clothes. When this answer began to be unsatisfactory, I complicated things a bit by conceding, for example, that since the person was wearing a dress, we might guess that he or she was a girl because, in this country, girls are the ones who more often wear dresses. As always, however, I concluded that one cannot know for certain without seeing under the person's clothes.

I was not the only person my children talked to, of course, and they were not dummies, so eventually they came to understand that I was playing a kind of game with them, and then we began to play the game together. One time I remember in particular, Emily brought me a magazine with a male face on the cover and teasingly said to me, "Look, Mom, it's a boy head." Knowing it was a game, I immediately started laughing and said to her, "What do you mean it's a boy head? I don't see any penis on that head. How can it be a boy head if it doesn't have a penis?" Then she started laughing too. But even if everyone treated these interactions playfully, the game had a serious subtext: an important distinction must be made between an attribute that is merely correlated with sex and an attribute that is definitional of sex. Attributes that are merely correlated with sex, like clothing and hairstyle, don't really matter; only your genitalia define you as male or female.

Both the liberation that can come from having a narrow bodily definition of sex and the imprisonment that can come from not having such a definition are strikingly illustrated by what happened to Jeremy on the day he decided to wear barrettes to nursery school. When Jeremy came to me that morning and asked me to put barrettes in his hair, the first thought that came into my mind was: "Hmmm. I wonder if Jeremy knows that barrettes are 'just for girls.'" The next thought was the script I imagined the good liberal parent would now begin to read from. "Jeremy," this good liberal script would say, "you're certainly welcome to wear these barrettes to nursery school if you want to. It's fine with me. But there's something I need to tell you to help you make your decision. Even though our family thinks boys and girls should be able to do anything they want as long as it doesn't hurt anybody or break anything, a lot of other people still have the old-fashioned idea that some things are just for girls and other things are just for boys, and (can you believe it?!) barrettes are actually one of the things these people think of as just for girls. Now just because that's what some people think about barrettes doesn't mean you shouldn't wear them. But you probably should know ahead of time that if you do wear them, you might get teased a bit."

I myself said none of this, however, because I had vowed long before, never, in the domain of sex and gender, to be the carrier of the culture to my children. So with barrettes in his hair, off Jeremy went to nursery school.

When Jeremy came home that day, I was dying to find out what, if anything, had happened, but I didn't want to ask because I didn't want to make a big deal of it. I waited and waited for Jeremy to bring it up spontaneously. But he never did, not that day, not the next day, not for a long time. Then I forgot about it until one of his teachers asked me at a parent-teacher get-together if Jeremy had ever described what happened on the day he wore barrettes to nursery school. Several times that day, another little boy had asserted that Jeremy must be a girl, not a boy, because "only girls wear barrettes." After repeatedly insisting that "Wearing barrettes doesn't matter; I have a penis and testicles," Jeremy finally pulled down his pants to make his point more convincingly. The other boy was not impressed. He simply said, "Everybody has a penis; only girls wear barrettes."

But I didn't try to "teach the body" only to provide our children with a stereotype-free definition of male and female. I also tried to teach the body as a stigma-free foundation for sexuality. . . .

By advancing our children's sex education and retarding their gender education, Daryl and I enabled them to learn their earliest lessons about sex and sexual difference without simultaneously learning the many cultural stereotypes and stigmas that typically accompany these lessons. But how were we to keep them from sliding over to the enemy side, so to speak, as they gradually began to hear the voice of the dominant culture? How, in other words, to keep them from forsaking these early lessons when they later began to realize, as they inevitably would, that their parents' beliefs about sex and sexual difference were different from those of most other people? This question brings me to the second phase of the children's inoculation process.

During this second phase, our overarching goal was to make our children skeptical of whatever conventional cultural messages about sex and gender they might be exposed to, whether from television, from books, from movies, from other people, or from anywhere else. More specifically, our goal was to provide them with the kind of critical feminist lens or framework that would predispose them to "read" the culture's conventional messages in an unconventional way. How did we go about trying to provide them with such a framework? In retrospect, four things we did seem particularly important.

The first thing we did—though I'm not sure we understood its relevance to our feminist goals when we did it—was to emphasize the theme of difference and diversity long before it was relevant to sex and gender. "Why are some of our friends not allowed to play in the nude, but we are?" our children would ask when they were young. "Why do other families say grace before meals but we don't? Why can cousin so-and-so drink Pepsi with dinner but we have to drink milk?" To these questions and dozens like them, our answer was always the same: Different people believe different things, and because they believe different things, they make up different rules for their children.

Few of these early diversity conversations focused on sex or gender. Nevertheless, they provided our kids with the underlying premise that different—and even contradictory—beliefs are the rule rather than the exception in a pluralistic society. This premise served as an excellent foundation for what we would later say about difference and diversity when our conversations turned to sex and gender, as they did when the kids started asking questions like: Why is some boy in Emily's nursery-school class not allowed to dress up in a princess costume for Halloween? Or, why is some girl in Jeremy's kindergarten class not allowed to sleep overnight in Jeremy's bedroom?

The second thing we did was to provide Emily and Jeremy with a non-gendered way of reframing the many conventional messages about male-female difference that they began to hear when they were three or four or five years old. These messages came in many variations, but they all boiled down to the same idea: Boys and girls are different from each other in innumerable ways, as are women and men. We always responded with a script something like the following: Yes, it's true, some girls don't like to play baseball. But you know what? Other girls like to play baseball a lot (including, for example, your Aunt Bev and Melissa who lives across the street), and some boys don't like to play baseball at all (including your dad and Melissa's brother Billy). As soon as our children began to mouth the conventional cultural stereotypes about male-female difference, we extended our earlier discussions of difference and diversity by telling them that it's not males and females who are different from each other. It's people who are different from each other.

The third thing we did was to help them to understand that all cultural messages about sex and gender (indeed, all cultural messages about everything) are created, whether now or in the distant past, by particular human beings with particular beliefs and biases. The appropriate stance to take toward such messages is thus not to assume that they are either true or relevant to your own personal life but to assume instead that they merely convey information about the beliefs and biases of their creators.

Perhaps the most obvious example of my trying to teach this stance occurred when I sat down to read to Emily from her first book of fairy tales. An older relative had given her this book when she was four years old, and although I knew it would expose her to many gender stereotypes she had never seen before, I didn't want to hold back from reading it because I thought that would indirectly and inappropriately be a criticism of the gift-giver. Besides, I thought Emily would probably enjoy the fairy tales immensely, just as I had when I was a child. Once again the challenge was how to get her own "reading" of the fairy tales to subvert the culture's messages about males and females rather than support them.

I gave Emily a little feminist lecture before I started to read. "The fairy tales in this book," I said, "are wonderfully exciting, and I think you'll like them a lot, but you need to understand before we read them that they were written a *long looooong* time ago by people who had some very peculiar ideas about girls and boys. In particular, the people who wrote these fairy tales seemed to think that the only thing that matters about girls is whether they're beautiful or not beautiful, and the other thing they seem to think about girls is that they are the kind of people who always get themselves into trouble and then need to be saved by boys, who—according to these fairy-tale writers anyway—are naturally brave and smart. Now, I haven't read these particular fairy tales yet, but I did read a lot of other fairy tales when I was little, and I'm willing to bet that if you listen really carefully, you'll hear lots and lots of stories where a brave, wise boy rescues a beautiful girl, but what you won't ever hear is even one story where a brave, wise girl rescues a beautiful boy.""

Emily loved the fairy tales, just as I thought she would, but after each one, she giggled with glee about how I had been right. "There's another one, Mom," she would say. "Aren't the people who made up these stories silly?"

Several years ago, a feminist colleague of mine was lamenting a question her preschool daughter had asked after watching *Mr. Rogers' Neighborhood* on television. "Why are kings royaler than queens?" her daughter had wanted to know. The question had troubled my colleague because she couldn't figure out how to use her daughter's question as a springboard for a feminist lesson. I knew immediately what I would say, but then I began to wonder what my kids would say, so I asked them (they were then maybe eleven and fourteen), and they both said basically the same thing: "Your friend should tell her daughter to think about who writes the script for *Mr. Rogers' Neighborhood*. If King Friday is more royal than Queen Sarah, it's not because kings *are* more royal than queens. It's because Mr. Rogers *thinks* kings are more royal than queens."

All this talk about difference and diversity is fine as far as it goes, but from a feminist perspective, not all beliefs and biases are equally valid. At some point, we also needed to convey to our children that the view of women and men represented by fairy tales, by the mass media, and by sexist and homophobic people of all ages everywhere is not only different or even "old-fashioned." It is plain and simply wrong. Accordingly, the fourth thing we did to provide our children with a critical feminist framework was to teach them about sexism and homophobia.

I distinctly remember how I introduced the concept of sexism to Emily because she immediately custom-fit my lesson to her own needs. I'm not sure why I chose the particular moment I did. Probably Emily had been quoting some classmate at nursery school who said that either Emily or some other girl couldn't do this activity or that because of her sex. Whatever the catalyst, I then read Emily a children's book I had been saving for just this occasion. The book was *Girls Can Be Anything,* by Norma Klein. The main characters are two kindergartners named Marina and Adam. Marina and Adam love to pretend that they are grown-up workers in a grown-up work environment. One day they're flying an airplane, another day they're staffing a hospital, a third day they're running a country. The plot has a certain redundancy. Both Marina and Adam want to pilot the airplane, but Adam says "girls can't be pilots . . . they have to be stewardesses"; both Marina and Adam want to be doctors, but Adam says "girls are always nurses"; and so on. I think you get the message. Luckily, Marina not only has feminist parents. She also has an abundance of extremely accomplished female relatives. Thus, when she complains to her parents at dinner about whatever sexist stereotype Adam asserted that day, her parents not only reply that of course girls can be pilots or doctors. They also remind her that one or another of her aunts is either a famous jet pilot who just logged her millionth mile (see her picture on the front page of the *New York Times*) or a famous heart surgeon who just performed her millionth heart transplant. I'm exaggerating a bit, but not much.

After we read this book together, Emily, then age four, spontaneously began to call anyone who said anything the least bit gender-stereotyped an "Adam Sobel," in the most contemptuous voice she could muster. Clearly Adam Sobelness (also known as sexism) was a concept she was ready for.

Denise A. Segura and
Jennifer L. Pierce

Chicana/o Family Structure and Gender Personality: Chodorow, Familism, and Psychoanalytic Sociology Revisited

Chicana/o Family Structure and Gender Personality

Chicanas and Chicanos come to maturity as members of a racial and ethnic minority in a social and historical context in which their political, economic, and cultural uniqueness is constantly undermined, denigrated, and violated. Since the annexation of northern Mexico by the United States in 1848, Chicanas and Chicanos have experienced second-class citizenship both politically and economically. Chicanas and Chicanos have faced discrimination in employment, education, and political participation. They have been and continue to be concentrated among the poor and the working class in the United States (Barrera 1979; Rochin and Castillo 1991). Furthermore, Chicanas and Chicanos maintain and affirm a distinct culture that emphasizes familism, *compadrazgo* [extended family ties], and a collectivist orientation that is devalued by the dominant culture's emphasis on individualism....

Much... research emphasizes the heterogeneity among Chicana/o families by immigrant status, urban/rural residence, household size, acculturation, and class status. Such empirical research also establishes important commonalities. In 1990, nearly 90 percent of Chicana/o families reported income below $50,000 to maintain families significantly larger, on the average, than the societal "norm" (4.03 persons in Chicana/o families compared with 3.12 persons in white families) (U.S. Bureau of the Census 1992, table 1). Half of all Chicana/o families in 1990 were maintained by $23,240 or less for a family of four while 25 percent lived below the poverty level ($13,359 for a family of four) (U.S. Bureau of the Census 1991a, 18, 25). In contrast, 8.1 percent of European-American families and 29.3 percent of black families lived below the poverty rate in 1990 (U.S. Bureau of the Census 1991b, 15). These figures indicate that Chicana/o families are primarily working class and often among the working poor; they provide a key socioeconomic context to the analysis of this community.

From Denise A. Segura and Jennifer L. Pierce, "Chicana/o Family Structure and Gender Personality: Chodorow, Familism, and Psychoanalytic Sociology Revisited," *Signs: Journal of Women in Culture and Society*, vol. 19, no. 1 (Autumn 1993), pp. 70, 72–81, 83–91. Copyright © 1993 by The University of Chicago. Reprinted by permission of The University of Chicago Press. Notes omitted.

Bolstered by empirical data, revisionist researchers often examine features commonly associated with both working-class and middle-class Chicana/o families, including familism (beliefs and behaviors associated with family solidarity), *compadrazgo* (extended family via godparents), *confianza* (a system of trust and intimacy), high Spanish language loyalty, a gender-specific division of labor, and high fertility. But most such research has focused on working-class families; the degree to which these traits vary by class has not been sufficiently explored. In view of the limited research on middle-class Chicana/o families, we limit our discussion to working-class families and caution that our analysis may be less relevant as income levels rise. Some evidence exists, however, that middle-class Chicana/o families display surprisingly high loyalty to the Spanish language and place a high premium on familism (Keefe and Padilla 1987); our analysis thus may resonate within this more privileged sector of the Chicana/o community.

Revisionist researchers typically analyze characteristics attributed to Chicana/o families within the context of Chicanas' and Chicanos' historically suppressed social, economic, and political opportunities, their historical clustering within certain geographic areas (the southwestern United States), and their limited political clout (Saragoza 1983; Baca Zinn and Eitzen 1987). This broader social context is important to an analysis of mothering and the reproduction of gendered personalities in Chicana/o families; this context helps to shape and define the unique constellation of features that characterize Chicana/o families. We begin by describing this constellation, which includes features such as familism, *compadrazgo,* and nonexclusive mothering. Then, by extending [Nancy] Chodorow's more recent argument (1989) about social specificity and mothering, we explore the psychological consequences this particular social context poses for the development of gender personality among Chicanas and Chicanos. We argue that in Chicana/o families the blending of gender identity and ethnic identity creates forms of masculine and feminine personality distinct from that of the European-American middle class.

The Constellation of Features in Chicana/o Families

Contemporary sociologists consider familism to be a primary characteristic of Chicana/o families (Griswold del Castillo 1984, 146). Maxine Baca Zinn observes that familism is observable in four ways: by macrocharacteristics such as large family size (demographic familism); by the presence of multigenerational households or extended households (structural familism); by the high value placed on family unity and solidarity (normative familism); and by the high level of interaction between family and kin networks (behavioral familism) (Baca Zinn 1982/83, 226–27).

Compadrazgo, another prominent feature of Chicana/o families and one associated with behavioral familism, refers to two sets of relationships with godparents who become "fictive" kin: *padrinos* and *ahiados* (godparents and their godchildren) and *compadres* (godparents and parents who become co-parents) (Falicov 1982). *Compadrazgo* relationships with godparents create connections between families, thereby enlarging Chicana/o family ties. According to Richard Griswold del Castillo, "godparents [are] required for the celebration of major religious occasions in a person's life: baptism, first communion and marriage" (1984, 42). At these times, godparents enter "into special religious, social and economic relationships with the godchild as well as the parents of the child." They act as co-parents, "providing discipline and emotional and financial support when needed." As *compadres,* they are expected to become the closest friends of the parents and members of the extended family (1984, 40–44). While *compadrazgo* is principally a feature of Roman Catholic Chicana/o families, non-Catholic Chicanas and Chicanos who go through baptism and marriage rituals may also gain *compadres....*

The continuing high fertility rate of Chicanas, for example, enhances their opportunities to acquire *compadres* and to affirm close connections to extended family members. In 1988, Hispanic women had an estimated fertility rate of 94 births per 1,000 women between the ages of 18 and 44, compared with European-American women's 67.5 births per 1,000 women (U.S. Bureau of the Census 1988). High fertility, thus, is one mechanism that reinforces the significance of familism and *compadrazgo* in Chicana/o communities. While *compadrazgo* may be changing, especially in its economic functions, Williams observes it remains an important resource for emotional support and cultural affirmation (Williams 1990, 138, 140).

Extended households and extensive family networks are other important features associated with Chicana/o familism. In their study on extended households or structural familism among whites, blacks, and Hispanics, Marta Tienda and Ronald Angel (1982) found that low-income Chicanas who headed families were more likely than European-Americans to live in households composed of several generations of kin. Charles Mindel (1980) compared European-American, African-American, and Mexican-American families and found that Mexican-Americans had the largest and most socially active extended family networks in several local geographic areas. This study and others emphasize the extensive interaction (behavioral familism) across kinship systems (fictive and real) in Chicana/o families (Horowitz 1983; Zavella 1987).

Behavioral familism reinforces what Zavella terms "the cultural principle of *confianza*" or the belief that "only certain people outside the immediate family are to be trusted with private information" (1987, 28). Mirandé suggests that the mistrust of outsiders to Chicana/o kin networks has developed historically "in response to the oppressive conditions of internal colonialism" (1985, 163). "Trust" that resides solely within Chicana/o families serves as an important strategy for cultural survival and resistance in the face of racism and other forms of domination by creating ties within and across kin networks (Bott 1971; Caulfield 1974). Extensive interaction across kin networks also enhances the opportunities for relatives other than the mother to become involved in child rearing and providing child care as well as emotional support. In times of crisis, members of the extended family provide physical and affective care for children and emotional and economic support for the parents (Sotomayor 1971; Keefe 1979; Wagner and Schaffer 1980).

Among Chicanas, mothering and paid employment are not mutually exclusive. In 1990, Chicanas' labor force participation rate was 50.6 percent while that of Chicanos was 79.6 percent (U.S. Bureau of the Census 1991a, table 2). Several researchers have observed that employed Chicanas and Chicanos rely on female kin for child care instead of on institutional arrangements (Zavella 1987; Segura 1988). A recent study of Chicana/o and European-American families in the Sunbelt region confirms this finding, but with a twist: Chicano fathers actively parent and care for their children more than Anglo fathers (Lamphere, Zavella, and Gonzalez 1993, chap. 6). The conditions under which this occurs are quite specific: female kin are not available, and men's work schedules allow them to assume child-care duties. It is possible that the higher participation of some Chicano men doing child care reflects their relatively higher representation in shift work (compared with Anglo men). On the other hand, it may also reflect a different cultural orientation. The greater willingness of Chicano fathers to engage in expanded parenting flows from their commitment to their families and familism and lack of *confianza* for nonfamily caretakers. While these parenting and child-care strategies used by Chicanas and Chicanos may not be exclusively cultural, but may also be economic strategies of a low-income group—shared to some extent by other disadvantaged groups—they are nevertheless important to consider in analyzing the reproduction of gender personality.

The practice of nonexclusive mothering, in particular, has critical implications for the development of feminine and masculine personalities in Chicana/o families. Multiple mother figures among Chicanas and Chicanos have been reported in numerous accounts. Griswold del Castillo (1984) discusses the important role of godmothers and godfathers in Chicana/o communities. Closeness between Chicanas and their grandmothers is described by many social narrators, including Diane Neumaier (1990), Lorna Dee Cervantes (1980), and Tey Diana Rebolledo (1983). Lisa Hernandez describes the critical grandmother-mother-daughter triad as a "process of transformation" integral to Chicana self-affirmation and empowerment (1988). That is, Chicanas want to affirm themselves "as Chicanas," women with a unique racial and ethnic history, language, and ways of relating to one another through close interaction with women in the kin networks.

Chicanas, Ethnicity, and Gender Identity

Like European-American women, Chicanas are more likely to identify with their daughters than with their sons. Daughters, in turn, identify with their mothers' female role. Because a Chicana's activity as a mother revolves around family and home, Viktor Gecas (1973) argues that these constitute a major arena for the daughter's definition of self. This psychological identification is framed within Chicanas' cultural practices and beliefs. For example, José Límon (1980) discusses the socializing function of a commonly played folk game, La Vieja Inés, which emphasizes Chicana-appropriate mothering roles. This game is usually played by girls and has two major roles: the prized role of *la mamá* and the stigmatized role of *la vieja Inés*. Other child players do not have names, for part of the game is for *la mamá* to assign them name of colors. If *la vieja Inés* can guess the color name of a child, a chase ensues, which ends with a capture by *la vieja Inés* or the safe return to *la mamá* (home). Límon notes that *la mamá* is often selected for her proven proficiency in assigning color names that have successfully eluded the previous guesses of *Inés*. He argues that this game is a "symbolic learning experience" in which Chicanas "learn" and "practice" how "to take responsibility for children by naming them and speaking for them against the world beyond this known kin group" (1980, 92).

Other important differences exist between European-American women and Chicanas. In many poor Chicana/o families, infants often sleep with parents until they are weaned (Johnson 1980). And the larger the family, the more likely young Chicana/o children are to sleep with their parents or with one another. While this theme is not well researched in academic accounts of Chicana/o family life, it shows up in many literary works (Anaya 1972; Elasser, MacKenzie, and Tixier Y Vigil 1980). Chicanas and Chicanos also exhibit a high degree of residential stability by remaining in or close to their community of origin for many years, or several generations (Keefe and Padilla 1987). Moreover, unmarried Chicanas and Chicanos tend to live with their families of origin until they get married. Interaction with primary kin, particularly the mother, intensifies once childbearing begins.

Because many Chicana/o families do not practice exclusive mothering, daughters often have several female attachment figures responsible for the teaching of gender-related cultural behaviors. Chicanas are sometimes as close, if not closer, to grandmothers or godmothers as they are to their own mothers. Marlene Zepeda's research (1979) indicates that grandmothers are important role models for young Chicanas, particularly with respect to culturally specific skills (speaking Spanish, cooking traditional foods, celebrating Mexican holidays), and that they form particularly strong ties to their daughters' children as opposed to the children of their sons.

Norma Alarcón (1985) also discusses the closeness of grandmother/ granddaughter relationships, particularly regarding culturally gendered role expectations. Grandmothers, by virtue of their age and long relationship with the family, are honored by others in the kin network. The grandmother/ granddaughter relationship is less tense than that of mothers and daughters. Mothers are directly responsible for teaching their daughters how to be Chicanas knowledgeable in cultural traditions and behaviors that signal their gender and ethnicity. Their transmission of a culture overlaid with patriarchal prerogatives can be hotly contested by their daughters, situated generationally in a different social and historical setting. Grandmothers stand one step away from the mother/daughter identity process; they offer granddaughters love and support without dramatically altering cultural messages.

A Chicana may experience herself, thus, not only as an extension of her mother but also of her grandmother. Depending on the extent of behavioral familism, a Chicana may also see herself in relation to her godmother and/or an aunt. Extending Chodorow's theory here suggests that, unlike European-American girls, Chicanas may not develop an inner psychic "triangular object relational constellation" of daughter/mother/father but, rather, a multi-object relational configuration of daughter/mother/aunt/grandmother/godmother/father. To recreate this internal psychic world as an adult, having children may be even more important to Chicanas than to European-American women, and maintaining relationships with other women in the *compadrazgo* system may be particularly crucial for Chicanas to fulfill their relational needs.

Furthermore, for the majority of Chicanas who are working-class, mothers and mothering are enveloped and cast in particular cultural representations, imagery, and symbols (Mirandé and Enríquez 1979; Melville 1980; Baca Zinn 1982). In Chicana/o literature and art and in Catholicism, women, particularly mothers, are represented as essentially sacred and holy. Chicanas are held accountable to *la madre*'s self-sacrificing and pure nature in the image of *La Virgen de Guadalupe* (the Catholic patroness of Mexico whose portrait graces many Mexican immigrant and Chicana/o houses and churches in the Southwest). *La Virgen* as both cultural and religious representation of the good mother frames this gendered/ethnic sense of self. Chicana/o culture identifies several images of "bad" women and mothers, including *La Llorona* (the weeping woman), to dramatically describe the evil fate in store for women who deviate from the norm of the "good" mother. *La Llorona* killed her children and committed suicide. She wanders for eternity, a condemned ghost, in search of her lost children. Both images, *La Virgen* and *La Llorona,* frame a cultural context for mothers and mothering in Chicana/o communities.

Mario García's historical research (1980) on Chicanas highlights women's responsibility to transmit Chicana/o–Mexican cultural values as well as to care for the family unit. Baca Zinn (1975, 1979) argues that Chicana/o families tend to be mother-centered, with women responsible for the majority of household and child-rearing decisions and tasks. These responsibilities form a complementary sphere to the work of men done for the family. Women's mothering occurs in a patriarchal context and is not a direct challenge to male providers but, rather, an assertion of her culturally gendered role. That is, among Chicanas and Chicanos, women's work in the home is often articulated as part of "doing Chicana" (Segura 1992), a claim legitimized by a shared sense of the Chicana/o culture as under assault by outside social pressures (Baca Zinn 1975, 1982; Segura 1992). The sense that a woman's mothering is part of her Chicana identity is bolstered by interaction across kin networks and the larger ethnic community that can result in Chicanas feeling more strongly motivated to mother than European-American middle-class women whose kinship ties are more dispersed. When Chicanas contest traditional patterns they can become caught between their desire for personal empowerment and their politically charged responsibility for cultural maintenance. Thus, the need or motivation to continue traditional patterns may be more complex for Chicanas inasmuch as it is one potential site for reinforcing Chicana/o culture and ethnicity (Segura 1992; Pesquera 1993).

Chicanos, Ethnicity, and Gender Identity

The psychological consequences the Chicana/o family constellation poses differs for the young Chicano. His early relationship with the mother differs from that of the young Chicana. Although he too may be mothered by more than one primary female caretaker, his maleness means that his female nurturers do not identify with him in the way they identify with their daughters. In *Hunger of Memory: The Education of Richard Rodriguez,* Rodriguez writes that from the time he was a little boy, his mother would "repeat the old Mexican dictum [to him] that men should be *feo, fuerte y formal*" (1982, 128). Roughly translated, this means rugged, strong, and steady, a man of responsibility and a good provider for the family. The process Rodriguez describes is found in other writings by Chicanos on "becoming masculine" (e.g., Villarreal 1959; Galarza 1971; Acosta 1972). Moreover, Gecas's (1973) research finds that young Chicanos are more likely than their sisters to identify with their fathers and with their potential male occupational roles. In sum, the Chicano boy must learn his gender identity as being not female—or not mother, not grandmother, and not godmother. Extending Chodorow's theoretical formulation, this suggests that the young Chicano must repress his identification and attachment with many women—not just one—and, at the same time, strive to achieve a masculine gender identification with his father and many other men.

Chicanos' personality development is in some ways similar to that of European-American men. Brooks Brennis and Samuel Roll (1975), for example, found that Chicanos tended to organize their internal psychic world around a highly visible, demarcated self that was seen as robust, randomly active, and engaged in contentious interactions with unfamiliar others. Chicanos' repression of several female objects instead of one, however, suggests that they may develop masculine identity differently than do European-American men. Divergent possibilities exist: nonexclusive mothering may make Chicanos more responsive to women—or conversely it may make them more disdainful. The presence of several female caretakers may actually ameliorate male contempt for women because the Chicano child is not completely dependent on any one woman. The opposing view is that nonexclusive mothering makes it much harder for the young Chicano boy than for his European-American counterpart to achieve a masculine identification because the energy involved in repressing feminine identification is greater—a difficulty exacerbated by the disadvantaged structural position of Chicanos. Baca Zinn (1979), for example, argues that machismo may be one response to the structural obstacles Chicano men face in achieving masculinity in a social world that has historically denied them equal participation. In Chodorow's model, boys' repression of their early identification with their mothers engenders a highly ambivalent stance toward women. With more women caring for the Chicano boy, the ambivalence could be greater, suggesting that Chicanos might be even more likely than European-American men to experience strong feelings of longing and disdain for women.

This scenario directly implicates machismo, the politically loaded notion that Chicanos are in some sense more dominating or macho than European-American men. Much of the early pejorative literature on Mexican national character employed psychoanalytic concepts to depict machismo as a problematic psychological component of Mexican men (Bermúdez 1955; Díaz-Guerrero 1955; Gilbert 1959). In a 1959 study based on interviews with nine Mexican men, G. M. Gilbert concluded there was "a pronounced tendency to either severely constricted affect or morbid-depressed-hypochondriacal types of response among older males ... this may be indicative of increasing importance and 'castration anxiety' as the males fail in the lifelong struggle to live up to the demands of machismo" (1959). Other early researchers constructed an image cast in the discourse of the "normative" wherein diverse Chicana/o families became the "Chicano family" ruled by "macho-dominated," authoritarian males demanding complete deference, respect, and obedience from wives and children (Humphrey 1944; Jones 1948; Peñalosa 1968).

From the vantage point of the 1990s, the findings of these early and influential studies read like ludicrous stereotypes rather than as valid descriptions of Chicana/o culture and people. As Baca Zinn, Mirandé, and others have concluded, however, the machismo stereotype contains a grain of truth. The most recent research on Chicana/o families confirms patriarchal privilege structurally, ideologically, and interpersonally (Zavella 1987; Williams 1990). Patriarchy within Chicana/o families does not constitute a culturally unique pathology (or machismo). In Baca Zinn's review of the social science literature on Chicana/o families, she argues that male domination/female subordination transcends any one cultural group. Indeed, the central tenet of feminist theorizing about the family is that the family is not simply a "haven in a heartless world" (Lasch 1977) but the "locus of struggle" and the source of psychological oppression of women (Hartmann 1981; Thorne and Yalom 1982). In this respect, Chicana/o families struggle over the meanings of gender and mothering in the same way that European-American working-class families do. Chicanas and Chicanos are unique, however, insofar as they simultaneously invoke and perceive themselves as reinforcing a distinct Chicana/o and Mexican culture.

Chicanos invoke "family" and "community" in ways that suggest a cultural and political overlap in masculine identity. Accounts of high-achieving Chicanos reveal considerable overlap between their desire to "help the community" and their wish to attain individual excellence. Themes of individual and group identity, family, and community responsibilities inform the autobiographies of prominent Chicanos such as activist-scholar Ernesto Galarza's *Barrio Boy* (1971), Chicano movement leader Rodolfo "Corky" Gonzales's *Yo Soy Joaquín* (1972), and Fred Ross's biography of labor leader César Chávez (1989). Chicano literary critic Ramón Saldívar analyzes what he terms the "themes of transformation and identity" in *Barrio Boy*, asserting that "the motifs of transformation and identity which might have been offered in terms of the individual, are transferred instead to the entire community within which the individuals exist, by which they are created, and which they in turn dialectically transform" (1990, 164). This suggests Chicanos are more likely to affirm their gender identity as masculine by pursuing their interests and affiliations in the immediate ethnic community. For example, Zavella (1989) suggests that Chicano political activists during the turbulent 1960s and 1970s established organizations to reconstruct *familia* and *carnalismo* (Chicano brotherhood).

This blending of gender identity with community also occurs with Chicanas. Writer Helena María Viramontes writes, "I want to do justice to their voices. I want to tell these women, in my own gentle way that I will fight for them, that they provide me with my own sense of humanity" (1990, 292). Similarly, in a personal account of her graduate school experiences, sociologist Gloria Cuádraz characterizes the importance of doing well in school as part of the larger struggle of her community rather than the more individualistic frame of her Anglo counterparts (Cuádraz and Pierce 1993). In a related vein, discussions of Chicana muralists highlight how their works typically express "both personal and collective expression" (Mesa-Baines 1990). Other accounts stress that Chicana political activism (e.g., running for school board, joining the Mothers of East Los Angeles, labor union organizing) is often spurred by Chicanas' desire to better the opportunities for their families and their communities (Pardo 1990; Segura and Pesquera 1992). The ideological commitment in Chicana/o communities to the intertwined notions of *familia* and community is emphasized in recent research on Chicano political activism and political consciousness. What this research suggests is that in the particular constellation of Chicana/o families the development of gender identity and group or ethnic identity are closely intertwined. Chicana mothers do not raise their children to be "independent" or "individualistic," as European-American mothers do (Anderson and Evans 1976). Instead Chicana/o mothers encourage their children to think and act communally—for the good of the family and the community (Ramírez and Castañeda 1974; Trueba and Delgado-Gaitan 1985). This, as well as the constellation of features associated with Chicana/o family structure —working-class status, large family size, familism, *compadrazgo,* nonexclusive mothering—helps explain why Chicanas and Chicanos often realize their interests, skills, and desires in the community and *la familia* instead of the larger public domain. Much of the current research on Chicana feminism highlights the "collective" orientation of Chicanas' struggles against oppression based on gender, race, ethnicity, and class—a struggle distinct from mainstream liberal feminism's focus on gender inequality and individual rights.

Our analysis shows the applicability of Chodorow's theoretical account of gender development to Chicana/o families. The crucial role of women emphasized by Chodorow is evident in Chicana/o families, but as a part of a unique constellation of features that together bear on the acquisition of gender identity and the related development of group identity. In particular, the psychological meaning of other women within the kin network must be taken into account.

References

Acosta, Oscar Zeta. 1972. *The Autobiography of a Brown Buffalo.* San Francisco: Straight Arrow.

Alarcón, Norma. 1985. "What Kind of Lover Have You Made Me, Mother? Toward a Theory of Chicanas' Feminism and Cultural Identity through Poetry." In *Women of Color Perspectives on Feminism and Identity,* ed. Audrey T. McClusky. Occasional Papers Series 1. Bloomington: University of Indiana Women's Studies Program.

Anaya, Rudolfo A. 1972. *Bless Me, Ultima.* Berkeley: Tonatiuh International.

Anderson, James, and Francis B. Evans. 1976. "Family Socialization and Educational Achievement in Two Cultures: Mexican-American and Anglo-American." *Sociometry* 39:209–22.

Baca Zinn, Maxine. 1975. "Chicanas: Power and Control in the Domestic Sphere." *De Colores: Journal of Emerging Raza Philosophies* 2:19–31.

———. 1979. "Chicano Family Research: Conceptual Distortions and Alternative Directions." *Journal of Ethnic Studies* 7:59–71.

———. 1982. "Chicano Men and Masculinity." *Journal of Ethnic Studies* 10:29–44.

———. 1982/83. "Familism among Chicanos: A Theoretical Review." *Humboldt Journal of Social Relations* 10:224–38.

Baca Zinn, Maxine, and Stanley D. Eitzen. 1987. *Diversity in American Families.* New York: Harper & Row.

Barrera, Mario. 1979. *Race and Class in the Southwest: A Theory of Racial Inequality.* Notre Dame, Ind.: University of Notre Dame Press.

Bermúdez, María. 1955. *La Vida del Mexicano.* Mexico City: Antigua Liberia Robredo.

Bott, Elizabeth. 1971. *Family and Social Networks.* 2d ed. New York: Free Press.

Brennis, Brooks, and Samuel Roll. 1975. "Ego Modalities in Manifest Dreams of Male and Female Chicanos." *Psychiatry* 38:172–85.

Caulfield, Mina Davis. 1974. "Imperialism, the Family and Cultures of Resistance." *Socialist Revolution* 2:67–85.

Cervantes, Lorna Dee. 1980. "Beneath the Shadow of the Freeway." In her *Emplumada,* 11–14. Pittsburgh: University of Pittsburgh Press.

Chodorow, Nancy. 1989. *Feminism and Psychoanalytic Theory.* New Haven, Conn.: Yale University Press.

Cuadráz, Gloria, and Jennifer Pierce. 1993. "From Scholarship Girls to Scholarship Women: Race, Class and Gender in Graduate Education." Paper presented at the National Association for Ethnic Studies conference, Salt Lake City, Utah, March 6.

Diaz-Guerrero, Rogelio. 1955. "Neurosis and the Mexican Family Structure." *American Journal of Psychiatry* 112 (December): 411–17.

Elasser, Nan, Kyle MacKenzie, and Yvonne Tixier Y Vigil. 1980. *Las Mujeres: Conversations from a Hispanic Community.* Old Westbury, N.Y.: Feminist Press.

Falicov, Celia Jaes. 1982. "Mexican Families." In *Ethnicity and Family Therapy,* ed. Monica McGoldrick, John K. Pearce, and Joseph Giordano, 134–63. New York: Guilford Press.

Galarza, Ernesto. 1971. *Barrio Boy.* Notre Dame, Ind.: University of Notre Dame Press.

García, Mario T. 1980. "The Chicana in American History: The Mexican Women of El Paso, 1880–1920—a Case Study." *Pacific Historical Review* 49:315–37.

Gecas, Viktor. 1973. "Self-Conceptions of Migrant Settled Mexican Americans." *Social Science Quarterly* 54(3):579–95.

Gilbert, G. M. 1959. "Sex Differences in Mental Health in a Mexican Village." *International Journal of Psychiatry* 3 (Winter): 208–13.

Gonzales, Rodolfo. 1972. *I Am Joaquín, Yo Soy Joaquín.* New York: Bantam.

Griswold del Castillo, Richard. 1984. *La Familia: Chicano Families in the Urban Southwest.* Notre Dame, Ind.: University of Notre Dame Press.

Hartmann, Heidi. 1981. "The Family as the Locus of Gender, Class, and Political Struggle: The Example of Housework." *Signs: Journal of Women in Culture and Society* 6(3):366–94.

Hernandez, Lisa. 1988. "Canas." In *Palabras Chicanas,* ed. Lisa Hernandez and Tina Benitez, 47–49. Berkeley: University of California, Berkeley, Mujeres in March Press.

Horowitz, Ruth. 1983. *Honor and the American Dream: Culture and Identity in a Chicano Community.* New Brunswick, N.J.: Rutgers University Press.

Humphrey, Norman D. 1944. "The Changing Structure of Detroit Mexican Families: An Index of Acculturation." *American Sociological Review* 9 (December): 622–26.

Johnson, Carmen Acosta. 1980. "Breast-feeding and Social Class Mobility: The Case of Mexican Migrant Mothers in Houston, Texas." In *Twice a Minority: Mexican American Women,* ed. Margarita B. Melville, 66–82. St. Louis: Mosby.

Jones, Robert. 1948. "Ethnic Family Patterns: The Mexican-American Family in the U.S." *American Journal of Sociology* 53 (May): 450–52.

Keefe, Susan E. 1979. "Urbanization, Acculturation and Extended Family Ties: Mexican Americans in Cities." *American Ethnologist* 6:349–45.

Keefe, Susan E., and Amado M. Padilla. 1987. *Chicano Ethnicity.* Albuquerque: University of New Mexico Press.

Lamphere, Louise, Patricia Zavella, and Felipe Gonzales, with Peter B. Evans. 1993. *Sunbelt Working Mothers: Reconciling Family and Factory.* Ithaca, N.Y.: Cornell University Press.

Lasch, Christopher. 1977. *Haven in a Heartless World.* New York: Basic.

Límon, José E. 1980. " 'La Vieja Inés,' a Mexican Folk Game: A Research Note." In *Twice a Minority: Mexican American Women,* ed. Margarita B. Melville, 88–94. St. Louis: Mosby.

Melville, Margarita B. 1980. "Introduction" and "Matresence." In *Twice a Minority: Mexican-American Women,* ed. Margarita B. Melville, 1–16. St. Louis: Mosby.

Mesa-Baines, Amalia. 1990. "Quest for Identity: Profile of Two Chicana Muralists: Based on Interviews with Judith F. Baca and Patricia Rodriguez." In *Signs from the Heart: California Chicano Murals,* ed. Eva Sperling Cockroft and Holly Barnet Sanchez, 69–82. Venice, Calif.: Social and Public Art Resource Center.

Mindel, Charles H. 1980. "Extended Familism among Urban Mexican Americans, Anglos, and Blacks." *Hispanic Journal of Behavioral Sciences* 2:21–34.

Mirandé, Alfredo. 1985. *The Chicano Experience: An Alternative Perspective.* Notre Dame, Ind.: University of Notre Dame Press.

Neumaier, Diane. 1990. "Judy Baca: Our People Are the Internal Exiles." In *Making Face, Making Soul—Haciendo Caras,* ed. Gloria Anzaldúa, 256–70. San Francisco: Aunt Lute Foundation.

Pardo, Mary. 1990. "Mexican American Women Grassroots Community Activists (Mothers of East Los Angeles)." *Frontiers: A Journal of Women's Studies* 11(1):1–7.

Peñalosa, Fernando. 1968."Mexican-American Family Roles." *Journal of Marriage and the Family* 30(4):680–88.

Pesquera, Beatríz M. 1993. " 'It Gave Me Confianza': Work Commitment and Identity." *Aztlán: Journal of Chicano Studies Research,* in press.

Ramírez, Manuel, III, and Alfredo Castañeda. 1974. *Cultural Democracy, Bicognitive Development, and Education.* New York: Academic Press.

Rebolledo, Tey Diana. 1983. "Abuelitas: Mythology and Integration in Chicano Literature." *Revista Chicano-Riquena* 11(3–4):148–58.

Rochin, Refugio I., and Monica D. Castillo. 1991. "Immigration, *Colonía* Formation and Latino Poor in Rural California: Evolving Immigration." Working Paper no. 91-38. University of California, Davis, Department of Agricultural Economics.

Rodriguez, Richard. 1982. *Hunger of Memory: The Education of Richard Rodriguez.* New York: Bantam.

Ross, Fred. 1989. *Conquering Goliath: Cesar Chavez and the Beginning.* Keene, Calif.: United Farm Workers.

Saldívar, Ramón. 1990. "Ideologies of the Self: Chicano Autobiography.: In his *Chicano Narrative: The Dialectics of Difference,* 154–70. Madison: University of Wisconsin Press.

Saragoza, Alex M. 1983. "The Conceptualization of the History of the Chicano Family." In *The State of Chicano Research on Family, Labor, and Migration: Proceedings of the First Stanford Symposium on Chicano Research and Public Policy,* ed. Armando Valdez, Alberto Camarillo, and Tomas Almaguer, 11–38. Stanford, Calif.: Stanford Center for Chicano Research.

Segura, Denise A. 1988. "Familism and Employment among Chicanas and Mexican Immigrant Women." In *Mexicanas at Work in the United States,* ed. Margarita B. Melville, 24–32. Houston: University of Houston, Mexican-American Studies.

———. 1992. "Chicanas in White Collar Jobs: 'You Have to Prove Yourself More.' " *Sociological Perspectives* 35:163–82.

Segura, Denise A., and Beatríz M. Pesquera. 1992. Beyond Indifference and Antipathy: The Chicana Feminist Movement and Chicana Feminist Discourse." *Aztlán: Journal of Chicano Studies Research* 19(2):69–88.

Sotomayor, Marta. 1971. "Mexican-American Interaction with Social Systems." In *La Causa Chicana: The Movement for Justice,* ed. Margaret M. Manfold, 148–60. New York: Family Service Association of America.

Thorne, Barrie, and Marilyn Yalom. 1982. *Rethinking the Family: Some Feminist Questions.* New York: Longman Press.

Tienda, Marta, and Ronald Angel. 1982. "Headship and Household Composition among Blacks, Hispanics and Other Whites." *Social Forces* 61:508–31.

Trueba, Henry T., and Concha Delgado-Gaitan. 1985. "Specialization of Mexican Children for Cooperation and Competition: Sharing and Copying." *Journal of Educational Equity and Leadership* 5:189–204.

U.S. Bureau of the Census. 1988. "Fertility of American Women." *Current Population Reports,* Series P-20 (June). Washington, D.C.: Government Printing Office.

———. 1991a. "The Hispanic Population in the United States: March 1990." *Current Population Reports,* Series P-20, no. 449 (May). Washington, D.C.: Government Printing Office.

———. 1991b. "Poverty in the United States: 1990.": *Current Population Reports,* Series P-60, no. 175. Washington, D.C.: Government Printing Office.

———. 1992. "Household and Family Characteristics: March 1991." *Current Population Reports,* Series P-20, no. 458 (February). Washington, D.C.: Government Printing Office.

Villarreal, José Antonio. 1959. *Pocho.* New York: Doubleday.

Viramontes, Helene María. 1990. "Nopalitos: The Making of Fiction." In *Making Faces, Making Soul—Haciendo Caras: Creative and Critical Perspectives by Women of Color,* ed. Gloria Anzaldúa, 291–94. San Francisco: Aunt Lute Foundation.

Wagner, Roland M., and Diane M. Schaffer. 1980. "Social Networks and Survival Strategies: An Exploratory Study of Mexican-American, Black and Anglo Female Family Heads in San Jose, California." In *Twice a Minority: Mexican American Women,* ed. Margarita B. Melville, 173–90. St. Louis: Mosby.

Williams, Norma. 1990. *The Mexican American Family: Tradition and Change.* New York: General Hall.

Zavella, Patricia. 1987. *Women's Work and Chicano Families: Cannery Workers of the Santa Clara Valley.* Ithaca, N.Y.: Cornell University Press.

Zepeda, Marlene. 1979. "Las Abuelitas." *Agenda* 6 (November/December): 10–13.

POSTSCRIPT

Can We Raise "Gender-Neutral" Children?

Clearly, people are different. We are different physically, intellectually, emotionally, culturally, and in many other ways. This includes our gender. Problems do not seem to arise when these differences are noticed or expressed; problems tend to arise when we put the word "only" in front as a clarifier. Someone is "only" a stay-at-home mom, arguably one of the most challenging—and, incidentally, unpaid—jobs there is. If someone is "only" a secretary at work, and the majority of secretaries are women, these attitudes translate into seeing women as less than men. Similarly, if a man shows sensitivity, he is accused of not being tough enough, or a "real" man. At the same time, many complain that most men do not communicate feelings enough or as effectively as they would like —forgetting, it seems, that they have been socialized in this way almost from birth.

Something to consider is how our feelings about gender role expectations and fulfillment relate to our feelings about a person's sexual orientation. Many people still relate gender to whether we are heterosexual, lesbian, gay, or bisexual, mostly because people who act in identifiably stereotypical manners can more easily be perceived to be a particular sexual orientation. People look at a "macho" football player and assume he is heterosexual; people look at a woman with short hair who is a construction worker and assume she is lesbian. As a result, there is the erroneous notion that gendered behavior determines or creates a person's sexual orientation. However, studies show repeatedly that this is not true. Having a boy learn how to cook or letting a girl join the middle school football team is not going to create gay kids any more than making a gay- or lesbian-identified individual learn to hunt or dance ballet is going to create heterosexual kids. Yet while the two are separate, they are related. Boys are called "faggot" from an early age if they do anything that digresses even slightly from the gender expectation. A "faggot" in popular terms does not do what the rest of the group does; he drinks less alcohol than the other guys; he stays home and studies rather than going out. In this way, a "faggot" is less than a male—he is a "womanly" male. Few people consider that this comment is not only homophobic but also degrading to women.

A wonderful study in how people relate to each other comes from watching small children play in a sandbox. They are there for a common goal—to do "something" within the community of the sandbox. They are different sexes, races, and ethnicities. These differences are irrelevant; in fact, the children will rarely even ask each other their names. What *is* important is, Do you have a shovel? Did you bring a pail? Can you support the common good of the sand pile?

To be sure, children notice differences. However, it is not until adults teach them that these differences mean something, either positive or negative, that biases begin to form. And biases do not serve anyone well, regardless of gender.

Suggested Readings

George Abrahams and Sheila Ahlbrand, *Boy v. Girl: How Gender Shapes Who We Are, What We Want, and How We Get Along* (Free Spirit Publishing, 2002).

Carole R. Beal, *Boys and Girls: The Development of Gender Roles* (McGraw-Hill, 1993).

Beverly Lyon Clark and Margaret R. Higonnet, eds., *Girls, Boys, Books, Toys: Gender in Children's Literature and Culture* (Johns Hopkins University Press, 1999).

Carol Gilligan, *In a Different Voice: Psychological Theory and Women's Development* (Harvard University Press, 1993).

Christina Hoff Sommers, *The War Against Boys: How Misguided Feminism Is Harming Our Young Men* (Touchstone Books, 2001).

Susan Hoy Crawford, *Beyond Dolls & Guns: 101 Ways to Help Children Avoid Gender Bias* (Heinemann, 1995).

Jyl J. Josephson, *Gender, Families, and State* (Rowman & Littlefield Publishing, 1996).

Mary Pipher, *Reviving Ophelia: Saving the Selves of Adolescent Girls* (Ballantine Books, 1995).

ISSUE 5

Does Divorce Create Long-Term Negative Effects for Children?

YES: Karl Zinsmeister, from "Divorce's Toll on Children," *The American Enterprise* (May/June 1996)

NO: David Gately and Andrew I. Schwebel, from "Favorable Outcomes in Children After Parental Divorce," *Journal of Divorce and Remarriage* (vol. 18, nos. 3–4, 1992)

ISSUE SUMMARY

YES: Karl Zinsmeister, editor in chief of *The American Enterprise*, points to research and surveys showing that not only is divorce much more harmful to children but also that children themselves say they would rather remain in a household where parents argue and fight than to have their parents break up.

NO: Educators David Gately and Andrew I. Schwebel highlight literature that demonstrates how going through a divorce can actually strengthen a child, helping to build her or his self-efficacy and level of self-esteem.

$\mathbf{I}$t is safe to say that the majority of the literature examining the effects of divorce discusses the negative effects divorce has not only on the two people who are separating but also on the couple's children.

Although every child's situation in divorce is unique, research has shown how children can be affected at different ages by divorce. Approximately twice as many children of divorced parents have emotional problems as children of parents who do not divorce. Babies may feel that their parents are upset and unhappy. Toddlers may be unable to achieve certain developmental milestones and experience an increase in nightmares, while preschoolers often blame themselves for the divorce. A child in puberty may feel like she or he needs to choose between her or his parents, labeling one the "good" and the other the "bad" parent. Teenagers may cope by using alcohol, drugs, and/or other behaviors.

While no one argues that divorce or the breakup of any long-term relationship is not an enormous challenge to everyone involved, some experts believe there is a silver lining to this otherwise dark cloud. For example, if there has been great discord and constant fighting in the household, a divorce can provide relief to the children who have been living in that highly stressful setting. If there has been physical violence, a divorce can provide comfort and safety for the child. Some experts have found children's self-esteem to actually increase after a divorce as the children recognize and realize that they have navigated through an enormous challenge successfully.

As you read the following selections, think about how important you feel that keeping an intact relationship is to the well-being of a child. Pay close attention to the language used by the authors in describing both divorce and the potential outcomes. Does any breakup or divorce guarantee emotional problems for a child of the separating couple, or, if parents take careful measures, can they help to ward off the deleterious effects of the separation? Do you think that parents should remain in the relationship, even if they are unhappy, until their child is older and leaves the house? Or should couples do what they feel is best for themselves and try to support their child as best they can? Think about your own family situation and how you were raised, as well as the experiences of peers around you. Did anyone in your life experience a separation or divorce? Do you remember how challenging or strengthening the experience was for this person?

In the following selection, Karl Zinsmeister cites resources and studies that show extensive negative effects of divorce on children, focusing in particular on emotional and behavioral changes. Talking exclusively about heterosexual marriages, he asserts that children of divorce have greater challenges negotiating relationships themselves once they are older, have a greater chance of choosing the "wrong" partner, and are much more likely to divorce themselves. David Gately and Andrew I. Schwebel do not dispute many of the deleterious effects of divorce or long-term relationship dissolution on children, but they question the methodology of the literature discussing these findings—much of which does not involve interviews of the children themselves but instead is colored by caregivers' views of how a divorce or breakup affects the children. Gately and Schwebel believe that children who go through divorce often have increased senses of responsibility, independence, and maturity than their counterparts whose parents have remained together.

Karl Zinsmeister  **YES**

Divorce's Toll on Children

Originally, notes family historian John Sommerville, marriage arose to create "security for the children to be expected from the union." Yet nowadays "the child's interest in the permanence of marriage is almost ignored." During the divorce boom that began in the mid-1960s, divorces affecting children went up even faster than divorces generally, and today *most* crack-ups involve kids. Since 1972, more than a million youngsters have been involved in a divorce *each year.*

The result is that at some time before reaching adulthood, around half of today's children will go through a marital rupture. Most of these youngsters will live in a single-parent home for at least five years. A small majority of those who experience a divorce eventually end up in a step-family, but well over a third of them will endure the extra trauma of seeing that second marriage break up.

The typical divorce brings what researcher Frank Furstenberg describes as "either a complete cessation of contact between the non-residential parent and child, or a relationship that is tantamount to a ritual form of parenthood." In nine cases out of ten the custodial parent is the mother, and fully half of all divorce-children living with their mom have had no contact with their father for at least a full year. Only one child in 10 sees his non-custodial parent as often as once a week. Overall, only about one youngster in five is able to maintain a close relationship with both parents.

Joint child custody receives a lot of publicity (it is now allowed in about half the states), but it remains unusual. In California, where it is much more common than anywhere else, only 18 percent of divorced couples have joint physical custody. Most divorced children still live solely with their mothers.

"For most men," sociologist Andrew Cherlin notes, "children and marriage are part of a package deal. Their ties to their children depend on their ties to their wives." Studies show that remarriage makes fathers particularly likely to reduce involvement with the children from their previous marriage.

Even when divorced parents do maintain regular contact with their children, truly cooperative child rearing is very rare. Most often, research shows, the estranged parents have no communication or mutual reinforcement. As a

From Karl Zinsmeister, "Divorce's Toll on Children," *The American Enterprise,* vol. 7, no. 3 (May/ June 1996), pp. 39–44. Copyright © 1996 by *The American Enterprise.* Reprinted by permission of *The American Enterprise,* a magazine of politics, business, and culture. http://www.TAEmag.com.

result, mother and father frequently undercut each other, intentionally or not, and parent-child relations are often unhealthy.

A series of interviews with children of divorce conducted by author/ photographer Jill Krementz illustrates this phenomenon. "My relationship with my parents has changed because now my mother does all the disciplining," says 14-year-old Meredith, "and sometimes she resents it—especially when we tell her how much fun we have with Dad. It's as if it's all fun and games with him because we're with him so little." Ari, also 14, confides, "I really look forward to the weekends because it's kind of like a break—it's like going to Disneyland because there's no set schedule, no 'Be home by 5:30' kind of stuff. It's open. It's free. And my father is always buying me presents." Zach, age 13, reports "whenever I want to see my other parent I can, and if I have a fight with one of them, instead of having to take off... I can just go eat at my Mom's house or my Dad's."

Other youngsters feel torn in two after a divorce, particularly in cases of joint custody where they must physically bounce back and forth between two houses. "It's hello, goodbye, hello, goodbye all the time," says one father. Gary Skoloff, chairman of the American Bar Association's family law section, explains that "joint custody was going to be a great panacea, the ultimate solution.... But it turned out to be the world's worst situation." The lack of a stable home has proved so harmful to children that several states, including California where the practice was pioneered, have recently revoked statutes favoring joint custody.

Fear and Loathing of Divorce Among the Young

Children's view of divorce is unambiguous: it's a disaster. In 1988, professor Jeanne Dise-Lewis surveyed almost 700 junior high school students, asking them to rate a number of life events in terms of stressfulness. The only thing students ranked as more stressful than parental divorce was death of a parent or close family member. Parental divorce received a higher rating than the death of a friend, being "physically hit" by a parent, feeling that no one liked them or being seriously injured.

The "fairy tale" believed by adults, says University of Michigan psychologist and divorce expert Neil Kalter, is that if they simply present new family set-ups to their children in a calm, firm way, the children will accept them. Actually, he says, that "is seen by the kids as a lot of baloney." Among the hundreds of children he's worked with in setting up coping-with-divorce programs for schools, "there are very few who have anything good to say about divorce." "Children are generally more traditional than adults," agrees Judith Wallerstein. "Children want both parents. They want family." If children had the vote, she says, there would be no such thing as divorce.

Indeed, Gallup youth surveys in the early 1990s show that three out of four teenagers age 13 to 17 think "it is too easy for people in this country to get divorced." Go into a typical high school today and ask some students what their most important wish for the future is and a surprising number will answer "that there wouldn't be so many divorces." Young Arizonan Cynthia Coan has lots of company when she says, "as a child of divorce, I cannot help but hope that the next generation of children will be spared what mine went through."

You'll sometimes hear the claim that divorce doesn't hurt children as much as conflict in a marriage. This is not supported by the evidence. "For kids," reports Kalter, "the misery in an unhappy marriage is usually less significant than the changes" after a divorce. "They'd rather their parents keep fighting and not get divorced." Even five years later, few of the youngsters in Wallerstein's study agreed with their parents' decision to separate. Only ten percent were more content after the split than before.

Contrary to popular perceptions, the alternative to most divorces is not life in a war zone. Though more than 50 percent of all marriages currently end in divorce, experts tell us that only about 15 percent of all unions involve high levels of conflict. In the vast number of divorces, then, there is no gross strife or violence that could warp a youngster's childhood. The majority of marital break-ups are driven by a quest for greener grass—and in these cases the children will almost always be worse off.

Many mothers and fathers badly underestimate how damaging household dissolution will be to their children. A 1985 British study that quizzed both parents and children found that the children reported being far more seriously upset by their parents' separation than the parents assumed. Despite the common perception that the best thing parents can do for their children is to make themselves happy, the truth is that children have their own needs that exist quite apart from those of their parents. One may argue that a parent should be allowed to rank his own needs above those of his children (though this is not the traditional understanding of how families should work). But one ought not cloak that decision with the false justification that one is thereby serving the children's best interests.

Wade Horn, former commissioner of the U.S. Administration for Children, Youth, and Families, illustrates how parents can be deluded in this way:

> Families used to come to me when I was practicing psychology, seeking advice about how to divorce. They would say, "We want a divorce because we really don't get along very well any more, and we understand that our child will be better off after we divorce than if we stay together." Rarely, if ever, did I hear a family say, "We're having conflict, but we have decided to work as hard as we can at solving our problems because we know that children of divorce are more disturbed than children of intact families."

A major reason parents are making this mistake is because that is what some authorities and many ideologues in the cause of family "liberation" have been telling them. "For years experts said, 'Once the initial trauma wears off, kids make adjustments,'" complains psychologist John Guidubaldi, past president of the National Association of School Psychologists. While it's true that kids make adjustments, Guidubaldi notes in the *Washington Post*, "so do people in prisons and mental institutions. The pertinent question is: Are those adjustments healthy? And the weight of the evidence has become overwhelming on the side that they aren't."

Short- and Long-Term Effects of Divorce on Children

The longer-term effects of divorce on children are something we've learned a lot about over the last decade. Guidubaldi, who orchestrated one of the large studies documenting these effects, concludes from his work that "the old argument of staying together for the sake of the kids is still the best argument.... People simply aren't putting enough effort into saving their marriages." Family scholar Nicholas Zill points out that "if you looked at the kind of long-term risk factors that divorce creates for kids and translated them to, say, heart disease, people would be startled."

In the early months after divorce, young children are often less imaginative and more repetitive. Many become passive watchers. They tend to be more dependent, demanding, unaffectionate, and disobedient than their counterparts from intact families. They are more afraid of abandonment, loss of love, and bodily harm. A significant number—in some studies a quarter—say they blame themselves for their parents' smash-up.

A small study conducted some years ago by University of Hawaii psychiatrist John McDermott sorted pre-schoolers who had been involved in a divorce a few months earlier into three categories. Three out of 16 children were judged to have weathered the initial storm essentially unchanged. Two of 16 became what he called "severely disorganized" and developed gross behavior problems. The rest, more than two-thirds, he categorized as "the sad, angry children." They displayed resentment, depression, and grief, were restless, noisy, possessive and physically aggressive.

In Judith Wallerstein's landmark study, almost half of the pre-schoolers still displayed heightened anxiety and aggression a full year after their parents' divorce. Forty-four percent "were found to be in significantly deteriorated psychological condition." All of the two- and three-year-olds showed acute regression in toilet training. They displayed unusual hunger for attention from strangers. Older pre-schoolers had become more whiny, irritable, and aggressive, and had problems with play.

Wallerstein's study also returned to its subjects five and 10 years later, and the collected results were quite staggering. In overview they look like this: initially, two-thirds of all the children showed symptoms of stress, and half thought their life had been destroyed by the divorce. Five years down the road, over a third were still seriously disturbed (even more disturbed than they had been initially, in fact), and another third were having psychological difficulties. A surprisingly large number remained angry at their parents.

After a decade, 45 percent of the children were doing well, 14 percent were succeeding in some areas but failing in others, and 41 percent were still doing quite poorly. This last group "were entering adulthood as worried, underachieving, self-deprecating, and sometimes angry young men and women." In addition to their emotional problems and depression, many felt sorrow over their childhoods and fear about their own marriage and childrearing prospects. About a third of the group had little or no ambition at the 10-year mark. Many expressed a sense of powerlessness, neediness, and vulnerability. Most of the ones who had reached adult age regarded their parents' divorce as a continuing major influence in their lives.

It should be noted that the 131 children in the study experienced divorce in what Wallerstein and associates call the "best of circumstances." Most of their parents were college educated, and at the beginning these children were achievers in school. None of the participants was initially being treated for psychiatric disorder. Most of the families were white and middle class; half regularly attended church or synagogue.

Even in families with all these advantages, divorce wreaks havoc among the young. Summarizing her findings on the offspring of broken marriages, Wallerstein has written that "it would be hard to find any other group of children—except, perhaps, the victims of a natural disaster—who suffered such a rate of sudden serious psychological problems." Other long-term studies teach similar conclusions. "Divorce," says psychiatrist McDermott, "is now the single largest cause of childhood depression." Marital disruption, quite clearly, can wound children for years.

A Catalogue of Behavioral Changes

Let's look more specifically at some of the changes in behavior that affect children of divorce. John Guidubaldi and Joseph Perry found in their survey of 700 youngsters that children of divorced parents performed worse than children of intact families on 9 of 30 mental health measures, showing, among other things, more withdrawal, dependency, inattention, and unhappiness, plus less work effort. Divorced students were more likely to abuse drugs, to commit violent acts, to take their own life, and to bear children out of wedlock.

A University of Pittsburgh study in the late 1980s found that there were 30 percent more duodenal ulcers and 70 percent more suicide attempts—both symptoms of serious psychological stress—among children who had lost a parent. In Wallerstein's middle-class sample, one-third of the girls with divorced parents became pregnant out of wedlock, and 8 percent had at least two abortions. Two-thirds of the girls had a history of delinquency, and almost 30 percent of the boys had been arrested more than once.

The National Survey of Children showed that more than 30 percent of the individuals whose parents separated or divorced before they were eight years old had received therapy by the time they were teenagers. Divorce-children are two to four times as numerous in psychiatric care populations as they are in society at large. In fact, more than 80 percent of the adolescents in mental hospitals, and 60 percent of the children in psychiatric clinics, have been through a divorce. And what is being treated in most cases is much more than just a short-term reaction: the average treatment takes place five years after their parents' marital breakup. At the fully adult age of 23, middle-class women whose mother and father had divorced were three times likelier to have a psychological problem than counterparts from intact families, according to a massive multi-year British study.

Schooling is another problem area. Children exposed to divorce are twice as likely to repeat a grade, and five times likelier to be expelled or suspended.

(Fully 15 percent of all teenagers living with divorced mothers have been booted from school at least temporarily, according to the National Survey of Children.) Even in Wallerstein's middle-class sample, 13 percent of the youngsters had dropped out of school altogether. Barely half of Wallerstein's subjects went on to college, far less than the 85 percent average for students in their high schools. Wallerstein concludes that 60 percent of the divorce-children in her study will fail to match the educational achievements of their fathers.

Children of divorce also frequently have problems with sexual identity. In most studies, boys seem to be harder hit than girls. Pre-school boys tend to be unpopular with male peers, to have difficulty gaining access to play groups, to spend more time with younger compatriots and females, and to engage in more activities traditionally considered to be feminine. Young boys tend to be more vehemently opposed to the divorce, to long more for their father, to feel rejected by him, and to feel uncertain about their masculinity. They are more likely than girls to become depressed and angry. Many later have problems developing intimacy, and build lifestyles of solitary interests and habits.

For girls there is a "sleeper effect"—beginning at adolescence, seemingly well-adjusted individuals often develop serious problems with sexuality, self-control, and intimacy. Kalter found higher rates of substance abuse, running away, and sexual activity among girls who had been through divorce, particularly when the father had departed early on. Wallerstein found that a "significant minority" of girls expressed insecurity, anger, or lack of self-respect in promiscuity, some gravitating to older men or a series of aimless sexual relationships. "I'm prepared for anything. I don't expect a lot," said one 20-year-old. "Love is a strange idea to me. Life is a chess game. I've always been a pawn."

Mavis Hetherington of the University of Virginia has found that girls have special problems when their divorced mothers remarry. She has also shown that the pattern of low self-respect and sexual precocity among girls with a divorced mother does *not* hold true among girls living with a solo mother due to death of the father—apparently it is active alienation from the father, more than his simple absence, that causes the disturbance. This fits well with psychologist Erik Erikson's view that it is less deprivation *per se* that is psychologically destructive than deprivation without redeeming significance.

Wallerstein points out that teenage girls often view their absent fathers with a combination of idealization and distrust.

> The idealized father that the young adolescent girl imagines is the exact opposite of the image that later becomes prominent in her mind as she grows older—namely, the father as betrayer.... Because daughters of divorce often have a hard time finding out what their fathers are really like, they often experience great difficulty in establishing a realistic view of men in general, in developing realistic expectations, and in exercising good judgment in their choice of partner.

Researcher Conrad Schwarz has hypothesized that children who are allied only with their same-sex parent (as a girl growing up with a divorced mother would be) tend to hold a chauvinistic and alienated view of the opposite sex.

Conversely, he suggests, children growing up with only opposite-sex parents (like boys living with divorced mothers) tend to have problems with gender identity and self-esteem. One study that fits this hypothesis found that college-age women who had experienced divorce in childhood were more prone to see men as unfeeling and weak than counterparts from intact families.

Female children of divorced parents are more likely to choose "inadequate husbands" and to have marital problems of their own. They are substantially likelier to have extensive premarital sexual experience and twice as likely to cohabit before marriage. They are more frequently pregnant at their weddings.

And both male and female children of divorce see their own marriages dissolve at significantly higher rates than counterparts who grew up in intact families. Partly this is attitudinal: One eight-year study of 1,300 men and women found that people who had watched their own parents divorce were much more tolerant of the idea of divorce, and that this tolerance translated into increased marital breakup.

The other thing that childhood divorce encourages, of course, is the avoidance of marriage. "My mom got remarried and divorced again, so I've gone through two divorces so far. And my father's also gotten remarried—to someone I don't get along with all that well. It's all made me feel that people shouldn't get married," 14-year-old Ari explained to Jill Krementz.

Divorces involving children thus set a whole train of losses into motion, transporting unhappy effects not only over the years but even across generations. And not even children fortunate enough to live in stable homes are wholly insulated from the turmoil. As writer Susan Cohen observes:

> Although I am not divorced and live in a conventional nuclear family with a husband and two children... divorce has been part of my daughter Sarah's life since she was two or three. Divorce is in her books, on her television programs, in her lessons at school, in her conversations with her friends, and in her questions to me.

Indeed, divorce is in the very air our children breathe—with lasting significance for their later views of love, families, and life.

**David Gately and
Andrew I. Schwebel**

Favorable Outcomes in Children
After Parental Divorce

SUMMARY. The present paper is based on a review of the literature that considers the short- and long-term effects parental divorce has on children. Most studies in this literature have identified unfavorable outcomes that develop in many areas of children's lives as they struggle to cope with their changed family situations. However, as children adjust to the challenges they face before, during, and after parental divorce, neutral and favorable outcomes are also possible in one or more areas of their lives. In fact, the literature review indicated that many investigators have identified certain strengths in children who had experienced parental divorce. In particular they have observed that following the divorce of their parents some children, in comparison to peers or their own pre-divorce development, have shown enhanced levels of functioning in four areas: maturity, self-esteem, empathy, and androgyny.

Over ten million divorces were granted in the United States during the 1980s (U.S. Bureau of the Census, 1990). The great number of people affected by divorce in the second half of the 20th century stimulated scholarly interest in this area. One topic that received considerable attention is the effects of parental divorce on children, a group affected at a rate of about one million per year since the mid 1970s (U.S. Bureau of Census, 1990).

Findings consistently show that children experience distress during the process of parental separation and divorce and that it is associated with a variety of short- and long-term negative outcomes (see reviews by Anthony, 1974; Fry & Addington, 1985; Kelly, 1988; Kurdek, 1981; Long & Forehand, 1987; Lopez, 1987; Santrock, 1987). Wallerstein and Blackeslee (1989) stated, "Almost all children of divorce regard their childhood and adolescence as having taken place in the shadow of divorce.... Almost half of the children entered adulthood as worried, underachieving, self-deprecating, and sometimes angry young men and women" (pp. 298-299).

In fact, studies indicate that children may experience difficulties in interpersonal relationships, school behavior, academic achievement, self-esteem, in

From David Gately and Andrew I. Schwebel, "Favorable Outcomes in Children After Parental Divorce," *Journal of Divorce and Remarriage,* vol. 18, nos. 3-4 (1992), pp. 57-63, 66-78. Copyright © 1992 by The Haworth Press, Inc. Reprinted by permission.

future life outlook, etc. Besides delineating the wide range of unfavorable outcomes that can develop in children before, during, and after the divorce, the literature also identifies factors that can moderate and exacerbate the problems children face.

Although much of the literature discusses children's struggle to cope with parental divorce and the unfavorable outcomes they may experience in one or more aspects of their lives, some children in adjusting to their changed circumstances before, during, and after parental divorce may also become strengthened in one or more areas. These individuals develop competencies or grow psychologically because of what they learn while undertaking the divorce-related challenges they face and/or because of the changes they experience in self-view as a result of successfully meeting the challenges.

Decades ago Bernstein and Robey (1962) suggested that successful coping with the demands presented by parental divorce can spur emotional and personality growth in children. Since then a number of investigators have found these favorable outcomes in youngsters relative either to their pre-divorce status or to matched peers from intact family backgrounds. (These include: Grossman, Shea, & Adams, 1980; Hetherington, 1989; Kelly & Wallerstein, 1976; Kurdek & Siesky, 1979, 1980a, 1980b, 1980c; MacKinnon, Stoneman & Brody, 1984; Reinhard, 1977; Richmond-Abbott, 1984; Rosen, 1977; Santrock & Warshak, 1979; Slater, Stewart, & Linn, 1983; Springer & Wallerstein, 1983; Wallerstein, 1984, 1985a, 1987; Wallerstein & Kelly, 1974, 1976, 1980b; Warshak & Santrock, 1983; Weiss, 1979.)

The present paper is based on a comprehensive review of the literature that investigated post-divorce outcomes in children. The review included literature generated from computer searches of the Psychological Abstracts and Family Resources and Educational Resources Information Center data bases. Manual searches of the Psychological Abstracts, The Inventory of Marriage and Family Literature, and the Social Sciences Index bases were conducted to supplement the computer searches. Finally, empirical and theoretical contributions published in books, chapters, and Dissertation Abstracts were reviewed. Following a brief assessment of this body of literature, the present paper focuses on those studies that reported favorable outcomes in children following parental divorce.

Most of the earliest investigations used a pathogenic model that viewed the divorced family as a deviation from the traditional 2-parent family, and attempted to link this "inferior" family structure to negative effects on children's adjustment and psychosocial development (Levitin, 1979). The picture of the effects of parental divorce on children were further colored in a negative way because these projects typically employed clinical samples and studied the crisis period immediately following divorce (Bernstein & Robey, 1962; Kalter, 1977; McDermott, 1968; Westman, 1972).

Later studies employing non-clinical samples showed that, although divorce is associated with an initial crisis reaction in most children, long-term consequences are variable (Hetherington, Cox, & Cox, 1982; Hetherington, 1989). While longitudinal studies demonstrated that parental divorce may have long-term negative effects on the social, emotional, and cognitive functioning of children (Guidubaldi & Cleminshaw, 1985; Hetherington, Cox, & Cox, 1985), they also showed that children may escape long-term negative outcomes if the crisis of divorce is not compounded by multiple stressors and continued adversity (Hetherington, 1979, 1989; Hetherington et al., 1982, 1985).

The finding that divorce does not necessarily result in long-term dysfunction led to a search for individual, family, and environmental factors that moderate children's adjustment. Researchers found the quality of adjustment related to: the child's gender and age at the time of separation/divorce (Guidubaldi & Perry, 1985; Hetherington et al., 1982, 1985; Kalter & Rembar, 1981; Wallerstein & Kelly, 1980a); the child's temperament, locus of control, interpersonal knowledge, and level of coping resources (Ankerbrandt, 1986; Hetherington, 1989; Kurdek & Berg, 1983; Kurdek, Blisk, & Siesky, 1981; Kurdek & Siesky, 1980a); the amount of interparental conflict prior to, during, and following separation/divorce (Emery, 1982; Hetherington et al., 1982; Jacobson, 1978; Wallerstein & Kelly, 1980b); the quality of parent-child relationships (Hess & Camara, 1979; Hetherington, Cox, & Cox, 1982; Wallerstein & Kelly, 1980a); the parents' mental and physical health (Guidubaldi & Cleminshaw, 1985; Guidubaldi & Perry, 1985); the type of custody arrangement (Ambert, 1984; Lowery & Settle, 1985; Santrock & Warshak, 1979; Santrock, Warshak, & Elliot, 1982; Warshak & Santrock, 1983; Wolchik, Braver, & Sandler, 1985); parental remarriage (Clingempeel & Segal, 1986; Hetherington et al., 1982; Santrock, Warshak, Lindbergh & Meadows, 1982); the number of major life changes experienced following divorce (Hetherington et al., 1985; Stolberg, Camplair, Currier, & Wells, 1987), including the amount of financial decline experienced by the post-divorce family (Desimone-Luis, O'Mahoney, & Hunt, 1979); and the social support available to both the parents and children (Isaacs & Leon, 1986).

Drawing upon the concept of stress, Wallerstein (1983a) and Peterson, Leigh, & Day (1984) developed models that could account for the absence of negative outcomes in children. For example, Wallerstein conceived of divorce as an acute social stressor that had consequences and made unique demands on children (differing from those associated with stressors like the death of a parent). Although families experiencing divorce and the loss of a parent pass through similar transitional stages (Schwebel, Fine, Moreland, & Prindle, 1988), studies comparing the short- and long-term effects on children of separation/divorce and death of a parent support Wallerstein's contention (Boyd & Parish, 1983; Felner, Stolberg, & Cowen, 1975; Hetherington, 1972; Mueller & Cooper, 1986; Rozendal, 1983).

Wallerstein (1983a, 1983b) described the sequence of adjustments a child must make: (1) acknowledge the marital disruption, (2) regain a sense of direction and freedom to pursue customary activities, (3) deal with loss and feelings of rejection, (4) forgive the parents, (5) accept the permanence of divorce and relinquish longings for the restoration of the pre-divorce family, and (6) come to feel comfortable and confident in relationships. The successful completion of these tasks, which allows the child to stay on course developmentally, depends on the child's coping resources and the degree of support available to help in dealing with the stressors. Of course, the divorce process also may include pre-separation distress, family conflict, and compromised parenting which both place children at risk and call for them to make adjustments well before the time when the legal divorce is granted (Block, Block, & Gjerde, 1986).

Reports describing protective factors that could mitigate negative outcomes for children following parental divorce complemented findings being described in stress research. More specifically, several authors (Garmezy, 1981; Rutter, 1987; Werner, 1989; Werner & Smith, 1982) found that some children, although exposed to multiple stressors that put them at risk, did not experience negative outcomes. Protective factors diminished the impact of these stressors. Although these investigators studied different stressors, their findings were remarkably similar and suggested that the factors which produce "resilience" in children-at-risk fit into three categories: (1) positive personality dispositions (e.g., active, affectionate, socially responsive, autonomous, flexible, intelligent; possessing self-esteem, an internal locus of control, self-control, and a positive mood); (2) a supportive family environment that encourages coping efforts; and (3) a supportive social environment that reinforces coping efforts and provides positive role models (Garmezy, 1981).

These protective factors reduce the likelihood of negative outcomes by means such as: decreasing exposure to or involvement with risk factors; opening of opportunities for successful task accomplishment and growth; and promoting self-esteem and self-efficacy through secure, supportive personal relationships (Rutter, 1987). Besides helping children avoid short-term harm, these resiliency-building factors strengthen children so they will cope more effectively with and master the stressful life events they will encounter in the future. This "steeling" effect is a favorable outcome that develops after an exposure to stressors of a type and degree that is manageable in the context of the child's capacities and social situation (Rutter, 1987).

The number of studies that identify favorable outcomes of any type of children following parental divorce is small in contrast to the number of studies that have reported unfavorable outcomes. To state the obvious, this difference in the volume of research reports primarily reflects the reality of what children face before, during, and after their parents' divorce. However, a small yet significant part of the difference may be due to the way science has addressed the question of children's outcomes. Specifically, the content of the literature has certainly been shaped, in part, by the fact that neither the pathological nor the stress models heuristically guide researchers to search for favorable outcomes (Kanoy & Cunningham, 1984; McKenry & Price, 1984, 1988; Scanzoni, Polonko, Teachman, & Thompson, 1988) and the fact that the research methods which have been typically employed are more likely to detect negative consequences than positive ones (Blechman, 1982; Kanoy & Cunningham, 1984). For instance, the wide use of measures that identify weaknesses (Blechman, 1982; Kanoy & Cunningham, 1984) and of subjects drawn from clinical samples, who are more maladjusted than their peers (Isaacs, Leon, & Donohue, 1987), makes the likelihood of detecting favorable outcomes unlikely (Kanoy & Cunningham, 1984).

A similar issue is presented by the tendency among researchers to neglect children as a source of data while, at the same time electing to use informants (eg., parents, teachers, clinicians) aware of children's family status (Kanoy &

Cunningham, 1984). Although parents' ratings of their elementary school children's adjustment is not related to the children's assessment of the emotional support they are receiving, the children's self-ratings of their adjustment are significant (Cowen, Pedro-Carroll & Alpert-Gillis, 1990). Teachers hold more negative expectations for children from divorced families than for their counterparts from intact families (Ball, Newman, & Scheuren, 1984) while parents and clinicians, in contrast to the children, tend to overestimate the negative effects of the divorce (Forehand, Brody, Long, Slotkin, & Fauber, 1986; Wolchik, Sandler, Braver, & Fogas, 1985). In fact, correlations between children's ratings of their own post-divorce adjustment and their parent's ratings are typically low (Kurdek & Siesky, 1980b), a finding consistent with correlations found between children's self-ratings and the ratings of adult informants in other areas of the literature (Achenbach, McConaughy, & Howell, 1987)....

The review of . . . the divorce-adjustment literature suggested four areas, in particular, in which children may experience favorable outcomes following their parents' divorce: in maturity, self-esteem, empathy, and androgyny. Each is discussed below.

Maturity

Intact families have an "echelon structure" in which parents form the executive unit. In the single-parent home this structure is replaced by a parent-child partnership that encourages children to assume more self and family responsibility and to participate more fully in important family decisions (Weiss, 1979). Such involvement fosters maturity which is evidenced by increased levels of responsibility, independence, and awareness of adult values and concerns.

Studies employing nonclinical samples have supported Weiss's conclusions. Kurdek and Siesky (1980a) reported that about 80% of the 132 5–19 year-old children they sampled (four years post-separation) believed they had assumed increased responsibilities after the divorce and learned to rely on themselves more. Their parents agreed, with about 75% of the 74 parents sampled rating their children as more mature and independent (Kurdek & Siesky, 1980b). Similar findings were reported by Rosen (1977), who assessed children 6–10 years after parental divorce, and by Reinhard (1977), who surveyed 46 adolescents three years post-divorce.

Children from single-parent families spend more time working in the home and taking care of siblings (Amato, 1987; Bohannon & Erikson, 1978; Hetherington, 1989; Zakariya, 1982). These chores can foster maturity in children, if they are age-appropriate and if the children receive adequate support. The maturity may exhibit itself in the form of an increased level of independence, realism, or identity development (Grossman et al., 1980). Single-parents further foster maturity when they (1) involve children in appropriate decision making and in a healthy range of other responsibilities in the post-divorce family (Bohannon & Erickson, 1978; Devall, Stoneman, & Brody, 1986; Hetherington, 1989; Kurdek & Siesky, 1979, 1980a; Reinhard, 1977; Wallerstein, 1985a; Weiss, 1979; Zakariya, 1982), and (2) allow children appropriate access to feelings that they, the adult caretakers, have as vulnerable individuals who may not always be able to meet the children's needs (Springer & Wallerstein, 1983; Wallerstein & Kelly, 1974).

Finally, a distinction is needed between pseudomaturity, a precocious adoption of adult roles and responsibilities, and maturity, an adaptive development that helps individuals cope more effectively. Pseudomaturity is seen in females from divorced families who display flirtatious and attention-seeking behavior with male interviewers (Hetherington, 1972), who engage in earlier and more frequent sexual activity (Boss, 1987; Hetherington, 1972; Kinnaird & Gerard, 1986) and who possess a greater likelihood of premarital pregnancy (Boss, 1987) than counterparts from intact families. Pseudomaturity is also found in both males and females from divorced families who engage in earlier and more frequent dating activity (Booth, Brinkerhoff, & White, 1984; Hetherington, 1972) and marry earlier (Boss, 1987; Glenn & Kramer, 1987) than peers from intact families.

Self-Esteem

Children may experience increased self-esteem in the aftermath of parental divorce because they cope effectively with changed circumstances, are asked to assume new responsibilities, successfully perform new duties, and so forth. Santrock and Warshak (1979) studied 6–11 year-old children, three years after their parents' divorce, and matched youngsters from intact, mother-custody and father-custody families. Father-custody boys demonstrated higher levels of self-esteem and lower levels of anxiety than intact family boys, while the opposite was true for girls. Slater et al. (1983) studied matched adolescents and found that boys from divorced family backgrounds possessed significantly higher levels of self-esteem than boys from intact and girls from both intact and divorced family backgrounds. Girls from divorced family backgrounds had lower levels of self-esteem than their counterparts from intact families. These results are consistent with Wallerstein and Kelly's (1980a).

One circumstance that appears to foster boys' increased self-esteem in post-divorce families is that they may be more heavily relied upon by custodial parents (most of whom are women) than girls, and as a result may gain a new position of increased responsibility and status. A study of children raised during the Great Depression indicated that older children were strengthened by assuming domestic responsibilities and part-time work (Elder, 1974).

Besides developing as a result of an individual's accomplishments, feelings of self-efficacy may also evolve from vicarious experience, verbal persuasion, and a reduction in the level of fear associated with performing particular behaviors (Bandura, Adams, & Beyer, 1977). Concretely, this suggests that divorcing parents benefit their children by modeling adaptive coping behavior (Kaslow & Hyatt, 1982) and by persuading children to be less fearful and to cope more effectively. Children are most likely to develop hardiness in facing post-divorce challenges if the demands upon them are moderate, if their parents support their efforts to perform new responsibilities, and if family members hold a positive view of divorce-related changes (Maddi & Kobasa, 1984).

Empathy

Some children in divorced and single-parent families show increased concern for the welfare of family members (Kurdek & Siesky, 1980b; Reinhard, 1977; Weiss, 1979). For example, Hetherington (1989) found older girls in divorced families, in contrast to peers, are more often involved in supportive and nurturing teaching, play, and caretaking activities with younger sisters and tend to help and share more frequently. Likewise, about 25% of Rosen's (1977) South African children sample reported they had gained a greater understanding of human emotions as a result of their parent's divorce 6 to 10 years earlier.

Although Wallerstein (1985b) suggested that children's increase in empathy does not extend beyond the parent-child relationship, Hetherington (1989) believes the increased empathy and sensitivity may reflect a more general orientation. The conditions prevalent during children's adjustment may determine the extent to which empathy develops and generalizes. If children are encouraged to provide age-appropriate emotional and practical support to family members, they may be able to extend themselves, gaining an understanding of others' feelings and, in this way, practice and refine their role- and perspective-taking skills. Hetherington and Parke (1979) suggested that more advanced role-taking skills are related to increased altruism, prosocial behavior, communication skills, moral standards, and empathetic understanding.

Androgyny

Necessity, encouragement from others, and the observation of models are among the factors that can lead children to shift away from stereotypical sex-role thinking and behavior and toward androgyny. This shift, in turn, can result in increased cognitive and behavioral flexibility (Bem, 1975; Bem & Lenney, 1976; Bem, Martyna, & Watson, 1976).

MacKinnon et al. (1984) investigated the effects of marital status and maternal employment on sex-role orientations in matched groups of mothers and children between 3 and 6 years old. While employment influenced mother's sex-role views, divorce appeared related to children's sex-role views. These authors suggested that the more androgynous sex-role views of the children in the post-divorce homes may stem from the mothers modeling more generalized sex-role behavior, or from the children assuming more nontraditional responsibilities.

Kurdek & Siesky (1980c) investigated the sex-role self-concepts of divorced single parents and their 10 to 19 year-old children, approximately four years post-separation. They found that custodial and noncustodial parents and their children possessed higher levels of self-reported androgyny, when compared to published norms, and that the boys and girls possessed more androgynous sex-role self-concepts than a comparison group of children from intact family backgrounds.

Richmond-Abbott (1984) found that the sex-role attitudes of children, ages 8 to 14, tended to reflect the liberal ones of their divorced, single-parent mothers. However, although the mothers stated that they wanted their children to behave in nontraditional ways, children were encouraged to pursue and tended to prefer sex-stereotyped chores and activities. This fits with the failure of others to find an effect of divorce on preadolescent female's sex-role orientation (Kalter, Riemer, Brickman, & Chen, 1985; Hetherington, 1972). Another finding, that the girls in the sample did foresee themselves engaging in nontraditional behaviors and occupations in the future, supports a conclusion that clear post-divorce increases in androgynous attitudes and behaviors may not emerge until children cope with adolescent identity issues.

Stevenson and Black (1988) conducted a meta-analysis of 67 studies that compared the sex-role development of children in father-present and father-absent homes. The applicability of their findings to the present issue is limited, however, by the fact that father absence because of divorce was not treated separately from father absence because of death or other reasons. Nonetheless, some conclusions they drew fit well with points made above. Specifically, father-absent female adolescents and young adults were slightly but consistently less feminine than their father-present peers in measures of traditionally feminine characteristics such as nurturance and expressiveness. Similarly, father-absent preschool boys, compared to their father-present peers, made fewer stereotypically sex-typed choices in picking toys and activities. However, older father-absent boys were more stereotypical than their father-present peers in their overt behavior, particularly in the expression of aggression. This latter difference could be reflecting the fact that in a mother-headed household an older boy may be asked to assume "man-of-the-house" duties.

In conclusion, the literature suggests that increased androgyny in children may develop following divorce if parents model nontraditional attitudes and behaviors or if children, by necessity and/or with parental encouragement, engage in nontraditional activities following divorce. While children in adolescence may struggle with androgynous thoughts, feelings, and behaviors, by their late teens and early twenties many will have worked through the issues. For example, two studies used by Stevenson and Black (1988) showed that college men who had experienced father absence reported fewer stereotypical vocational preferences. Finally, methodology has affected findings: While data collected from parents and teachers suggest that father-absent boys' behavior is more stereotypical than father-present boys', self-report measures indicate the opposite. In this connection, teachers' assessments have differed depending on whether they thought they were rating a child from a divorced or an intact home (Ball et al., 1984; Santrock & Tracy, 1978).

Research and Treatment Implications

Research is needed to identify a full list of favorable outcomes that can emerge following children's adjustment to parental divorce. Longitudinal studies would be desirable, especially those using matched comparison groups of intact family children while controlling for possible confounding variables, including parental conflict and family SES.

Hurley, Vincent, Ingram, and Riley (1984) categorize interventions designed to cope with unfavorable consequences in children following parental divorce as either therapeutic or preventative. The therapeutic approaches, which include psychodynamic and family systems interventions, focus on treating psychopathology, while the preventative approaches help healthy children avoid significant dysfunction by coping effectively with the normal post-divorce crisis reaction. Preventative interventions take the form of school-based support groups for children (Cantor, 1977; Gwynn & Brantley, 1987; Moore & Sumner, 1985; Pedro-Carroll & Cowen, 1985) or school and community-based support groups for parents (Davidoff & Schiller, 1983; Omizo & Omizo, 1987) and families (Magid, 1977; Stolberg & Cullen, 1983). Outcome studies show that parents, children, and group leaders believe support groups decrease distress and dysfunction in children (Cantor, 1977; Freeman, 1984; Gwynn & Brantly, 1987; Magid, 1977; Omizo & Omizo, 1987; Pedro-Carroll & Cowen, 1985). At this point, mental health workers could draw from the literature and design a third type of intervention: ones aimed at promoting favorable outcomes in children who must adjust to their parents' divorce.

References

Achenbach, T. M., McConaughy, S. H., & Howell, C. T. (1987). Child/adolescent behavioral and emotional problems: Implications of cross-informant correlations for situational specificity. *Psychological Bulletin, 101,* 213–232.

Amato, P. R. (1987). Family processes in one-parent, stepparent, and intact families: The child's point of view. *Journal of Marriage and the Family, 49,* 327–337.

Ambert, A. M. (1984). Longitudinal changes in children's behavior toward custodial parents. *Journal of Marriage and the Family,* (May), 463–467.

Ankenbrandt, M. J. (1986). Learned resourcefulness and other cognitive variables related to divorce adjustment in children. *Dissertation Abstracts International, 47* B, DA8628750, 5045.

Anthony, E. J. (1974). Children at risk from divorce: A review. In E. J. Anthony & C. Koupernik (Eds.), *The child in his family: Children at psychiatric risk* (Vol. 3), 461–478. N.Y.: John Wiley & Sons.

Ball, D. W., Newman, J. M., Scheuren, W. J. (1984). Teachers' generalized expectations of children of divorce. *Psychological Reports, 54,* 347–352.

Bandura, A., Adams, N. E., & Beyer, J. (1977). Cognitive processes mediating behavioral changes. *Journal of Personality and Social Psychology, 35,* 125–139.

Bem, S. L. (1975). Sex-role adaptability: One consequence of psychological androgyny. *Journal of Personality and Social Psychology, 31,* 634–643.

Bem, S. L. & Lenney, E. (1976). Sex typing and the avoidance of cross-sex behavior. *Journal of Personality and Social Psychology, 33,* 48–54.

Bem, S. L., Martyna, W., & Watson, C. (1976). Sex typing and androgyny: Further explorations of the expressive domain. *Journal of Personality and Social Psychology, 34,* 1016–1023.

Bernstein, N. & Robey, J. (1962). The detection and management of pediatric difficulties created by divorce. *Pediatrics, 16,* 950–956.

Blechman, E. A. (1982). Are children with one parent at psychiatric risk? A methodological review. *Journal of Marriage and the Family, 44,* 179–195.

Block, J. H., Block, J., & Gjerde, P. F. (1986). The personality of children prior to divorce: A prospective study. *Child Development, 57,* 827–840.

Bohannon, P. & Erickson, R. (1978, Jan.) Stepping in. *Psychology Today, 11,* 53–59.

Booth, A., Brinkerhoff, D. B., White, L. K. (1984). The impact of parental divorce on courtship. *Journal of Marriage and the Family, 46,* 85–94.

Boss, E. R. (1987). The demographic characteristics of children of divorce. *Dissertation Abstracts International, 48 1026A, DA8714900.*

Boyd, D. A. & Parish, T. (1983). An investigation of father loss and college students' androgyny scores. *The Journal of Genetic Psychology, 145*, 279–280.

Cantor, D. W. (1977). School based groups for children of divorce. *Journal of Divorce, 1*, 183–187.

Clingempeel, W. G. & Segal, S. (1986). Stepparent-stepchild relationships and the psychological adjustment of children in stepmother and stepfather families. *Child Development, 57*, 474–484.

Cowen, E., Pedro-Carroll, J., & Alpert-Gillis, L. (1990). Relationships between support and adjustment among children of divorce. *Journal of Child Psychology and Psychiatry, 31*, 727–735.

Davidoff, I. F. & Schiller, M. S. (1983). The divorce workshop as crisis intervention: A practical model. *Journal of Divorce, 6*, 25–35.

Desimone-Luis, J., O'Mahoney, K., & Hunt, D. (1979). Children of separation and divorce: Factors influencing adjustment. *Journal of Divorce, 3*, 37–41.

Devall, E., Stoneman, Z., & Brody, G. (1986). The impact of divorce and maternal employment on pre-adolescent children. *Family Relations, 35*, 153–159.

Elder, G. H. (1974). *Children of the great depression*. Chicago: University of Chicago Press.

Emery, R. E. (1982). Interparental conflict and the children of discord and divorce. *Psychological Bulletin, 92*, 310–330.

Felner, R. D., Stolberg, A., & Cowen, E. L. (1975). Crisis events and school mental health referral patterns of young children. *Journal of Consulting and Clinical Psychology, 3*, 305–310.

Forehand, R., Brody, G., Long, N., Slotkin, J., & Fauber, R. (1986). Divorce/divorce potential and interparental conflict: The relationship to early adolescent social and cognitive functioning. *Journal of Adolescent Research, 1*, 389–397.

Freeman, R. (1984). Children in families experiencing separation and divorce: An investigation of the effects of brief intervention. Family Service Association of Metropolitan Toronto (Ontario).

Fry, P. S. & Addington, J. (1985). Perceptions of parent and child adjustment in divorced families. *Clinical Psychology Review, 5*, 141–157.

Garmezy, N. (1981). Children under stress: Perspective on antecedents and correlates of vulnerability and resistance to psychopathology. In A. I. Rabin, J. Arnoff, A. N. Barclay, & R. A. Zucker (Eds.), *Further explorations in personality* (pp. 196–269). N.Y.: Wiley.

Glenn, N. D. & Kramer, K. B. (1987). The marriage and divorce of children of divorce. *Journal of Marriage and the Family, 49*, 811–825.

Grossman, S. M., Shea, J. A., & Adams, G. R. (1980). Effects of parental divorce during early childhood on the ego development and identity formation of college students. *Journal of Divorce, 3*, 263–271.

Guidubaldi, J. & Cleminshaw, H. (1985). Divorce, family health, and child adjustment. *Family Relations, 34*, 35–41.

Guidubaldi, J. & Perry, J. D. (1985). Divorce and mental health sequelae for children: A two-year follow-up of a nationwide sample. *Journal of American Academy of Child Psychiatry, 24* (5), 531–537.

Gwynn, C. A. & Brantley, H. T. (1987). Effects of a divorce group intervention for elementary school children. *Psychology in the Schools, 24*, 161–164.

Hess, R. D. & Camara, K. A. (1979). Post-divorce family relationships as mediating factors in the consequences of divorce for children. *Journal of Social Issues, 35* (4), 79–95.

Hetherington, E. M. (1972). Effects of father absence on personality development in adolescent daughters. *Developmental Psychology, 7*, 313–326.

Hetherington, E. M. (1979). Divorce: A child's perspective. *American Psychologist, 34*, 851–858.

Hetherington, E. M. (1989). Coping with family transitions: Winners, losers, and survivors. *Child Development, 60*, 1–14.

Hetherington, E. M., Cox, M., & Cox, R. (1982). Effects of divorce on parents and children. In M. Lamb (Ed.), *Nontraditional families: Parenting and child development* (233–288). Hillsdale, N.J.: Erlbaum.

Hetherington, E. M., Cox, M., & Cox, R. (1985). The long-term effects of divorce and remarriage on the adjustment of children. *Journal of the American Academy of Child Psychiatry, 24* (5), 518–530.

Hetherington, E. M. & Parke, R. D. (1979). *Child psychology: A contemporary viewpoint.* New York: McGraw-Hill Inc.

Hurley, E. C., Vincent, L. T., Ingram, T. L., & Riley, M. T. (1984). Therapeutic interventions for children of divorce. *Family Therapy, 9,* 261–268.

Isaacs, M. B. & Leon, G. (1986). Social networks, divorce, and adjustment: A tale of three generations. *Journal of Divorce, 9,* 1–16.

Isaacs, M. B., Leon, G., & Donohue, A. M. (1987). Who are the "normal" children of divorce? On the need to specify population. *Journal of Divorce, 10,* 107–119.

Jacobson, D. S. (1978). The impact of marital separation/divorce on children: II. Interparental hostility and child adjustment. *Journal of Divorce 2*(1), 3–19.

Kalter, N. (1977). Children of divorce in an outpatient psychiatric population. *American Journal of Orthopsychiatry, 47,* 40–51.

Kalter, N. & Rembar, J. (1981). The significance of a child's age at the time of divorce. *American Journal of Orthopsychiatry, 51,* 85–100.

Kalter, N., Riemer, B., Brickman, A., & Chen, J. W. (1985). Implications of parental divorce for female development. *Journal of the American Academy of Child Psychiatry, 24,* 538–544.

Kanoy, K. W. & Cunningham, J. L. (1984). Consensus or confusion in research on children and divorce: Conceptual and methodological issues. *Journal of Divorce, 74,* 45–71.

Kaslow, F. & Hyatt, R. (1982). Divorce: A potential growth experience for the extended family. *Journal of Divorce, 6,* 115–126.

Kelly, J. B. (1988). Longer-term adjustment in children of divorce: Converging findings and implications for practice. *Journal of Family Psychology, 2,* 119–140.

Kelly, J. B. & Wallerstein, J. S. (1976). The effects of parental divorce: Experiences of the child in early latency. *American Journal of Orthopsychiatry, 46,* 20–32.

Kinnaird, K. L. & Gerrard, M. (1986). Premarital sexual behavior and attitudes toward marriage and divorce among young women as a function of their mothers' marital status. *Journal of Marriage and the Family, 48,* 757–765.

Kurdek, L. A. (1981). An integrative perspective on children's divorce adjustment. *American Psychologist, 36,* 856–866.

Kurdek, L. A. & Berg, B. (1983). Correlates of children's adjustment to their parents' divorce. In L. A. Kurdek (Ed.). *Children and Divorce* (pp. 47–60). San Francisco: Jossey-Bass Inc., Publishers.

Kurdek, L. A., Blisk, D., & Siesky, A. E. (1981). Correlates of children's long-term adjustment to their parents' divorce. *Developmental Psychology, 17,* 565–579.

Kurdek, L. A. & Sieksy, A. E. (1979). An interview study of parents' perceptions of their children's reactions and adjustment to divorce. *Journal of Divorce, 3,* 5–17.

Kurdek, L. A. & Siesky, A. E. (1980a). Children's perceptions of their parents' divorce. *Journal of Divorce, 3,* 339–379.

Kurdek, L. A. & Siesky, A. E. (1980b). Effects of divorce on children: The relationship between parent and child perspectives. *Journal of Divorce, 4,* 85–99.

Kurdek, L. A. & Siesky, A. E. (1980c). Sex-role self-concepts of single divorced parents and their children. *Journal of Divorce, 3,* 249–261.

Levitin, T. E. (1979). Children of divorce. *Journal of Social Issues, 35,* 1–25.

Long, N. & Forehand, R. (1987). The effects of parental divorce and parental conflict on children: An overview. *Developmental and Behavioral Pediatrics, 8,* 292–296.

Lopez, F. G. (1987). The impact of parental divorce on college student development. *Journal of Counseling and Development, 65,* 484–486.

Lowery, C. R. & Settle, S. A. (1985). Effects of divorce on children: Differential impact of custody and visitation patterns. *Family Relations, 34,* 455–463.

MacKinnon, C. E., Stoneman, Z., & Brody, G. H. (1984). The impact of maternal employment and family form on children's sex-role stereotypes and mothers' traditional attitudes. *Journal of Divorce, 8,* 51–60.

Maddi, S. R. & Kobasa, S. C. (1984). *The hardy executive: Health under stress.* Chicago: Dorsey Professional Books.

Magid, K. M. (1977). Children facing divorce: A treatment program. *Personnel and Guidance Journal, 55,* 534–536.

McDermott, J. F. (1968). Parental divorce in early childhood. *American Journal of Psychiatry, 124,* 1424–1432.

McKenry, P. C. & Price, S. J. (1984). The present state of family relations research. *Home Economics Journal, 12,* 381–402.

McKenry, P. C. & Price, S. J. (1988). Research bias in family science: Sentiment over reason. *Family Science Review, 1,* 224–233.

Moore, N. E. & Sumner, M. G. (1985). *Support group for children of divorce: A family life enrichment group model.* Paper presented at Annual Meeting of the National Association of Social Workers, New Orleans.

Mueller, D. & Cooper, P. W. (1986). Children of single parent families: How they fare as young adults. *Family Relations, 35,* 169–176.

Omizo, M. M. & Omizo, S. A. (1987). Effects of parents' divorce group participation on child-rearing attitudes and children's self-concepts. *Journal of Humanistic Education and Development, 25,* 171–179.

Pedro-Carroll, J. L. & Cowen, E. L. (1985). The children of divorce intervention program: An investigation of the efficacy of a school based prevention program. *Journal of Consulting and Clinical Psychology, 53,* 603–611.

Peterson, G., Leigh, G. K., & Day, R. D. (1984). Family stress theory and the impact of divorce on children. *Journal of Divorce, 7,* 1–20.

Reinhard, D. (1977). The reaction of adolescent boys and girls to the divorce of their parents. *Journal of Clinical Child Psychology, 6,* 21–23.

Richmond-Abbott, M. (1984). Sex-role attitudes of mothers and children in divorced, single-parent families. *Journal of Divorce, 8,* 61.

Rosen, R. (1977). Children of divorce: What they feel about access and other aspects of the divorce experience. *Journal of Clinical Child Psychology, 6,* 24–27.

Rozendal, F. G. (1983). Halos vs. stigmas: Long-term effects of parent's death or divorce on college students' concepts of the family. *Adolescence, 18,* 948–955.

Rutter, M. (1987). Psychosocial resilience and protective mechanisms. *American Journal of Orthopsychiatry, 57,* 316–331.

Santrock, J. W. (1987). The effects of divorce on adolescence: Needed research perspectives. *Family Therapy, 14,* 147–159.

Santrock, J. W. & Tracy, R. L. (1978). Effects of children's family structure status on the development of stereotypes by teachers. *Journal of Educational Psychology, 70,* 754–757.

Santrock, J. W. & Warshak, R. A. (1979). Father custody and social development in boys and girls. *Journal of Social Issues, 35,* 112–125.

Santrock, J. W., Warshak, R. A., & Elliot, G. L. (1982). Social development and parent child interactions in father-custody and stepmother families. In M. Lamb (Ed.), *Nontraditional families: Parenting and child development.* Hillsdale, N.J.: Erlbaum, 289–314.

Santrock, J. W., Warshak, R. A., Lindbergh, C., & Meadows, L. (1982). Children's and parents' observed social behavior in stepfather families. *Child Development, 53,* 472–480.

Scanzoni, J., Polonko, K., Teachman, J. T., & Thompson, L. (1988). *The sexual bond: Rethinking families and close relationships.* Newbury Park, CA: Sage Publications Inc.

Schwebel, A. I., Fine, M., Moreland, J. R., & Prindle, P. (1988). Clinical work with divorced and widowed fathers: The adjusting family model. In P. Bronstein & C. Cowen (Eds.), *Fatherhood today: Men's changing role in the family.* New York: Wiley, 299–319.

Slater, E. J., Stewart, K., & Linn, M. (1983). The effects of family disruption on adolescent males and females. *Adolescence, 18,* 933.

Springer, C. & Wallerstein, J. S. (1983). Young adolescents' responses to their parents' divorce. In L. A. Kurdek (Ed.), *Children and divorce.* San Francisco: Jossey-Bass, 15–27.

Stevenson, M. R. & Black, K. N. (1988). Paternal absence and sex-role development: A meta-analysis. *Child Development, 59,* 795–814.

Stolberg, A., Camplair, C., Currier, K., & Wells, M. (1987). Individual, familial, and environmental determinants of children's post-divorce adjustment and maladjustment. *Journal of Divorce, 11,* 51–70.

Stolberg, A. L. & Cullen, P. M. (1983). Preventive interventions for families of divorce: The divorce adjustment project. *New Directions for Child Development, 19,* 71–81.

U.S. Bureau of the Census (1990). *Statistical abstract of the U.S.: 1990.* Washington, D.C.

Wallerstein, J. (1983a). Children of divorce: Stress and developmental tasks. In N. Garmezy and M. Rutter (Eds.), *Stress, coping, and development.* New York: McGraw-Hill Inc., 265–302.

Wallerstein, J. (1983b). Children of divorce: The psychological tasks of the child. *American Journal of Orthopsychiatry, 53,* 230–243.

Wallerstein, J. (1984). Children of divorce: Preliminary report of a ten-year follow-up of young children. *American Journal of Orthopsychiatry, 54*(3), 444–458.

Wallerstein, J. (1985a). Children of divorce: Preliminary report of a ten-year follow-up of older children and adolescents. *Journal of American Academy of Child Psychiatry, 24*(5), 545–553.

Wallerstein, J. (1985b). The overburdened child: Some long-term consequences of divorce. *Social Work, 30*(2), 116–123.

Wallerstein, J. (1987). Children of divorce: Report of a ten-year follow-up of early latency-age children. *American Journal of Orthopsychiatry, 57,* 199–211.

Wallerstein, J. & Blackeslee, S. (1989). *Second chances.* New York: Ticknor & Fields.

Wallerstein, J. & Kelly, J. (1974). The effects of divorce: The adolescent experience. In J. Anthony & C. Koupernik (Eds.), *The child in his family: Children at psychiatric risk* (Vol. 3). N.Y.: Wiley.

Wallerstein, J. & Kelly, J. (1976). The effects of divorce: Experiences of the child in later latency. *American Journal of Orthopsychiatry, 46*(2), 256–269.

Wallerstein, J. & Kelly, J. (1980a). *Surviving the Breakup.* New York: Basic Books Inc.

Wallerstein, J. & Kelly, J. (1980b, Jan.) California's children of divorce. *Psychology Today,* 67–76.

Warshak, R. & Santrock, J. W. (1983). The impact of divorce in father-custody and mother-custody homes: The child's perspective. In L. Kurdek (Ed.), *Children and divorce,* San Francisco: Jossey-Bass Inc., Publishers, 29–45.

Weiss, R. (1979). Growing up a little faster: The experience of growing up in a single-parent household. *Journal of Social Issues, 35*(4), 97–111.

Werner, E. E. (1989). High-risk children in young adulthood: A longitudinal study from birth to 32 years. *American Journal of Orthopsychiatry, 59,* 72–81.

Werner, E. E. & Smith, B. S. (1982). *Vulnerable but invincible: A study of resilient children.* New York: McGraw-Hill Inc.

Westman, J. C. (1972). Effect of divorce on child's personality development. *Medical Aspects of Human Sexuality, 6,* 38–55.

Wolchik, S. & A., Braver, S., & Sandler, I. (1985). Maternal versus joint custody: Children's postseparation experiences and adjustment. *Journal of Clinical Child Psychology, 14,* 5–10.

Wolchik, S. A., Sandler, I., Braver, S., & Fogas, B. (1985). Events of parental divorce: Stressfulness ratings by children, parents, and clinicians. *American Journal of Community Psychology, 14,* 59–74.

Zakariya, S. B. (1982, Sept.). Another look at the children of divorce: Summary report of school needs of one-parent children. *Principal, 62,* 34–38.

POSTSCRIPT

Does Divorce Create Long-Term Negative Effects for Children?

Raising children is among the most challenging jobs a person can have in her or his lifetime. With that in mind, one must consider how an individual or couple makes the decision to have children. Some people plan meticulously, save their money, and have a child when they feel they are as ready as they will ever be. Some people are faced with a surprise pregnancy and decide they are ready even if they had not planned for it. Some spend exorbitant amounts of money on alternative fertilization methods or adoption agencies. Some people end up with children they did not expect to raise, like grandparents raising their grandchild for one reason or another. Still other people are in relationships that are not working out and think that having a child will strengthen the relationship.

There is no crystal ball to see into the future, and there are no guarantees in life. Most couples who enter a relationship with the intention of a long-term commitment will usually work hard to make it work. Some will do so successfully, and others will not.

If a couple breaks up "well," with little or no animosity, there is a greater likelihood that the couple will be able to negotiate coparenting in a way that will best serve both of them, their future partners or spouses, and their child or children. Again, there are no guarantees—and no direct correlations. A couple can be absolutely atrocious to each other during a breakup, and the child can end up just fine. A couple can be respectful and thoughtful in negotiating the breakup, and the child can end up depressed and with other emotional challenges. Clearly, the issue merits additional research, using more current methodology, reviewing the many different relationship structures in which children are raised, and including children themselves in the process.

Suggested Readings

Patrick F. Fagan and Robert Rector, "The Effects of Divorce on America," *The Backgrounder, No. 1373* (The Heritage Foundation, 2000).

E. Mavis Hetherington, *For Better or for Worse, Divorce Reconsidered* (W. W. Norton & Company, 2002).

Karen S. Peterson, "Divorce Need Not End in Disaster," *USA Today* (January 30, 2002).

Judith S. Wallerstein, Julia M. Lewis, and Sandra Blakeslee, *The Unexpected Legacy of Divorce* (Hyperion, 2000).

The National Association of the Deaf

The National Association of the Deaf, established in 1880, is the oldest and largest constituency organization safeguarding the accessibility and civil rights of 28 million deaf and hard of hearing Americans in education, employment, health care, and telecommunications.

http://www.nad.org

The Alexander Graham Bell Association for the Deaf and Hard of Hearing

The Alexander Graham Bell Association for the Deaf and Hard of Hearing is an international membership organization and resource center on hearing loss and spoken language approaches and related issues.

http://www.agbell.org

The Intersex Society of North America

The Intersex Society of North America is devoted to systemic change to end shame, secrecy, and unwanted genital surgeries for people born with atypical reproductive anatomies.

http://www.isna.org

The Family Research Council (FRC)

The Family Research Council (FRC) champions marriage and family as the foundation of civilization, the seedbed of virtue, and the wellspring of society. FRC shapes public debate and formulates public policy that values human life and upholds the institutions of marriage and the family.

http://www.frc.org

Concerned Women for America

The mission of Concerned Women for America is to protect and promote Biblical values among all citizens—first through prayer, then education, and finally by influencing society—thereby reversing the decline in moral values in the United States.

http://www.cwfa.org

PART 2

Parental Decisions

*A*mong the greatest responsibilities of being a parent is making decisions that the parent believes to be in the best interest of her or his
child. These decisions can affect children's education, health and well-
being, and manner of expressing who they are. As a result, parents are
often open to scrutiny by individuals inside and outside their families
for making decisions that some may agree with and others may not. This
part examines three particularly challenging parental decisions.

- Should Parents Be Allowed to Opt Out of Vaccinating Their Kids?

- Should Parents of Deaf Children Choose Cochlear Implant
  Surgery?

- Should Parents Surgically Alter Their Intersex Infants?

ISSUE 6

Should Parents Be Allowed to Opt Out of Vaccinating Their Kids?

YES: Barbara Loe Fisher, from "Children at Risk for Adverse Reactions Should Be Given a Pass Without Penalty," *Insight on the News* (April 24, 2000)

NO: Steven P. Shelov, from "That Would Open the Door for Epidemics of Some Deadly Childhood Diseases," *Insight on the News* (April 24, 2000)

ISSUE SUMMARY

YES: Barbara Loe Fisher, cofounder and president of the National Vaccine Information Center, argues that the risks involved with vaccinating children need to be weighed by their parents. She asserts that in some states government policies relating to vaccinations for children discount the parents' rights to choose what is best for their children and that parents should be allowed to decide whether or not to have their children vaccinated.

NO: Steven P. Shelov, chairman of the Department of Pediatrics at the Maimonides Medical Center in New York City, points to the vast number of diseases, disorders, and deaths that are preventable thanks to vaccines early in life. He maintains that parents should trust in science and the extensive research that has been done on these vaccines and make every effort to ensure that their children are vaccinated.

Vaccines were created to strengthen the immune system so that diseases that previously resulted in serious physical and mental disabilities could be stopped before they affected the body. One of these diseases, smallpox, has not been a problem in the United States since the 1960s. Vaccines work by introducing a small amount of a bacterium or virus that is very weak. This causes the body to create antibodies that would attack the disease were it to be contracted. Antibodies can also be created by having a particular disease. This is why children who have chicken pox once will not get it again in their lives. With other infections, an individual may need a booster shot at different times in their lives.

There are currently 11 vaccinations that children are given before they are two years old, which are delivered in as many as 16 doses. These immunizations protect against such potentially serious infections as measles, mumps, chicken pox, and hepatitis B.

The Centers for Disease Control and Prevention (CDC) estimate that between 37 and 56 percent of children in the United States have not been fully immunized by the time they are two years old. Parents are required to have their children vaccinated before the children can be enrolled in school or in day care. However, some babies and toddlers end up in day-care settings that are not licensed. Without the requirement, some children will not end up having the vaccinations. We see this, in particular, in low-income (particularly urban) areas where diseases that are uncommon in most parts of the United States today are more likely to occur in disproportionate numbers due to improper vaccination of the children living in the community.

Some parents do not feel that they should be required to have their children immunized. They believe that the risks of having such a young infant injected with an infection like hepatitis B are too great, especially if neither parent is in the high-risk population for the infection. Other people feel that the financial burden on parents to vaccinate their children against infections they believe their children are highly unlikely to contract is too great. Since only about half of health insurance plans cover childhood vaccines, the cost can add up for a low-income family. Others argue that the financial burden is not as great, since many public health departments offer vaccines for free or on a sliding fee scale. In addition, federal dollars are allocated in the hundreds of millions to provide free vaccinations to uninsured children and to educate parents about the need for childhood immunizations. They also maintain that spending money on vaccines today will save money down the line. According to the National Academy of Sciences' Institute of Medicine, every $1 spent on vaccinations saves $10 in healthcare-related costs later in the child's life.

As with any health-related procedure, there are risks involved in vaccinating an infant or child. Some children do suffer injuries or even die as a result of receiving a vaccination. In response to this, Congress passed the National Childhood Vaccine Injury Act in 1986. This act was designed to help ensure vaccine safety and availability and to provide financial recompense for the people or families of children injured or killed by vaccination. In addition, medical professionals are required to report significant adverse reactions they witness as a result of certain vaccines. In the first seven years after this act, the CDC received more than 20,000 reports.

In the following selections, Barbara Loe Fisher argues that parents should be allowed to opt out of vaccinating their children because of the potential risks involved. She states that regardless of what science says, a parent needs to determine whether or not even a small risk is too much in the case of her or his own child. Steven P. Shelov, believes that current data show a lower risk for the types of negative reactions that a small percentage of children have had to various vaccinations. He warns against making a decision that he feels puts children at higher risk for infections and diseases based on such a low incidence of negative vaccination reactions.

Barbara Loe Fisher

 **YES**

Children at Risk for Adverse Reactions Should Be Given a Pass Without Penalty

P arents do not want their children to be injured or die from a disease or a vaccination. As guardians of their children until those children are old enough to make life-and-death decisions for themselves, parents take very seriously the responsibility of making informed vaccination decisions for the children they love. That responsibility includes becoming educated about the relative risks of diseases when compared to the vaccines aimed at preventing them.

Like every encounter with a viral or bacterial infection, every vaccine containing lab-altered viruses or bacteria has an inherent ability to cause injury or even death. Vaccination either can produce immunity without incident or can result in mild to severe brain and immune-system damage, depending upon the vaccine or combination of vaccines given, the health of the person at the time of vaccination and whether the individual is generically or otherwise biologically at risk for developing complications.

The fact that vaccines can cause injury and death officially was acknowledged in the United States in 1986 when Congress passed the National Childhood Vaccine Injury Act, creating a no-fault federal compensation system for vaccine-injured children to protect the vaccine manufacturers and doctors from personal-injury lawsuits. Since then, the system has paid out more than $1 billion to 1,000 families, whose loved ones have died or been harmed by vaccines, even though three out of four applicants are turned away.

Since 1990, between 12,000 and 14,000 reports of hospitalizations, injuries and deaths following vaccination are made to the federal Vaccine Adverse Event Reporting System, or VAERS, annually, but it is estimated that only between 1 and 10 percent of all doctors make reports to VAERS. Therefore, the number of vaccine-related health problems occurring in the United States every year may be more than 1 million.

In the late 1980s, the Institute of Medicine, or IOM, and the National Academy of Sciences convened committees of physicians to study existing medical knowledge about vaccines and, in 1991 and 1994, IOM issued historic reports confirming vaccines can cause death, as well as a wide spectrum of brain

From Barbara Loe Fisher, "Children at Risk for Adverse Reactions Should Be Given a Pass Without Penalty," *Insight on the News* (April 24, 2000). Copyright © 2000 by News World Communications, Inc. Reprinted by permission of *Insight on the News*.

and immune-system damage. But the most important conclusion, which deserves greater public attention and congressional action, was: "The lack of adequate data regarding many of the [vaccine] adverse events under study was a major concern to the committee. [T]he committee encountered many gaps and limitations in knowledge bearing directly or indirectly on the safety of vaccines."

Because so little medical research has been conducted on vaccine side effects, no tests have been developed to identify and screen out vulnerable children. As a result, public-health officials have taken a "one-size-fits-all" approach and have aggressively implemented mandatory vaccination laws while dismissing children who are injured or die after vaccination as unfortunate but necessary sacrifices "for the greater good." This utilitarian rationale is of little comfort to the growing number of mothers and fathers who watch their once-healthy, bright children get vaccinated and then suddenly descend into mental retardation, epilepsy, learning and behavior disorders, autism, diabetes, arthritis and asthma. Some adverse reactions are fatal.

As vaccination rates have approached 98 percent for children entering kindergarten in many states, there is no question that mass vaccination in the last quarter-century has suppressed infectious diseases in childhood, eradicating polio in the Western hemisphere and lowering the number of cases of measles from a high of more than 400,000 cases in 1965 to only 100 in 1999. Yet, even as infectious-disease rates have fallen, rates of chronic disease and disability among children and young adults have risen dramatically.

A University of California study published by the U.S. Department of Education in 1996 found that "the proportion of the U.S. population with disabilities has risen markedly during the last quarter-century. [T]his recent change seems to be due not to demographics, but to greater numbers of children and young adults reported as having disabilities." The study concluded the change was due to "increases in the prevalence of asthma, mental disorders (including attention-deficit disorder), mental retardation and learning disabilities that have been noted among children in recent years."

Instead of epidemics of measles and polio, we have epidemics of chronic autoimmune and neurological disease: In the last 20 years rates of asthma and attention-deficit disorder have doubled, diabetes and learning disabilities have tripled, chronic arthritis now affects nearly one in five Americans and autism has increased by 300 percent or more in many states. The larger unanswered question is: To what extent has the administration of multiple doses of multiple vaccines in early childhood—when the body's brain and immune system is developing at its most rapid rate—been a cofactor in epidemics of chronic disease? The assumption mass-vaccination policies have played no role is as unscientific and dangerous as the assumption that an individual child's health problems following vaccination are only coincidentally related to the vaccination.

Questions about vaccination only can be answered by scientific research into the biological mechanism of vaccine injury and death so that pathological profiles can be developed to distinguish between vaccine-induced health problems and those that are not. Whether the gaps in scientific knowledge about vaccines will be filled in this decade or remain unanswered in the next depends upon the funding and research priorities set by Congress, the National Institutes of Health and industry.

With the understanding that medical science and the doctors who practice it are not infallible, today's better-educated health-care consumer is demanding more information, more choices and a more equal decision-making partnership with doctors. Young mothers, who are told that their children must be injected with 33 doses of 10 different vaccines before the age of 5, are asking questions such as: "Why does my 12-hour-old newborn infant have to be injected with hepatitis B vaccine when I am not infected with hepatitis B and my infant is not an IV-drug user or engaging in sex with multiple partners—the two highest risk groups for hepatitis B infection?" And: "Why does my 12-month-old have to get chicken-pox vaccine when chicken pox is a mild disease and once my child gets it he or she will be immune for life?"

Informed parents know that hepatitis B is not like polio and that chicken pox is not like smallpox. They know the difference between taking a risk with a vaccine for an adult disease that is hard to catch, such as the blood-transmitted hepatitis B, and using a vaccine to prevent a devastating, highly contagious childhood disease such as polio.

All diseases and all vaccines are not the same and neither are children. Parents understand the qualitative difference between options freely taken and punishing dictates. They are calling for enlightened, humane implementation of state vaccination laws, including insertion of informed-consent protections that strengthen exemptions for sincerely held religious or conscientious beliefs. This is especially critical for parents with reason to believe that their child may be at high risk for dying or being injured by one or more vaccines but cannot find a doctor to write an exemption.

Informed consent has been the gold standard in the ethical practice of medicine since World War II, acknowledging the human right for individuals or their guardians to make fully informed, voluntary decisions about whether to undergo a medical procedure that could result in harm or death. To the extent that vaccination has been exempted from informed-consent protections and vaccine makers and doctors have been exempted from liability for vaccine injuries and deaths, the notion that a minority of individuals are expendable in service to the majority has prevented a real commitment of will and resources to develop ways to screen out vulnerable children and spare their lives. It is not difficult to understand why some parents resist offering up their children as sacrifices for a government policy that lacks scientific and moral integrity.

But even as educated health-care consumers are asking for more information and choices, mechanisms are being set up to restrict those choices. Government-operated, electronic vaccine-tracking systems already are in place in most states, using health-care identifier numbers to tag and track children without the parent's informed consent in order to enforce use of all government-recommended vaccines now and in the future. Health-maintenance organizations are turning down children for health insurance and federal entitlement programs are economically punishing parents who cannot show proof their child got every state-recommended vaccine. Even children who have suffered severe vaccine reactions are being pressured to get revaccinated or be barred from getting an education.

Drug companies and federal agencies are developing more than 200 new vaccines, including ones for gonorrhea and herpes that will target 12-year-olds. On March 2, President Clinton joined with the international pharmaceutical industry, multinational banks and the Bill and Melinda Gates Foundation to launch the Millennium Vaccine Initiative with several billion dollars committed to vaccinating all children in the world with existing and future vaccines, including those in accelerated development for AIDS, tuberculosis and malaria.

With so many unanswered questions about the safety and necessity of giving so many vaccines to children, the right to informed consent to vaccination takes on even greater legal and ethical significance as we head into the 21st century. In a broader sense, the concept of informed consent transcends medicine and addresses the constitutional concept of individual freedom and the moral concept of individual inviolability. If the state can tag, track down and force individuals into being injected with biological agents of unknown toxicity today, will there by an limit on what individual freedoms the state can take away in the name of the greater good tomorrow?

Parents, who know and love their children better than anyone else, have the right to make informed, voluntary vaccination decisions for their children without facing state-sanctioned punishment. Whether a child is hurt by a vaccine or a disease, it is the mother and father—not the pediatrician, vaccine maker or public-health official—who will bear the lifelong grief and burden of what happens to that child.

Steven P. Shelov

 **NO**

That Would Open the Door for Epidemics of Some Deadly Childhood Diseases

Some parents today are in a quandary regarding the need for immunizing their children. They need not be.

True, recent media stories about an increase in childhood autism associated with immunizations and other illnesses have led some to question the need to give their children the full range of vaccinations required by most school districts in the country. In addition, numerous others have had unfortunate experiences with their own children or relatives with respect to a bad reaction to an immunization. Yet, it is important to keep all these issues and incidents in perspective and not to erode public confidence in immunizing our children. In fact, if the U.S. population or any population regards immunizing children as optional, we risk having large numbers of children becoming vulnerable to the most deadly diseases known to man. As a practicing pediatrician, I am passionately opposed to that. The following are a few questions some skeptical parents are asking about the vaccination issue:

What would happen if I did not have my child immunized? Without immunizations there would be a significant possibility that your child would contract some of the diseases that are now waiting to come back. These include: whooping cough (pertussis), tetanus, polio, measles, mumps, German measles (rubella), bacterial meningitis and diphtheria.

These illnesses all may injure children severely, leaving them deaf, blind, paralyzed or they even may cause death. For example, in 1960 there were more than 1.5 million cases of measles and more than 400 deaths associated with this disease. As a result of our active immunization process in 1998 the United States had only 89 cases of measles and there were no deaths.

Why should I accept any risk of immunization for my child when other children already are immunized? Won't that protect my child? It is important to understand the concept of herd immunity and public health vs. individual risk. Individual risk is always a possibility with any procedure, medication, new activity or vaccine. The key to any program or new intervention is to minimize the risk. There is no question that vaccines are the safest, most risk-free type of medication ever developed. Nevertheless, occasionally—very occasionally—

children have been known to experience a bad, or adverse, reaction to a vaccine. In some cases—polio vaccine, for example—one in 1 million doses appears to have been associated with vaccine-related mild polio disease. The reactions to other vaccines also have been very, very small, though nevertheless significant for the child or family who have experienced one.

It is not, however, good public policy to give those few at-risk situations priority over the goal of protecting the population as a whole from those diseases. If the pool of unimmunized children becomes large enough, then the disease itself may reemerge in those unimmunized children, possibly in epidemic proportions. This has occurred in countries where immunizations have been allowed to decrease; most recently pertussis (whopping cough) resurfaced in Europe. Failure to immunize a child not only puts that child at risk of illness but also increases the potential for harm to other children who are not able to be vaccinated because they are too young or too ill or to those who in rare cases are vaccinated but the vaccination fails to provide the expected protection.

Are immunizations safe? Don't they hurt? Reactions to vaccines may occur, but they usually are mild. Serious reactions are very, very rare but also may occur. Remember, the risks from these potentially dangerous childhood illnesses are far greater than any risk of serious reaction from immunization. Even though immunizations may hurt a little when they are given, and your baby may cry for a few minutes, and there might be some swelling, protecting your child's health is worth a few tears and a little temporary discomfort.

Isn't it better that children get a disease such as chicken pox to give them a permanent immunity? If a child gets the disease, the danger is that the child may develop serious complications from the disease. The immunity conferred following the recommended immunization schedule will give excellent immunity and not place the child at risk.

Is it true that hepatitis B vaccine can cause autism or juvenile diabetes, sudden infant death syndrome, or SIDS, multiple sclerosis or asthma? There have been occasional reports in the media associating this vaccine with all of the above illnesses. Scientific research has not found any evidence linking the hepatitis B vaccine to autism, SIDS, multiple sclerosis, juvenile diabetes or asthma. In fact, SIDS rates have declined during the same time period that the hepatitis B vaccine has been recommended for routine immunization. Although some media have circulated reports that health authorities in France have stopped giving the hepatitis vaccine to children, that is not true. French health officials did not stop giving the hepatitis vaccine but decided not to administer the vaccine in the schools and recommended that the vaccine be given in medical settings.

Is there a link between measles vaccine and autism? No. There is no scientifically proven link between measles vaccine and autism. Autism is a chronic developmental disorder often first identified in toddlers ages 18 months to 30 months. The MMR (mumps, measles, rubella vaccine) is administered just before the peakage of autism that has caused some parents to assume a causal relationship, but a recent study in a British journal showed there was no association between the MMR vaccine and autism.

It is assumed that there has been an increase in the diagnosis of autism because the definition for who would fall under that category has changed. In addition, parents and medical professionals are more aware of this condition and are more likely to pursue that diagnosis. Though there may be an increase in the number of children who have autism, there have been many studies completed that show that the MMR does not cause autism.

Aren't measles, mumps and rubella relatively harmless illnesses? Measles is a highly contagious respiratory disease. It causes a rash, high fever, cough and runny nose. In addition, it can cause encephalitis, which leads to convulsions, deafness or mental retardation in one to two children of every 2,000 who get it. Of every 1,000 people who get measles, one to two will die. MMR can prevent this disease. Mumps is less serious than measles but may cause fever, headache and swelling of one or both sides of the jaw. Four to 6 percent of those who get mumps will get meningitis, which puts the child at risk for significant disability and potential retardation. In addition, inflammation of the testicles occurs in four of every 10 adult males who get mumps, and mumps may result in hearing loss that usually is permanent. The effects of rubella are mild in children and adults—causing only a minor rash—but the major reason to prevent rubella in the community is to prevent exposure of pregnant women to children who have rubella. When contracted by a pregnant woman, rubella may infect her unborn baby, leading to a significant potential for mental retardation and a host of serious defects. This devastating disease, known as congenital rubella syndrome, essentially has been eliminated with the use of rubella vaccine.

Given that measles, rubella and mumps essentially have disappeared from the United States and therefore are uncommon, why should we continue to immunize? The measles virus continues to be present in other countries outside the United States. Given the large number of immigrants to this country, the potential for exposure to measles remains a real potential. Just a few weeks ago several young children who recently emigrated from the United Kingdom came into one of our pediatrician's offices. Due to the decrease in immunization vigilance in the United Kingdom against measles, these young children were infected with measles, and they put at risk the other infants and children in the waiting room of this busy pediatrician's office. If those other children contract measles, they will be at risk for developing serious sequela of the disease. And, should they develop the disease, they potentially will expose others as well. A mini-epidemic could have been caused by these infected children with measles.

Should parents be able to choose not to vaccinate their child without being barred from enrolling that child in school? Immunizing children is a public-health issue. Public-health laws in all 50 states require immunization of children as a condition of school enrollment. This is as it should be, since public health must take precedence. Immunizations have a clear community benefit and, therefore, individual preferences should not be permitted to expose the public to the hazards of infectious diseases.

In summary, it is clear that the risk of exposing children to infectious disease should there be a decline in immunizations is a risk to which the population of the United States should not be exposed. It always is regrettable when an individual case of an adverse event occurs no matter what might have taken place. These adverse events clearly affect the child and obviously the family as well, and there indeed is always an outcry when this does occur. However, as with all safe, proven interventions, an exception could always occur given a normal risk ratio.

It would be actual malpractice and poor public-health philosophy and practice to consider not immunizing our children against the potentially deadly infectious diseases. We should be thankful to our research scientists, epidemiologists, and medical and pharmaceutical industry for the skill and care with which these important vaccines have been developed and the care with which the vaccine policies have been developed and monitored. There is no question in my mind that immunizations are one of the most important ways parents can protect their children against serious diseases. Without immunizations the children of the United States would be exposed to deadly diseases that continue to occur throughout the world.

POSTSCRIPT

Should Parents Be Allowed to Opt Out of Vaccinating Their Kids?

In 2002 the journal *Pediatrics* reported that newborn babies' immune systems are more than strong enough to handle receiving one or more vaccinations. The experts quoted in this study maintain that if a baby received all 11 available vaccines at one time, she or he would "use up" only about 0.1 percent of the immune system. This is, they say, because the B cells and T cells, which fight off infection and start being produced while the infant is still in utero, are constantly being regenerated.

For some people, this information adds fuel to the fire behind their argument that vaccinations should be mandatory for all children and that parents should not be able to keep their children from being vaccinated. However, this information does not necessarily mean anything to parents who either do not trust medicine, do not feel that even the smallest risk is worth taking when it comes to their own child, or whose cultural or religious beliefs do not support medical interventions of this kind. As a result, the debate on this issue continues to go back and forth.

You may not yet have children, although you may have children in your families. Think about how you feel about this issue. Were the children in your life vaccinated as babies? Were you? Do you plan on having your own children vaccinated? Why, or why not?

There is a saying that goes, "Hindsight is 20/20." In other words, it is easier to look back on how we handled a particular situation or were treated in our own lives and base our values, beliefs, and decisions on the outcome of that situation. Quite simply, our vision is clear (or "20/20") when we have some personal experience with a topic or issue. For example, someone who was not vaccinated as a baby and ended up with whooping cough may have feelings about whether or not children should be vaccinated that come from their personal experience. Someone who was not vaccinated and never had a disease growing up may base her or his opinions on that experience, as will someone who was vaccinated and remained healthy, without any adverse side-effects to the vaccine. It is important to keep this hindsight perspective in mind when determining how we feel about any sensitive topic.

Suggested Readings

American Academy of Pediatrics, "Why Immunize?" Fact sheet, available online at http://www.aap.org/advocacy/releases/whyimmunize.htm.

Stephanie Cave and Deborah Mitchell, *What Your Doctor May Not Tell You About Children's Vaccinations* (Warner Books, 2001).

Daniel R. Feikin, Dennis C. Lezotte, Richard F. Hamman, Daniel A. Salmon, Robert T. Chen, and Richard E. Hoffman, "Individual and Community Risks of Measles and Pertussis Associated With Personal Exemptions to Immunization," *Journal of the American Medical Association* (vol. 284, 2000).

Sharon G. Humiston and Cynthia Good, *Vaccinating Your Child: Questions and Answers for the Concerned Parent* (Peachtree Publishers, 2000).

Institute for Health Freedom, *Vaccinating Children: Where Do We Draw the Line?* Accessible online at `http://forhealthfreedom.org/Publications/Children/Vaccine.html`.

Aviva Jill Romm, *Vaccinations: A Thoughtful Parent's Guide: How to Make Safe, Sensible Decisions About the Risks, Benefits, and Alternatives* (Inner Traditions International Limited, 2001).

Diane Rozario, *The Immunization Resource Guide: Where to Find Answers to All Your Questions About Childhood Vaccinations* (Patter Publications, 2000).

ISSUE 7

Should Parents of Deaf Children Choose Cochlear Implant Surgery?

YES: Alexander Graham Bell Association for the Deaf and Hard of Hearing, from "Kids and Cochlear Implants: Getting Connected," a Brochure of the Alexander Graham Bell Association for the Deaf and Hard of Hearing, `http://www.agbell.org/information/kids_cochlear.pdf` (2001)

NO: National Association of the Deaf, from "NAD Position Statement on Cochlear Implants," `http://www.nad.org/infocenter/newsroom/positions/CochlearImplants.html` (October 6, 2000)

ISSUE SUMMARY

YES: The Alexander Graham Bell Association for the Deaf and Hard of Hearing, an international membership organization and resource center on hearing loss and spoken language, maintains that a cochlear device can lead to greater hearing and speech capability throughout a person's life.

NO: The National Association of the Deaf, the oldest and largest constituency organization focusing on accessibility and civil rights of Americans who are deaf or hard of hearing, argues that the cochlear implant treats deafness as a disability and ignores the historical and cultural aspects of deaf life.

There are no truly accurate statistics on how many people in the United States are deaf or hard of hearing. A recent estimate from the Centers for Disease Control and Prevention's (CDC's) National Center for Health Statistics indicates that approximately 13 percent of the population under age 18 has some kind of hearing impairment. Deafness can be caused by any number of factors. More than 100 hereditary syndromes can cause a child to be born deaf. Different infections can cause hearing loss. For example, in the 1960s, a rubella epidemic caused an increase in the number of children born deaf or hard of hearing. Some other illnesses can cause hearing loss at different times throughout a person's life. Long-term exposure to loud sounds, such as construction noises and music, can also lead to hearing loss as one grows older. Some deaf people do not know what caused their deafness.

In 1984, a device called the cochlear implant was approved for use in people who were 18 years old or older. A cochlear implant is different from a hearing aid. Cochlear implants are designed to deliver electrical signals directly to the auditory nerve, thereby bypassing the area of the inner ear that is not enabling the person to hear without an assisted device. Just over 10 years later, in 1995, the age requirements were reduced dramatically to age two and older after research revealed that earlier implantation would be most beneficial to parents choosing cochlear implantation for their children. The medical argument is that by the age of two, children have already passed the critical period for auditory input in language acquisition. Currently, the minimum age at which an infant can be surgically implanted with a cochlear device is 18 months, although some medical professionals will implant infants under the age of 12 months.

For some people, deaf and hearing alike, the cochlear implant was heralded as a "cure" for deafness—that the implant would enable deaf children to hear and speak and therefore negotiate more effectively through the world. They feel that the cochlear implant eliminates the need for a deaf child and her or his parents to learn sign language, as well as the need for the deaf person to have interpreting services throughout her or his educational, vocational, and social life.

Other people resent the classification of deafness as a disability. Unlike those with other so-called disabilities, deaf people have a community, language, culture, and history. There are also social norms within deaf culture, beyond simply having a different language, that affect daily interactions and values—just as in any other culture. As a result, many deaf, hard of hearing, and hearing people do not welcome the cochlear implant and feel that it is an attempt to eradicate deaf culture.

Whether you agree or disagree with the use of cochlear implants is an important question to consider; however, at issue here is whether or not you feel that parents have the right to make this decision for their infants. On the one hand, a child may grow up wondering what it would have been like to have grown up culturally deaf. On the other hand, a child may be grateful that their parents made this decision for them. In the end, should parents be able to determine this for their children because the best chance for cochlear implant success seems to be between birth and age two? Or should parents opt to leave their children as they were born and let the children decide when they are older whether or not they wish to have the implant?

In the following selections, the Alexander Graham Bell Association for the Hard of Hearing outlines the benefits of cochlear implants, including improved hearing, speech, and lip-reading ability. The National Association of the Deaf argues that while technology is important, the cochlear implant is not appropriate for all people, nor does it provide speech or the capacity to understand language in a way that is equivalent to a child that is born hearing. The Association recognizes the historical and cultural significance of being deaf and does not see deafness as a disability.

Kids and Cochlear Implants: Getting Connected

What Is a Cochlear Implant?

A cochlear implant is an electronic device designed to provide enhanced sound detection and the potential for greater speech understanding to children with severe to profound hearing loss who obtain negligible benefit from hearing aids. Unlike hearing aids that deliver amplified sounds to the ear, cochlear implants bypass the damaged parts of the ear and send electrical signals directly to the hearing nerve (auditory nerve), which relays this information to the part of the brain that is responsible for hearing. Cochlear implants have been approved for use in children since June 1990. Currently, approximately 7,000 children in the United States have been implanted.

How Do Cochlear Implants Work?

A cochlear implant converts speech, music, and environmental sounds into electrical signals and sends these signals to the hearing nerve, where the signals are interpreted as sound by the brain. A cochlear implant works in this way:

1. Sound (signals) are received by the microphone.
2. Electrical pulses that represent the energy contained in sound signals are sent from the microphone to the speech processor.
3. The speech processor selects and codes the most useful portions of the sound signals.
4. Code is sent to the transmitter.
5. Transmitter sends code across skin to receiver/stimulator.
6. Receiver/stimulator converts code to electrical signals.
7. Electrical signals are sent to electrode array in the cochlea to stimulate hearing nerve fibers.
8. Signals are recognized as sounds by the brain....

From Alexander Graham Bell Association for the Deaf and Hard of Hearing, "Kids and Cochlear Implants: Getting Connected" (2001). Reviewed by: John K. Niparko, M.D., The Johns Hopkins University, Baltimore, MD. Copyright © 2001 by Alexander Graham Bell Association for the Deaf and Hard of Hearing, 3417 Volta Place, NW, Washington, DC 20007-2778. http://www.agbell.org. Reprinted by permission.

How Do I Know if My Child Is a Candidate for a Cochlear Implant?

Children who are candidates for a cochlear implant must:

- Have a profound sensorineural hearing loss in both ears.
- Receive little or no benefit from hearing aids (usually determined through a trial period of using two hearing aids) as indicated by whether age-appropriate communication skills are developing.
- Be of an age that will allow the clinical team from an implant center to determine if preverbal behaviors or speech recognition abilities are developing through the use of using hearing aids.
- Have an intact auditory nerve as indicated by CT- or MRI-scans.
- Be healthy enough to tolerate surgery (typically an outpatient procedure).
- Have had active middle-ear disease (otitis) brought under control (if applicable).

Additionally, their families must possess a clear understanding of the benefits and limitations of a cochlear implant, and have the time to accommodate pre-implant evaluations and postoperative follow-up services. Children undergo audiological, medical, and psychological procedures to determine implant candidacy, and the time involved in completing these procedures varies with the age and abilities of the child.

Some centers require assurance from the family that the child's home and educational environment will rely on spoken language (an oral approach) to ensure the best possible outcomes from the implant....

What Does the Surgery Involve?

Surgery

Cochlear implant surgery is typically performed under general anesthesia and lasts for approximately 2½ hours. The procedure can be performed in either an inpatient or outpatient setting and carries the normal risks of major ear surgery requiring general anesthesia. The surgeon exposes the mastoid bone behind the ear canal and drills open a channel to the inner ear. The electrodes are threaded into the inner ear and the receiver coil is placed in the bone behind the ear. The skin is closed over the receiver-stimulator. A pressure bandage is placed to reduce swelling around the incision. Most children go home the same day or spend no more than one night in the hospital.

Device Fitting

After four to six weeks to allow for healing around the surgical site, the process of "fitting" the external parts takes place. During the fitting session, the headpiece and microphone are placed over the implant. The speech processor is connected to the headpiece and the audiologists' computer. Measurements are used to program the speech processor for the individual child. The speech processor is disconnected from the audiologist's computer and rechargeable or disposable batteries are then inserted. The child can then take the implant system home....

Follow-Up Services

Once the speech processor is set, the child requires intensive auditory and speech training. Implanted children require this communication training to help them jumpstart their language and listening skills, which they were not able to fully develop prior to the implant....

What Are the Benefits Associated With Cochlear Implants?

Although there is a wide range of performance in children using cochlear implants, the benefits for most users include sound awareness, environmental sound recognition, enhanced lipreading abilities, speech recognition (understanding the speech of others without lipreading), and improved speech production. Today, advances in implant technology enable more children to maximize these benefits and develop spoken language skills.

Even though thousands of children have received cochlear implants, surgeons and audiologists are currently unable to predict before surgery the degree of benefit an individual child will receive from an implant. Factors affecting implant performance include:

- Age at implantation and whether the child has had some experience with effective hearing previously
- Postoperative (re)habilitation
- Primary mode of communication
- Educational setting
- Length of implant use

Research suggests that implantation works best for children who are prelingually deaf and are implanted at the earliest possible age after performance limitations with hearing aids are determined. Of special importance when considering implantation is the critical period for speech and language development (0–6 years old). Before becoming a candidate for an implant, children must complete a six-month trial period with hearing aids to see whether or not this technology can provide them with satisfactory sound. Children may be considered candidates for an implant if the hearing aid trial period has failed to promote more age-appropriate listening and speaking.

Currently, the minimum age for implantation is eighteen months. However, the promising results demonstrated by children implanted at an early age has promoted the trend to lower the age of implantation with some centers implanting under the age of twelve months. With a renewed focus on early identification of hearing loss, and the passing of early identification legislation at the federal level (the "Walsh Bill"), many more children will be identified with hearing loss soon after birth. It is likely, as a result, that as the age of identification decreases, so too will the age of implantation in an effort to tap natural language learning abilities that are maximal during a child's first six-year "critical period".

How Much Do Cochlear Implants Cost?

Cochlear implants are covered benefits in most medical insurance policies and in most states' Medicaid plans. Currently, the cost for evaluation, implantation, and follow-up programs and (re)habilitation is approximately $40,000. Included in these costs are audiological testing, medical examinations, surgical fees, anesthesiologist, operating room and hospital charges, and follow-up programs. Auditory and speech training is sometimes not covered by medical insurance.

Follow-up care after the first year includes testing and monitoring and occasional reprogramming of the device. Like any child with a hearing loss, children with cochlear implants will need ongoing therapy to ensure maximum listening and speech skills.

Clearly, cochlear implantation carries with it financial costs. However, the ability for a child with hearing loss to participate fully in the hearing world—hearing the leaves rustle, cars honk, birds sing—can be associated with substantial cost savings associated with later rehabilitation, education, and vocational opportunities....

How Can I Expect My Child to Perform With a Cochlear Implant?

Summary of the Current Research

The results of a recent study demonstrate that early implantation promotes the acquisition of speaking and listening skills.

— Indiana University Cochlear Implant Research Team, 1999

A correlation has been observed between the length of cochlear implant experience and the rate of full-time placement in mainstream classrooms (i.e., the longer a child has an implant, the more likely he or she is to be mainstreamed) and a negative correlation has been found between the length of implant experience and the number of hours of special education support used by fully mainstreamed children (i.e., the longer the child has an implant, the fewer hours he or she is likely to require of special education services).

— Johns Hopkins University Cochlear Implant Research Team, 1999

Rapid improvement in both speech production and language acquisition has been observed in children implanted before five years of age....

— NY League for the Hard of Hearing Research Team, 1998

When compared with prelingually deafened children who were implanted at the mean age of 6.1, the children implanted before the age of 3 showed higher overall improvement in the perception of all parts of speech. Providing a cochlear implant to deaf children at a young age is beneficial to their auditory development.

— New York University School of Medicine researchers, 1995

Both children who are prelingually or postlingually deafened derive significant benefit from cochlear implants as demonstrated on speech perception tasks and speech production measures.

— University of Iowa researchers, 1995

The cochlear implant has had a dramatic impact on improving the acquisition and use of spoken language by deaf children, with positive ripple effects socially and psychologically.

— Indiana University Cochlear Implant Research Team, 1993

NO ◀

National Association of the Deaf

NAD Position Statement on Cochlear Implants

The NAD [National Association of the Deaf] recognizes that diversity within the deaf community itself, and within the deaf experience, has not been acknowledged or explained very clearly in the public forum. Deafness is diverse in its origin and history, in the adaptive responses made to it, and in the choices that deaf adults and parents of deaf children continue to make about the ever-increasing range of communication and assistive technology options. Diversity requires mutual respect for individual and/or group differences and choices.

The NAD welcomes all individuals regardless of race, religion, ethnic background, socioeconomic status, cultural orientation, mode of communication, preferred language use, hearing status, educational background, and use of technologies. The NAD also welcomes deaf, hard of hearing and hearing family members, educators, and other professionals serving deaf and hard of hearing children and adults.

The NAD subscribes to the wellness model upon which the physical and psychosocial integrity of deaf children and adults is based. The general public needs information about the lives of the vast majority of deaf and hard of hearing individuals who have achieved optimal adjustments in all phases of life, have well-integrated and healthy personalities, and have attained self-actualizing levels of functioning, all with or without the benefits of hearing aids, cochlear implants, and other assistive devices.

The NAD recognizes all technological advancements with the potential to foster, enhance, and improve the quality of life of all deaf and hard of hearing persons. During the past three decades, technological developments such as closed captioning, email and the Internet, two-way pagers, text telephones, telecommunications relay services, video interpreting services, visual alerting devices, vibro-tactile devices, hearing aids, amplification devices, audio loop and listening systems have had an important role in leveling the playing field. The role of the cochlear implant in this regard is evolving and will certainly change in the future. Cochlear implants are not appropriate for all deaf and hard of hearing children and adults. Cochlear implantation is a technology that represents a tool to be used in some forms of communication, and not a cure for deafness. Cochlear implants provide sensitive hearing, but do not, by themselves, impart the ability to understand spoken language through listening alone. In addition, they do not guarantee the development of cognition or reduce the benefit of emphasis on parallel visual language and literacy development.

The NAD recognizes the rights of parents to make informed choices for their deaf and hard of hearing children, respects their choice to use cochlear implants and all other assistive devices, and strongly supports the development of the whole child and of language and literacy. Parents have the right to know about and understand the various options available, including all factors that might impact development. While there are some successes with implants, success stories should not be over-generalized to every individual.

Rationale

The focus of the 2000 NAD position statement on cochlear implants is on preserving and promoting the psychosocial integrity of deaf and hard of hearing children and adults. The adverse effects of inflammatory statements about the deaf population of this country must be addressed. Many within the medical profession continue to view deafness essentially as a disability and an abnormality and believe that deaf and hard of hearing individuals need to be "fixed" by cochlear implants. This pathological view must be challenged and corrected by greater exposure to and interaction with well-adjusted and successful deaf and hard of hearing individuals.

The media often describe deafness in a negative light, portraying deaf and hard of hearing children and adults as handicapped and second-class citizens in need of being "fixed" with cochlear implants. There is little or no portrayal of successful, well adjusted deaf and hard of hearing children and adults without implants. A major reason implantation and oral language training have been pursued so aggressively by the media, the medical profession, and parents is not simply because of the hoped-for benefits that come with being able to hear in a predominantly hearing society but more because of the perceived burdens associated with being deaf.

Because cochlear implant technology continues to evolve, to receive mainstream acceptance, and to be acknowledged as part of today's reality, it is urgent to be aware of and responsive to the historical treatment of deaf persons. This perspective makes it possible to provide more realistic guidelines for parents of deaf and hard of hearing children and for pre-lingually and post-lingually deafened adults.

Wellness Model

Many deaf and hard of hearing people straddle the "deaf and hearing worlds" and function successfully in both. There are many people with implants who use sign language and continue to be active members of the deaf community and who ascribe to deaf culture and heritage. There are many deaf and hard of hearing individuals, with and without implants, who are high-achieving professionals, talented in every imaginable career field. They, too, are successfully effective parents, raising well-adjusted deaf, hard of hearing and hearing children. As citizens, they continue to make contributions to improve the quality of life for society at large. Deaf and hard of hearing individuals throughout the ages have demonstrated psychological strength and social skills when surviving and overcoming society's misconceptions, prejudices, and discriminatory attitudes and behaviors, thus attesting to their resilience, intelligence, and integrity.

Given the general lack of awareness about the reality of the wellness model, the NAD strongly urges physicians, audiologists, and allied professionals to refer parents to qualified experts in deafness and to other appropriate resources so that parents can make fully informed decisions—that is, decisions that incorporate far more than just the medical-surgical. Such decisions involve language preferences and usage, educational placement and training opportunities, psychological and social development, and the use of technological devices and aids.

The Cochlear Implant

The most basic aspect of the cochlear implant is to help the user perceive sound, i.e., the sensation of sound that is transmitted past the damaged cochlea to the brain. In this strictly sensorineural manner, the implant works: the sensation of sound is delivered to the brain. The stated goal of the implant is for it to function as a tool to enable deaf children to develop language based on spoken communication.

Cochlear implants do not eliminate deafness. An implant is not a "cure" and an implanted individual is still deaf. Cochlear implants may destroy what remaining hearing an individual may have. Therefore, if the deaf or hard of hearing child or adult later prefers to use an external hearing aid, that choice may be removed.

Unlike post-lingually deafened children or adults who have had prior experience with sound comprehension, a pre-lingually deafened child or adult does not have the auditory foundation that makes learning a spoken language easy. The situation for those progressively deafened or suddenly deafened later in life is different. Although the implant's signals to the brain are less refined than those provided by an intact cochlea, an individual who is accustomed to receiving signals about sound can fill in certain gaps from memory. While the implant may work quite well for post-lingually deafened individuals, this result just cannot be generalized to pre-lingually deafened children for whom spoken language development is an arduous process, requiring long-term commitment by parents, educators, and support service providers, with no guarantee that the desired goal will be achieved.

Parents

Parents face challenges when their child is born deaf or becomes deaf. At least ninety percent of deaf and hard of hearing children are born to hearing parents who usually want their children to be like themselves, to understand sound, to use their voices and verbally express their thoughts through spoken language, and to hear the voices and spoken language of those around them.

However, language and communication are not the same as speech, nor should the ability to speak and/or hear be equated with intelligence, a sense of well-being and lifelong success. Communication and cognition are vital ingredients of every child's development, regardless of the mode in which it is expressed, i.e., visual or auditory.

Despite the pathological view of deafness held by many within the medical profession, parents would benefit by seeking out opportunities to meet and get to know successful deaf and hard of hearing children and adults who are fluent in sign language and English, both with and without implants. The NAD encourages parents and deaf adults to research other options besides implantation. If implantation is the option of choice, parents should obtain all information about the surgical procedure, surgical risks, post-surgical auditory and speech training requirements, and potential benefits and limitations so as to make informed decisions.

Cochlear implant surgery is a beginning, not an end. The surgery decision represents the beginning of a process that involves a long-term, and likely, life-long commitment to auditory training, rehabilitation, acquisition of spoken and visual language skills, follow-up, and possibly additional surgeries. Whatever choices parents make, the primary goal should be to focus on the "whole child" and early language development/literacy and cognitive development. The absence of visual language opportunities can result in developmental delays that can be extremely difficult to reverse. Since the first six years are critical for language acquisition and usage, concurrent acquisition of visual and written language skills should be stressed.

Further improvements to cochlear implant technology and greater experience with educating and supporting pre-lingually deafened children and adults may later result in better outcomes for both of these populations than are achieved at present. In the meantime, though, parents of deaf and hard of hearing children need to be aware that a decision to forego implantation for their children does not condemn their children to a world of meaningless silence. Regardless of whether or not a deaf or hard of hearing child receives an implant, the child will function within both the hearing and the deaf communities. For these reasons, parents of pre-lingually deaf children presently have a reasonable basis upon which to decline implantation for their child. Parents must feel comfortable with their decision, whether they choose implantation or not.

Once parents have arrived at a decision, they want their decision to be validated. They seek reassurances often solely from within the medical and professional hearing health care community. This is a serious and major concern to the NAD. By releasing this position statement, the NAD seeks to alert, educate, and inform parents about deafness and the deaf community.

Recommendations

The NAD hereby makes the following recommendations for action:

Professional Training

Medical professionals have historically been the first point of contact for parents of deaf children. Their expertise is valuable but is primarily limited only to their medical areas of expertise. They should not be viewed as, nor should they function as, experts with regard to larger issues such as the educational, psychological, social, and linguistic needs of the deaf child. Medical professionals may be experts regarding the mysteries of the inner ear, but they are not experts regarding the inner lives of deaf children and adults. Psychological, social, educational, cultural and communication aspects of deafness, including the wellness model, must be a significant part of every medical school curriculum, especially within the specialty of otolaryngology. In-service training programs should be implemented for all interdisciplinary staff at cochlear implant centers that would include guidance and counseling methods with parents of deaf children and adults considering cochlear implants. These training programs should be conducted by professional counselors who are trained, qualified, and competent to work and communicate with deaf and hard of hearing children and adults and their families.

Early Assessment of Hearing Aid Benefit

It is widely understood and accepted that a trial period of hearing aid use is necessary prior to cochlear implantation. Advanced digital hearing aids should be explored. The NAD encourages that this effort be earnest and of appropriate duration for adequate assessment by objective testing and skilled observation of behaviors and communication skills. This assessment is complicated by the child's lack of prior auditory experience, and inability to communicate what s/he is hearing. The length of this trial period will vary with the individual. Further research by the medical and educational communities regarding objective hearing assessment and hearing aid trials is strongly encouraged.

Cochlear Implant Team

Candidacy assessment and surgery must be performed in a medical setting that has a close working relationship with a team of professionals that will provide ongoing long-term support to implant recipients. To be a responsible implant center, caution must be taken when describing the potential benefits of implantation, including risks, limitations, and long-term implications. Parents of deaf children and adults must be assisted in developing realistic and appropriate expectations. Critical to both pediatric and adult cochlear implantation and the long-range medical, audiological, psychological, social, emotional, educational, and vocational adjustment is access to implant centers fully complemented by an interdisciplinary staff, including rehabilitation specialists, psychologists and counselors. Implant center personnel must also work with and involve deafness professionals in education and in the helping professions. It takes a coordinated team of specialists, parents, educators and counselors to raise an implanted child and to support an implanted adult over an extended period of time. The implant team is also morally obligated to recognize when the implant experience has been unsuccessful and provide alternate strategies for language training.

Habilitation

An essential component of the cochlear implant process is habilitation. Parents and professionals must make a long-term commitment to integrating listening strategies throughout the child's day at home and at school. It is important to recognize that a newly implanted child is unable to understand spoken language through listening alone. Therefore parents and professionals should continue to use sign language to ensure age-appropriate psychological, social, cognitive, and language development.

Insurance Coverage

The NAD recommends that medical insurance carriers also provide fair and equitable coverage for hearing aid devices and associated support services.

Media

Reporters, journalists, anchors and directors of newspapers, television networks and film are encouraged to research and prepare their material more carefully and without bias. There is a serious need for a more balanced approach to fact-finding and reporting.

Research

Longitudinal research is critically needed, including a more thorough analysis of those for whom the implant is not working. Future research should involve highly controlled, manufacturer-independent and unbiased research on the long-term outcomes of childhood implants on auditory and communicative development, academic and intellectual development and achievement, psychological, social and emotional adjustment, and interpersonal relationship functioning. Comparative research on children without implants receiving parallel support services should also be conducted, especially those for whom sign language is the primary form of communication. Research findings relative to children with and without cochlear implants in educated lay terms must be made available and disseminated to deaf individuals, to parents of implanted children, to those in the helping professions, and to those contemplating implants.

Parents

The NAD knows that parents love and care deeply about their deaf children. Since the decision to perform implant surgery on the deaf child is made for the child, it is necessary for parents to become educated about cochlear implants— the potential benefits, the risks, and all the issues that they entail. During this critical education process, parents have both the need and the right to receive unbiased information about the pros and cons of cochlear implants and related matters. The NAD knows that parents want to make informed decisions. Parents also would benefit by opportunities to interact with successful deaf and hard of hearing adults, as well as with parents of deaf and hard of hearing children.

Deafness is irreversible. Even with the implant and increased sound perception, the child is still deaf. Cochlear implants are not a cure for deafness. The most serious parental responsibility from the very beginning is total commitment to, and involvement with, their child's overall development and well-being. Throughout the developmental years, the deaf child—implanted or not, mainstreamed or not—should receive education in deaf studies, including deaf heritage, history of deafness and deaf people, particularly stories and accounts of deaf people who have succeeded in many areas of life.

Support Services

Parents must understand that, after suitability testing and the decision-making process, the actual surgical procedure is just the beginning—a prelude to a lifetime proposition for the child and years of commitment by the parents. Implanted children are still deaf and will continue to require educational, psychological, audiological assessment, auditory and speech training, and language support services for a long period of time. Services for families and children should be provided in a manner that is consistent with standards set by the Individuals with Disabilities Education Act (IDEA), with focus on the whole child and the family. It is imperative that psychological support be available, including counseling services. Such services are to be available throughout the child's developmental years, often until adulthood.

Visual Environment

The NAD has always and continues to support and endorse innovative educational programming for deaf children, implanted or not. Such programming should actively support the auditory and speech skills of children in a dynamic and interactive visual environment that utilizes sign language and English. In closing, the NAD asserts that diversity in communication modes and cultures is our inherent strength, and that mutual respect and cooperation between deaf, hard of hearing, and hearing individuals ultimately benefit us all.

POSTSCRIPT

Should Parents of Deaf Children Choose Cochlear Implant Surgery?

Achild who grows up deaf often feels separate from her or his peers, particularly once the child is in a school that is not specifically for deaf children. Few people know and use American Sign Language (ASL), including some hearing parents of deaf children. As a result, many children will go through school—and adults will go through their careers—using an interpreter to communicate effectively with their hearing counterparts. For some deaf people, this is a natural part of living in a mostly hearing world. For others, the desire to hear and communicate by speaking is stronger.

Some deaf people are bilingual and bicultural, communicating in ASL and in spoken English, and negotiating well within both deaf and hearing cultures. This includes some children whose parents have chosen to have the cochlear implant done—yet whose parents recognize the cultural aspect of deafness and both learn and have their children learn ASL. Other deaf people barely know sign language because their parents did not use it, and they were sent to schools that attempted to teach them to lip-read and speak without having ASL as a part of their lives.

Do you see deafness as a disability, something that should be overcome to enable all children and adults to hear? Or do you see it as a community and culture that the medical profession and society should not attempt to eliminate? The question can apply to many other groups that are not a part of the power majority in a given society. What do you think you would discover if you asked a group of African Americans whether they wish they had been born white? a group of lesbian, gay, and bisexual individuals whether they wish they had been born heterosexual? a group of women whether they wish they had been born men? It would be very hard to say, in retrospect, whether any individual would want to change who they are. Certainly a person of color would appreciate not being the target of racism, or a lesbian, gay, or bisexual person the target of homophobia. Yet the richness of a culture and a community often outweighs the social or economic benefits of being in a power majority, as does the pride of being who one is even when society refers to one's group as a "minority" group.

Remember, though, that the issue here is whether or not parents have the right to make this decision for their children. Adults make hard decisions throughout their lives. Pregnant women may have amniocentesis, a test during the pregnancy, to determine whether or not the fetus has any significant genetic or other health concerns. Armed with that information, the pregnant woman needs to decide, often with a partner, whether to carry the pregnancy to term or whether to have an abortion. Similarly, parents are often faced with decisions for their infants that may affect their children in later life, including whether or not to circumcise a male baby, which vaccinations their infant should have—and whether or not to have their deaf child implanted with a cochlear device. Do you think these are decisions that parents should be making for their children? If not all, which decisions do you think are appropriate for parents to make for their children, and why?

Suggested Readings

Dianne J. Allum, ed., *Cochlear Implant Rehabilitation in Children and Adults* (reprint, Whurr Publications, 1998).

Jack Gannon, *Deaf Heritage: A Narrative History of Deaf America* (National Association of the Deaf, 1981).

Roy K. Holcomb, Thomas K. Holcomb, and Samuel K. Holcomb, *Deaf Culture Our Way* (Dawn Sign Press, 1998).

Paddy Ladd, *Understanding Deaf Culture: In Search of Deafhood* (Multilingual Matters, 2002).

Harlan Lane, *The Mask of Benevolence: Disabling the Deaf Community* (DawnSign Press, 2000).

Mary Ellen Nevins and Patricia M. Chute, eds., *Children With Cochlear Implants in Educational Settings (School-Age Children Series)* (Singular Publishing Group, 1996).

Debara L. Tucci, Amy McConkey Robbins, Karen Iler Kirk, and Nancy K. Mellon, in John K. Niparko, ed., *Cochlear Implants: Principles & Practices* (Lippincott, Williams & Wilkins, 2000).

Ila Parasnis, ed., *Cultural and Language Diversity and the Deaf Experience* (Cambridge University Press, 1998).

Sue Schwartz, ed., *Choices in Deafness: A Parents' Guide to Communication Options* (Woodbine House, 1996).

Note: *There is an excellent film about the cochlear implant decision-making process and debate called,* Sound and Fury, *produced by Elizabeth Owen. It has aired on* PBS *several times; watch your local listings if this topic is of interest to you.*

ISSUE 8

Should Parents Surgically Alter Their Intersex Infants?

YES: Amicur Farkas, B. Chertin, and Irith Hadas-Halpren, from "One-Stage Feminizing Genitoplasty: Eight Years of Experience With Forty-Nine Cases," *The Journal of Urology* (June 2001)

NO: Alice Domurat Dreger, from " 'Ambiguous Sex'—or Ambivalent Medicine? Ethical Issues in the Treatment of Intersexuality," *Hastings Center Report* (May–June 1998)

ISSUE SUMMARY

YES: Amicur Farkas, B. Chertin, and Irith Hadas-Halpren, faculty of the Ben-Gurion University in Jerusalem, Israel, see ambiguous genitalia as a true emergency. They assert that feminizing surgery should be done on an infant with congenital adrenal hyperplasia to ensure that as an adult woman she will have sexual functioning and be able to give birth.

NO: Alice Domurat Dreger, assistant professor in the Lyman Briggs School at Michigan State University, explores the ethics in recommending to parents that they should have their children's genitals altered surgically. With so little education available about the true meaning and options relating to children born with ambiguous genitalia, she wonders if any parents who decide that their child should have the surgery are truly giving informed consent.

T he term *intersex* is often more recognizable by its historical term, *hermaphrodite*, a term still used by many medical professionals. In Greek mythology, Hermaphroditus was the son of Hermes and Aphrodite. A nymph named Salmacis fell in love with Hermaphroditus, but he did not feel the same. Salmacis prayed that they would never be separated—so when Hermaphroditus swam in her stream, she combined with him to create a person with male and female characteristics in one body. Most individuals born with ambiguous or mixed genitalia and chromosomal structures prefer to be called intersex rather than hermaphrodite, the latter of which is considered by many intersex individuals to be negative. However, some intersex individuals have reclaimed the word *hermaphrodite* to describe themselves, just as members of other minority groups have reclaimed epithets as a way of asserting their power.

It is estimated that every year in the United States, approximately 65,000 babies are born with ambiguous genitalia. However, reliable statistics on the true incidence of intersexuality are limited. While attention to intersexuality and the medical, psychological, and social issues relating to intersexual individuals have increased dramatically over the last 10 years, disagreement still exists on how parents should respond when they are told that their infants have ambiguous genitalia.

Support for surgical sex assignment is rooted in the work of psychologist John Money. In 1967, Money conducted an experiment in gender identity involving an infant whose genitalia was not ambiguous at birth but deformed severely by a botched circumcision. In this now-notorious case, Money maintained that gender identity was fluid for the first few months of life. Money asserted that by completing the castration, providing the child with hormones, and raising the child as a girl, the child would "become" female. At the time, the case received a lot of attention and was declared a success when, at follow-up, Money noted that the then-nine-year-old girl was adjusting "normally."

About 30 years later, two other researchers, Milton Diamond and Keith Sigmundson, found that the child with whom Money had worked ended up depressed and confused by her strong feelings that she was actually male. Once the truth was revealed to her, she was extremely relieved. Her parents arranged for the surgeries and other treatments that would enable her to transition back to male. Now an adult male, he is living with his wife and their children, whom he adopted.

As you read the selections, consider the reasoning behind each argument. There is the so-called locker room viewpoint—that adolescents have a tough enough time navigating through adolescence, why make it even harder by subjecting them to further torment in the locker room where their ambiguous genitalia would be revealed? There are also parents who believe that children should remain intact until they are older and can decide for themselves what, if anything, to do about their ambiguous genitalia.

In the following selections, Amitur Farkas, B. Chertin, and Irith Hadas-Halpren, provide a detailed description of what they call "feminizing" surgery. They believe that having this type of surgery is best for patients to ensure both cosmetic contentment and satisfactory intercourse. Alice Domurat Dreger asserts that the desire to select a biological sex for an infant comes from our society's discomfort with anything with which we are unfamiliar. She believes that viewing intersexuality as an infirmity to be fixed rather than an expression of the diversity of human biology results in surgical procedures that result in genital mutilation rather than assignment.

Amicur Farkas, B. Chertin,
and Irith Hadas-Halpren

One-Stage Feminizing Genitoplasty: Eight Years of Experience With Forty-Nine Cases

The neonate with sexual ambiguity represents an enigmatic but true emergency in pediatric urology. In recent years several techniques of 1-stage feminizing genitoplasty have been described. Successful reconstruction depends on accurate preoperative recognition of the anatomy while the main area of interest is the location of the vaginal opening into the urogenital sinus and its relationship to the pelvic floor and external sphincter mechanism. Passerini-Glazel, and Gonzales and Fernandes described their techniques of 1-stage feminizing genitoplasty. The primary features of both techniques are the use of preputial skin in combination with the distal part of the urogenital sinus to construct a vaginal introitus and to avoid the frequent complications associated with previous types of operations, such as vaginal stenosis and injury of the urethral sphincter. We retrospectively analyzed the results of our modification of these techniques.

Materials and Methods

Between 1991 and 1998, 49 patients underwent 1-stage feminizing genitoplasty at our department. All patients were referred following complete evaluation of gender, and chromosomal and biochemical data by pediatric endocrinologists. Of the 49 patients 44 had congenital adrenal hyperplasia (CAH) due to 21-hydroxylase deficiency in 33 and 11-hydroxylase deficiency in 11, 3 were true hermaphrodites and 2 were adolescents with different degrees of the androgen insensitivity syndrome. All patients with CAH and the true hermaphrodites had 46 XX karyotype, and those with androgen insensitivity syndrome had 46 XY karyotype. The true hermaphrodites and androgen insensitivity syndrome patients were referred to us after surgical removal of the contradictory gonads and internal duct structure before the genitoplasty. Mean age was 0.9 $\pm$ 0.3 years, of the patients with CAH and 13 $\pm$ 2.3 of the remainder. Before surgical correction all patients underwent transabdominal pelvic ultrasound only to provide

From Amicur Farkas, B. Chertin, and Irith Hadas-Halpren, "One-Stage Feminizing Genitoplasty: Eight Years of Experience With Forty-Nine Cases," *The Journal of Urology*, vol. 165 (June 2001), pp. 2341–2346. Copyright © 2001 by American Urological Association, Inc. Reprinted by permission of Lippincott Williams & Wilkins. References omitted.

information for surgical decision making regarding status of the internal genitalia, length and anatomical position of the vagina, and whether the vaginal junction with the urogenital sinus was distal or proximal to the pelvic floor. The ultrasound technique and results have been reported previously.

The patients with CAH underwent panendoscopy as an initial and integral step of the feminizing genitoplasty. The communication of the vagina and urogenital sinus was localized using a 10Fr pediatric cytoscope. In the majority of cases the cystocope was passed into the vaginal cavity. At that point the telescope was removed from the sheath and a 6Fr silicone Foley catheter was inserted into the vaginal cavity through the cytoscope sheath and its balloon was inflated to 2 cc. The cytoscope sheath was then pulled back and the catheter was clamped at the distal end of the urogenital sinus to avoid balloon deflation. The distal end of the catheter was cut off to enable complete removal of the cytoscope sheath. In some cases with a small vaginal opening a Fogarty catheter was used with the cytoscope inserted only as far as the opening and not into the vaginal cavity. After the cytoscope was removed an 8 to 10Fr silicone Foley was inserted into the bladder in the conventional manner. Of the 44 patients with CAH 41 had vaginal confluence at the level of the verumontanum and 3 had high vaginal confluence according to Powell types II and III classification. The patients were placed in an exaggerated lithotomy position and surgery was performed via the perineal approach by a senior urologist (A. F.) or under his personal supervision.

The operation begins with vertical incisions of the phallic skin on ventral and dorsal surfaces and degloving of the phallus circumferentially. The ventral incision is extended to the bottom of the labioscrotal folds in a Y shape and then terminates in an inverted U shaped perineal flap to provide good exposure of the urogenital sinus. The urogenital sinus including the vagina and urethra is then completely mobilized *en bloc* from the corporeal bodies. The dissection is done between the 2 crura of corpora cavernosa and mobilization continues below the lower rami of the pubis. Thereafter the dissection between the lateral and posterior walls of the sinus, including the vagina and the anterior rectal wall, is completed circumferentially so the posterior wall of the vagina can be brought to the perineum without tension.

At this point clitoroplasty is performed using the technique of Kogan et al. The plane of cleavage is developed between the corpora and dorsal neurovascular bundle via Buck's fascia, taking care to preserve the tunica of the corporeal body. Subsequently resection of the corpora is performed from the glans to the proximal part passing the bifurcation. The stumps of the corpora are placed and sutured by running 5-zero polyglactin sutures below the pubic bone. The proximal phallic skin sutured to the preputial skin and left around the glans clitoris corona creates a preputial hood. To avoid rectal injury and bleeding from the spongiosal tissue, traction 5-zero polyglactin sutures are placed on the urogenital sinus to bring the deeper structures to a more superficial level. All of this part of the procedure is done during meticulous palpation of the balloon of the Foley or Fogarty catheter, which is inserted into the vagina and serves as a guide during dissection.

The posterior vaginal wall is opened over the balloon between the traction sutures, and the connection between the vagina and urogenital sinus is closed from the internal surface of the vagina. The vagina is opened into an adequate caliber to prevent future stenosis. The previously dissected posterior inverted U is sutured to the dorsal vaginal wall. The redundant distal part of the urogenital sinus is partially opened on the dorsal surface leaving a long enough urethra. The inverted open strip of epithelium is sutured to the anterior and lateral vaginal walls enabling creation of a wet and wide introitus. The preputial and phallic skin is completely split down the midline, and sutured around the clitoris and to the lateral epithelial edges of the aforementioned urogenital strips to create the labia minora. The lateral labioscrotal skin can be brought down and sutured to the corners between the posterior U flap and lateral skin to form the labia majora....

Results

Mean operating time was 145 minutes (range 120 to 180) and average hospitalization period was 4 to 5 days. Preoperative ultrasound provided the correct data regarding vaginal and internal genitalia anatomy in all of our cases, and the exact communication between the vagina and urogenital sinus was demonstrated in 41 of 44 (93%) with CAH. In 1 patient anterior rectal wall injury occurred intraoperatively and was immediately closed without further complications. The only immediate postoperative complication was mild wound infection of the buttock area in 3 cases. Mean followup was 4.7 ± 2.6 years. In 1 case total clitoris loss was later observed, and 2 patients presented with repeat clitoromegalia due to inadequate androgen suppression. All patients who underwent our modification of genitoplasty have had successful cosmetic and early functional results. In those cases with CAH who reached puberty repeat examinations showed normal menstruation, a wet and wide introitus and no evidence of fibrosis or scarring of the perineum. In the smaller girls we were able to calibrate the vaginal opening easily with a 20 to 22Fr bougie. No patient had urinary tract infection, and to date all patients are continent including those with a high vagina. None of the girls with CAH has yet achieved intercourse age and, therefore, we have no information regarding sexual satisfaction, possibility of vaginal delivery and psychosocial aspects of these forms of intersexuality. Both patients with partial AIS who presented initially with a small phallus and adequate vagina are now 18 and 22 years old, and report satisfactory sexual intercourse experiences.

Discussion

Existence of ambiguous genitalia is an emergency situation necessitating a team approach, which can provide quick identification of the genetic sex and biochemical profile. One of the most common causes of genital ambiguity is CAH, and today several surgical techniques are available for reconstruction. Feminizing genitoplasty should provide an adequate opening for the vagina into the perineum, create a normal-looking wet introitus, fully separate the urethral orifice from the vagina, remove phallic erectile tissue while preserving glandular innervation and blood supply, and prevent urinary tract complications.

Successful reconstruction depends on good knowledge of the anatomy of the urogenital sinus, particularly the location of the communication of the vagina to the urogenital sinus in relation to the pelvic floor and rectum. The surgeon must know whether the vagina is long enough to reach the perineum without any tension through a perineal approach and without compromising the pelvic floor and urethral continence mechanism. To provide the necessary information we perform only ultrasound in our patients.

The optimal time for genitoplasty is controversial. A few authors advise neonatal genitoplasty because of the presence of neonatal hypertrophy of the external and internal genitalia due to maternal and placental hyperstimulation with estrogens, and apparent easy vaginal mobilization.

In contrast, others suggest deferring definitive reconstruction of the intermediate and high vagina until after puberty. To spare our patients and parents the anxiety we endeavor to perform genitoplasty at around age 6 months when the child reaches 5 to 6 kg, as the risk of anesthesia at this age is negligible. Modern anesthesiology produces negligible risks in neonates and recently we started to operate on patients at age 3 months.

Historically, genital reconstruction in patients with CAH involved a 2-stage operation. At stage 1 simple amputation or reduction of the clitoris was performed in the neonatal period with the vaginoplasty being postponed until an older age. Currently, many authors recommend 1-stage genitoplasty, which can be done early in life using the perineal approach in the majority of cases even those with high vaginal confluence. We had no difficulty reaching the posterior wall of the vagina of those patients in the exaggerated lithotomy position via the perineal approach, especially as we made no effort to dissect and separate its communication with the urogenital sinus as described originally by Passerini-Glazel. Preservation of the megaloclitoris is advantageous once 1-stage genitoplasty is performed, as it enables easy dissection and *en bloc* mobilization of the urogenital sinus. The remaining redundant phallic and preputial skin after removal of the erectile tissue provides excellent material for reconstruction of the introitus and labia. Those cases referred to our hospital after clitorectomy or clitorous reduction were more challenging for reconstruction and are not included in this report.

Endoscopy is a crucial step in genitoplasty, which identifies the anatomy and enables insertion of a Foley or Fogarty catheter into the vagina through the communication to the urogenital sinus. We inserted the 10Fr cystoscope into the vagina so that a Foley catheter could be inserted into the vagina via the cystoscope sheath. The balloon of the Foley catheter that is used in the majority of our cases was bigger than that of the Fogarty catheter. This maneuver enables easier and safer localization of the posterior vaginal wall and prevents rectal injury.

Since 1989 different modifications of feminizing genitoplasty have become popular and replaced the classical Hendren and Crawford technique, decreased the percent of vaginal stenosis to negligible levels and improved the cosmetic appearance of the external genitalia. We have improved a few steps of the previously reported operations. Complete mobilization of the urogenital sinus *en bloc* including the vagina and urethra makes it possible to bring the sinus to the perineum and avoid the difficult step of dissection between the anterior vagina wall and overlying urethra and bladder neck. The connecting fistula between the urethra and vagina is closed from the internal surface of the vagina after opening the posterior vaginal wall. It is difficult to evaluate the failure and existence of a new fistula in small girls but to date no fistula has occurred in our adolescent and adult patients. Rink and Adams and Passerini-Glazel mention that fibrosis is the main reason for vaginal stenosis. The fact that we use the healthy posterior vaginal wall to create the vaginal opening instead of the distal fibrotic vaginal portion, which creates the fistula to the sinus, also prevents further stenosis. We use the inverted distal open strip of the urogenital sinus to create a wet introitus, which at the end of the operation has nearly a 320 degree circumference of epithelial tissue or preputial skin and, therefore, prevents vaginal stenosis.

One of the most important goals of feminizing genitoplasty is to provide sexual satisfaction and normal vaginal delivery. Our patients who have reached puberty have normal appearing external genitalia and clitoris. Only 2 patients had repeat clitomegalia due to inadequate androgen suppression necessitating reoperation to reduce the glandular part of the clitoris. Since none of our children has yet reached the age of sexual relations and childbearing, we cannot assess these results of our technique. However both XY patients with AIS who underwent identical feminizing genitoplasty are now 18 and 22 years old, and report normal and satisfactory intercourse.

Conclusions

Our modification of feminizing genitoplasty enables nearly all children presenting with ambiguous genitalia, 1-stage reconstruction early in life with good cosmetic and functional results. Undoubtedly the outcome of vaginoplasty should be reevaluated later.

NO

Alice Domurat Dreger

"Ambiguous Sex"—or Ambivalent Medicine?

W hat makes us "female" or "male," "girls" or "boys," "women" or "men"—our chromosomes, our genitalia, how we (and others) are brought up to think about ourselves, or all of the above? One of the first responses to the birth of a child of ambiguous sex by clinicians, and parents, is to seek to "disambiguate" the situation: to assign the newborn's identity as either female or male, surgically modify the child's genitalia to conform believably to that sex identity, and provide other medical treatment (such as hormones) to reinforce the gender decided upon. The assumptions that underly efforts to "normalize" intersexual individuals and the ethics of "treatment" for intersexuality merit closer examination than they generally receive.

࿔

A number of events have lately aroused substantial public interest in intersexuality (congenital "ambiguous sex") and "reconstructive" genital surgery. Perhaps the most sensational of these is the recent publication of unexpected long-term outcomes in the classic and well-known "John/Joan" case.[1] "John" was born a typical XY male with a twin brother, but a doctor accidentally ablated John's penis during a circumcision at age eight months. Upon consultation with a team of physicians and sexologists at the Johns Hopkins Hospital (circa 1963) it was decided that given the unfortunate loss of a normal penis John should be medically reconstructed and raised as a girl—"Joan." Surgeons therefore removed John/Joan's testes and subsequently subjected Joan to further surgical and hormonal treatments in an attempt to make her body look more like a girl's. The team of medical professionals involved also employed substantial psychological counseling to help Joan and the family feel comfortable with Joan's female gender. They believed that Joan and the family would need help adjusting to her new gender, but that full (or near-full) adjustment could be achieved.

For decades, the alleged success of this particular sex reassignment had been widely reported by Hopkins sexologist John Money and others as proof that physicians could essentially create any gender out of any child, so long

From Alice Domurat Dreger, "'Ambiguous Sex'—or Ambivalent Medicine? Ethical Issues in the Treatment of Intersexuality," *Hastings Center Report* (May–June 1998), pp. 24–35. Adapted from the Epilogue in *Hermaphrodites and the Medical Invention of Sex* (Harvard University Press, 1998). Copyright © 1998 by Alice Domurat Dreger. Reprinted by permission of Harvard University Press, Cambridge, MA.

as the cosmetic alteration was performed early. Money and others repeatedly asserted that "Johns" could be made into "Joans" and "Joans" into "Johns" so long as the genitals looked "right" and everyone agreed to agree on the child's assigned gender. The postulates of this approach are summarized succinctly by Milton Diamond and Keith Sigmundson: "(1) individuals are psychosexually neutral at birth and (2) healthy psychosexual development is dependent on the appearance of the genitals" (p. 298). While not a case of congenital intersexuality, the John/Joan case was nevertheless used by many clinicians who treat intersexuality as proof that in intersex cases the same postulates should hold. The keys seemed to be surgical creation of a believable sexual anatomy and assurances all around that the child was "really" the assigned gender.

But reports of the success of John/Joan were premature—indeed, they were wrong. Diamond and Sigmundson recently interviewed the person in question, now an adult, and report that Joan had in fact chosen to resume life as John at age fourteen. John, now an adult, is married to a woman and, via adoption, is the father of her children. John and his mother report that in the Joan-years, John was never fully comfortable with a female gender identity. Indeed, Joan actively attempted to resist some of the treatment designed to ensure her female identity; for instance, when prescribed estrogens at age twelve, Joan secretly discarded the feminizing hormones. Depressed and unhappy at fourteen, Joan finally asked her father for the truth, and upon hearing it, "All of a sudden everything clicked. For the first time things made sense, and I understood who and what I was" (p. 300). At his request, John received a mastectomy at age fourteen, and for the next two years underwent several plastic surgery operations aimed at making his genitals look more masculine.[2]

Diamond and Sigmundson are chiefly interested in using this new data to conclude that "the evidence seems overwhelming that normal humans are not psychosocially neutral at birth but are, in keeping with their mammalian heritage, predisposed and biased to interact with environmental, familial, and social forces in either a male or female mode."[3] In other words, sexual nature is not infinitely pliable; biology matters.

In their report, Diamond and Sigmundson also take the opportunity of publication to comment on the problem of the lack of long-term follow-up of cases like these. But what is also troubling is the lack of ethical analysis around cases like this—particularly around cases of the medical treatment of intersexuality, a phenomenon many orders of magnitude more common than traumatic loss of the penis. While there have been some brief discussions of the ethics of deceiving intersex patients (that discussion is reviewed below), the medical treatment of people born intersexed has remained largely ignored by ethicists. Indeed, I can find little discussion in the literature of any of the ethical issues involved in "normalizing" children with allegedly "cosmetically offensive" anatomies. The underlying assumption grounding this silence appears to be that "normalizing" procedures are necessarily thoroughly beneficent and that they present no quandaries. This article seeks to challenge that assumption and to encourage interested parties to reconsider, from an ethical standpoint, the dominant treatment protocols for children and adults with unusual genital anatomy.

Frequency of Intersexuality

Aside from the apparent presumption that "normalizing" surgeries are necessarily good, I suspect that ethicists have ignored the question of intersex treatment because like most people they assume the phenomenon of intersexuality to be exceedingly rare. It is not. But how common is it? The answer depends, of course, on how one defines it. Broadly speaking, intersexuality constitutes a range of anatomical conditions in which an individual's anatomy mixes key masculine anatomy with key feminine anatomy. One quickly runs into a problem, however, when trying to define "key" or "essential" feminine and masculine anatomy. In fact, any close study of sexual anatomy results in a loss of faith that there is a simple, "natural" sex distinction that will not break down in the face of certain anatomical, behavioral, or philosophical challenges.[4]

Sometimes the phrase "ambiguous genitalia" is substituted for "intersexuality," but this does not solve the problem of frequency, because we still are left struggling with the question of what should count as "ambiguous." (How small must a baby's penis be before it counts as "ambiguous"?) For our purposes, it is simplest to put the question of frequency pragmatically: How often do physicians find themselves unsure which gender to assign at birth? One 1993 gynecology text estimates that "in approximately 1 in 500 births, the sex is doubtful because of the external genitalia."[5] I am persuaded by more recent, well-documented literature that estimates the number to be roughly 1 in 1,500 live births.[6]

The frequency estimate goes up dramatically, however, if we include all children born with what some physicians consider cosmetically "unacceptable" genitalia. Many technically nonintersexed girls are born with "big" clitorises, and many technically nonintersexed boys are born with hypospadic penises in which the urethral opening is found somewhere other than the very tip of the penis.

Historical Background

I came to this topic as a historian and philosopher of science. My initial interest was actually in learning how British and French medical and scientific men of the late nineteenth century dealt with human hermaphroditism. The late nineteenth century was a time when the alleged naturalness of European social sex borders was under serious challenge by feminists and homosexuals and by anthropological reports of sex roles in other cultures. I wanted to know what biomedical professionals did, at such a politically charged time, with those who *inadvertently* challenged anatomical sex borders.

The answer is that biomedical men tried their best to shore up the borders between masculinity and femininity.[7] Specifically, the experts honed in on the ovarian and testicular tissues and decided that these were the key to any body's sexual identity. The "true sex" of most individuals thus by definition settled nicely into one of the two great and preferred camps, no matter how confusing the rest of their sexual anatomies. People with testicular tissue but with some otherwise "ambiguous" anatomy were now labeled "male pseudo-hermaphrodites"—that is, "true" males. People with ovarian tissue but with some otherwise ambiguous anatomy were labeled "female pseudo-hermaphrodites"—"true" females.

By equating sex identity simply with gonadal tissue, almost every body could be shown really to be a "true male" or a "true female" in spite of mounting numbers of doubtful cases. Additionally, given that biopsies of gonads were not done until the 1910s and that Victorian medical men insisted upon histological proof of ovarian and testicular tissue for claims of "true hermaphroditism," the only "true hermaphrodites" tended to be dead and autopsied hermaphrodites.

Nevertheless, new technologies—specifically laparotomies and biopsies—in the 1910s made this approach untenable. It now became possible (and, by the standing rules, necessary) to label some living people as "true" hermaphrodites via biopsies, and disturbed physicians noted that no one knew what to do with such people. There was no place, socially or legally, for true hermaphrodites. Moreover, physicians found case after case of extremely feminine-looking and feminine-acting women who were shown upon careful analysis to have testes and no ovaries. The latter were cases of what today is called androgen-insensitivity syndrome (AIS), also known as testicular feminization syndrome. We now know that individuals with AIS (roughly 1/60,000[8]) have an XY ("male") chromosomal complement and testes, but their androgen receptors cannot "read" the masculinizing hormones their testes produce. Consequently, *in utero* and throughout their lives, their anatomy develops along apparently "feminine" pathways. AIS is often not discovered until puberty, when these girls do not menstruate and a gynecological examination reveals AIS. Women with AIS look and feel very much like "typical" women, and in a practical, social, legal, and everyday sense they are women, even though congenitally they have testes and XY chromosomes.

In the 1910s, physicians working with intersexuality realized that assigning these women to the male sex (because of their testes) or admitting living "true hermaphrodites" (because of their ovotestes) would only wreak social havoc. Consequently, in practice the medical profession moved away from a strict notion of gonadal "true sex" toward a pragmatic concept of "gender" and physicians began to focus their attentions on gender "reconstruction." Elaborate surgical and hormonal treatments have now been developed to make the sexual anatomy more believable, that is, more "typical" of the gender assigned by the physician.

Dominant Treatment Protocols

Thus the late twentieth century medical approach to intersexuality is based essentially on an anatomically strict psychosocial theory of gender identity. Contemporary theory, established and disseminated largely via the work of John Money[9] and endorsed by the American Academy of Pediatrics,[10] holds that gender identity arises primarily from psychosocial rearing (nurture), and not directly from biology (nature); that all children must have their gender identity fixed very early in life for a consistent, "successful" gender identity to form; that from very early in life the child's anatomy must match the "standard" anatomy for her or his gender; and that for gender identity to form psychosocially boys primarily require "adequate" penises with no vagina, and girls primarily require a vagina with no easily noticeable phallus.[11]

Note that this theory presumes that these rules *must* be followed if intersexual children are to achieve successful psychosocial adjustment appropriate to their assigned gender—that is, if they are to act like girls, boys, men, and women are "supposed" to act. The theory also by implication presumes that there are definite acceptable and unacceptable roles for boys, girls, men, and women, and that this approach *will* achieve successful psychosocial adjustment, at least far more often than any other approach.

Many parents, especially those unfamiliar with sex development, are bothered by their children's intersexed genitals and receptive to offers of "normalizing" medical treatments. Many also actively seek guidance about gender assignment and parenting practices. In the United States today, therefore, typically upon the identification of an "ambiguous" or intersexed baby teams of specialists (geneticists, pediatric endocrinologists, pediatric urologists, and so on) are immediately assembled, and these teams of doctors decide to which sex/gender a given child will be assigned. A plethora of technologies are then used to create and maintain that sex in as believable a form as possible, including, typically, surgery on the genitals, and sometimes later also on other "anomalous" parts like breasts in an assigned male; hormone monitoring and treatments to get a "cocktail" that will help and not contradict the decided sex (and that will avoid metabolic dangers); and fostering the conviction among the child's family and community that the child is indeed the sex decided —"psychosocial" rearing of the child according to the norms of the chosen sex. Doctors typically take charge of the first two kinds of activities and hope that the child's family and community will successfully manage the all-critical third.

Clinicians treating intersexuality worry that any confusion about the sexual identity of the child on the part of relatives will be conveyed to the child and result in enormous psychological problems, including potential "dysphoric" states in adolescence and adulthood. In an effort to forestall or end any confusion about the child's sexual identity, clinicians try to see to it that an intersexual's sex/gender identity is permanently decided by specialist doctors within forty-eight hours of birth. With the same goals in mind, many clinicians insist that parents of intersexed newborns be told that their ambiguous child *does* really have a male or female sex, but that the sex of their child has just not yet "finished" developing, and that the doctors will quickly figure out the "correct" sex and then help "finish" the sexual development. As the sociologist Suzanne Kessler noted in her ground-breaking sociological analysis of the current treatment of intersexuality, "the message [conveyed to these parents]...is that the trouble lies in the doctor's ability to determine the gender, not in the baby's gender per se."[12] In intersex cases, Ellen Hyun-Ju Lee concludes, "physicians present a picture of the 'natural sex,' either male or female, despite their role in actually constructing sex."[13]

Because of widespread acceptance of the anatomically strict psychosocial theory of treatment, the practical rules now adopted by most specialists in intersexuality are these: genetic males (children with Y chromosomes) must have "adequate" penises if they are to be assigned the male gender. When a genetic male is judged to have an "adequate" phallus size, surgeons may operate, sometimes repeatedly, to try to make the penis look more "normal." If their penises are determined to be "inadequate" for successful adjustment as males, they are assigned the female gender and reconstructed to look female. (Hence John to Joan.) In cases of intersexed children assigned the female sex/gender, surgeons may "carve a large phallus down into a clitoris" (primarily attempting to make the phallus invisible when standing), "create a vagina using a piece of colon" or other body parts, "mold labia out of what was a penis," remove any testes, and so on.[14]

Meanwhile, genetic females (that is, babies lacking a Y chromosome) born with ambiguous genitalia are declared girls—no matter how masculine their genitalia look. This is done chiefly in the interest of preserving these children's potential feminine reproductive capabilities and in bringing their anatomical appearance and physiological capabilities into line with that reproductive role. Consequently, these children are reconstructed to look female using the same general techniques as those used on genetically male children assigned a female role. Surgeons reduce "enlarged" clitorises so that they will not look "masculine." Vaginas are built or lengthened if necessary, in order to make them big enough to accept average-sized penises. Joined labia are separated, and various other surgical and hormonal treatments are directed at producing a believable and, it is hoped, fertile girl.

What are the limits of acceptability in terms of phalluses? Clitorises—meaning simply phalluses in children labeled female—are frequently considered too big if they exceed one centimeter in length.[15] Pediatric surgeons specializing in treating intersexuality consider "enlarged" clitorises to be "cosmetically offensive" in girls and therefore they subject these clitorises to surgical reduction meant to leave the organs looking more "feminine" and "delicate."[16] Penises—meaning simply phalluses in children labeled male—are often considered too small if the stretched length is less than 2.5 centimeters (about an inch). Consequently, genetically male children born at term "with a stretched penile length less than 2.5 [centimeters] are usually given a female sex assignment."[17]

Roughly the same protocols are applied to cases of "true" hermaphroditism (in which babies are born with testicular and ovarian tissue). Whereas the anatomico-materialist metaphysics of sex in the late nineteenth century made true hermaphrodites an enormous problem for doctors and scientists of that time, clinicians today believe that "true hermaphrodites" (like "pseudo-hermaphrodites") can be fairly easily retrofitted with surgery and other treatment to either an acceptable male or acceptable female sex/gender.

One of the troubling aspects of these protocols are the asymmetric ways they treat femininity and masculinity. For example, physicians appear to do far more to preserve the reproductive potential of children born with ovaries than that of children born with testes. While genetically male intersexuals often have infertile testes, some men with micropenis may be able to father children if allowed to retain their testes.[18]

Similarly, surgeons seem to demand far more for a penis to count as "successful" than for a vagina to count as such. Indeed, the logic behind the tendency to assign the female gender in cases of intersexuality rests not only on the belief that boys need "adequate" penises, but also upon the opinion among surgeons that "a functional vagina can be constructed in virtually everyone [while] a functional penis is a much more difficult goal."[19] This is true because much is expected of penises, especially by pediatric urologists, and very little of vaginas. For a penis to count as acceptable—"functional"—it must be or have the potential to be big enough to be readily recognizable as a "real" penis. In addition, the "functional" penis is generally expected to have the capability to become erect and flaccid at appropriate times, and to act as the conduit through which urine and semen are expelled, also at appropriate times. The urethral opening is expected to appear at the very tip of the penis. Typically, surgeons also hope to see penises that are "believably" shaped and colored.

Meanwhile, very little is needed for a surgically constructed vagina to count among surgeons as "functional." For a constructed vagina to be considered acceptable by surgeons specializing in intersexuality, it basically just has to be a hole big enough to fit a typical-sized penis. It is not required to be self-lubricating or even to be at all sensitive, and certainly does not need to change shape the way vaginas often do when women are sexually stimulated. So, for example, in a panal discussion of surgeons who treat intersexuality, when one was asked, "How do you define successful intercourse? How many of these girls actually have an orgasm, for example? a member of the panel responded, "Adequate intercourse was defined as successful vaginal penetration."[20] All that is required is a receptive hole.

Indeed, clinicians treating intersex children often talk about vaginas in those children as the absence of a thing, as a space, a "hole," a place to put something. That is precisely why opinion holds that "a functional vagina can be constructed in virtually everyone"—because it is relatively easy to construct an insensitive hole surgically. (It is not always easy to keep them open and uninfected.) The decision to "make" a female is therefore considered relatively fool-proof, while "the assignment of male sex of rearing is inevitably difficult and should only be undertaken by an experienced team" who can determine if a penis will be adequate for "successful" malehood.[21]

The Problem of "Normality"

The strict conception of "normal" sexual anatomy and "normal" sex behavior that underlies prevailing treatment protocols is arguably sexist in its asymmetrical treatment of reproductive potential and definitions of anatomical "adequacy." Additionally, as Lee and other critics of intersex treatment have noted, "[d]ecisions of gender assignment and subsequent surgical reconstruction are inseparable from the heterosexual matrix, which does not allow for other sexual practices or sexualities. Even within heterosexuality, a rich array of sexual practices is reduced to vaginal penetration."[22] Not surprisingly, feminists and intersexuals have invariably objected to these presumptions that there is a "right" way to be a male and a "right" way to be a female, and that children who challenge these categories should be reconstructed to fit into (and thereby reinforce) them.

Indeed, beside the important (and too often disregarded) philosophical-political issue of gender roles, there is a more practical one: how does one decide where to put the boundaries on acceptable levels of anatomical variation? Not surprisingly, the definition of genital "normality" in practice appears to vary among physicians. For example, at least one physician has set the minimum length of an "acceptable" penis at 1.5 centimeters.[23]

Indeed, at least two physicians are convinced (and have evidence) that any penis is a big enough penis for male adjustment, if the other cards are played right. Almost a decade ago Justine Schober (neé Reilly), a pediatric urologist now based at the Hamot Medical Center in Erie, Pennsylvania, and Christopher Woodhouse, a physician based at the Institute of Urology and St. George's Hospital in London, "interviewed and examined 20 patients with the primary diagnosis of micropenis in infancy" who were labeled and raised as boys. Of the post-pubertal (adult) subjects, "All patients were heterosexual and they had erections and orgasms. Eleven patients had ejaculations, 9 were sexually active and reported vaginal penetration, 7 were married or cohabitating and 1 had fathered a child."[24]

Schober and Woodhouse concluded that "a small penis does not preclude normal male role" and should not dictate female gender reassignment. They found that when parents "were well counseled about diagnosis they reflected an attitude of concern but not anxiety about the problem, and they did not convey anxiety to their children. They were honest and explained problems to the child and encouraged normality in behavior. We believe that this is the attitude that allows these children to approach their peers with confidence" (p. 571).

Ultimately, Schober and Woodhouse agreed with the tenet of the psychosocial theory that assumes that "the strongest influence for all patients [is] the parental attitude." But rather than making these children into girls and trying to convince the parents and children about their "real" feminine identity, Schober and Woodhouse found that "the well informed and open parents...produced more confident and better adjusted boys." We should note that these boys were not considered "typical" in their sex lives: "The group was characterized by an experimental attitude to [sexual] positions and methods.... The group appears to form close and long-lasting relationships. They often attribute partner sexual satisfaction and the stability of their relationships [with women partners] to their need to make extra effort including nonpenetrating techniques" (p. 571).

"Ambiguous" genitalia do not constitute a disease. They simply constitute a failure to fit a particular (and, at present, a particularly demanding) definition of normality. It is true that whenever a baby is born with "ambiguous" genitalia, doctors need to consider the situation a *potential* medical emergency because intersexuality may signal a potentially serious metabolic problem, namely congenital adrenal hyperplasia (CAH), which primarily involves an electrolyte imbalance and can result in "masculinization" of genetically female fetuses. Treatment of CAH may save a child's life and fertility. At the birth of an intersex child, therefore, adrenogenital syndrome must be quickly diagnosed and treated, or ruled out. Nonetheless, as medical tests advise, "of all the conditions responsible for ambiguous genitalia, congenital adrenal hyperplasia is the only one that is life-threatening in the newborn period," and even in cases of CAH the "ambiguous" genitalia themselves are not deadly.[25]

As with CAH's clear medical issue, doctors now also know that the testes of AIS patients have a relatively high rate of becoming cancerous, and therefore AIS needs to be diagnosed as early as possible so that the testes can be carefully watched or removed. However, the genitalia of an androgen-insensitive person are not diseased. Again, while unusual genitalia may *signal* a present or potential threat to health, in themselves they just *look* different. As we have seen, because of the perception of a "social emergency" around an intersex birth, clinicians take license to treat nonstandard genitalia as a medical problem requiring prompt correction. But as Suzanne Kessler sums up the situation, intersexuality does not threaten the patient's life; it threatens the patient's culture.

Psychological Health and the Problem of Deception

Clearly, in our often unforgiving culture intersexuality can also threaten the patient's psyche; that recognition is behind the whole treatment approach. Nevertheless, there are two major problems here. First, clinicians treating intersex individuals may be far more concerned with strict definitions of genital normality than intersexuals, their parents, and their acquaintances (including lovers). This is evidenced time and again, for example, in the John/Joan case:

> John recalls thinking, from preschool through elementary school, that physicians were more concerned with the appearance of Joan's genitals than was Joan. Her genitals were inspected at each visit to The Johns Hopkins Hospital. She thought they were making a big issue out of nothing, and they gave her no reason to think otherwise. John recalls thinking: "Leave me be and then I'll be fine.... It's bizarre. My genitals are not bothering me; I don't know why it is bothering you guys so much."[26]

Second, and more basically, it is not self-evident that a psychosocial problem should be handled medically or surgically. We do not attempt to solve the problems many dark-skinned children will face in our nation by lightening their skins. Similarly, Cheryl Chase has posed this interesting question: when a baby is born with a severely disfigured but largely functional arm, ought we quickly remove the arm and replace it with a possibly functional prosthetic, so that the parents and child experience less psychological trauma?[27] While it is true that genitals are more psychically charged than arms, genitals are also more easily and more often kept private, whatever their state. Quoting the ideas of Suzanne Kessler, the pediatric urologist Schober argues in a forthcoming work that "surgery makes parents and doctors more comfortable, but counseling makes people comfortable too, and [it] is not irreversible." She continues: "Simply understanding and performing good surgeries is not sufficient. We must also know when to appropriately perform or withhold surgery. Our ethical duty as surgeons is to do no harm and to serve the best interests of our patient. Sometimes, this means admitting that a 'perfect' solution may not be attainable."[28]

Ironically, rather than alleviating feelings of freakishness, in practice the way intersexuality is typically handled may actually produce or contribute to many intersexuals' feelings of freakishness. Many intersexuals look at these two facts: (1) they are subject, out of "compassion," to "normalizing" surgeries on an emergency basis without their personal consent, and (2) they are often not told the whole truth about their anatomical conditions and anatomical histories. Understandably, they conclude that their doctors see them as profound freaks and that they must really be freaks. H. Martin Malin, a professor in clinical sexology and a therapist at the Child and Family Institute in Sacramento, California, has found this to be a persistent theme running through intersexuals' medical experience.

> As I listened to [intersexuals'] stories, certain leit motifs began to emerge from the bits of their histories. They or their parents had little, if any, counseling. They thought they were the only ones who felt as they did. Many had asked to meet other patients whose medical histories were similar to their own, but they were stonewalled. They recognized themselves in published case histories, but when they sought medical records, were told they could not be located. . . .
>
> The patients I was encountering were not those whose surgeries resulted from life-threatening or seriously debilitating medical conditions. Rather, they had such diagnoses as "micropenis" or "clitoral hypertrophy." These were patients who were told—when they were told anything—that they had vaginoplasties or clitorectomies because of the serious psychological consequences they would have suffered if surgery had not been done. But the surgeries *had* been performed—and they were reporting longstanding psychological distress. They were certain that they would rather have had the "abnormal" genitals they [had] had than the "mutilated" genitals they were given. They were hostile and often vengeful towards the professionals who had been responsible for their care and sometimes, by transference, towards me. They were furious that they had been lied to.[29]

Given the lack of long-term follow-up studies it is unclear whether a majority of intersexuals wind up feeling this way, but even if only a small number do we must ask whether the practice of deception and "stonewalling" is essentially unethical.

Why would a physician ever withhold medical and personal historical information from an intersexed patient? Because she or he believes that the truth is too horrible or too complicated for the patient to handle. In a 1988 commentary in the *Hastings Center Report,* Brendan Minogue and Robert Tarszewski argued, for example, that a physician could justifiably withhold information from a sixteen-year-old AIS patient and/or her parents if he believed that the patient and/or family was likely to be incapable of handling the fact that she has testes and an XY chromosomal complement.[30] Indeed, this reasoning appears typical among clinicians treating intersexuality; many continue to believe that talking truthfully with intersexuals and their families will undo all the "positive" effects of the technological efforts aimed at covering up doubts. Thus despite intersexuals' and ethicists' published, repeated objections to deception, in 1995 a medical student was given a cash prize in medical ethics by the Canadian Medical Association for an article specifically advocating deceiving AIS patients (including adults) about the biological facts of their conditions. The prize-winner argued that "physicians who withhold information from AIS patients are not actually lying; they are only deceiving" because they *selectively withhold* facts about patients' bodies.[31]

But what this reasoning fails to appreciate is that hiding the facts of the condition will not necessarily prevent a patient and family from thinking about it. Indeed, the failure on the part of the doctor and family to talk honestly about the condition is likely only to add to feelings of shame and confusion. One woman with AIS in Britain writes, "Mine was a dark secret kept from all outside the medical profession (family included), but this [should] not [be] an option because it both increases the feelings of freakishness and reinforces the isolation."[32] Similarly, Martha Coventry, a woman who had her "enlarged" clitoris removed by surgeons when she was six, insists that "to be lied to as a child about your own body, to have your life as a sexual being so ignored that you are not even given the decency of an answer to your questions, is to have your heart and soul relentlessly undermined."[33]

Lying to a patient about his or her biological condition can also lead to a patient unintentionally taking unnecessary risks. As a young woman, Sherri Groveman, who has AIS, was told by her doctor that she had "twisted ovaries" and that they had to be removed; in fact, her testes were removed. At the age of twenty, "alone and scared in the stacks of a [medical] library," she discovered the truth of her condition. Then "the pieces finally fit together. But what fell apart was my relationship with both my family and physicians. It was not learning about chromosomes or testes that caused enduring trauma, it was discovering that I had been told lies. I avoided all medical care for the next 18 years. I have severe osteoporosis as a result of a lack of medical attention. This is what lies produce."[34]

Similarly, as B. Diane Kemp—"a social worker with more than 35 years' experience and a woman who has borne androgen insensitivity syndrome for 63 years"—notes, "secrecy as a method of handling troubling information is primitive, degrading, and often ineffective. Even when a secret is kept, its existence carries an aura of unease that most people can sense...Secrets crippled my life."[35]

Clearly, the notion that deception or selective truth-telling will protect the child, the family, or even the adult intersexual is extraordinarily paternalistic and naive, and, while perhaps well-intentioned, it goes against the dominant trend in medical ethics as those ethics guidelines are applied to other, similar situations. In what other realms are patients regularly not told the medical names for their conditions, even when they ask? As for the idea that physicians should not tell patients what they probably "can't handle," would a physician be justified in using this reasoning to avoid telling a patient she has cancer or AIDS?

In their commentary in the *Hastings Center Report* Sherman Elias and George Annas pointed out that a physician who starts playing with the facts of a patient's condition may well find himself forced to lie or admit prior deception. "Practically," Elias and Annas wrote, "it is unrealistic to believe that [the AIS patient] will not ultimately learn the details of her having testicular syndrome. From the onset it will be difficult to maintain the charade."[36] They also note that without being told the name and details of her condition any consent the AIS patient gives will not truly be "informed." As an attorney Groveman too argues "that informed consent laws mandate that the patient know the truth before physicians remove her testes or reconstruct her vagina."[37]

Informed Consent and Risk Assumption

It is not at all clear if all or even most of the intersex surgeries done today involve what would legally and ethically constitute informed consent. It appears that few intersexuals or their parents are educated, before they give consent, about the anatomically strict psychosocial model employed. The model probably ought to be described to parents as essentially unproven insofar as the theory remains unconfirmed by broad-based, long-term follow-up studies, and is directly challenged by cases like the John/Joan case as well as by ever-mounting "anecdotal" reports from former patients who, disenfranchised and labeled "lost to follow-up" by clinicians, have turned to the popular press and to public protest in order to be heard. Of course, as long as intersex patients are not consistently told the truth of their conditions, there is some question about whether satisfaction can be assessed with integrity in long-term studies.

At a finer level, many of the latest particular cosmetic surgeries being used on intersexed babies and children today remain basically unproven as well, and need to be described as such in consent agreements. For example, a team of surgeons from the Children's Medical Center and George Washington University Medical School has reported that in their preferred form of clitoral "recession" (done to make "big" clitorises look "right"), "the cosmetic effect is excellent" but "late studies with assessment of sexual gratification, orgasm, and general psychological adjustment are unavailable...and remain in question."[38] In fact the procedure may result in problems like stenosis, increased risk of infections, loss of feeling, and psychological trauma. (These risks characterize all genital surgeries.)

This lack of long-term follow-up is the case not only for clitoral surgeries; David Thomas, a pediatric urologist who practices at St. James's University Hospital and Infirmary in Leeds, England, recently noted that same problem with regard to early vaginal reconstructions: "So many of these patients are lost to follow-up. If we do this surgery in infancy and childhood, we have an obligation to follow these children up, to assess what we're doing."[39] There is a serious ethical problem here: risky surgeries are being performed as standard care and are not being adequately followed-up.[40]

The growing community of open adult intersexuals understandably question whether anyone should have either her ability to enjoy sex or her physical health risked without personal consent just because she has a clitoris, penis, or vagina that falls outside the standard deviation. Even if we *did* have statistics that showed that particular procedures "worked" a majority of the time we would have to face the fact that part of the time they would not work, and we need to ask whether that risk ought to be assumed on behalf of another person.

Beyond "Monster Ethics"

In a 1987 article on the ethics of killing one conjoined twin to save the other, George Annas suggested (but did not advocate) that one way to justify such a procedure would be to take "the monster approach." This approach would hold that conjoined twins are so grotesque, so pathetic, any medical procedure aimed at normalizing them would be morally justified.[41] Unfortunately, the present treatment of intersexuality in the U.S. seems to be deeply informed by the monster approach; ethical guidelines that would be applied in nearly any other medical situation are, in cases of intersexuality, ignored. Patients are lied to; risky procedures are performed without follow-up; consent is not fully informed; autonomy and health are risked because of unproven (and even disproven) fears that atypical anatomy will lead to psychological disaster. Why? Perhaps because sexual anatomy is not treated like the rest of human anatomy, or perhaps because we simply assume that any procedure which "normalizes" an "abnormal" child is merciful. Whatever the reason, the medical treatment of intersexuality and other metabolically benign, cosmetically unusual anatomies needs deep and immediate attention.

We can readily use the tools of narrative ethics to gain insight into practices surrounding intersexuality. There are now available many autobiographies of adult intersexuals.[42] Like that of John/Joan, whether or not they are characteristic of long-term outcomes these autobiographies raise serious questions about the dominant treatment protocols.

Narrative ethics also suggests that we use our imaginations to think through the story of the intersexual, to ask ourselves, if we were born intersexed, what treatment we would wish to have received. Curious about what adult nonintersexuals would have chosen for themselves, Suzanne Kessler polled a group of college students regarding their feelings on the matter. The women were asked, "Suppose you had been born with a larger than normal clitoris and it would remain larger than normal as you grew to adulthood. Assuming that the physicians recommended surgically reducing your clitoris, under what circumstances would you have wanted your parents to give them permission to do it?" In response,

> About a fourth of the women indicated they would not have wanted a clitoral reduction under *any* circumstance. About half would have wanted their clitoris reduced *only* if the larger than normal clitoris caused health problems. Size, for them, was not a factor. The remaining forth of the sample

could imagine wanting their clitoris reduced if it were larger than normal, but *only* if having the surgery would *not* have resulted in a reduction in pleasurable sensitivity.[43]

Meanwhile, in this study, "the men were asked to imagine being born with a smaller than normal penis and told that physicians recommended phallic reduction and a female gender assignment." In response,

> All but one man indicated they would not have wanted surgery under any circumstance. The remaining man indicated that if his penis were 1 cm. or less *and he were going to be sterile,* he would have wanted his parents to give the doctors permission to operate and make him a female. (p. 36)

Kessler is cautious to note that we need more information to assess this data fully, but it does begin to suggest that given the choice most people would reject genital cosmetic surgery for themselves.

As an historian, I also think we need to consider the historical and cultural bases for genital conformity practices, and realize that most people in the U.S. demonstrate little tolerance for practices in other cultures that might well be considered similar. I am, of course, talking about the recent passage of federal legislation prohibiting physicians from performing "circumcision" on the genitalia of girls under the age of eighteen, *whether or not the girls consent or personally request the procedure.* African female genital "cutting" typically involves, in part, excision of the clitoral tissue so that most or all clitoral sensation will be lost. While proponents of this traditional female genital "cutting" have insisted this practice is an important cultural tradition—analogous to male circumcision culturally—advocates of the U.S. law insist it is barbaric and violates human rights. Specifically, in the federal legislation passed in October 1996 Congress declared that: "Except as provided in subsection (b), whoever knowingly circumcises, excises, or infibulates the whole or any part of the labia majora or labia minora or clitoris of another person who has not attained the age of 18 years shall be fined under this title or imprisoned not more than 5 years, or both."[44]

Subsection "b" specifies that: "A surgical operation is not a violation of this section if the operation is (1) necessary to the health of the person on whom it is performed, and is performed by a person licensed in the place of its performance as a medical practitioner; or (2) performed on a person in labor or who has just given birth and is performed for medical purposes connected with that labor or birth."

Surgeons treating intersexuality presumably would argue that the procedures they perform on the genitals of girls (which clearly include excision of parts of the clitoris) are indeed "necessary to the health of the person on whom it is performed." While it is easy to condemn the African practice of female genital mutilation as a barbaric custom that violates human rights, we should recognize that in the United States medicine's prevailing response to intersexuality is largely about genital conformity and the "proper" roles of the sexes. Just as we find it necessary to protect the rights and well-being of African girls, we must now consider the hard questions of the rights and well-being of children born intersexed in the United States.

As this paper was in process, the attention paid by the popular media and by physicians to the problems with the dominant clinical protocols increased dramatically, and many more physicians and ethicists have recently come forward to question those protocols. Diamond and Sigmundson have helpfully proposed tentative new "guidelines for dealing with persons with ambiguous genitalia."[45]

As new guidelines are further developed, it will be critical to take seriously two tasks. First, as I have argued above, intersexuals must not be subjected to different ethical standards from other people simply because they are intersexed. Second, the experiences and advice of adult intersexuals must be solicited and taken into consideration. It is incorrect to claim, as I have heard several clinicians do, that the complaints of adult intersexuals are irrelevant because they were subjected to "old, unperfected" surgeries. Clinicians have too often retreated to the mistaken belief that improved treatment technologies (for example, better surgical techniques) will eliminate ethical dilemmas surrounding intersex treatment. There is far more at issue than scar tissue and loss of sensation from unperfected surgeries.

References

1. Milton Diamond and H. Keith Sigmundson, "Sex Reassignment at Birth: Long-Term Review and Clinical Implications," *Archives of Pediatrics and Adolescent Medicine* 15 (1997): 298–304.
2. For a more in-depth biography, see John Colapinto, "The True Story of John/Joan," *Rolling Stone*, 11 December 1997, pp. 55ff.
3. Diamond and Sigmundson, "Sex Reassignment," p. 303.
4. I discuss this at length in Dreger, *Hermaphrodites and the Medical Invention of Sex* (Cambridge, Mass.: Harvard University Press, 1998); see especially prologue and chap. 1.
5. See Ethel Sloane, *Biology of Women,* 3rd ed. (Albany: Delmar Publishers, 1993), p. 168. According to Denis Grady, a study of over 6,500 women athletes competing in seven different international sports competitions showed an incidence of intersexuality of one in 500 women, but unfortunately Grady does not provide a reference to the published data from that study (Denise Grady, "Sex Test," *Discover,* June 1992, pp. 78–82). That sampled population should not simply be taken as representative of the whole population, but this number is certainly higher than most people would expect.
6. Anne Fausto-Sterling, *Body Building: How Biologists Construct Sexuality* (New York: Basic Books, forthcoming 1999), chap. 2; Fausto-Sterling, "How Dimorphic Are We?" *American Journal of Human Genetics* (forthcoming); and personal communication. The highest modern-day estimate for frequency of sexually ambiguous births comes from John Money, who has posited that as many as 4 percent of live births today are of "intersexed" individuals (cited in Anne Fausto-Sterling, "The Five Sexes," *The Sciences* 33 [1993]: 20–25). Money's categories tend to be exceptionally broad and poorly defined, and not representative of what most medical professionals today would consider to be "intersexuality."
7. Dreger, *Hermaphrodites,* chaps. 1–5; for a summary of the scene in Britain in the late-nineteenth century, see Dreger, "Doubtful Sex: The Fate of the Hermaphrodite in Victorian Medicine," *Victorian Studies* 38 (1995): 335–69.
8. Stuart R. Kupfer, Charmain A. Quigley, and Frank S. French, "Male Pseudohermaphroditism," *Seminars in Perinatology* 16 (1992): 319–31, at 325.

9. For summaries and critiques of Money's work on intersexuality, see especially: Cheryl Chase, "Affronting Reason," in *Looking Queer: Image and Identity in Lesbian, Bisexual, Gay and Transgendered Communities,* ed. D. Atkins (Binghamton, N.Y.: Haworth, 1998); "Hermaphrodites with Attitude: Mapping the Emergence of Intersex Political Activism," *GLQ* 4, no. 2 (1998): 189–211; Anne Fausto-Sterling, "How to Build a Man," in *Science and Homosexualities,* ed. Vernon A. Rosario (New York: Routledge, 1997), pp. 219–25; and Ellen Hyun-Ju Lee, "Producing Sex: An Interdisciplinary Perspective on Sex Assignment Decisions for Intersexuals" (Senior Thesis, Brown University, 1994).

10. American Academy of Pediatrics (Section on Urology), "Timing of Elective Surgery on the Genitalia of Male Children with Particular Reference to the Risks, Benefits, and Psychological Effects of Surgery and Anesthesia," *Pediatrics* 97, no. 4 (1996): 590–94.

11. For example, see Patricia K. Donahoe. "The Diagnosis and Treatment of Infants with Intersex Abnormalities," *Pediatric Clinics of North America* 34 (1987): 1333–48.

12. Suzanne J. Kessler, "The Medical Construction of Gender: Case Management of Intersexed Infants," *Signs* 16 (1990); 3–26; compare the advice given by Cynthia H. Meyers-Seifer and Nancy J. Charest, "Diagnosis and Management of Patients with Ambiguous Genitalia." *Seminars in Perinatology* 16 (1992): 332–39.

13. Lee, "Producing Sex," p. 45.

14. Melissa Hendricks, "Is It a Boy or a Girl?" *John Hopkins Magazine* (November, 1993): 10–16, p. 10.

15. Barbara C. McGillivray, "The Newborn with Ambiguous Genitalia," *Seminars in Perinatology* 16 (1991): 365–68, p. 366.

16. Kurt Newman, Judson Randolph, and Kathryn Anderson, "The Surgical Management of Infants and Children with Ambiguous Genitalia." *Annals of Surgery* 215 (1992): 644–53, pp. 651 and 647.

17. Meyers-Seifer and Charest, "Diagnosis and Management," p. 337. See also Kupfer, Quigley, and French, "Male Pseudohermaphroditism," p. 328; Rajkumar Shah, Morton M. Woolley, and Gertrude Costin, "Testicular Feminization: The Androgen Insensitivity Syndrome," *Journal of Pediatric Surgery* 27 (1992): 757–60, p. 757.

18. Justine Schober, personal communications; for data on this, see Justine M. Reilly and C. R. J. Woodhouse, "Small Penis and the Male Sexual Role," *Journal of Urology* 142 (1989): 569–71.

19. Robin J. O. Catlin, *Appleton & Lange's Review for the US-MILE Step 2* (East Norwalk, Connecticut: Appleton & Lange, 1993), p. 49.

20. See the comments of John P. Gearhart in M. M. Bailez, John P. Gearhart, Claude Migeon, and John Rock, "Vaginal Reconstruction After Initial Construction of the External Genitalia in Girls with Salt-Wasting Adrenal Hyperplasia," *Journal of Urology* 148 (1992): 680–84, p. 684.

21. Kupfer, Quigley, and French, "Male Pseudohermaphroditism," p. 328.

22. Lee, "Producing Sex," p. 27.

23. See Donahoe, "The Diagnosis and Treatment of Infants with Intersex Abnormalities."

24. Reilly and Woodhouse, "Small Penis," p. 569.

25. Patricia K. Donahoe, David M. Powell, and Mary M. Lee, "Clinical Management of Intersex Abnormalities," *Current Problems in Surgery* 28 (1991): 515–79, p. 540.

26. Diamond and Sigmundson, "Sex Reassignment," pp. 300–301.

27. Cheryl Chase, personal communication.

28. Quoted in Justine M. Schober, "Long-Term Outcome of Feminizing Genitoplasty for Intersex," *Pediatric Surgery and Urology: Long Term Outcomes,* ed. Pierre D. E. Mouriquand (Philadelphia: William B. Saunders, forthcoming).

29. H. M. Malin, personal communication of 1 January 1997 to Justine M. Schober, quoted in Schober, "Long-Term Outcome."

30. Brendan P. Minogue and Robert Taraszewski, "The Whole Truth and Nothing But the Truth?" (Case Study), *Hasting Center Report* 18, no. 5 (1998): 34–35.

31. Anita Natarajan, "Medical Ethics and Truth Telling in the Case of Androgen Insensitivity Syndrome," *Canadian Medical Association Journal* 154 (1996): 568–70. (For responses to Natarajan's recommendations by AIS women and a partner of an AIS woman, see *Canadian Medical Association Journal* 154 [1996]: 1829–33.)

32. Anonymous, "Be Open and Honest with Sufferers," *British Medical Journal* 308 (1994): 1041–42.

33. Martha Coventry, "Finding the Words," *Chrysalis: The Journal of Transgressive Gender Identities* 2 (1997): 27–30.

34. Sherri A. Groveman, "Letter to the Editor," *Canadian Medical Association Journal* 154 (1996): 1829, 1832.

35. B. Diane Kemp, "Letter to the Editor," *Canadian Medical Association Journal* 154 (1996): 1829.

36. Sherman Elias and George J. Annas. "The Whole Truth and Nothing But the Truth?" (Case Study), *Hastings Center Report* 18, no. 5 (1988): 35–36, p. 35.

37. Groveman, "Letter to the Editor," p. 1829.

38. Newman, Randolph, and Anderson, "Surgical Management," p. 651.

39. "Is Early Vaginal Reconstruction Wrong for Some Intersex Girls?" *Urology Times* (February 1997): 10–12.

40. Intersexuals are understandably tired of hearing that "long-term follow-up data is needed" while the surgeries continued to occur. On this, see especially the guest commentary by David Sandberg, "A Call for Clinical Research," *Hermaphrodites with Attitude* (Fall/Winter 1995–1996): 8–9, and the many responses of intersexuals in the same issue.

41. George J. Annas, "Siamese Twins: Killing One to Save the Other" (At Law), *Hastings Center Report* 17, no. 2 (1987): 27–29.

42. See, for example, M. Morgan Holmes, "Medical Politics and Cultural Imperatives: Intersex Identities beyond Pathology and Erasure" (M. A. Thesis, York University, 1994); Chase, "Hermaphrodites with Attitude": Geoffrey Cowley, "Gender Limbo," *Newsweek,* 19 May 1997, pp. 64–66; Natalie Angier, "New Debate Over Surgery on Genitals," *New York Times,* 13 May 1997; "Special Issue: Intersexuality," *Chrysalis: The Journal of Transgressive Gender Identities* 2 (1997). Intersexual autobiographies are also from peer support groups, including the Intersex Society of North America. For information about support groups see the special issue of *Chrysalis,* vol. 2, 1997.

43. Suzanne J. Kessler, "Meanings of Genital Variability," *Chrysalis: The Journal of Transgressive Gender Identities* 2 (1997): 33–37.

44. Omnibus Consolidated Appropriations Bill, H. R. 3610, P. L. 104–208.

45. Milton Diamond and Keith Sigmundson, "Management of Intersexuality: Guidelines for Dealing with Persons with Ambiguous Genitalia," *Archives of Pediatric and Adolescent Medicine* 151 (1997): 1046–50.

POSTSCRIPT

Should Parents Surgically Alter Their Intersex Infants?

Regardless of whether parents choose to alter their child's ambiguous genitalia or whether they choose to let their child decide later in life whether or not to have surgery, the experience of having an infant with ambiguous genitalia usually takes parents by surprise. For many parents, especially those who have little or no information about ambiguous genitalia, the experience can be quite alarming to them. Other parents struggle with the decisions but in the end feel good about the choices they make.

The support for assigning a sex surgically seems to be based in a portion of society's strong viewpoints on the role penis size plays in not just being able to define a child as male but also in a male child's sense of his own "maleness." In fact, nearly all infants born with ambiguous genitalia whose biological sex is determined surgically are made female because, quite simply, the surgery is better and easier. Moreover, parents and medical professionals alike struggle with the implications of a male child born with a micropenis. It is clear that some adults are motivated strongly by trying to avoid embarrassment for their male child. It would be better, they feel, to create a girl rather than leave an intact boy with an "inferior" penis.

Thirty years ago, the standard operating procedure was to select a biological sex at birth based on genital appearance alone. Today, with greater capacity for chromosomal and other types of testing, many medical professionals and associations are taking a much more conservative approach to dealing with a child born with ambiguous genitalia. Diamond and Sigmundson suggest the following guidelines for working with infants with ambiguous genitalia:

- **A complete physical is necessary.** This includes, they suggest, taking a thorough history of the patient's family. The physical should look not just at the external genitalia but also at the internal systems as they exist, at genetic structures, and at the endocrine system. They argue that many cases of intersexuality go undetected. This can avoid surprises and additional challenges later in the child's life.
- **Parents should be given full information on intersexuality and start being counseled immediately.** Intersexuality is among many conditions where medical professionals often withhold information until the final outcome and conclusions are drawn. Diamond and Sigmundson recommend full disclosure from the onset and immediate and ongoing counseling to help parents understand what intersexuality is, that they are not alone, and that many people with ambiguous genitalia grow up to live happy lives.

- **Medical professionals need to respect confidentiality, even within the hospital setting.** While giving the family the clear message that having an intersex child is nothing to be embarrassed about, medical professionals must be careful about not treating the family as a novelty.
- **Assign sex based on the most likely outcome.** This is an important distinction to make for parents who may have felt ambivalent about having a child of one sex versus the other. If they are disappointed with a child of one sex and would prefer to have the other, they must understand clearly that having an intersex child is not an opportunity for sex selection and that there is a potentially disastrous outcome if the assignment is based on desire for a son or daughter rather than the child's true nature.

Above all Diamond and Sigmundson they discourage medical professionals and parents from opting for genital surgery for cosmetic rather than medical reasons.

Suggested Readings

Lenore Abramsky, Sue Hall, Judith Levitan, and Theresa M. Marteau, "What Parents Are Told After Prenatal Diagnosis of a Sex Chromosome Abnormality: Interview and Questionnaire Study," Available online at http://www.bmj.com/cgi/content/full/322/7284/463.

John Colapinto, *As Nature Made Him: The Boy Who Was Raised as a Girl* (HarperCollins Publishing, 2000).

M. Diamond and K. Sigmundson, "Management of Intersexuality: Guidelines for Dealing With Individuals With Ambiguous Genitalia," *Archives of Pediatrics and Adolescent Medicine* (June 10, 2002).

Alice Domurat Dreger, ed., *Intersex in the Age of Ethics* (University Publishing Group, 1999).

Anne Fausto-Sterling, "The Five Sexes, Revisited," *Sciences* (July 2000).

Anne Fausto-Sterling, *Sexing the Body: Gender Politics and the Construction of Sexuality* (Basic Books, 2000).

Melissa Hendricks, "Into the Hands of Babes," *Johns Hopkins Magazine* (September 2000).

Katherine A. Mason, "The Unkindest Cut: Intersexuals Launch a Movement to Stop Doctors From 'Assigning' Sex With a Scalpel," *New Haven Advocate* (March 29, 2001).

John Money, "Ablatio Penis: Normal Male Infant Sex-Reassigned as a Girl," *Archives of Sexual Behavior* (1975).

E. Nussbaum, "A Question of Gender," *Discover* (January 2000).

The Child Rights Information Network (CRIN)

The Child Rights Information Network (CRIN) is a global network that disseminates information about the Convention on the Rights of the Child and child rights among nongovernmental organizations, United Nations agencies, intergovernmental organizations, educational institutions, and other child rights experts.

http://www.crin.org

UNICEF

UNICEF is mandated by the United Nations General Assembly to advocate for the protection of children's rights, to help meet their basic needs, and to expand their opportunities to reach their full potential.

http://www.unicef.org

Planned Parenthood Federation of America

Planned Parenthood Federation of America is the oldest and largest voluntary reproductive health organization in the United States.

http://www.plannedparenthood.org

Eagle Forum

Eagle Forum's mission is to enable conservative and pro-family men and women to participate in the process of self-government and public policy making.

http://www.eagleforum.org

PART 3

Children's Rights

*M*any parents say that a significant challenge of parenting is watching a child grow up and begin the developmentally appropriate separating and individuating that continue throughout an individual's life. But before we are adults, what rights do we have as infants? As children? As adolescents? Should government have the power to make laws that give children rights with which parents do not agree? The questions in this part examine the rights of children and teens in two specific areas.

- Should the Senate Ratify the Convention on the Rights of the Child?

- Should Minors Be Required to Get Their Parents' Permission in Order to Obtain an Abortion?

ISSUE 9

Should the Senate Ratify the Convention on the Rights of the Child?

YES: United States Fund for UNICEF, from "United Nations Convention on the Rights of the Child: Frequently Asked Questions," *United States Fund for UNICEF* (1998)

NO: Catherina Hurlburt, from "U.N. Convention on the Rights of the Child: A Treaty to Undermine the Family," a Policy Paper of Concerned Women for America (September 2001)

ISSUE SUMMARY

YES: The United States Fund for UNICEF, a United Nations agency working for the protection of children's rights, points to the successes that governments around the world have had in using the Convention on the Rights of the Child to promote children's rights and improve children's lives in general. UNICEF contends that the Convention reinforces parental rights and promotes values and norms with which no one could take issue, such as freedom from discrimination, access to adequate health care, and protection from physical harm and abduction.

NO: Catherina Hurlburt, a writer for Concerned Women for America (CWFA), maintains that the Convention on the Rights of the Child gives government more power over children's rights than parents would have. In giving children the right to "express their views freely in all matters," the Convention would, she argues, usurp parental authority and give children too much independence.

In 1989 the General Assembly of the United States adopted the Convention on the Rights of the Child. It provides guidelines for worldwide norms that nations who ratify the Convention would agree to incorporate on behalf of children living in their countries. Among these norms are children's rights to adequate nutrition, education, and healthcare, and protection from exploitative employment situations as well as from any kind of violence, abuse, or kidnapping.

To date, the Convention has been ratified by 191 countries. In countries where the Convention is being used, sample results include new justice codes for children, changes in laws relating to child prostitution and pornography, and increased training for professionals who come into contact with children, such as legal professionals, judges, and police officers. The only two countries who have not yet ratified the treaty are the United States and Somalia.

Opponents to the Convention believe that by ratifying this type of treaty, the United States would then fall under the jurisdiction of the United Nations and be forced to enact laws relating to children that may not reflect the United States' democratic system. Opponents are also concerned that ratifying the Convention would take power away from parents and give it to the government —or worse, to children themselves. They believe that children are too young to understand the consequences of and responsibilities involved in many of the areas discussed in the Convention.

As you read the following selections, consider your own upbringing. Do you think it would have been affected in any way had there been a Convention on the Rights of the Child? In what ways do you think this Convention could help children whose situations may be different from yours? In what ways do you think it could hurt? If you were a parent, would you want the United States to ratify this Convention?

In the following selections, the United States Fund for UNICEF maintains that ratifying the Convention can only enhance the lives of children living in the United States. UNICEF believes that the rights of parents are maintained and that ratifying the Convention would reaffirm the United States' position as a worldwide leader in human rights protections. Catherina Hurlburt finds the motivation behind the Convention more suspect. It would, she believes, put children's needs and power above their parents' and enable governments to enact laws that would rescind inherent parental rights.

United Nations Convention on the Rights of the Child: Frequently Asked Questions

Q: What is the United Nations Convention on the Rights of the Child?

A: The Convention on the Rights of the Child (CRC), a human rights treaty adopted by the United Nations a decade ago, has been used by countries around the world to help promote the rights of children, strengthen government efforts to serve families, and build upon the efforts of non-governmental organizations (NGOs) on behalf of children. The Convention sets forth basic norms and standards which individual nations agree to pursue on behalf of their children.

Emphasizing the primacy and importance of the role and authority of parents, the treaty calls for governments to respect the responsibilities, rights and duties of parents to provide direction and guidance for the development of their children. In addition, it calls on governments to develop policies conducive to family and community environments that will allow children to grow up in an atmosphere of happiness, love, and understanding. The CRC's internationally recognized norms include:

- protection from violence, abuse, and abduction;
- protection from hazardous employment and exploitation;
- adequate nutrition;
- free compulsory primary education;
- adequate health care;
- equal treatment regardless of gender, race or cultural background;
- the right to express opinions and freedom of thought in matters affecting them;
- safe exposure/access to leisure, play, culture, and art.

Recognizing the special vulnerability of children and their need for guidance, all of these goals are expressed with respect to the child's age and maturity —the child's best interests are always the paramount concern.

Q: How has the Convention been used to help children?

The treaty is being used in a variety of ways around the world to help children. For example,

- In Rwanda, children have been moved out of adult detention centers where they had been held for alleged war offenses, and have been transferred to special juvenile institutions where they were allotted lawyers to defend them.
- In Belgium and Germany, laws inspired by the Convention extended the national jurisdiction in cases of child prostitution and pornography.
- In Romania, adoption laws were amended, magistrates were trained for juvenile delinquency and child abuse cases and reforms were made to the child protection system.
- In Sri Lanka, the parliament unanimously passed four bills to bring about sweeping changes in existing laws related to child abuse, child labor and adoption.
- In Vietnam, the Ministry of Justice is working with UNICEF and nongovernmental organizations to review the judicial process for juveniles, as well as to train judges, police, and other legal professionals on how to apply the Convention.
- El Salvador, Peru, and Bolivia have all enacted new justice codes for children.

Q: What is the Convention's status in the United States and globally?

The CRC is the most widely and rapidly ratified human rights treaty in history, with 191 participating nations. Only two countries, Somalia and the United States, have not ratified this celebrated agreement. However, since Somalia currently does not have the governmental capacity to ratify a treaty, the United States stands alone as the only remaining nation that can ratify the Convention.

Q: Why hasn't the United States ratified the Convention? What is holding it up?

The United States signed the Convention on the Rights of the Child in February 1995. The next step, consideration by the Senate Foreign Relations Committee, has been delayed due to procedural and political barriers. Procedurally, it is the general policy of the United States to thoroughly evaluate the constitutionality and potential impact of a treaty prior to giving its consent for ratification. Much like our own Constitution which requires judicial interpretation, the CRC also requires interpretation which necessitates this type of diligent analysis and examination.

Due, in part, to this lengthy review process, it can take several years for a treaty to be ratified, and if the treaty is controversial (or portrayed as controversial), it can become politicized—which often lengthens the process even more. For example, the Convention on the Prevention and Punishment of the Crime of Genocide took more than 30 years to be ratified in the United States, and the Convention on the Elimination of All Forms of Discrimination Against Women (CEDAW), which was signed by the United States 19 years ago, still has not been ratified. Moreover, the U. S. Government will typically consider only one human rights treaty at a time. . . .

In addition to the extensive analysis and lengthy ratification process, two factors have created obstacles to moving the CRC ahead expeditiously —widespread misconceptions about the Convention's intent, provisions, and potential impact; and political opposition. These factors have resulted in opposition to the treaty within the Senate and in some sectors of the public. Consequently, the Administration has not prioritized nor pursued ratification by forwarding the treaty to the Senate Foreign Relations Committee for consideration. In addition, the chairman of the Committee has indicated that he will refuse to consider the Convention.

Q: What are the most common claims made about the Convention by its opposition?

A small number of organizations have spearheaded the effort in opposition to U. S. ratification of the Convention on the Rights of the Child. Typically using a campaign of misrepresentations, these organizations have made a significant effort to minimize the treaty's value and to portray it as a threat to the American family. In general, the treaty's opponents base their opposition to the Convention largely on unsubstantiated claims regarding national sovereignty and interference in the parent-child relationship. The treaty's opposition claims that:

- the Convention would enable the United Nations to usurp national and state sovereignty;
- the Convention undermines parental authority;
- the Convention would allow and encourage children to sue parents, have abortions, etc.;
- the Convention would enable the United Nations to dictate how we raise and teach children.

These claims and perceptions are false and are likely the result of misconceptions, erroneous information, and a lack of understanding about how international human rights treaties are implemented in the United States. Notably, in many cases, the Convention's opponents criticize provisions which were added by the Reagan Administration during the drafting process in an effort to reflect the rights American citizens have under the U. S. Constitution.

Q: Does the Convention threaten our national sovereignty? Will the United Nations control our laws and children?

The Convention contains no language or mandates regarding how a country should implement the treaty. Therefore, each country determines how and when the treaty is to be implemented. Neither the United Nations nor the Committee on the Rights of the Child (the international body established to monitor the Convention) would have dominion, power, or enforcement authority over the United States or its citizens. Ultimately, the Convention obligates the federal government to make sure that the provisions of the treaty are fulfilled. There is no international enforcement mechanism.

Moreover, the Supreme Court has ruled that, under the Supremacy Clause of our Constitution, no treaty can "override" our Constitution (Reid v. Covert, 354 U.S. 1 (1957)). Furthermore, the United States has historically regarded treaties such as this Convention to be non-self-executing, which means that the text of a treaty itself does not directly become part of U. S. law. The Convention would only be implemented through domestic legislation, regulatory action, and judicial opinion.

Q: Does the Convention threaten a parent's authority or rights? Does it threaten the parent-child relationship?

The Convention repeatedly emphasizes the primacy and importance of the role and authority of the family. There is ample language throughout the Convention to support this....

For example, part of the Convention's preamble affirms "...the family, as the fundamental group of society and the natural environment for the growth and well-being of all its members and particularly children, should be afforded the necessary protection and assistance so that it can fully assume its responsibilities within the community; the child, for the full and harmonious development of his or her personality, should grow up in a family environment, in an atmosphere of happiness, love and understanding." The best evidence of this principle is found in article 5 which reads, "States Parties shall respect the responsibilities, rights and duties of parents or, where applicable, the members of the extended family...to provide, in a manner consistent with the evolving capacities of the child, appropriate direction and guidance in the exercise by the child of the rights recognized in the present Convention."...

Q: What does the Convention say on the issue of abortion?

In order to be utilized as an international agreement and to provide the needed flexibility to conform to the many cultures and legal systems of the world, the Convention on the Rights of the Child was designed to be adaptable. This requires a degree of neutrality in certain areas, one of which is the issue of abortion. This effort to keep the Convention "abortion neutral" has been reviewed by various legal experts and deemed feasible.

For the purposes of this treaty, the standard of when a child's life begins is determined by each nation which ratifies the Convention. The Holy See was one of the first states to ratify the Convention, and many countries, such as Ireland and the Philippines, which have strict abortion laws have also ratified the

Convention. Conversely, countries such as Sweden and France, which recognize their citizens' right to abortion, have ratified the Convention as well.

Q: What about capital punishment for minors?

Article 37 of the Convention on the Rights of the Child provides an explicit prohibition on the use of capital punishment for minors. In the United States, this standard conflicts with the constitutional right of individual states to execute those who are convicted of committing capital crimes while under the age of 18 (16 being the minimum).

This conflict was addressed in 1992 when the United States ratified the Covenant on Civil and Political Rights, which also has a prohibition on the execution of minors. To address this conflict, the Bush Administration chose to take a reservation on this specific issue, and the Senate gave its advice and consent to this reservation. This essentially means that the United States did not ratify this part of the treaty. A similar action would likely be taken while ratifying the children's convention.

Q: Why should the United States ratify the Convention on the Rights of the Child?

The United States has some of the best programs and laws in the world to protect its children. However, many U. S. children still face considerable adversity. Our children suffer from some of the highest rates of poverty, hunger and infant mortality in the industrialized world. Three American children die every day due to abuse and neglect, and nearly three quarters of all the murders of children in industrialized countries occur in the United States. More can to be done in order to safeguard our most physically, politically, and socially vulnerable citizens.

The Convention on the Rights of the Child has been used by governments and organizations around the world to improve the situation of children. In some countries, the treaty has facilitated direct changes in laws, policies and programs. In others, it has gone further and helped change the way governments and citizens view and prioritize children. Notably, the treaty itself does not directly create these changes, but the people and governments in each individual nation in a manner and timeframe determined by each sovereign government.

In the United States, the Convention would establish a useful framework and set clear goals by which officials at all levels of government, private organizations, and individuals can form domestic policies and programs addressing the specific needs of families and children in the United States. The reporting requirements of the treaty would compel our nation to re-evaluate the situation of children and develop action plans to make crucial improvements. Consequently, ratification of the Convention in concert with appropriate legislative measures would promote a more supportive social and legislative environment for families and would assist in making children more of a national priority.

In addition to the potential domestic benefits, U. S. ratification would help enhance America's role as an international leader in human rights by allowing the United States to participate in the international body set up to monitor the Convention, and by encouraging further progress in the countries which have already ratified the treaty.

The Convention offers a catalyst which will help fortify our national and international efforts to improve the lives of children and support the family environment.

 **NO**

U.N. Convention on the Rights of the Child: A Treaty to Undermine the Family

"Parents are the principal violators of our rights!"[1]

On November 20, 1989, the U.N. General Assembly adopted the *U.N. Convention on the Rights of the Child* (CRC). This document deems children (age 18 and under) as autonomous from their parents, who supposedly stamp out their "rights," and asserts the government is children's savior. Madeleine Albright, then-U.S. Ambassador to the United Nations, signed it nearly six years later on February 16, 1995. It awaits consideration by the U.S. Senate Foreign Relations Committee. If the CRC passes out of that committee, it will go before the full Senate for a final vote on ratification.

If ratified, the United States is obligated to uphold and enforce the *Convention*. Article VI of the United States Constitution states:

> This Constitution, and the Laws of the United States which shall be made in Pursuance thereof; and all Treaties made, or which shall be made, under the Authority of the United States, shall be the supreme Law of the Land; and the Judges in every State shall be bound thereby, any Thing in the Constitution or Laws of any State to the Contrary notwithstanding.

Clearly, the signing of treaties is a very serious matter. The U.S. Supreme Court has ruled treaties supersede federal and state laws. Because of a treaty's power, the Constitution requires ratification by two-thirds of the Senate, rather than just a simple majority.

The Clinton administration regarded the CRC quite favorably. Sen. Hillary Rodham Clinton (D-New York) is a former chairman of the Washington-based Children's Defense Fund, a liberal advocacy group, where she supported the *Convention*. The George W. Bush administration, however, has taken a strong pro-family stand at the United Nations. At the 2001 U.N. Special Session on Children, which touted the CRC, U.S. Ambassador E. Michael Southwick called for "emphasizing the vital role the family plays in the upbringing of children." Regarding the CRC, Ambassador Southwick stated, "As a non-party to the Convention, the United States does not accept obligations based on it, nor do we accept that it is the best or only framework for developing programs and policies to benefit children.... [W]e believe the text goes too far when it asserts entitlements based on the economic, social and cultural rights contained in the Convention and other instruments."[2] ...

With CRC supporters calling for ratification, citizens must be vigilant in urging their senators not to ratify this invasive treaty, lest we cede our parental rights—and children's well being—to a committee of foreign "experts."

The Committee on the Rights of the Child

Each nation that ratifies this treaty must submit to the authority of the Committee on the Rights of the Child. The Committee was created "for the purpose of examining the progress made by States Parties [nations] in achieving the realization of the obligations undertaken in the present Convention" (Article 43). In other words, it judges how well a ratifying nation is obeying the CRC.

The Committee consists of 10 "experts" in areas covered by the CRC, such as child development and education. Each signatory nation nominates one individual, then 10 are chosen from that group according to an "equitable geographical distribution" and variety of "principal legal systems" (Article 43). Therefore, an individual nation will never have a guaranteed voice on the committee. Members serve four-year terms and are eligible for re-election.

Article 43 also allows the Committee on the Rights of the Child to establish its own procedures. It normally meets annually to assess progress of nations that have ratified the CRC. Those countries must provide progress reports within two years of ratification, and every five years thereafter (Article 44). As Committee reports show, the language of the CRC is elastic—subject to interpretation according to the members' opinions....

The *Convention on the Rights of the Child* goes beyond simply safeguarding society for children. It delves into the personal affairs of the family, pitting children against parents, thus endangering their innocence and well being. It would make the government the national guardian of children, charged with determining "the best interests of the child" (Article 3), subject to U.N. interpretation. Yet the Committee's definition of a child's best interests is often very different from a parent's definition. Witness the following rulings.

Parental rights   The Preamble to the CRC upholds the family as the "fundamental group of society and the natural environment for the growth and well-being of... children." Article 5 urges "respect [for] the responsibilities, rights and duties of parents." But Article 12 establishes the child's "right to express [his or her own views] freely in all matters affecting the child." The Committee consistently usurps parental authority by viewing children as autonomous agents, capable of making adult decisions and dealing with adult situations. Its rulings stand in stark contrast to the traditional concept, upheld in America, that children are "minors" in need of parental protection.

Nevertheless, the CRC Committee insists on giving children autonomous decision-making power. For example, it called for Belize to create "an independent child-friendly mechanism... accessible to children to deal with complaints of violations of their rights and to provide remedies for such violations."[3] The Dominican Republic told the Committee it envisioned a "special police force ... to guarantee the freedom of opinion of children."[4]

Article 16 prohibits "arbitrary or unlawful interference with his or her privacy." The Committee called on Japan to introduce legislative measures to guarantee the child's right to privacy, "especially in the family, in schools, and in child-care institutions."[5] This provision could make parental consent laws for abortion illegal, endangering young girls' lives.

The CRC also usurps parental authority in the following areas.

Discipline

Article 19 calls upon countries "to protect the child from all forms of physical or mental violence ... while in the care of parent(s), legal guardian(s) or any other person who has the care of the child." It does not ban corporal punishment, or spanking. However the CRC Committee does. In its country reports, it called for legislation against spanking in Bolivia (para. 21), Luxembourg (para. 31), Austria (para. 256), Congo (para. 39), the United Kingdom,[6] Tanzania (para. 39), Bhutan,[7] Monaco (para. 27), and Turkey,[8] among others. But Denmark outlawed parents' right to use corporal punishment in 1997,[9] which the Committee praised.[10]

"Concerning corporal punishment," the Palau delegate reported to the Committee, "some parents complained that the Convention on the Rights of the Child was taking away their right to rear their children in a disciplined manner.... [P]arents were worried that if they used corporal punishment, they would be taken to court."[11] Experience in other nations justifies their apprehension. The Committee censured Canada twice (in 1995[12] and 2000) for legally permitting spanking.[13] In 2001, at the request of child-welfare officials, police in Ontario took seven children, ages 6 to 14, from their parents, who are Church of God members. The children screamed in protest as police dragged them away. Outside the courthouse, other young children held signs reading, "Anti-Abuse, Pro-Discipline," calling for the return of the seven children. They returned home a few weeks later, after their parents agreed not to spank while the case was before the courts.[14]

Clarifying the church's view of spanking, Rev. Henry Hildebrandt, the family's pastor, said Proverbs 13:24—"He that spareth his rod hateth his son" —is a direction to parents, but "it doesn't mean something that would bruise them."[15] When officials questioned more parents, 26 mothers and 74 children fled for the United States.[16] While not binding in law, the CRC carries significant weight on nations to modify their laws.

"Gender discrimination" and homosexuality   The CRC Committee urges nations to end so-called gender discrimination, which generally works out as favoring girls over boys and normalizing homosexuality as equivalent to heterosexuality. For example, in its report it said Bolivia's "use of biological criterion ... to set different ages of maturity [in policies] for boys and girls" was "gender-based discrimination" (para. 16). It also recommended that Austria re-think its age of sexual consent to ensure legislation is as conducive to girls' "rights" as it is to boys' (para. 16).

Further, leftists define gender as a social construct that can be changed through education and law, thus legitimizing homosexuality.[17] The Commit-tee's actions support this effort. In October 2000, the Committee said to the United Kingdom while it "notes the Isle of Man's intention to reduce the le-gal age for consent to homosexual relations from 21 to 18 years, it remains concerned about the disparity... between the ages of consent to heterosexual (16 years) and homosexual relations." Further, it recommended legislation to "prevent discrimination based on the grounds of sexual orientation."[18]...

Abortion   Paragraph 9 of the Preamble to the CRC recognizes "the child, by reason of his physical and mental immaturity, needs special safeguards and care, including appropriate legal protection, before as well as after birth." How-ever, the Committee has used Article 24's provision for "health care services" and "family planning education and services" to urge "reproductive health care and services" for adolescents in country reports for Maldives (para. 39), Japan (para. 21), Belize (para. 25), Congo (para. 55) and Bhutan (para. 44-45).

Further, the Committee demands reproductive services for children *with-out parental knowledge or consent*. It recommended Austria pass laws for "med-ical counseling and treatment without parental consent."[19] In Guatemala, the Committee urged that reproductive health include "confidential counseling, care and rehabilitation facilities that are accessible without parental consent."[20] It called for the same in Turkey.[21]

Nevertheless, CRC supporter Marian Wright Edelman, president of the Children's Defense Fund, mocks "opponents of the CRC [who] have made bizarre claims that it gives children an international legal right to abortion."[22]

But that claim is not bizarre. In fact, the Committee has questioned na-tions, such as Saudi Arabia and Latvia, about their abortion laws. Not long after its criticism of Guatemala, the U.N. Human Rights Committee demanded the country legalize abortion.[23] Moreover, this repetition of "reproductive rights, care and services" at U.N. conferences and in documents is a calculated cam-paign to legalize abortion-on-demand. Court documents from the pro-abortion Center for Reproductive Law and Policy (CRLP) reveal its strategy to estab-lish "customary law" through repetition of phrases like "reproductive health and rights" in international documents. Indeed, CRLP's lawsuit to overturn the "Mexico City Policy," which prohibits U.S. funding for overseas abortion pro-motion and provision, asserts "generally recognized international legal norms may, if endorsed and accepted by the vast majority of nations, become part of customary international law and thus binding on the United States even if it does not ratify or endorse those norms."[24]

Sex education   Article 13 provides the child's unlimited "right to freedom of expression; this right shall include freedom to seek, receive and impart infor-mation and ideas of all kinds, regardless of frontiers, either orally, in writing or in print, in the form of art, or through any other media of the child's choice."

Based on this provision, the Committee asked Lesotho if it had "succeeded in convincing the population on the need to have sexual education."[25] The Committee also said England violated Article 12 (child's right to express opinion) by allowing parents to withdraw their children from parts of sex education courses.[26]

Education   The American Bar Association determined that curriculum requirements in Article 29 of the CRC could make religious schools in the United States illegal.[27] Article 14 provides the right to "manifest one's religion or beliefs," and Article 30 gives children the right to "profess and practice his or her own religion." With the freedom of expression provisions, the CRC would give children the legal right to rebel against their parents about attending church or observing religious practices.

The Committee has called on governments to implement human rights education, especially the CRC, in school curricula. If governments follow this request, students will graduate indoctrinated with the "rights-based approach" notion—that they are entitled to have government provide for all their needs.

The Committee has mandated that governments ratify and implement the *Convention on the Elimination of All Forms of Discrimination Against Women*, or CEDAW, another dangerous treaty. It also urges governments to alter civil, criminal and penal codes to fall in line with the CRC. This usurps the U.S. republican form of government. Though the United Nations cannot enforce compliance through fines or jail, it does so through international pressure. Nicaragua provides a clear-cut example. Max Padilla was Nicaragua's Minister of the Family and delegate to the United Nations at past conferences. He promoted pro-family and pro-life values. Norway and other European nations did not like Padilla's advocacy and threatened to withhold aid if his government did not fire him. Hence, Padilla lost his position. Today, the organization Save the Children-Norway, a CRC sympathizer, has moved in to Nicaragua to "sensitize" its government officials to children's rights.[28]

Protect Children and Oppose the CRC

Other than Somalia, the United States is the only nation that has not ratified the CRC. The treaty's supporters argue that the United States should ratify it as a symbol of support for "human rights." Edelman claims its provisions are more "aspirational than mandatory."[29] However, the Committee's rulings and countries' subsequent actions show the opposite. Further, Edelman wrote, "We should lead, not lag the rest of the world in the care and protection of children."[30] However, not ratifying this dangerous treaty is an act of leadership. The United States provides more protection for children than any other nation. Consider those nations that have ratified the CRC and their horrible records on protecting children. The only thing that the CRC guarantees is a foothold for leftist organizations to separate children from families with moral or religious lifestyles.

The United States Constitution and current laws are sufficient to govern its people. This nation rests on the belief that civil government has a duty to protect man's *inalienable* rights. Indeed, our founding documents presuppose that rights are God-given. They are not created by our government—or the United Nations. The egregious crimes committed against children in other nations are not lawful here. Thus, there is no need to ratify a treaty that attempts to do what our existing laws have already accomplished.

Notes

1. A coalition of nongovernmental organizations (NGOs) has developed the "Say Yes" media campaign to publicize and garner support for the *U.N. Convention on the Rights of the Child* (CRC). A video presentation at the 2001 Special Session on children featured the Salvadoran youth who made the statement. The Special Session is a follow-up to the 1990 U.N. World Summit for Children, which followed the adoption of the CRC. CWA sent representatives to both conferences to advocate for the family and promote pro-life principles—in order to protect *all* children from the events' dangerous ideas.

2. Ambassador E. Michael Southwick, Deputy Assistant Secretary of State for International Organization Affairs, *Statement in the Preparatory Committee for the General Assembly Special Session on the Children's World Summit*, 1 February 2001 (http://www.un.int/usa/01_015.htm).

3. *Concluding Observations of the Committee on the Rights of the Child: Belize*, CRC/C/15/Add.99 (Geneva, Switzerland: Office of the United Nations High Commissioner for Human Rights, 10 May 1999), para. 11.

4. U.N. Office at Geneva press release, "Committee on Rights of Child Concludes Consideration of Report of Dominican Republic."

5. Japan, para. 36.

6. *Concluding Observations of the Committee on the Rights of the Child: United Kingdom of Great Britain and Northern Ireland*, CRC/C/15/Add.34 (Geneva, Switzerland: Office of the United Nations High Commissioner for Human Rights, 15 February 1995), para. 30–31.

7. *Concluding Observations of the Committee on the Rights of the Child: Bhutan*, CRC/C/15/Add.157 (Geneva, Switzerland: Office of the United Nations High Commissioner for Human Rights, 8 June 2001), para. 41.

8. *Concluding Observations of the Committee on the Rights of the Child: Turkey*, CRC/C/15/Add.152 (Geneva, Switzerland: Office of the United Nations High Commissioner for Human Rights, 8 June 2001), para. 48.

9. U.N. Office at Geneva press release, "Committee on Rights of Child Concludes Dialogue With Denmark on Compliance With Convention."

10. *Concluding Observations of the Committee on the Rights of the Child: Denmark*, CRC/C/15/Add.151 (Geneva, Switzerland: Office of the United Nations High Commissioner for Human Rights, 8 June 2001), para. 6.

11. U.N. Office at Geneva press release, "Committee on Rights of Child Completes Examination of Report of Palau," 23 January 2001.

12. *Concluding Observations of the Committee on the Rights of the Child: Canada*, CRC/C/15/Add.37 (Geneva, Switzerland: Office of the United Nations High Commissioner for Human Rights, 20 June 1995), para. 25.

13. Joe Woodard, "The U.N. Quietly Wages War on Religion," *The Calgary Herald*, 11 August 2001.

14. William Claiborne, "Canadians Flee in Spanking Dispute," *The Washington Post*, 2 August 2001, A3.

15. John Saunders, "Police remove seven children from their home," *The Globe and Mail,* 6 July 2001.

16. Jon Bricker, "100 flee after kids seized," *The National Post,* 16 July 2001.

17. Austin Ruse, "Radical Theorists and Policy Makers Promote Idea of 'Five Genders,'" Catholic Family & Human Rights Institute (C-Fam) *Friday Fax* 4, no. 18 (20 April 2001).

18. *Concluding Observations of the Committee on the Rights of the Child: United Kingdom of Great Britain and Northern Ireland (Isle of Man),* CRC/C/15/Add.134 (Geneva, Switzerland: Office of the United Nations High Commissioner for Human Rights, 16 October 2000), para. 22-23.

19. Austria, para. 15.

20. *Concluding Observations of the Committee on the Rights of the Child: Guatemala,* CRC/C/15/Add.154 (Geneva, Switzerland: Office of the United Nations High Commissioner for Human Rights, 8 June 2001), para. 45.

21. Turkey, para. 53–54.

22. Marian Wright Edelman, "Symposium: Should the Senate ratify the Convention on the Rights of the Child?", *Insight on the News,* 16 April 2001, 42.

23. Woodard.

24. Austin Ruse, "Federal Lawsuit Reveals Long-Time U.N. Strategy of Pro-Abortionists," C-Fam *Friday Fax* 4, no. 27 (22 June 2001).

25. U.N. Office at Geneva press release, "Committee on Rights of Child Concludes Review of Situation in Lesotho," 18 January 2001.

26. United Kingdom of Great Britain and Northern Ireland, para. 14.

27. Diane Sabom, "Symposium: Should the Senate ratify the Convention on the Rights of the Child?", *Insight on the News,* 16 April 2001, 41.

28. "Nicaragua: UNICEF-Backed Meeting to Educate Officials on Child Rights," *U.N. Wire,* 20 August 2001.

29. Edelman.

30. Ibid.

POSTSCRIPT

Should the Senate Ratify the Convention on the Rights of the Child?

It is striking to note that the United States is joined by Somalia as the only two countries that have not ratified the Convention on the Rights of the Child. Clearly, these countries' situations are significantly different and, very likely, any reasons for not ratifying are just as different. The U.S. State Department keeps tabs on the human rights violations of nearly 200 countries around the world receiving aid from the United States in the annual *Country Reports on Human Rights Practices.* At the same time, however, there is no report available on the United States itself. How do you think the United States is doing on human rights practices? If there were such a report, what do you think it would say?

A Convention on the Rights of the Child should, by its very definition, elicit widespread support. After all, who can argue with protecting children from abuse, neglect, and other horrors? Yet there is something about this Convention—indeed, in many of the U.S. government policies—that raises enough concerns with parents to incite fear and mistrust rather than presumed support. Many warn that it is imperative that we review this perceived separation between parents and state to see whether or not we might be able to do a more effective job of making children's safety and quality of life a priority without undue government intervention.

How do you think one could go about creating policies that would be embraced by both policymakers and parents? Do you think that one group should give in and offer priority to the other by virtue of whom they represent? What kinds of changes do you think would have to be made to the Convention in order to secure the additional support to sign on—if you think the United States should sign on at all?

Suggested Readings

Philip Alston, *Promoting Human Rights Through Bills of Rights: Comparative Perspectives* (Oxford University Press, 2000).

Sharon Detrick, *A Commentary on the United Nations Convention on the Rights of the Child* (Kluwer Law International, 1999).

Deirdre Frottell, *Revisiting Children's Rights—10 Years of the UN Convention on the Rights of the Child* (Kluwer Law International, 2001).

United Nations, *The Universal Declaration of Human Rights* (1948). Available online at http://www.unhchr.ch/udhr/lang/eng.htm.

ISSUE 10

Should Minors Be Required to Get Their Parents' Permission in Order to Obtain an Abortion?

YES: Teresa Stanton Collett, from Testimony Before the Subcommittee on the Constitution, Committee on the Judiciary, U.S. House of Representatives (September 6, 2001)

NO: Planned Parenthood Federation of America, Inc., from "Fact Sheet: Teenagers, Abortion, and Government Intrusion Laws," Planned Parenthood Federation of America, Inc., http://www.plannedparenthood.org/library/ABORTION/laws.html (August 1999)

ISSUE SUMMARY

YES: Teresa Stanton Collett, professor at South Texas College of Law, testifies in front of the U.S. House of Representatives in support of the federal Child Custody Protection Act. She advocates parental involvement in a minor's pregnancy, regardless of the girl's intention to carry or terminate the pregnancy. Parental involvement, Collett maintains, is not punitive; rather, it offers the girl herself additional protection against injury and sexual assault. Minors tend to have less access to information and education than adults; without this information and education, they are not able to provide truly "informed" consent, concludes Collett.

NO: Planned Parenthood Federation of America, Inc., the oldest and largest reproductive health organization in the United States, argues that parental notification and consent laws keep girls from exercising their legal right to access abortion. Notifying parents of their daughter's intent to terminate a pregnancy puts many girls at risk for severe punishment, expulsion from the home, or even physical violence. Planned Parenthood contends that, just as minors have the power to give their consent for other surgical procedures, they should be able to give their own consent to terminate a pregnancy.

In 1973 the United States Supreme Court decision *Roe v. Wade* guaranteed a woman's right to access abortion without restriction during the first trimester. The decision did not mention, however, the age of the woman seeking the abortion. A number of individual states, therefore, have statutes that require a girl under the age of 18 to either receive one or both parents' or legal guardians' consent in order to obtain an abortion, or to notify one or both parents.

A later Supreme Court decision, *Belotti v. Baird*, upheld the rights of states to place these restrictions on girls—provided there is an option for a "judicial bypass." This means that a girl can appear before a judge and either demonstrate that she is mature enough to make the decision to have an abortion or explain why notifying her parents would be detrimental to her. As the *Belotti* decision says, "[if] the court decides the minor is not mature enough to give informed consent, she must be given the opportunity to show that the abortion is in her best interest. If she makes this showing, the court must grant her bypass petition." Confidentiality is guaranteed, so that a girl's parents do not know that she has gone to court. Currently, 42 states have laws on their books about obtaining consent from or notifying at least one parent. Of these, 10 are currently not enforced. Thirty-eight states provide for a judicial bypass.

Any discussions around abortion rights are rooted in the fundamental support or opposition to abortion itself. It can be challenging, therefore, to separate out the question of abortion from the question of whether or not minors can make an informed decision. Even adults who consider themselves to be pro-choice may support an adult woman's right to choose whether to carry or terminate a pregnancy, while feeling differently about girls under the age of 18 being able to make this decision for themselves. Others are clear on their belief that abortion is wrong regardless of the circumstance or age of the girl or woman involved. And still others believe that any girl or woman, regardless of age, is able and has the right to make this personal decision for herself. Many encourage girls considering abortion to talk with their parent(s) or another trusted adult. However, the reality is that many girls know that doing so would create a significant conflict in their family setting.

Specific to the debate around parental notification is the issue of someone other than a parent facilitating an abortion for a girl under the age of 18. Supporters of parental notification laws believe that such legislation would prevent this from happening. Opponents agree that it would, and that it would be wrong to prosecute a family member for helping a niece or granddaughter under the age of 18 obtain an abortion.

In the following selections, Theresa Stanton Collett uses her knowledge of laws in different states to demonstrate what she feels is widespread support for parental involvement laws, focusing in particular on the Child Custody Protection Act. Planned Parenthood Federation of America, Inc., believes that since minors are able to access other medical care without parental consent, an abortion procedure should be no exception.

Prepared Testimony of
Teresa Stanton Collett

UNITED STATES HOUSE OF REPRESENTATIVES
Committee on the Judiciary
Subcommittee on the Constitution
Congressman Steve Chabot, Subcommittee Chair
September 6, 2001

... I am honored to have been invited to testify on H.R. 476, the "Child Custody Protection Act." ... My testimony represents my professional knowledge and opinion as a law professor who writes on the topic of family law, and specifically on the topic of parental involvement laws. It also represents my experience in assisting the legislative sponsors of the Texas Parental Notification Act during the legislative debates prior to passage of the act, and as a member of the Texas Supreme Court Subadvisory Committee charged with proposing court rules implementing the judicial bypass created by the Texas act....

It is my opinion that the Child Custody Protection Act will significantly advance the legitimate health and safety interests of young girls experiencing an unplanned pregnancy. It will also safeguard the ability of states to protect their minor citizens through the adoption of effective parental involvement statutes....

Parental Rights to Control Medical Care of Minors

Just this past year, in a case involving the competing claims of parents and grandparents to decisionmaking authority over a child, the United States Supreme Court described parents' right to control the care of their children

From U.S. House of Representatives. Committee on the Judiciary. Subcommittee on the Constitution. *H.R. 476, the "Child Custody Protection Act."* Hearing, September 6, 2001. Washington, DC: Government Printing Office, 2001. Notes omitted.

as "perhaps the oldest of the fundamental liberty interests recognized by this Court." In addressing the right of parents to direct the medical care of their children, the Court has stated:

> Our jurisprudence historically has reflected Western civilization concepts of the family as a unit with broad parental authority over minor children. Our cases have consistently followed that course; our constitutional system long ago rejected any notion that a child is "the mere creature of the State" and, on the contrary, asserted that parents generally "have the right, coupled with the high duty, to recognize and prepare [their children] for additional obligations." *Surely, this includes a "high duty" to recognize symptoms of illness and to seek and follow medical advice. The law's concept of the family rests on a presumption that parents possess what a child lacks in maturity, experience, and capacity for judgment required for making life's difficult decisions.*

It is this need to insure the availability of parental guidance and support that underlies the laws requiring a parent be notified or give consent prior to the performance of an abortion on his or her minor daughter. The national consensus in favor of this position is illustrated by the fact that there are parental involvement laws on the books in forty-three of the fifty states. Of the statutes in these forty-three states, eight have been determined to have state or federal constitutional infirmities. Therefore the laws of thirty-five states are in effect today. Nine of these states have laws that empower abortion providers to decide whether to involve parents or allow notice to or consent from people other than parents or legal guardians. These laws are substantially ineffectual in assuring parental involvement in a minor's decision to obtain an abortion. However, parents in the remaining twenty-six states are effectively guaranteed the right to parental notification or consent in most cases.

Widespread Public Support

There is widespread agreement that as a general rule, parents should be involved in their minor daughter's decision to terminate an unplanned pregnancy. This agreement even extends to young people, ages 18 to 24. To my knowledge, no organizations or individuals, whether abortion rights activists or pro-life advocates, dispute this point. On an issue as contentious and divisive as abortion, it is both remarkable and instructive that there is such firm and long-standing support for laws requiring parental involvement.

Various reasons underlie this broad and consistent support. As Justices O'Connor, Kennedy, and Souter observed in *Planned Parenthood v. Casey,* parental consent and notification laws related to abortions "are based on the quite reasonable assumption that minors will benefit from consultation with their parents and that children will often not realize that their parents have their best interests at heart." This reasoning led the Court to conclude that the Pennsylvania parental consent law was constitutional. Two of the benefits achieved by parental involvement laws include improved medical care for young girls seeking abortions and increased protection against sexual exploitation by adult men.

Improved Medical Care of Minors Seeking Abortions

Medical care for minors seeking abortions is improved by parental involvement in three ways. First, parental involvement laws allow parents to assist their daughter in the selection of a healthcare provider. As with all medical procedures, one of the most important guarantees of patient safety is the professional competence of those who perform the medical procedure or administer the medical treatment. In *Bellotti v. Baird,* the United States Supreme Court acknowledged the superior ability of parents to evaluate and select appropriate abortion providers.

For example, the National Abortion Federation recommends that patients seeking an abortion confirm that the abortion will be performed by a licensed physician in good standing with the state Board of Medical Examiners, and that he or she have admitting privileges at a local hospital not more than twenty minutes away from the location where the abortion is to occur. A well-informed parent seeking to guide her child is more likely to inquire regarding these matters than a panicky teen who just wants to no longer be pregnant.

Parental involvement laws also insure that parents have the opportunity to provide additional medical history and information to abortion providers prior to performance of the abortion.

> The medical, emotional, and psychological consequences of an abortion are serious and can be lasting; this is particularly so when the patient is immature. An adequate medical and psychological case history is important to the physician. Parents can provide medical and psychological data, refer the physician to other sources of medical history, such as family physicians, and authorize family physicians to give relevant data.

Abortion providers, in turn, will have the opportunity to disclose the medical risks of the various procedures to an adult who can advise the girl in giving her informed consent to the procedure ultimately selected. Parental notification or consent laws insure that the abortion providers inform a mature adult of the risks and benefits of the proposed treatment, after having received a more complete and thus more accurate medical history of the patient.

The third way in which parental involvement improves medical treatment of pregnant minors is by insuring that parents have adequate knowledge to recognize and respond to any post-abortion complication that may develop. In a recent ruling by a Florida intermediate appellate court upholding that state's parental involvement law, the court observed:

> The State proved that appropriate aftercare is critical in avoiding or responding to post-abortion complications. Abortion is ordinarily an invasive surgical procedure attended by many of the risks accompanying surgical procedures generally. If post-abortion nausea, tenderness, swelling, bleeding, or cramping persists or suddenly worsens, a minor (like an adult) may need medical attention. A guardian unaware that her ward or a parent unaware that his minor daughter has undergone an abortion will be at a serious disadvantage in caring for her if complications develop. An adult who has been kept in the dark cannot, moreover, assist the minor in following the

abortion provider's instructions for post-surgical care. Failure to follow such instructions can increase the risk of complications. As the plaintiffs' medical experts conceded, the risks are significant in the best of circumstances. While abortion is less risky than some surgical procedures, abortion complications can result in serious injury, infertility, and even death.

Abortion proponents often claim that abortion is one of the safest surgical procedures performed today. However, the actual rate of many complications is simply unknown. At least one American court has held that a perforated uterus is a "normal risk" associated with abortion. Untreated, a perforated uterus may result in an infection, complicated by fever, endometritis, and parametritis. "The risk of death from postabortion sepsis [infection] is highest for young women, those who are unmarried, and those who undergo procedures that do not directly evacuate the contents of the uterus.... A delay in treatment allows the infection to progress to bacteremia, pelvic abscess, septic pelvic thrombophlebitis, disseminated intravascular coagulophy, septic shock, renal failure, and death."

Without the knowledge that their daughter has had an abortion, parents are incapable of insuring that the minor obtain routine post-operative care or of providing an adequate medical history to physicians called upon to treat any complications the girl might experience.

Increased Protection From Sexual Assault

In addition to improving the medical care received by young girls dealing with an unplanned pregnancy, parental involvement laws are intended to afford increased protection against sexual exploitation of minors by adult men. National studies reveal that "[a]lmost two thirds of adolescent mothers have partners older than 20 years of age." In a study of over 46,000 pregnancies by school-age girls in California, researchers found that "71%, or over 33,000, were fathered by adult post-high-school men whose mean age was 22.6 years, an average of 5 years older than the mothers.... Even among junior high school mothers aged 15 or younger, most births are fathered by adult men 6-7 years their senior. *Men aged 25 or older father more births among California school-age girls than do boys under age 18.*" Other studies have found that most teenage pregnancies are the result of predatory practices by men who are substantially older.

Abortion providers have resisted any reporting obligation to insure that men who unlawfully impregnant minors are identified and prosecuted. Just [recently] a lawsuit was filed in Arizona alleging that Planned Parenthood failed to report the sexual molestation of a twelve-year-old leading to her continued molestation and impregnation. If true, this conduct is consistent with the position of many abortion providers who argue that encouraging medical care through insuring confidentiality is more important than insuring legal intervention to stop the sexual abuse. While seemingly well intentioned, this reasoning fails since the ultimate result of this approach is to merely address a symptom of the sexual abuse (the pregnancy) while leaving the cause unaffected. The minor, no longer pregnant, then returns to the abusive relationship, with no continuing contact with an adult (other than the abuser) knowing of her plight. The clinic won't tell, the police and parents don't know, and the girl, still under the abuser's influence, is too confused or afraid to tell. . . .

States adopting parental involvement laws have come to the reasonable conclusion that secret abortions do not advance the best interests of most minor girls. This is particularly reasonable in light of the fact that most teen pregnancies are the result of sexual relations with adult men, and many of these relationships involve criminal conduct. Parental involvement laws insure that parents have the opportunity to protect their daughters from those who would victimize their daughters again and again and again. The Child Custody Protection Act would insure that men cannot deprive these minors of this protection by merely crossing state lines.

Effectiveness of Judicial Bypass

In those few cases where it is not in the girl's best interest to disclose her pregnancy to her parents, state laws generally provide the pregnant minor the option of seeking a court determination that either involvement of the girl's parent is not in her best interest, or that she is sufficiently mature to make decisions regarding the continuation of her pregnancy. This is a requirement for parental consent laws under existing United States Supreme Court cases, and courts have been quick to overturn laws omitting adequate bypass.

Opponents of the Child Custody Protection Act have argued that its passage would endanger teens since parents may be abusive and many teens would seek illegal abortions. This is a phantom fear. Parental involvement laws are on the books in over two-thirds of the states, some for over twenty-years, and there is no case where it has been established that these laws led to parental abuse or to self-inflicted injury. Similarly, there is no evidence that these laws have led to an increase in illegal abortions.

It [is] often asserted that parental involvement laws do not increase the number of parents notified of their daughters' intentions to obtain abortions, since minors will commonly seek judicial bypass of the parental involvement requirement. Assessing the accuracy of this claim is difficult since parental notification or consent laws rarely impose reporting requirements regarding the use of judicial bypass. The Idaho parental consent law enacted in 2000 is one of the few exceptions to this general rule. Based upon the reporting required under that law, no abortions obtained by minors were pursuant to a judicial bypass. From September 1, 2000 through April 3, 2001, thirty-three minors have been reported as obtaining an abortion in Idaho. Thirty-one of these abortions were performed after obtaining parental consent. One minor was legally emancipated and did not need parental consent, and one report did not indicate the nature of the consent obtained prior to performance of the abortion.

Obtaining comparable information in states having parental involvement laws with no mandatory reporting requirement is difficult. State agencies will not accumulate such information absent a legislative mandate. Nonetheless, it is safe to say that the use of judicial bypass to avoid parental involvement varies significantly among the states. While commonly used in Massachusetts, judicial bypass is seldom used in many states. In 1999, 1,015 girls got abortions in Alabama with a parent's approval and 12 with a judge's approval, according to state health department records. Indiana also has few bypass proceedings according to an informal study. In Pennsylvania, approximately 13,700 minors obtained abortions from 1994 through 1999. Of these only about seven percent or 1,000 girls bypassed parental involvement via court order. Texas implemented its Parental Notification Act in 2000. During the state legislative hearings, the Texas Family Planning Council submitted a study indicating that a parent accompanied 69% of minors seeking abortions in Texas. After passage of the Texas Parental Notification Act, 96% of all minors seeking an abortion in Texas involved a parent.

Conclusion

By passage of the Child Custody Protection Act, Congress will protect the ability of the citizens in each state to determine the proper level of parental involvement in the lives of young girls facing an unplanned pregnancy.

Experience in states having parental involvement laws has shown that, when notified, parents and their daughters unite in a desire to resolve issues surrounding an unplanned pregnancy. If the minor chooses to terminate the pregnancy, parents can assist their daughters in selecting competent abortion providers, and abortion providers may receive more comprehensive medical histories of their parents. In these cases, the minors will more likely be encouraged to obtain post-operative check-ups, and parents will be prepared to respond to any complications that arise.

If the minor chooses to continue her pregnancy, involvement of her parents serves many of the same goals. Parents can provide or help obtain the necessary resources for early and comprehensive prenatal care. They can assist their daughters in evaluating the options of single parenthood, adoption, or early marriage. Perhaps most importantly, they can provide the love and support that is found in the many healthy families of the United States.

Regardless of whether the girl chooses to continue or terminate her pregnancy, parental involvement laws have proven desirable because they afford greater protection for the many girls who are pregnant due to sexual assault. By insuring that parents know of the pregnancy, it becomes much more likely that they will intervene to insure the protection of their daughters from future assaults.

In balancing the minor's right to privacy and her need for parental involvement, the majority of states have determined that parents should know before abortions are performed on minors. This is a reasonable conclusion and well within the states' police powers. However, the political authority of each state stops at its geographic boundaries. States need the assistance of the federal government to insure that the protection they wish to afford their children is not easily circumvented by strangers taking minors across state lines.

The Child Custody Protection Act has the unique virtue of building upon two of the few points of agreement in the national debate over abortion: the desirability of parental involvement in a minor's decisions about an unplanned pregnancy, and the need to protect the physical health and safety of the pregnant girl. I urge members of this committee to vote for its passage.

NO ↩

Teenagers, Abortion, and Government Intrusion Laws

O f all the abortion-related policy issues facing decision-makers in this country today, parental consent or notification before a minor may obtain an abortion is perhaps the most difficult. Few would deny that most teenagers, especially younger ones, would benefit from adult guidance when faced with an unwanted pregnancy. Few would deny that such guidance ideally should come from the teenager's parents. Unfortunately, we do not live in an ideal world.

In the 30 states with laws in effect that mandate the involvement of at least one parent in the abortion decision, teenagers who cannot tell their parents must either travel out of state or obtain approval from a judge—known as a "judicial bypass" procedure—to obtain an abortion. The result is almost always a delay that increases both the cost of the abortion and the physical and emotional health risk to the teenager, since an earlier abortion is a safer one (Paul, *et al.,* 1999).

Currently, anti-choice members of Congress are seeking to make it even more difficult for minors living in states with mandatory parental consent laws to obtain an abortion with the so-called "Child Custody Protection Act" (CCPA). The bill would make it a federal crime to transport a minor across state lines for an abortion unless the parental involvement requirements of her home state had been met. If the bill were enacted, persons convicted would be subject to imprisonment, fines, and civil suits (H. R. 1218, 1999; S. 661, 1999).

Requiring Parental Consent for Abortion Is Not Consistent With State Laws Regulating a Range of Medical Services for Minors

Parental involvement proponents contend that parents have a right to decide what medical services their minor children receive. However, states have long recognized that many minors have the capacity to consent to their own medical care and that, in certain critical areas such as mental health, drug and/ or alcohol addiction, and treatment for sexually transmitted infections (STIs) and pregnancy, entitlement to confidential care is a public health necessity (Donovan, 1998).

The informed consent of a patient, if competent, has always been a prerequisite to medical treatment. The common law assumed that a minor was not wise enough or mature enough to determine his or her medical needs and gave the right to consent to the parent or guardian. However, except in the area of abortion, there have never been criminal penalties for treating a minor on her own consent.

Various exceptions to the common law rule currently exist. In fact, many states have passed laws that protect providers from civil liability for providing care in specific areas. Implicit in the passage of these laws is the recognition that a minor can give an informed, competent consent. For example:

- Approximately 23 states and the District of Columbia grant minors the authority to consent to contraceptive services.
- Approximately 27 states and the District of Columbia authorize a pregnant minor to obtain prenatal care and delivery services without parental consent or notification.
- Forty-nine states and the District of Columbia give minors the authority to consent to the diagnosis and treatment of sexually transmitted infections. (Donovan, 1998)

Many of these laws allow minors to give consent to treatments that involve greater medical risk than a first-trimester abortion, such as surgical interventions during pregnancy and Caesarean sections. Nevertheless, many of these same states require parental consent for abortion.

Most Teenagers Having Abortions Already Involve Their Parents, Even When Not Required to Do So by Law

A minority of teenagers do not involve their parents. They make this decision because such involvement would not be in their best interests. A 1991 study of unmarried minors having abortions in states without parental involvement laws found that:

- Sixty-one percent of the respondents reported that at least one of their parents knew about their abortion.
- Of these minors who did not inform their parents of their abortions, 30 percent had histories of violence in their families, feared the occurrence of violence, or were afraid of being forced to leave their homes.
- Minors who did not tell their parents were also disproportionately older (aged 16 or 17), white, and employed.
- Among the respondents who did not inform their parents of their pregnancies, all consulted someone in addition to clinic staff about their abortions, such as their boyfriend (89 percent), an adult (52 percent), or a professional (22 percent). (Henshaw & Kost, 1992)

Some states go as far as to require the notification of both parents. These states ignore the realities of teenagers' lives.

- In 1998, approximately 19.8 million children under the age of 18 lived with only one parent (U. S. Census Bureau, 1998).
- In 1993, 31 percent of all births occurred out of wedlock. One study found that 20 percent of unmarried fathers had little to no contact with their children (Doherty *et al.,* 1998).
- An even greater number of children live with a single parent subsequent to divorce—6.6 million in 1994. A 1990 study found that one-third of divorced fathers had no contact with their children during the previous year (Doherty *et al.,* 1998).
- In Minnesota, more than one-quarter of the teenagers who sought judicial bypass were accompanied by one parent, who was most often divorced or separated. According to the federal district court that reviewed Minnesota's law, many of the custodial parents feared that notification would "bring the absent parent back into the family in an intrusive and abusive way" (*Hodgson v. Minnesota,* 1986).

Even if a teenager is able and willing to involve one or both parents, the procedures required by some state parental consent or notification laws make compliance impossible for some, if not most, teenagers.

- Requiring that teenagers either obtain notarized evidence that parents have been notified, or present a death certificate for a deceased parent may present impossible logistical barriers for a young teenager or cause serious delay.
- A requirement that the physician personally locate and notify the parents could easily both delay the procedure and increase the cost.

Parental Consent Laws Cause Dangerous Delays for Teens Seeking Abortion

Experience shows that most teenagers who feel they cannot involve their parents still manage to obtain confidential abortion services. Whether they travel to other states or obtain judicial approval, the results are the same: delays that can greatly increase both the physical and emotional health risks as well as the costs.

- The manner in which each state enforces its judicial bypass laws is erratic. In Minnesota, the federal district court found that the state courts "denied only an infinitesimal proportion of the petitions brought since 1981" (ACLU, 1986). A study in Massachusetts found that only nine of the 477 abortion requests studied had been denied (Yates & Pliner, 1988). However, a Ohio report found that the percentage of waivers denied ranged from 100 percent to 2 percent, depending on the county in which the petition was filed (Rollenhagen, 1992).

- While nationwide most minors seeking judicial approval receive it, the process is unwieldy and, most importantly, time-consuming. Court proceedings in Minnesota routinely delayed abortions by more than one week, and sometimes up to three weeks (ACLU, 1986).
- In Minnesota, the proportion of second-trimester abortions among minors terminating their pregnancies increased by 18 percent following enactment of a parental notification law. Likewise, since Missouri's parental consent law went into effect in 1985, the proportion of second-trimester abortions among minors increased from 19 percent in 1985 to 23 percent in 1988 (Donovan, 1992).

The Child Custody Protection Act Harms Children

In March 1999, the Child Custody Protection Act was reintroduced in the House of Representatives (H.R. 1218) and the Senate (S. 661). The bill would make it a federal crime to transport a minor across state lines to obtain abortion services without fulfilling the parental consent or notice requirements of her home state.... [T]he House of Representatives passed the bill by a vote of 276 to 150, but President Clinton threatened to veto it, and the Senate never took it up for consideration (Eilperin, 1999). On June 23, 1999, the House Judiciary Committee passed the CCPA, defeating five proposed amendments including those that would create exceptions for grandparents, siblings, aunts and uncles, and religious leaders who assist minors in obtaining abortions (Superville, 1999). On June 30, the legislation passed in the House of Representatives again, this time by a vote of 270 to 159—a differential not sufficient to override a presidential veto (Eilperin, 1999). Although, if passed, the Act would only affect a small percentage of women seeking abortion services—minors account for fewer than one in 10 abortions performed—the impact of the Act would be dramatic.

- The Child Custody Protection Act would subject to criminal penalties anyone—a grandparent, sibling, member of the clergy, or medical professional—who assists a minor in traveling across state lines to receive an abortion. Because 86 percent of U. S. counties lack an abortion provider (Henshaw, 1998), many minors cross state lines to obtain, from the nearest provider, basic abortion services they require. Whether the issue is convenience or avoidance of parental consent laws, however, the CCPA is designed to impede access to safe and legal abortion services by forcing a young woman to deal with a crisis pregnancy on her own, rather than seeking the support of a trusted friend or family member.
- Because the Act would impose fines, imprisonment, and/or civil suits on those found in violation of it, it would deter responsible, caring adults from assisting a minor out of fear of prosecution.

- The CCPA also raises a number of constitutional and legal questions, particularly those related to issues of federalism. The legislation effectively requires the federal government to take sides on policies that are made by individual states—policies on which states are diametrically opposed. Such action on behalf of the federal government would be unprecedented, and raises serious implications for states' rights. (Saul, 1998)

References

ACLU—American Civil Liberties Union Foundation Reproductive Freedom Project. (1986). *Parental Consent Laws: Their Catastrophic Impact on Teenagers' Right to Abortion.* New York: ACLU.

Child Custody Protection Act, H. R. 1218, 106th Cong., 1st Sess. (1999).

———, S. 661, 106th Cong., 1st Sess. (1999).

Doherty, William J., *et al.* (1998). "Responsible Fathering: An Overview and Conceptual Framework." *Journal of Marriage and the Family,* 60(2): 277–292.

Donovan, Patricia. (1992). *Our Daughters' Decisions: The Conflict in State Law on Abortion and Other Issues.* New York: Alan Guttmacher Institute.

———. (1998). "Teenagers' Right to Consent to Reproductive Health Care." *Issues in Brief.* Washington, DC: Alan Guttmacher Institute.

Eilperin, Juliet. (1999, July 1). "House Acts to Bar Interstate Transport of Teens to Evade Abortion Laws." *Washington Post,* p. A06.

Henshaw, Stanley K. (1998). "Abortion Incidence and Services in the United States, 1995–1996." *Family Planning Perspectives,* 30 (6): 263–270 & 287.

Henshaw, Stanley K. & Kathryn Kost. (1992). "Parental Involvement in Minors' Abortion Decisions." *Family Planning Perspectives,* 24(5): 196–207 & 213.

Hodgson v. Minnesota, 648 F. Supp. 756 (D. Minn. 1986).

Makinson, Carolyn. (1985). "The Health Consequences of Teenage Fertility." *Family Planning Perspectives,* 17(3): 132–139.

Paul, Maureen, *et al.* (1999). *A Clinician's Guide to Medical and Surgical Abortion.* New York: Churchill Livingstone.

Rollenhagen, Mark. (1992, June 18). "Clinics Fight Notification Rule By Filing Suit." *Plain Dealer,* p. 1C.

Saul, Rebekah. (1998). "The Child Custody Protection Act: A 'Minor' Issue at the Top of the Anti-Abortion Agenda." *Guttmacher Report on Public Policy,* 1(4): 1–2 & 7.

Superville, Darlene. (1999, June 23, accessed 1999, July 1). "Teen Abortion Bill Clears House Committee." *Associated Press* [Online].

U. S. Census Bureau. (1998). "Marital Status and Living Arrangements: March 1998." *Current Population Reports,* Series P-20, No. 433.

Yates, Suzanne & Anita J. Pliner. (1988). "Judging Maturity in the Courts: The Massachusetts Consent Statute." *American Journal of Public Health,* 78(6): 646–649.

POSTSCRIPT

Should Minors Be Required to Get Their Parents' Permission in Order to Obtain an Abortion?

The abortion debate, like many other controversies, is often viewed in extremes. One is pro-choice, or one is antichoice. There is no gray area in between. At the same time, however, introducing a minor into the discussion often alters the discussion—particularly the younger the girl is who is seeking the abortion. In some cases, the younger a girl is, the more protection adults may feel she needs. In other cases, the younger she is, the more likely some abortion opponents might be to make an exception, citing a preference for the "necessary evil" of abortion over letting a 14-year-old girl become a parent.

An important factor to keep in mind is the fact that not everyone has sexual intercourse by choice. While many abortion opponents will make an exception for pregnancies that are caused by rape or incest, others maintain that a pregnancy is a pregnancy and that no potential life should be punished even if it were conceived in a violent manner. If a state law requires that a parent be notified, and the parent who is notified is the one who caused the pregnancy, then parental notification may have stopped an abortion only to put a girl's safety or life in jeopardy. On the other hand, in cases of incest, parental notification could help to bring rape or incest—which are all too frequently hidden or kept private—out into the open so that it will not happen again, and the perpetrator, if known, can be arrested and the abuse stopped.

Legislating personal decisions is, as always, a slippery slope. How far do we go? How do laws legislating one behavior or type of procedure affect others? For example, parental consent is currently not required in order for a minor to obtain birth control. Controversy remains around one particular type of birth control, Emergency Contraception, formerly known as the "morning-after" pill. Emergency Contraception is not an abortion; it prevents pregnancy from happening. In fact, if a woman is pregnant without knowing it, has unprotected intercourse, and then takes Emergency Contraception, her pregnancy should not be affected by the Emergency Contraception. At the same time, however, since one of the ways in which Emergency Contraception works is by preventing a fertilized egg from implanting, those who believe that life begins at conception argue that Emergency Contraception is the same thing as abortion. Therefore, the door that is open to parental notification and consent laws remains open to support for parental notification or consent before Emergency Contraception can be dispensed. This in turn could lead to legislation requiring parental notification or consent for birth control pills and condoms.

In an ideal world, people would not have sex before they are old enough and established enough in their lives to be able to manage the potential consequences of being in a sexual relationship. In an ideal world, abortion would not be necessary because no pregnancy would be unplanned or come as the result of rape or incest. However, we do not live in an ideal world. People, regardless of age, have unprotected sex or use contraception incorrectly. People, regardless of age, are raped and sexually abused. Women, regardless of age, have pregnancies that may need to be terminated for medical reasons. In some households, the revelation of an unplanned pregnancy can result in violence against the pregnant teen and/or her partner.

Is there a solution between these two extremes that could enable parents to show their care and support of their adolescents while at the same time letting them make their own decisions? Where do your feelings about abortion in general come into play in your thoughts on this matter?

Suggested Readings

American Civil Liberties Union, *Parental Involvement Laws*. Fact sheet available online at http://www.aclu.org/issues/reproduct/parent_inv.html.

Focus on the Family, "Talking Points for Laws Requiring Parental Involvement in Minor Abortions," *Citizen Link* (2000). Available online at http://www.family.org/cforum/research/papers/a0012619.html.

David J. Garrow, *Liberty and Sexuality: The Right to Privacy and the Making of Roe v. Wade* (University of California Press, 1998).

Deborah Haas-Wilson, "The Impact of State Abortion Restrictions on Minors' Demand for Abortions," *Journal of Human Resources* (vol. 31, no. 1, January 1999).

N. E. H. Hull and Peter Charles Hoffer, *Roe v. Wade: The Abortion Rights Controversy in American History* (University Press of Kansas, 2001).

NARAL, *Government-Mandated Parental Involvement in Family Planning Services Threatens Young People's Health*. Fact sheet available online at http://www.naral.org/mediaresources/fact/parental.html.

Annette Tomal, "Parental Involvement Laws and Minor and Non-Minor Teen Abortion and Birth Rates," *Journal of Family and Economic Issues* (vol. 20, no. 2, Summer 1999).

Parents, Families and Friends of Lesbians and Gays (PFLAG)

Parents, Families and Friends of Lesbians and Gays (PFLAG) promotes the health and well-being of gay, lesbian, bisexual, and transgender individuals, and their families and friends.

http://www.pflag.org

Focus on the Family

The mission of Focus on the Family is "to cooperate with the Holy Spirit in disseminating the Gospel of Jesus Christ to as many people as possible, and, specifically, to accomplish that objective by helping to preserve traditional values and the institution of the family."

http://www.family.org

The National Gay and Lesbian Task Force

The National Gay and Lesbian Task Force is a national, nonprofit organization working for the civil rights of gay, lesbian, bisexual, and transgender people, with the vision and commitment to building a powerful political movement.

http://www.ngltf.org

Lambda Legal

Lambda Legal is a national organization committed to achieving full recognition of the civil rights of lesbian, gay, bisexual, and transgender individuals, as well as people living with HIV or AIDS, through impact litigation, education, and public policy work.

http://www.lambdalegal.org

PART 4

Lesbian and Gay Families

*N*ot too long ago, the words lesbian *and* gay *appearing in front of the word* families *would have been considered oxymoronic. For some people, it still does. Others see diverse family structures as social progress. There are a number of issues that remain in the news today relating specifically to the rights of lesbian and gay individuals to have legal and social recognition in the context of family and relationships. This part examines two of these questions.*

- Should Same-Sex Couples Be Allowed to Marry Legally?

- Should Lesbian and Gay Couples Be Allowed to Adopt?

ISSUE 11

Should Same-Sex Couples Be Allowed to Marry Legally?

YES: Lambda Legal Defense and Education Fund, from "Talking About the Freedom to Marry: Why Same-Sex Couples Should Have Equality in Marriage," Lambda Legal Defense and Education Fund, `http://www.lambdalegal.org/cgi-bin/iowa/documents/record?record=47` (June 20, 2001)

NO: Robert P. George, from "The 28th Amendment: It Is Time to Protect Marriage, and Democracy, in America," *National Review* (July 23, 2001)

ISSUE SUMMARY

YES: The Lambda Legal Defense and Education Fund, a national civil rights organization for lesbian, gay, bisexual, and transgender individuals, as well as people living with HIV or AIDS, supports the right of two individuals to marry legally, regardless of the genders of the two people involved. The organization states that same-sex couples deserve the same social, legal, and financial benefits that heterosexual couples have.

NO: Princeton University professor Robert P. George asserts that marriage has historically been, and ever should be, between a man and a woman. He argues that recognizing a same-sex union as a legal marriage would destroy the institution of marriage as it has always been known, taking with it the moral values supporting marriage. A constitutional amendment is, in George's opinion, the only sure way of protecting the institution of heterosexual marriage.

Depending on the poll or survey, more than half of people living in the United States are thought to be supportive of—or at the very least, not against— gay rights. Many believe that any person should have the same rights as anyone else, regardless of their race, age, gender—or sexual orientation. When this discussion moves into the arena of same-sex marriage, however, those beliefs start to waiver a bit.

Currently, no state in the United States allows for same-sex marriage. A challenge to the Hawaii State Constitution, maintaining that marriage laws were discriminatory, failed. A similar effort failed in Alaska. Vermont became the first state to make civil unions legal between two people of the same sex. Although a same-sex couple cannot have a marriage license or refer to their union as a marriage, the benefits are the same as they would be for a heterosexual marriage.

When the law passed in 2000, hundreds of couples went to Vermont in order to have civil unions. However, once they left Vermont, their union was—from a legal standpoint—null and void. This is due in great part to the Defense of Marriage Act, which was signed into law in 1996 by then-President Bill Clinton. This act says that no state is required to recognize a same-sex union, and it defines marriage as being between a man and a woman only. In anticipation of efforts to have state recognition of civil unions, over 30 states have passed legislation saying that they would not recognize a same-sex union that took place in another state.

An alliance of conservative groups is currently campaigning for a 28th amendment to the U.S. Constitution, which would prevent same-sex couples from getting married legally. The proposed Federal Marriage Amendment reads, in part, "Marriage in the United States shall consist only of the union of a man and a woman. Neither this Constitution or the constitution of any state, nor state or federal law, shall be construed to require that marital status or the legal incidents thereof be conferred upon unmarried couples or groups."

Supporters of the amendment believe that marriage is a moral institution—and that at the heart of this morality is heterosexuality. They argue that among the goals of marriage is procreation; therefore, it should be entered into by two reproductively compatible individuals. Others believe that homosexuality is wrong and that recognizing same-sex marriage validates homosexuality. Still other supporters of the amendment may believe that same-sex couples should be able to unite but not call it "marriage."

Opponents to the amendment believe that this amendment violates the human rights of lesbian, gay, and bisexual individuals. If same-sex couples work, pay taxes, enter into lifetime commitments, and raise children, why should they not be afforded the same social and legal benefits and status as heterosexual couples?

Do you think that the government has a right to dictate who we can and cannot marry? Should lesbian and gay couples be grateful for what they do have in many states—domestic partner benefits at work, antidiscrimination laws relating to housing and hiring, and more—and let the marriage argument go? Would having this type of amendment open the door for other marriage restrictions, such as marriage between two people of very different ages, religions, or races?

In the following selections, the Lambda Legal Defense and Education Fund states that same-sex marriage would be no threat to heterosexual marriage and that a constitutional amendment would be discriminatory. Robert P. George staunchly defends the institution of heterosexual marriage and supports the amendment as a safety net for traditional values and for what he feels is the only appropriate context for marriage.

Talking About the Freedom to Marry:
Why Same-Sex Couples Should Have
Equality in Marriage

T oday, same-sex couples are not allowed to marry in any state—no matter how long they have been together, no matter how committed they are to their relationship or their children, no matter how much they have already assumed the same responsibilities as different-sex married couples, and no matter how much their families need the protections and benefits that come with civil marriage.

Same-sex couples want the right to marry for the same reasons different-sex couples do.

Same-sex couples want to get married for the same variety of reasons as any other couple: they seek the security and protection that come from a legal union both for themselves and for any children they may have; they want the recognition from family, friends and the outside world that comes with a marriage; and they seek the structure and support for their emotional and economic bonds that a marriage provides. All gay people, whether in a relationship today or not, whether they would choose marriage or not, deserve to have the same choice that all heterosexuals have.

The government should fully recognize same-sex couples as it does different-sex couples.

Marriage is a civil right that belongs to everyone. Loving, committed same-sex couples form families and provide emotional and economic support for each other and for their children just like other couples do. When different-sex couples apply for a marriage license, the state does not ask them whether their relationship is worthy of its recognition, because the government has no business deciding whom a person should marry. That is a completely private, personal choice that every individual has the right to make for him or herself—a basic principle that should be as true for same-sex couples as for other couples.

This inequality in access to marriage should end, just as our nation has abolished prior discriminatory exclusions.

This is not the first instance of unlawful governmental interference with the freedom to marry. Less than forty years ago, many states prohibited interracial couples from legally marrying. In *Loving v. Virginia,* a married interracial couple was arrested in Virginia and faced up to five years in prison. The state court upheld their conviction because it found interracial relationships to be "unnatural":

> "Almighty God created the races white, black, yellow, malay and red, and he placed them on separate continents. And but for the interference with his arrangement there would be no cause for such marriages. The fact that he separated the races shows that he did not intend for the races to mix."

Similar arguments are used against recognizing same-sex relationships today. But the U.S. Supreme Court held in its 1967 decision in the case that restricting marriage to same-race couples was unlawful discrimination. The government's restriction of marriage to different-sex couples is discriminatory as well. The choice of a marriage partner belongs to each individual, not to the state.

Responses to Some Possible Concerns and Comments

"Tradition" is not a reason to deny marriage to same-sex couples.

Marriage was "traditionally" defined as a union of two people of the same religion or the same race, or one in which wives were the property of their husbands. Those "traditional" elements of marriage changed to reflect this nation's core principles of equality for all people. Marriage should be defined to include the committed relationships of same-sex couples as well.

Raising children is one of many reasons for marriage, and same-sex couples do raise children.

Marriage is not only about procreation—many people marry who cannot have or choose not to have children. Marriage is about love between two adults who want to live in a committed relationship, with or without children. The state extends the same marital protections to couples who are infertile or couples who are past childbearing age that it extends to couples intending to have multiple children. It is also a fact that more and more lesbian and gay couples are raising children together. Marriage would create automatic protections for these children that now may have to be created through adoption or elaborate legal documents.

The right to a civil marriage is not a right to a religious ceremony.

Couples who wish legal recognition for their marriage must first get a license issued by the government and then have an authorized person marry them. This is a civil marriage. Depending on the state, the person who marries the couple may be a government official (such as a justice of the peace or city hall official) or an otherwise authorized individual (such as some clergy). But if the couple asks a clergyperson to marry them, that clergyperson can always say no, meaning that the couple would have to ask some other authorized person.

- Religious groups retain the right to marry or not to marry couples, as they wish, according to their religious principles.
- Though many faiths do perform marriage ceremonies for same-sex couples, at present these marriages have no legal recognition because they have not been licensed by the government, and thus are not civil marriages.
- Religions should not dictate who gets a marriage license from the state, just as the state should not dictate which marriage any religion performs or recognizes.

For those couples desiring the full structure and status of marriage, domestic partner benefits are inadequate.

In certain cities, states or companies, there is limited recognition of relationships between unmarried partners, often including both different-sex couples and same-sex couples. As domestic partners, couples may gain access to health care coverage and certain other basic family benefits. But many couples wish to structure their families around a broader set of rights and responsibilities. For these couples, domestic partnership is no substitute for civil marriage.

Civil unions are an important step forward, but separate is still unequal.

Vermont offers "civil unions" to same-sex couples. Civil unions provide a set of rights and responsibilities within Vermont that parallels marriage. This is an important step forward. It is not marriage, however, and its implications beyond Vermont have yet to be determined by the courts. It is a separate and unequal institution, setting same-sex couples apart for second-class citizenship in the eyes of others, which will carry over into how such couples are treated in other areas of their lives. Having the choice to marry is full equality. A separate, gay-only institution is not.

The sky will not fall because of equality for same-sex couples.

When opponents are desperate for arguments, they resort to familiar "the sky will fall" claims, such as the argument that allowing same-sex couples to marry could be followed by demands to legalize polygamy. This is a scare tactic, not an argument. Same-sex *couples* want the freedom to marry that is currently taken for granted by different-sex *couples*. The issue is about legal recognition for *couples*.

Allowing same-sex couples to marry does not destabilize marriage.

Allowing all families access to marriage, if they believe the structures and protections of marriage are appropriate for them, promotes stability for communities overall. Same-sex couples build their lives together like other couples, working hard at their jobs, volunteering in their neighborhoods, and valuing the responsibilities and love that their family commitments provide to them and to the children they may have. These families have everyday concerns, like being financially sound, emotionally and physically healthy, and protected by adequate health insurance. These concerns heighten when there are children in the family. Marriage provides tangible protections that address many of these concerns. Promotion of support and security for families is a benefit to the entire community; it does not de-stabilize other families. Equal access to marriage will also emphasize equality and non-discrimination for all of society.

Robert P. George

 **NO**

The 28th Amendment: It Is Time to Protect Marriage, and Democracy, in America

Marriage is so central to the well-being of children—and society as a whole —that it was, until recently, difficult to imagine that it might be necessary to mount a national political campaign to protect the institution from radical redefinition. Yet today it can scarcely be denied that such a campaign is needed.

Everybody knows that marriage is in trouble. The rise of divorce, illegitimacy, and cohabitation have all taken a toll. If the institution of marriage in our society is to be restored to good health, a reversal of trends and tendencies in all of these areas is required. Still, there is something unique in the threat posed by the movement for "same-sex marriage."

At the core of the traditional understanding of marriage in our society is a *principled* commitment to monogamy and fidelity. Marriage, as embodied in our customs, laws, and public policies, is intelligible and defensible as a one-flesh union whose character and value give a man and a woman *moral reasons* (going beyond mere subjective preferences or sentimental motivations) to pledge sexual exclusivity, fidelity, and permanence of commitment. Yet any argument for revising our law to treat homosexual relations as marital will implicitly do what clearheaded and honest proponents of "same-sex marriage" explicitly acknowledge: It will deny that there are such moral reasons. Any such argument would have to treat marriage as a purely private matter designed solely to satisfy the desires of the "married" parties. If that is the case, there is no principled reason marriage need imply exclusivity, fidelity, permanence, or even a limit of two people.

Thoughtful people *on both sides of the debate* recognize this. It is evident, then, that legal recognition of same-sex marriages, far from making marriage more widely available (as well-intentioned but misguided conservative advocates of same-sex marriage say they want to do), would in effect abolish the institution, by collapsing the moral principles at its foundation.

So while it is true, as Bill Bennett among others has acknowledged, that marriage in the past 35 years or so has been damaged more severely by heterosexual immorality and irresponsibility than by homosexual activism, it is also true that same-sex marriage, were it to be instituted, would strike a blow against the institution more fundamental and definitive even than the disastrous policy of "no-fault" divorce.

What can be done?

It is noteworthy that proponents of same-sex marriage have sought to change public policy through judicial decree. Where they have won, they have won through the courts. Where the issue has been settled in the court of public opinion, they have lost. The lesson is clear: If the institution of marriage is to be preserved, a campaign to settle the issue democratically at the national level must be mounted—and quickly.

At the time the U.S. Constitution was adopted, it was taken for granted that marriage is the union of a man and a women ordered to the rearing of children in circumstances conducive to moral uprightness. Its legal incidents and civil effects were part of the common law and regulated by the states. There was no need at the time for marriage to be expressly defined or protected by federal law or the Constitution. Consequently, the word "marriage" does not appear in the Constitution (nor, for that matter, does the word "family"). Our forefathers shared the consensus of humanity, which viewed marriage as a union between sexually complementary persons—that is, persons of opposite sexes. The common law that we inherited from England was clear about marriage as the union of man and woman: "Marriage . . . includes the reciprocal duties of husband and wife."

Only in the last decade has our country's time-honored recognition that marriage is, in its very essence, the union of male and female come under attack in the courts. In the earliest phase of this campaign, activists tried to establish a right of marriage for same-sex partners through lawsuits in state courts premised on state constitutional guarantees. The strategy was to get some state supreme court to recognize same-sex marriage. Other states would then be compelled to recognize these "marriages," because of the constitutional requirement that states extend "Full Faith and Credit" to one another's "public Acts, Records, and judicial Proceedings."

The supreme court of Hawaii, purporting to interpret the state constitution, went so far as to hold in 1993 that the state's marriage law "discriminated on the basis of sex." A lower court acting on its instructions then found the marriage law unconstitutional—but stayed its order pending appeal. In the end, though, the courts did not get the final say. In 1998, the people of Hawaii, by a very substantial majority (69 to 31 percent), enacted a state constitutional amendment affirming the heterosexual character of marriage. Hawaii's same-sex marriage case had to be dismissed.

Undaunted, attorneys for homosexual activist groups continued to press the issue in other venues. In Alaska, a trial judge read that state's constitution to include a fundamental right to "choose a life partner." Again, the voters responded by backing a constitutional amendment defining marriage as the union of a man and a woman—by 68 to 32 percent. Other states, such as California, passed similar amendments by wide margins without even facing an immediate legal threat.

Having been stopped by the democratic process in Hawaii and Alaska, homosexual activists decided to press their legal case in a state where it is very difficult for voters to amend the state constitution: Vermont. On December 20, 1999, the Vermont supreme court decided that the Vermont constitution requires the state either to grant marriage licenses to same-sex couples or to give them all of the benefits of marriage. The Vermont legislature chose the latter response to this judicial dictate: It passed, and the governor signed, a "civil unions" law that amounts to same-sex marriage in all but name.

The Vermont law, which took effect on July 1, 2000, contained no residency requirements for entering into a civil union. In the first six months, over 1,500 couples entered into civil unions. Only 338 involved at least one Vermont resident. The vast majority of Vermont civil unions, then, have been entered into by non-Vermont couples. Some of them will surely file suit in their home states to demand legal recognition of their Vermont status.

There is still an obstacle in the activists' path. The U.S. Constitution explicitly gives Congress the authority to make exceptions to the Full Faith and Credit Clause. So in 1996, Congress passed (and President Clinton signed, albeit reluctantly and without fanfare) the Defense of Marriage Act. That legislation defines marriage for purposes of federal law as the union of a man and a woman, and says that no state is required to recognize another state's same-sex marriages (though it does not forbid states to create same-sex marriages or recognize out-of-state same-sex marriages or civil unions). Subsequently, 34 states have enacted laws that deny recognition to same-sex marriages granted out of state.

But activists are putting forward a number of theories to persuade judges to declare the Defense of Marriage Act, and the state acts, unconstitutional. They may well succeed. The same year the Defense of Marriage Act was passed, the U.S. Supreme Court handed down *Romer v. Evans.* The case concerned a Colorado constitutional amendment forbidding the state government or localities to pass "gay rights" laws. The Court concluded that the amendment could be explained only on the basis of irrational "animus" toward homosexuals. The Defense of Marriage Act could surely be characterized the same way by socially liberal federal judges.

There is also the prospect of same-sex marriage migrating from abroad. On April 1, 2001, the Netherlands became the first country in the world to recognize same-sex marriage as such. The law requires only one of the parties to be a resident of the Netherlands. Ordinarily, a marriage validly entered into anywhere is valid everywhere. Our country has a public-policy exception to this rule, which allows states with a policy against same-sex marriage to decline to recognize it; but this exception may not cover states that—like Massachusetts —haven't enacted explicit bans on the importation of same-sex marriage. In addition, given the current culture of the American legal profession, there is good reason to expect that many American judges will eventually reason their way around the public-policy exception in favor of the legal arguments crafted for them by activist attorneys and other supporters of same-sex marriage.

The momentum of the movement to redefine and, in effect, abolish marriage has brought America to a crossroads. Evan Wolfson, former head of the marriage project at the Lambda Legal Defense and Education Fund, says he will file more lawsuits: "We have it within our reach to marry within five years." The judicial assault on marriage is accelerating and encompassing every dimension of our legal system—state, federal, and international law.

Time to Amend

The only sure safeguard against this assault is to use the ultimate democratic tool available to the American people: a constitutional amendment. Pro-marriage activists are inclined to back an amendment that would read: "Marriage in the United States shall consist only of the union of a man and a woman. Neither this constitution or the constitution of any state, nor state or federal law, shall be construed to require that marital status or the legal incidents thereof be conferred upon unmarried couples or groups."

The first sentence simply states that marriage anywhere in the United States consists only of male-female couples. This would prevent any state from introducing same-sex marriage by, for example, recognizing a Dutch same-sex marriage. The name and substance of "marriage" is reserved to husband and wife alone.

The second sentence seeks to prevent the judicial abuse of statutory or constitutional law to force the extension of marriage to include non-marital relationships. The word "construed" indicates that the intention is to preclude a judge or executive-branch official from inferring a requirement of same-sex marriage, or something similar, from a state or federal law.

The expression "legal incidents" is intended to convey the consequences "either usually or naturally and inseparably" dependent upon marriage. The Supreme Court has called "incidents of marriage" those "government benefits (e.g., Social Security benefits), property rights (e.g., tenancy by the entirety, inheritance rights), and other, less tangible benefits (e.g., legitimization of children born out of wedlock)" that follow upon marital status. Another example would be the marital privilege against being forced to testify against one's spouse.

The amendment would not prevent private corporations from treating same-sex couples as married couples for purposes of health-care benefits, nor the extension of hospital visitation privileges to same-sex partners. If a benefit is not made to depend on marriage, it can be applied more generally. What the amendment prevents is the automatic, across-the-board qualification of same-sex partners for whatever marital benefits happen to exist.

The Federal Marriage Amendment has a very narrow purpose. It seeks to prevent one very specific abuse of power by the courts, to make sure that on an issue of this importance, they don't confer a victory on the Left that it has not won in a fair contest in the forum of democratic deliberation. The amendment is intended to return the debate over the legal status of marriage to the American people—where it belongs. This amendment would have prevented the Vermont supreme court from ordering the legislature to grant the benefits of marriage to same-sex couples, but would not prevent a fair democratic struggle to decide the question of civil unions one way or the other in Vermont or any other state.

Why, some will ask, should we not go further, and use constitutional amendment to settle the issue of civil unions once and for all at the national level? While the legal recognition of non-marital sexual acts and relationships undermines the institution of marriage and should be opposed, the actual threat of the imposition of same-sex marriage and civil unions comes from the courts, not the legislatures. The amendment is thus tailored to the threat at hand. Moreover, it does not depart from principles of federalism, under which family law is, for the most part, a state matter. State autonomy on family-law matters is preserved.

As a practical matter, the chances of passing a more comprehensive amendment are small. Moreover, some potential allies would perceive an amendment as offending democratic principles if it were to reach beyond the abuse of judicial power in this area. We should not fear the democratic resolution of the question of marriage. If we lose the people on this question, constitutional law will not save us.

If state and federal judges remain free to manufacture marriage law as they please, the prestige of liberal sexual ideology in the law schools and other elite sectors of our society will eventually overwhelm conventional democratic defenses. The only sure means of preserving the institution of marriage for future generations of Americans is a federal constitutional amendment protecting marriage as the union of a man and a woman.

POSTSCRIPT

Should Same-Sex Couples Be Allowed to Marry Legally?

It is important to know that opinions and beliefs on this issue are not necessarily formed by a person's own sexual orientation. Not all lesbian, gay, and bisexual people support legal marriage. Some feel very strongly that marriage is a heterosexual institution and that same-sex couples are imitating heterosexual ones when they have union or commitment ceremonies. Many heterosexual individuals believe that same-sex couples should be able to marry if they wish. Calling the union anything other than a marriage, they believe, would make it a separate, unequal arrangement.

There have been nearly 10,000 amendments to the Constitution proposed since 1789. Among these was an amendment in 1912 that would have made marriage between races illegal and another in 1914 that would have made it illegal to get divorced. How do you think the United States would look today if either of these amendments had been ratified? How do you find an amendment prohibiting same-sex marriage similar to or different from either of these proposed amendments?

When you think about how you feel about this issue, on what are you basing your beliefs? If you know someone who is lesbian, gay, or bisexual, or are lesbian, gay, or bisexual yourself, how does this affect your opinion? If you are a member of a particular faith group, what kinds of messages have you received about homosexuality and same-sex marriage? Have these messages helped you to form your opinion?

Suggested Readings

William N. Eskridge and William N. Eskridge, Jr., *Equality Practice: Civil Unions and the Future of Gay Rights* (Routledge, 2001).

Stanley N. Kurtz, "What Is Wrong With Gay Marriage?" *Commentary* (September 2000).

Jonathan Goldberg Hiller, *The Limits to Union: Same-Sex Marriage and the Politics of Civil Rights (Law, Meaning, and Violence)* (University of Michigan Press, 2002).

Mark Strasser, *Constitutional Interpretation at the Crossroads on Same-Sex Marriages, Civil Unions, and the Rule of Law (Issues on Sexual Diversity and the Law)* (Praeger Publishing Text, 2002).

Andrew Sullivan, ed., *Same-Sex Marriage: Pro and Con* (Vintage Books, 1997).

ISSUE 12

Should Lesbian and Gay Couples Be Allowed to Adopt?

YES: American Civil Liberties Union, from "ACLU Fact Sheet: Overview of Lesbian and Gay Parenting, Adoption, and Foster Care," American Civil Liberties Union, http://www.aclu.org/issues/gay/parent.html (April 6, 1999)

NO: Timothy J. Dailey, from "Homosexual Parenting: Placing Children at Risk," *Insight* (October 30, 2001)

ISSUE SUMMARY

YES: The American Civil Liberties Union (ACLU), an organization that works to preserve the individual rights and liberties of all Americans, points to a growing area of scientific literature that maintains that children who are raised by one or two lesbian or gay parents are just as well off as children who are raised by heterosexual parents. Findings demonstrate, they say, that parents' sexual orientation has no bearing on their ability to raise a child, or on a child's own sexual orientation or gender identity—nor does it affect children's emotional development or educational abilities.

NO: Timothy J. Dailey, senior writer/analyst for cultural studies for the Family Research Council, points to studies showing that children do much better in family settings that include both a mother and a father and that the sexual behaviors same-sex parents engage in make them, by definition, inappropriate role models for children. He maintains that the purpose of a marriage is to create children biologically and that since a gay or lesbian couple cannot do this without outside assistance, they do not make suitable parents.

Recently, talk-show host and child advocate Rosie O'Donnell helped to revive the discussion around lesbian and gay adoption and parenting by coming out on national television as a lesbian. O'Donnell, a mother of three adopted children with a fourth on the way, was moved by the plight of a male couple living in Florida that has served as foster parents to four children. Although permitted to serve as foster parents, this couple cannot legally adopt the children in the state of Florida because both partners are male. Nearly 3,500 children remain in the foster system in Florida awaiting adoption.

There is a range of feelings about who should or should not parent children, whether this involves single or two-parent relationships, heterosexual or same-sex couples. Some individuals feel on one hand that children should be raised by a man and a woman who are married. At the opposite end of the moral spectrum, they feel, is a gay or lesbian individual or couple. Starting with the premise that homosexuality is wrong, they feel that such a relationship is an inappropriate context in which to raise children. For some of these opponents of lesbian and gay parenting, homosexuality is defined by behaviors. Because they fear that sexual orientation and behaviors can be learned, they also fear that a child raised by a lesbian or gay couple will be more likely to turn out as lesbian or gay.

Other people do not believe that a person's sexual orientation determines her or his ability to parent. Whether a person is raised by one parent, two men, two women, or a man and a woman is less important than any individual's or couple's ability to love, support, and care for a child. They oppose the concept that a heterosexual couple in which there is abuse or where there are inappropriate sexual boundaries would be considered preferable to a lesbian or gay couple in a long-term, committed relationship who care for each other and their children. They point to the fact that most lesbian, gay, and bisexual adults were raised by heterosexual parents. Therefore, they believe, being raised by a lesbian or gay couple will not create lesbian, gay, or bisexual children any more than being raised by a heterosexual, married couple would guarantee heterosexuality.

As you read this issue, think about what you consider to be the characteristics of a good parent. Can these characteristics only be found in heterosexual relationships, or can they be fulfilled by a same-sex relationship? Does the gender of a same-sex relationship affect your feelings on the subject? For example, do you find two women raising a child more or less threatening than two men? Why, or why not?

In the following selections, the ACLU responds to a number of myths about the ability of same-sex partners to parent within the context of child development and family research. The ACLU maintains that two parents that share responsibilities, challenges, and rewards are likely to be effective adoptive or biological parents, regardless of the genders and sexual orientations of the individuals. Timothy J. Dailey asserts that the research on which the ACLU bases its conclusions is flawed. Concluding that gay men are sexually promiscuous, he believes that such men make poor role models and parents for children. Lesbians, he believes, are ineffective parents because with two mothers a child is raised without the presence and influence of a father figure, which many theorists argue is vital to the psychosocial development of children, male and female.

ACLU Fact Sheet: Overview of Lesbian and Gay Parenting, Adoption, and Foster Care

The last decade has seen a sharp rise in the number of lesbians and gay men forming their own families through adoption, foster care, artificial insemination and other means. Researchers estimate that the total number of children nationwide living with at least one gay parent ranges from six to 14 million.

At the same time, the United States is facing a critical shortage of adoptive and foster parents. As a result, hundreds of thousands of children in this country are without permanent homes. These children languish for months, even years, within state foster care systems that lack qualified foster parents and are frequently riddled with other problems. In Arkansas, for example, the foster care system does such a poor job caring for children that it has been placed under court supervision.

Legal and Policy Overview of Lesbian and Gay Parenting

Many states have moved to safeguard the interests of children with gay or lesbian parents. For example, at least 21 states have granted second-parent adoptions to lesbian and gay couples, ensuring that their children can enjoy the benefits of having two legal parents, especially if one of the parents dies or becomes incapacitated.

Recognizing that lesbians and gay men can be good parents, the vast majority of states no longer deny custody or visitation to a person based on sexual orientation. State agencies and courts now apply a "best interest of the child" standard to decide these cases. Under this approach, a person's sexual orientation cannot be the basis for ending or limiting parent-child relationships unless it is demonstrated that it causes harm to a child—a claim that has been routinely disproved by social science research. Using this standard, more than 22 states to date have allowed lesbians and gay men to adopt children either through state-run or private adoption agencies.

Nonetheless, a few states—relying on myths and stereotypes—have used a parent's sexual orientation to deny custody, adoption, visitation and foster care.

For instance, two states (Florida and New Hampshire) have laws that expressly bar lesbians and gay men from ever adopting children. In a notorious 1993 decision, a court in Virginia took away Sharon Bottom's 2-year-old son simply because of her sexual orientation, and transferred custody to the boy's maternal grandmother. And Arkansas has just adopted a policy prohibiting lesbians, gay men, and those who live with them, from serving as foster parents.

Research Overview of Lesbian and Gay Parenting[1]

All of the research to date has reached the same unequivocal conclusion about gay parenting: the children of lesbian and gay parents grow up as successfully as the children of heterosexual parents. In fact, not a single study has found the children of lesbian or gay parents to be disadvantaged because of their parents' sexual orientation. Other key findings include:

- There is no evidence to suggest that lesbians and gay men are unfit to be parents.
- Home environments with lesbian and gay parents are as likely to successfully support a child's development as those with heterosexual parents.
- Good parenting is not influenced by sexual orientation. Rather, it is influenced most profoundly by a parent's ability to create a loving and nurturing home—an ability that does not depend on whether a parent is gay or straight.
- There is no evidence to suggest that the children of lesbian and gay parents are less intelligent, suffer from more problems, are less popular, or have lower self-esteem than children of heterosexual parents.
- The children of lesbian and gay parents grow up as happy, healthy and well-adjusted as the children of heterosexual parents.

A Crisis in Adoption and Foster Care

Right now there is a critical shortage of adoptive and foster parents in the United States. As a result, many children have no permanent homes, while others are forced to survive in an endless series of substandard foster homes. It is estimated that there are 500,000 children in foster care nationally, and 100,000 need to be adopted.[2] But last year there were qualified adoptive parents available for only 20,000 of these children.[3] Many of these children have historically been viewed as "unadoptable" because they are not healthy white infants. Instead, they are often minority children and/or adolescents, many with significant health problems.[4]

There is much evidence documenting the serious damage suffered by children without permanent homes who are placed in substandard foster homes. Children frequently become victims of the "foster care shuffle," in which they are moved from temporary home to temporary home. A child stuck in permanent foster care can live in 20 or more homes by the time she reaches 18. It is not surprising, therefore, that long-term foster care is associated with increased emotional problems, delinquency, substance abuse and academic problems.[5]

In order to reach out and find more and better parents for children without homes, adoption and foster care policies have become increasingly inclusive over the past two decades. While adoption and foster care were once viewed as services offered to infertile, middle-class, largely white couples seeking healthy same-race infants, these policies have modernized. In the past two decades, child welfare agencies have changed their policies to make adoption and foster care possible for a much broader range of adults, including minority families, older individuals, families who already have children, single parents (male and female), individuals with physical disabilities, and families across a broad economic range. These changes have often been controversial at the outset. According to the [Child Welfare League of America] CWLA, "at one time or another, the inclusion of each of these groups has caused controversy. Many well-intended individuals vigorously opposed including each new group as potential adopters and voiced concern that standards were being lowered in a way that could forever damage the field of adoption."[6]

As a result of the increased inclusiveness of modern adoption and foster care policies, thousands of children now have homes with qualified parents.

Myths vs. Facts

Myth: The only acceptable home for a child is one with a mother and father who are married to each other.

Fact: Children without homes do not have the option of choosing between a married mother and father or some other type of parent(s). These children have neither a mother nor a father, married or unmarried. There simply are not enough married mothers and fathers who are interested in adoption and foster care. Last year only 20,000 of the 100,000 foster children in need of adoption were adopted, including children adopted by single people as well as married couples. Our adoption and foster care policies must deal with reality, or these children will never have stable and loving homes.

Myth: Children need a mother and a father to have proper male and female role models.

Fact: Children without homes have neither a mother nor a father as role models. And children get their role models from many places besides their parents. These include grandparents, aunts and uncles, teachers, friends, and neighbors. In a case-by-case evaluation, trained professionals can ensure that the child to be adopted or placed in foster care is moving into an environment with adequate role models of all types.

Myth: Gays and lesbians don't have stable relationships and don't know how to be good parents.

Fact: Like other adults in this country, the majority of lesbians and gay men are in stable committed relationships.[7] Of course some of these relationships have problems, as do some heterosexual relationships. The adoption and foster care screening process is very vigorous, including extensive home visits and interviews of prospective parents. It is designed to screen out those individuals who are not qualified to adopt or be foster parents, for whatever reason. All of the evidence shows that lesbians and gay men can and do make good parents. The American Psychological Association, in a recent report reviewing the research, observed that "not a single study has found children of gay or lesbian parents to be disadvantaged in any significant respect relative to children of heterosexual parents," and concluded that "home environments provided by gay and lesbian parents are as likely as those provided by heterosexual parents to support and enable children's psychosocial growth."[8] That is why the Child Welfare League of America, the nation's oldest children's advocacy organization, and the North American Council on Adoptable Children say that gays and lesbians seeking to adopt should be evaluated just like other adoptive applicants.

Myth: Children raised by gay or lesbian parents are more likely to grow up gay themselves.

Fact: All of the available evidence demonstrates that the sexual orientation of parents has no impact on the sexual orientation of their children and that children of lesbian and gay parents are no more likely than any other child to grow up to be gay.[9] There is some evidence that children of gays and lesbians are more tolerant of diversity, but this is certainly not a disadvantage. Of course, some children of lesbians and gay men will grow up to be gay, as will some children of heterosexual parents. These children will have the added advantage of being raised by parents who are supportive and accepting in a world that can sometimes be hostile.

Myth: Children who are raised by lesbian or gay parents will be subjected to harassment and will be rejected by their peers.

Fact: Children make fun of other children for all kinds of reasons: for being too short or too tall, for being too thin or too fat, for being of a different race or religion or speaking a different language. Children show remarkable resiliency, especially if they are provided with a stable and loving home environment. Children in foster care can face tremendous abuse from their peers for being parentless. These children often internalize that abuse, and often feel unwanted. Unfortunately, they do not have the emotional support of a loving permanent family to help them through these difficult times.

Myth: Lesbians and gay men are more likely to molest children.

Fact: There is no connection between homosexuality and pedophilia. All of the legitimate scientific evidence shows that. Sexual orientation, whether heterosexual or homosexual, is an adult sexual attraction to others. Pedophilia, on the other hand is an adult sexual attraction to children. Ninety percent of child abuse is committed by heterosexual men. In one study of 269 cases of child sexual abuse, only two offenders were gay or lesbian. Of the cases studied involving molestation of a boy by a man, 74 percent of the men were or had been in a heterosexual relationship with the boy's mother or another female relative. The study concluded that "a child's risk of being molested by his or her relative's heterosexual partner is over 100 times greater than by someone who might be identifiable as being homosexual, lesbian, or bisexual."[10]

Myth: Children raised by lesbians and gay men will be brought up in an "immoral" environment.

Fact: There are all kinds of disagreements in this country about what is moral and what is immoral. Some people may think raising children without religion is immoral, yet atheists are allowed to adopt and be foster parents. Some people think drinking and gambling are immoral, but these things don't disqualify someone from being evaluated as an adoptive or foster parent. If we eliminated all of the people who could possibly be considered "immoral," we would have almost no parents left to adopt and provide foster care. That can't be the right solution. What we can probably all agree on is that it is immoral to leave children without homes when there are qualified parents waiting to raise them. And that is what many gays and lesbians can do.

Notes

1. See American Psychological Association, *Lesbian and Gay Parenting: A Resource for Psychologists,* District of Columbia, 1995; Child Welfare League of America, *Issues in Gay and Lesbian Adoption: Proceedings of the Fourth Annual Pierce-Warwick Adoption Symposium,* District of Columbia, 1995.

2. Petit, M. & Curtis, P., *Child Abuse and Neglect: A Look at the States, 1997 CWLA Stat Book,* Child Welfare League of America, Washington, D.C., 1997, p. 72, 124.

3. Petit, *supra* note 2.

4. Sokoloff, B., "Antecedents of American Adoption," *The Future of Children*, Vol. 3, No. 1 (1993), pp. 17–26; Cole, E. & Donley, K., "History Values, and Placement Policy Issues in Adoption," in *The Psychology of Adoption*, Eds., David Brodzinsky & Marshall Schecter (New York: Oxford University Press, 1990), pp. 273–294.

5. Eagle, R., "The Separation Experience of Children in Long Term Care: Theory, Resources, and Implications for Practice," *The American Journal of Orthopsychiatry*, Vol. 64, pp. 421–434 (1994); Robert, G., et al., "A Foster Care Resource Agenda for the '90's," *Child Welfare*, Vol. LXXIII, No. 5, pp. 525–552 (1994).

6. *Issues in Gay and Lesbian Adoption*, Child Welfare League of America, Washington, D.C., 1995, p. 2.

7. Overlooked Opinions, "The Gay Market," *Chicago*, January 1992.

8. American Psychological Association, *Lesbian and Gay Parenting: A Resource for Psychologists* (1995).

9. See Bailey, J. M., Bobrow, D., Wolfe, M., & Mikach, S. (1995), "Sexual Orientation of Adult Sons of Gay Fathers," *Developmental Psychology*, 31, 124–129; Bozett, F. W. (1987), *Children of Gay Fathers*, F. W. Bozett. (Ed.), *Gay and Lesbian Parents* (pp. 39–57), New York: Praeger; Gottman, J. S. (1991), "Children of Gay and Lesbian Parents," F. W. Bozett & M. B. Sussman, (Eds), *Homosexuality and Family Relations* (pp. 177–196), New York: Harrington Park Press; Golombok, S., Spencer, A., & Rutter, M. (1983), "Children in Lesbian and Single-Parent Households: Psychosexual and Psychiatric Appraisal," *Journal of Child Psychology and Psychiatry*, 24, 551–572; Green, R. (1978), "Sexual Identity of 37 Children Raised by Homosexual or Transsexual Parents," *American Journal of Psychiatry*, 135, 692–697; Huggins, S. L. (1989), "A Comparative Study of Self-Esteem of Adolescent Children of Divorced Lesbian Mothers and Divorced Heterosexual Mothers," F. W. Bozett (Ed.), *Homosexuality and the Family* (pp. 123–135), New York: Harrington Park Press; Miller, B. (1979), "Gay Fathers and Their Children," *The Family Coordinator*, 28, 544–52; Paul, J. P. (1986).

10. Carole Jenny, et al., "Are Children at Risk for Sexual Abuse by Homosexuals?" *Pediatrics*, Vol. 94, No. 1 (1994); see also David Newton, "Homosexual Behavior and Child Molestation: A Review of the Evidence," *Adolescence*, Vol. XIII, No. 49 at 40 (1978) ("A review of the available research on pedophilia provides no basis for associating child molestation with homosexual behavior.")

Timothy J. Dailey

 **NO**

Homosexual Parenting: Placing Children at Risk

Anumber of studies in recent years have purported to show that children raised in gay and lesbian households fare no worse than those reared in traditional families. Yet much of that research fails to meet acceptable standards for psychological research; it is compromised by methodological flaws and driven by political agendas instead of an objective search for truth....

The presence of methodological defects—a mark of substandard research —would be cause for rejection of research conducted in virtually any other subject area. The overlooking of such deficiencies in research papers on homosexual failures can be attributed to the "politically correct" determination within those in the social science professions to "prove" that homosexual households are no different than traditional families.

However, no amount of scholarly legerdemain contained in an accumulation of flawed studies can obscure the well-established and growing body of evidence showing that both mothers and fathers provide unique and irreplaceable contributions to the raising of children. Children raised in traditional families by a mother and father are happier, healthier, and more successful than children raised in non-traditional environments....

Harmful Aspects of the Homosexual Lifestyle

The evidence demonstrates incontrovertibly that the homosexual lifestyle is inconsistent with the proper raising of children. Homosexual relationships are characteristically unstable and are fundamentally incapable of providing children the security they need.

Homosexual promiscuity Studies indicate that the average male homosexual has hundreds of sex partners in his lifetime, a lifestyle that is difficult for even "committed" homosexuals to break free of and which is not conducive to a healthy and wholesome atmosphere for the raising of children....

- In their study of the sexual profiles of 2,583 older homosexuals published in *Journal of Sex Research,* Paul Van de Ven et al. found that "the modal range for number of sexual partners ever [of homosexuals] was 101–500." In addition, 10.2 percent to 15.7 percent had between 501 and 1000 partners. A further 10.2 percent to 15.7 percent reported having had more than 1000 lifetime sexual partners.[1]
- A survey conducted by the homosexual magazine *Genre* found that 24 percent of the respondents said they had had more than 100 sexual partners in their lifetime. The magazine noted that several respondents suggested including a category of those who had more than 1,000 sexual partners.[2] ...

Promiscuity among homosexual couples   Even in those homosexual relationships in which the partners consider themselves to be in a committed relationship, the meaning of "committed" typically means something radically different than in heterosexual marriage.

- In *The Male Couple,* authors David P. McWhirter and Andrew M. Mattison report that in a study of 156 males in homosexual relationships lasting from one to thirty-seven years:

> Only seven couples have a totally exclusive sexual relationship, and these men all have been together for less than five years. Stated another way, all couples with a relationship lasting more than five years have incorporated some provision for outside sexual activity in their relationships.[3]

Most understood sexual relations outside the relationship to be the norm, and viewed adopting monogamous standards as an act of oppression. . . .

Comparison of homosexual 'couples' and heterosexual spouses   Lest anyone suffer the illusion that any equivalency between the sexual practices of homosexual relationships and traditional marriage exists, the statistics regarding sexual fidelity within marriage are revealing:

- In *Sex in America,* called by the *New York Times* "the most important study of American sexual behavior since the Kinsey reports," Robert T. Michael et al. report that 90 percent of wives and 75 percent of husbands claim never to have had extramarital sex.[4]
- A nationally representative survey of 884 men and 1,288 women published in *Journal of Sex Research* found that 77 percent of married men and 88 percent of married women had remained faithful to their marriage vows.[5]
- In *The Social Organization of Sexuality: Sexual Practices in the United States,* E. O. Laumann et al. conducted a national survey that found that 75 percent of husbands and 85 percent of wives never had sexual relations outside of marriage.[6] . . .

While the rate of fidelity within marriage cited by these studies remains far from ideal, there is a magnum order of difference between the negligible lifetime fidelity rate cited for homosexuals and the 75 to 90 percent cited for married couples. This indicates that even "committed" homosexual relationships display a fundamental incapacity for the faithfulness and commitment that is axiomatic to the institution of marriage....

A Political Agenda: Redefining Marriage

It is not the intention of homosexual activists simply to make it possible for homosexuals and lesbians to partake of conventional married life. By their own admission they aim to change the essential character of marriage, removing precisely the aspects of fidelity and chastity that promote stability in the relationship and the home:

- Paula Ettelbrick, former legal director of the Lambda Legal Defense and Education Fund, has stated, "Being queer is more than setting up house, sleeping with a person of the same gender, and seeking state approval for doing so.... Being queer means pushing the parameters of sex, sexuality, and family, and in the process transforming the very fabric of society."[7]
- According to homosexual writer and activist Michelangelo Signorile, the goal of homosexuals is:

  > To fight for same-sex marriage and its benefits and then, once granted, redefine the institution of marriage completely, to demand the right to marry not as a way of adhering to society's moral codes but rather to debunk a myth and radically alter an archaic institution.... The most subversive action lesbian and gay men can undertake... is to transform the notion of "family" entirely.[8]

... The instability, susceptibility to disease, and domestic violence that is disproportionate in homosexual and lesbian relationships would normally render such households unfit to be granted custody of children. However, in the current social imperative to rush headlong into granting legitimacy to the practice of homosexuality in every conceivable area of life, such considerations are often ignored.

But children are not guinea pigs to be used in social experiments in redefining the institution of marriage. They are vulnerable individuals with vital emotional and developmental needs. The great harm done by denying them both a mother and a father in a committed marriage will not easily be reversed, and society will pay a grievous price for its ill-advised adventurism.

Children Need a Mom and a Dad

Attempts to redefine the very nature of the family ignore the accumulated wisdom of cultures and societies from time immemorial, which testifies that the best way for children to be raised is by a mother and father who are married to each other. The importance of the traditional family has been increasingly verified by research showing that children from married two-parent households do better academically, financially, emotionally, and behaviorally. They delay sex longer, have better health, and receive more parental support.[9]

Homosexual or lesbian households are no substitute for a family: Children also need both a mother and a father. [Psychologist David] Blankenhorn discusses the different but necessary roles that mothers and fathers play in children's lives: "If mothers are likely to devote special attention to their children's present physical and emotional needs, fathers are likely to devote special attention to their character traits necessary for the future, especially qualities such as independence, self-reliance, and the willingness to test limits and take risks." Blankenhorn further explains:

> Compared to a mother's love, a father's love is frequently more expectant, more instrumental, and significantly less conditional.... For the child, from the beginning, the mother's love is an unquestioned source of comfort and the foundation of human attachment. But the father's love is almost a bit farther away, more distant and contingent. Compared to the mother's love, the father's must frequently be sought after, deserved, earned through achievement.[10] ...

The complementary aspects of parenting that mothers and fathers contribute to the rearing of children are rooted in the innate differences of the two sexes, and can no more be arbitrarily substituted than can the very nature of male and female. Accusations of sexism and homophobia notwithstanding, along with attempts to deny the importance of both mothers and fathers in the rearing of children, the oldest family structure of all turns out to be the best.

In his analysis of human cultures, the eminent Harvard sociologist Pitirim Sorokin argued that no society has ceased to honor the institution of marriage and survived. Sorokin considered traditional marriage and parenting as the fulfillment of life's meaning for both individuals and society:

> Enjoying the marital union in its infinite richness, parents freely fulfill many other paramount tasks. They maintain the procreation of the human race. Through their progeny they determine the hereditary and acquired characteristics of future generations. Through marriage they achieve a social immortality of their own, of their ancestors, and of their particular groups and community. This immortality is secured through the transmission of their name and values, and of their traditions and ways of life to their children, grandchildren, and later generations.[11]

In the 1981 Apostolic Exhortation *Familiaris Consortio*, Pope John Paul II summarized the importance of marriage-based families:

> The family has vital and organic links with society since it is its foundation and nourishes it continually through its role of service to life: It is from the family that citizens come to birth and it is within the family that they find the first school of the social virtues that are the animating principle of the existence and development of society itself.[12]

None of this is possible in homosexual or lesbian households, which are by definition incapable of creating progeny and contributing to the "procreation of the human race." Any children found in such households are of necessity obtained either from married couples or otherwise through the sexual union of male and female, artificially or otherwise. Thus such households are ironically dependent upon the very womb of society—the union of male and female—that they wish so fervently to deny.

In *It Takes a Village,* Hillary Rodham Clinton refers, perhaps inadvertently, to indelible "laws of nature" when she observes that "every society requires a critical mass of families that fit the traditional ideal." Similarly, an organism needs a critical mass of healthy cells to survive, and—as every oncologist knows —the fewer abnormal cells the better. In a democratic society, those who choose to cohabit in "alternative" familial arrangements such as same-sex unions have the freedom to do so. But toleration is one thing; promotion and "celebration" are another. To entrust children to such arrangements is wholly beyond the pale. As history shows, a society that champions such unions at the expense of traditional families does so at its own peril. But with the formidable forces of nature, culture, and history arrayed against them, such efforts to remake the most fundamental institution of society are not likely, in the end, to prevail.

Notes

1. Paul Van de Ven et al., "A Comparative Demographic and Sexual Profile of Older Homosexually Active Men," *Journal of Sex Research* 34 (1997): 354.
2. "Sex Survey Results," *Genre* (October 1996), quoted in "Survey Finds 40 percent of Gay Men Have Had More Than 40 Sex Partners," *Lambda Report*, January 1998, p. 20.
3. David P. McWhirter and Andrew M. Mattison, *The Male Couple: How Relationships Develop* (Englewood Cliffs: Prentice-Hall, 1984), pp. 252, 253.
4. Robert T. Michael et al., *Sex in America: A Definitive Survey* (Boston: Little, Brown & Company, 1994).
5. Michael W. Wiederman, "Extramarital Sex: Prevalence and Correlates in a National Survey," *Journal of Sex Research* 34 (1997): 170.
6. E. O. Laumann et al., *The Social Organization of Sexuality: Sexual Practices in the United States* (Chicago: University of Chicago Press, 1994), p. 217.
7. Paula Ettelbrick, quoted in William B. Rubenstein, "Since When Is Marriage a Path to Liberation?" *Lesbians, Gay Men, and the Law,* (New York: The New Press, 1993), pp. 398, 400.
8. Michelangelo Signorile, "Bridal Wave," *Out,* December 1994.
9. See the following: Sara McLanahan and Gary Sandfeur, *Growing Up with a Single Parent: What Hurts, What Helps* (Cambridge: Harvard University Press, 1994), p. 45; Pat Fagan, "How Broken Families Rob Children of Their Chances for Prosperity," Heritage Foundation *Backgrounder* No. 1283, June 11, 1999, p. 13; Dawn Upchurch et al., "Gender and Ethnic Differences in the Timing of First Sexual Intercourse," *Family Planning Perspectives* 30 (1998): 121–127; Jeanne M. Hilton and Esther L. Devall, "Comparison of Parenting and Children's Behavior in Single-Mother, Single-Father, and Intact Families," *Journal of Divorce and Remarriage* 29 (1998): 23–54; Jane Mauldon, "The Effect of Marital Disruption on Children's Health," *Demography* 27 (1990): 431–446; Frank Furstenberg, Jr., and Julien Teitler, "Reconsidering the Effects of Marital Disruption: What Happens to Children of

Divorce in Early Adulthood?" *Journal of Family Issues* 15 (June 1994); Elizabeth Thomson et al., "Family Structure and Child Well-Being: Economic Resources vs. Parental Behaviors," *Social Forces* 73 (1994): 221–42.

10. David Blankenhorn, *Fatherless America* (New York: Basic Books, 1995), p. 219.

11. Pitirim Sorokin, *The American Sex Revolution* (Boston: Porter Sargent Publishers, 1956), pp. 6, 77–105.

12. John Paul II, Apostolic Exhortation, *Familiaris Consortio,* December 15, 1981, Section 42. Quoted by Robert H. Knight in "Gay 'Marriage': Hawaii's Assault on Matrimony," *Family Policy,* February 1996, p. 5.

POSTSCRIPT

Should Lesbian and Gay Couples Be Allowed to Adopt?

Parenting is an area that has so many unknown factors, influences, and outcomes. Two-parent, high-income families sometimes have children that grow up with emotional and/or behavioral problems. Single parents can raise healthy, well-adjusted children. Some heterosexual couples raise children effectively, and some do not; some lesbian or gay couples raise children effectively, and some do not.

While there is much research exploring correlations between economic health, number of parents, and other factors, literature reviewing the connections between a parent's sexual orientation and her or his ability to parent remains inconclusive. There are studies maintaining that children need to be raised by a married, heterosexual couple, and there are studies asserting that a same-sex couple can do just as effective a job.

There is also insufficient information about homosexuality itself, and the effects that having a lesbian, gay, or bisexual parent may or may not have on a child. The lack of information and plethora of misinformation breed fear. When people are afraid, they want to protect—in this case, people who do not understand the bases of sexual orientation feel they need to protect children. In doing so, they sometimes make decisions that are not always in the best interest of the child. For example, in 1996, a divorced heterosexual couple living in Florida was battling over custody of their 11-year-old daughter. The male partner had recently completed an eight-year prison sentence for the murder of his first wife, and he had married his third. His ex-wife, however, had since met and partnered with a woman. A judge determined that the man and his new wife would provide a more appropriate home for the child than the child's mother because she was in a relationship with another woman. In the end, the judge believed that the child would do best in a home with a mother and a father even though the father was convicted of second-degree murder and accused of sexually molesting his daughter from his first marriage.

How do you feel about this? If you feel that heterosexual couples are more appropriate parents than same-sex couples, how would the fact that one of the heterosexual partners had committed a capital crime affect your opinion? Can these situations be judged best on a case-by-case basis? Or, do certain rules and judgments apply to most, of not all, cases?

Sometimes, we argue for what we think "should be" in a given situation. A challenge arises when comparing the "should be" to the "is"—what we think is best as opposed to the reality. If you feel that heterosexual married couples make the best parents, what should be done with those same-sex couples that are providing a loving, stable home for their children? Would it be best to leave the child where she or he is, or do you think the child would be better off removed from her or his existing family structure and placed with a heterosexual couple? Clearly, this is a discussion and debate that will continue as more and more same-sex couples not only adopt but also have biological children of their own.

Suggested Readings

American Academy of Pediatrics, Committee on Psychosocial Aspects of Child and Family Health, "Coparent or Second-Parent Adoption by Same-Sex Parents" (2002). Accessible online at http://www.aap. org/policy/020008t.html.

P. A. Belcastro et al., "A Review of Data Based Studies Addressing the Effects of Homosexual Parenting on Children's Sexual and Social Functioning," *Journal of Divorce and Remarriage* (vol. 20, 1993).

Susan Golombok and Fiona L. Tasker, "Do Parents Influence the Sexual Orientation of Their Children? Findings From a Longitudinal Study of Lesbian Families," *Developmental Psychology* (vol. 32, 1996).

Human Rights Campaign Foundation, State of the Family (HRC FamilyNet, 2002). Accessible online at http://www.hrc.org/familynet/ library.asp?ID=271.

Suzanne M. Johnson and Elizabeth O'Connor, *The Gay Baby Boom: The Psychology of Gay Parenthood* (New York University Press, 2002).

Sheryl L. Sultan, *The Right of Homosexuals to Adopt: Changing Legal Interpretations of "Parent" and "Family."* Accessible online at http://www.tourolaw.edu/publications/Suffolk/vol10/ part3_txt.htm.

F. Tasker and S. Golombok, "Adults Raised as Children in Lesbian Families," *Developmental Psychology* (vol. 31, 1995).

Lynn D. Wardle, "The Potential Impact of Homosexual Parenting on Children," *University of Illinois Law Review* (University of Illinois, 1997). Accessible online at http://www.rcf.usc.edu~biblarz/soc169/ wardlearticle.pdf.

On the Internet . . .

The National Marriage Project

The mission of the National Marriage Project is to strengthen the institution of marriage by providing research and analysis that informs public policy, educates the American public, and focuses attention on the decline of marriage as an institution.

http://marriage.rutgers.edu

The Alternatives to Marriage Project

The Alternatives to Marriage Project is a national, nonprofit organization for unmarried people, including people who choose not to marry, cannot marry, or are among those who live together before marriage.

http://www.unmarried.org

PART 5

Miscellaneous Relationship Issues

*T*here are a myriad of issues that come up in relationships. The discussions and debates surrounding how we conduct ourselves in relationships are rooted deeply in how we were raised, our spiritual and cultural values and beliefs, and our past experiences with relationships. This part offers a look at two questions that are asked primarily within the context of heterosexual relationships.

- Should People Not Cohabit Before Getting Married?

- Do Women and Men Communicate Differently?

ISSUE 13

Should People Not Cohabit Before Getting Married?

YES: David Popenoe and Barbara Dafoe Whitehead, from "Should We Live Together? What Young Adults Need to Know About Cohabitation Before Marriage: A Comprehensive Review of Recent Research," 2d ed., A Report of the National Marriage Project (2002)

NO: Dorian Solot and Marshall Miller, from "What the Research Really Says About Cohabitation," A Report of the Alternatives to Marriage Project (2002)

ISSUE SUMMARY

YES: David Popenoe and Barbara Dafoe Whitehead, codirectors of the National Marriage Project, assert that living together before marriage can contribute to a higher chance of divorce down the line, leads to less satisfying relationships, and is contributing to a deterioration in society's regard for the institution of marriage.

NO: Dorian Solot and Marshall Miller, cofounders of the Alternatives to Marriage Project, maintain that our society overemphasizes marriage, discriminating against people who wish to commit to another person and remain unmarried.

Living together before marriage is a decision many heterosexual couples face. (Because same-sex couples cannot marry legally in the United States, this issue will refer to heterosexual couples exclusively). The trend over the past 40 years has moved dramatically away from marriage and more toward cohabitation. According to one source, the number of cohabiting, nonmarried couples increased by almost 700 percent. The majority of people who cohabit outside of marriage are adults between the ages of 24 and 35.

Supporters for cohabitation as a viable option for couples recognize that the reasons for cohabiting before or without marriage depend on the individual couple. Social trends have been changing around sexuality in general—so while some people still promote abstinence until marriage, it is much more common today for a couple to be sexually active before their wedding. Some people may feel that marriage is too big of a commitment and do not wish to make this commitment. Others may have witnessed divorce growing up and feel that while they want to be committed to someone, they do not believe in the institution of marriage. Others may believe that marriage is a social construct, one that focuses more on the thousands of dollars many people spend on caterers, dining halls, and wedding attire more than on the commitment between the two people. Some may simply wish to be committed to someone but do not wish to be married, and so forth. There may be many other reasons why people may choose to live together either before or instead of getting married.

Opponents to cohabitation before marriage tend to believe that cohabiting is a prescription for an unsuccessful relationship. They point to studies that show cohabiting relationships do not last as long as marriage relationships. Many point to religious connections, saying that the less religious a couple is, the more likely they will be to cohabit before marriage. In some Christian denominations, engaging in certain sexual behaviors outside of the context of marriage is considered a sin; with the assumption that sex will take place in cohabiting relationships, they are considered sinful by default. Opponents also assert that there is a higher risk for violence in the home, depression, and dissatisfaction in relationships among women who cohabit rather than marry.

What do you think is the difference between cohabiting and marriage? If a couple exchanges rings and pledges commitment to each other without having witnesses or a religious leader endorsing their pledges, is their relationship less valid than a couple who has a large ceremony and reception in front of 200 guests? What do you think makes for an enduring relationship? Can it be lifelong without marriage, or should marriage be the expected norm or goal for heterosexual couples?

In the following selections, David Popenoe and Barbara Dafoe Whitehead make a distinction between cohabitation that is a precursor to marriage and cohabitation that is chosen as an alternative to marriage. While they do not believe that cohabitation before an intended marriage causes significant damage to a marriage relationship, they maintain that a cohabiting relationship in place of marriage is destined for failure, leading to dissatisfaction for both partners and problems with any children that may be born as a result of the union. Dorian Solot and Marshall Miller address some of the arguments people raise who favor marriage over a long-term committed relationship outside of marriage. They argue that the data cited are flawed and that their assertions are based on outdated and moralistic viewpoints.

**David Popenoe and
Barbara Dafoe Whitehead**

YES

Should We Live Together?

Executive Summary

Cohabitation is replacing marriage as the first living together experience for young men and women. When blushing brides walk down the aisle at the beginning of the new millennium, well over half have already lived together with a boyfriend.

For today's young adults, the first generation to come of age during the divorce revolution, living together seems like a good way to achieve some of the benefits of marriage and avoid the risk of divorce. Couples who live together can share expenses and learn more about each other. They can find out if their partner has what it takes to be married. If things don't work out, breaking up is easy to do. Cohabiting couples do not have to seek legal or religious permission to dissolve their union.

Not surprisingly, young adults favor cohabitation. According to surveys, most young people say it is a good idea to live with a person before marrying.

But a careful review of the available social science evidence suggests that living together is not a good way to prepare for marriage or to avoid divorce. What's more, it shows that the rise in cohabitation is not a positive family trend. Cohabiting unions tend to weaken the institution of marriage and pose special risks for women and children. Specifically, the research indicates that:

- Living together before marriage increase the risk of breaking up after marriage.
- Living together outside of marriage increases the risk of domestic violence for women, and the risk of physical and sexual abuse for children.
- Unmarried couples have lower levels of happiness and wellbeing than married couples.

Because this generation of young adults is so keenly aware of the fragility of marriage, it is especially important for them to know what contributes to marital success and what may threaten it. Yet many young people do not know the basic facts about cohabitation and its risks. Nor are parents, teachers, clergy

From David Popenoe and Barbara Dafoe Whitehead, "Should We Live Together? What Young Adults Need to Know About Cohabitation Before Marriage: A Comprehensive Review of Recent Research," 2d ed., A Report of the National Marriage Project (2002). Copyright © 2002 by The National Marriage Project at Rutgers University. Reprinted by permission.

and others who instruct the young in matters of sex, love and marriage well acquainted with the social science evidence. . . .

Should We Live Together?

What Young Adults Need to Know About Cohabitation Before Marriage: A Comprehensive Review of Recent Research

Living together before marriage is one of America's most significant and unexpected family trends. By simple definition, living together—or unmarried cohabitation—is the status of couples who are sexual partners, not married to each other, and sharing a household. By 2000, the total number of unmarried couples in America was almost four and three-quarters million, up from less than half a million in 1960.[1] It is estimated that about a quarter of unmarried women between the ages of 25 and 39 are currently living with a partner and about half have lived at some time with an unmarried partner (the data are typically reported for women but not for men). Over half of all first marriages are now preceded by cohabitation, compared to virtually none earlier in the century.[2] . . .

Unlike divorce or unwed childbearing, the trend toward cohabitation has inspired virtually no public comment or criticism. It is hard to believe that across America, only thirty years ago, living together for unmarried, heterosexual couples was against the law.[3] And it was considered immoral—living in sin—or at the very least highly improper. Women who provided sexual and housekeeping services to a man without the benefits of marriage were regarded as fools at best and morally loose at worst. A double standard existed, but cohabiting men were certainly not regarded with approbation.

Today, the old view of cohabitation seems yet another example of the repressive Victorian norms. The new view is that cohabitation represents a more progressive approach to intimate relationships. How much healthier women are to be free of social pressure to marry and stigma when they don't. How much better off people are today to be able to exercise choice in their sexual and domestic arrangements. How much better off marriage can be, and how many divorces can be avoided, when sexual relationships start with a trial period.

Surprisingly, much of the accumulating social science research suggests otherwise. What most cohabiting couples don't know, and what in fact few people know, are the conclusions of many recent studies on unmarried cohabitation and its implications for young people and for society. Living together before marriage may seem like a harmless or even a progressive family trend until one takes a careful look at the evidence.

How Living Together Before Marriage May Contribute to Marital Failure

The vast majority of young people today want to marry and have children. And many if not most see cohabitation as a way to test marital compatibility and improve the chances of long-lasting marriage. Their reasoning is as follows: Given the high levels of divorce, why be in a hurry to marry? Why not test marital compatibility by sharing a bed and a bathroom for a year or even longer? If it doesn't work out, one can simply move out. According to this reasoning, cohabitation weeds out unsuitable partners through a process of natural deselection. Over time, perhaps after several living-together relationships, a person will eventually find a marriageable mate.

The social science evidence challenges the popular idea that cohabiting ensures greater marital compatibility and thereby promotes stronger and more enduring marriages. Cohabitation does not reduce the likelihood of eventual divorce; in fact, it is associated with a higher divorce risk. Although the association was stronger a decade or two ago and has diminished in the younger generations, virtually all research on the topic has determined that the chances of divorce ending a marriage preceded by cohabitation are significantly greater than for a marriage not preceded by cohabitation. A 1992 study of 3,300 cases, for example, based on the 1987 National Survey of Families and Households, found that in their marriages prior cohabitors "are estimated to have a hazard of dissolution that is about 46% higher than for noncohabitors." The authors of this study concluded, after reviewing all previous studies, that the enhanced risk of marital disruption following cohabitation "is beginning to take on the status of an empirical generalization."[4]

More in question within the research community is why the striking statistical association between cohabitation and divorce should exist. Perhaps the most obvious explanation is that those people willing to cohabit are more unconventional than others and less committed to the institution of marriage. These are the same people, then, who more easily will leave a marriage if it becomes troublesome. By this explanation, cohabitation doesn't cause divorce but is merely associated with it because the same types of people are involved in both phenomena.

There is substantial empirical support for this position. Yet, in most studies, even when this "selection effect" is carefully controlled statistically, a negative effect of cohabitation on later marriage stability still remains. And no positive contribution of cohabitation to marriage has been ever been found.[5]

The reasons for a negative "cohabitation effect" are not fully understood. One may be that while marriages are held together largely by a strong ethic of commitment, cohabiting relationships by their very nature tend to undercut this ethic. Although cohabiting relationships are like marriages in many ways—shared dwelling, economic union (at least in part), sexual intimacy, often even children—they typically differ in the levels of commitment and autonomy involved. According to recent studies, cohabitants tend not to be as committed as married couples in their dedication to the continuation of the relationship and reluctance to terminate it, and they are more oriented toward their own personal autonomy.[6] It is reasonable to speculate, based on these studies, that once this low-commitment, high-autonomy pattern of relating is learned, it becomes hard to unlearn....

The results of several studies suggest that cohabitation may change partners' attitudes toward the institution of marriage, contributing to either making marriage less likely, or if marriage takes place, less successful. A 1997 longitudinal study conducted by demographers at Pennsylvania State University concluded, for example, "cohabitation increased young people's acceptance of divorce, but other independent living experiences did not." And "the more months of exposure to cohabitation that young people experienced, the less enthusiastic they were toward marriage and childbearing."[7]

Particularly problematic is serial cohabitation. One study determined that the effect of cohabitation on later marital instability is found only when one or both partners had previously cohabited with someone other than their spouse.[10] A reason for this could be that the experience of dissolving one cohabiting relationship generates a greater willingness to dissolve later relationships. People's tolerance for unhappiness is diminished, and they will scrap a marriage that might otherwise be salvaged. This may be similar to the attitudinal effects of divorce; going through a divorce makes one more tolerant of divorce....

An important caveat must be inserted here. There is a growing understanding among researchers that different types and life-patterns of cohabitation must be distinguished clearly from each other. Cohabitation that is an immediate prelude to marriage, or prenuptial cohabitation—both partners plan to marry each other in the near future—is different from other forms. There is some evidence to support the proposition that living together for a short period of time with the person one intends to marry has no adverse effects on the subsequent marriage. Cohabitation in this case appears to be very similar to marriage; it merely takes place during the engagement period.[9] This proposition would appear to be less true, however, when one or both of the partners has had prior experience with cohabitation, or brings children into the relationship.

Cohabitation as an Alternative to Marriage

According to the latest information available, 46% of all cohabitations in a given year can be classified as precursors to marriage.[10] Most of the remainder can be considered some form of alternative to marriage, including trial marriages, and their number is increasing. This should be of great national concern, not only for what the growth of cohabitation is doing to the institution of marriage but for what it is doing, or not doing, for the participants involved. In general, cohabiting relationships tend in many ways to be less satisfactory than marriage relationships.

Except perhaps for the short term prenuptial type of cohabitation, and probably also for the post-marriage cohabiting relationships of seniors and retired people who typically cohabit rather than marry for economic reasons,[11] cohabitation and marriage relationships are qualitatively different. Cohabiting couples report lower levels of happiness, lower levels of sexual exclusivity and sexual satisfaction, and poorer relationships with their parents.[12] One reason is that, as several sociologists not surprisingly concluded after a careful analysis, in unmarried cohabitation "levels of certainty about the relationship are lower than in marriage."[13] ...

Still not fully known by the public at large is the fact that married couples have substantial benefits over the unmarried in labor force productivity, physical and mental health, general happiness, and longevity.[14] There is evidence that these benefits are diluted for couples who are not married but merely cohabiting.[15] Among the probable reasons for the benefits of marriage, as summarized by University of Chicago demographer Linda Waite,[16] are:

- *The long-term contract implicit in marriage.* This facilitates emotional investment in the relationship, including the close monitoring of each other's behavior. The longer time horizon also makes specialization more likely; working as a couple, individuals can develop those skills in which they excel, leaving others to their partner.
- *The greater sharing of economic and social resources by married couples.* In addition to economies of scale, this enables couples to act as a small insurance pool against life uncertainties, reducing each person's need to protect themselves from unexpected events.
- *The better connection of married couples to the larger community.* This includes other individuals and groups (such as in-laws) as well as social institutions such as churches and synagogues. These can be important sources of social and emotional support and material benefits.

In addition to missing out on many of the benefits of marriage, cohabitors may face more serious difficulties. Annual rates of depression among cohabiting couples are more than three times what they are among married couples.[17] And women in cohabiting relationships are more likely than married women to suffer physical and sexual abuse. Some research has shown that aggression is at least twice as common among cohabitors as it is among married partners.[18] Two studies, one in Canada and the other in the United States, found that women in cohabiting relationships are about nine times more likely to be killed by their partner than are women in marital relationships.[19]

Again, the selection factor is undoubtedly strong in findings such as these. But the most careful statistical probing suggests that selection is not the only factor at work; the intrinsic nature of the cohabiting relationship also plays a role. As one scholar summed up the relevant research, "regardless of methodology.... cohabitors engage in more violence than spouses.[20]

Why Cohabitation Is Harmful for Children

Of all types of cohabitation, that involving children is by far the most problematic. In 2000, 41% of all unmarried-couple households included a child under eighteen, up from only 21% in 1987.[21] For unmarried couples in the 25–34 age group the percentage with children is higher still, approaching half of all such households.[22] By one recent estimate nearly half of all children today will spend some time in a cohabiting family before age 16.[23]

One of the greatest problems for children living with a cohabiting couple is the high risk that the couple will break up.[24] Fully three quarters of children born to cohabiting parents will see their parents split up before they reach age sixteen, whereas only about a third of children born to married parents face a similar fate. One reason is that marriage rates for cohabiting couples have been plummeting. In the last decade, the proportion of cohabiting mothers who go on to eventually marry the child's father declined from 57% to 44%.[25]

Parental break up, as is now widely known, almost always entails a myriad of personal and social difficulties for children, some of which can be long lasting. For the children of a cohabiting couple these may come on top of a plethora of already existing problems. Several studies have found that children currently living with a mother and her unmarried partner have significantly more behavior problems and lower academic performance than children in intact families.[26]

It is important to note that the great majority of children in unmarried-couple households were born not in the present union but in a previous union of one of the adult partners, usually the mother.[27] This means that they are living with an unmarried "stepfather" or mother's boyfriend, with whom the economic and social relationships are often tenuous. For example, unlike children in stepfamilies, these children have few legal claims to child support or other sources of family income should the couple separate.

Child abuse has become a major national problem and has increased dramatically in recent years, by more than 10% a year according to one estimate.[28] In the opinion of most researchers, this increase is related strongly to changing family forms. Surprisingly, the available American data do not enable us to distinguish the abuse that takes place in married-couple households from that in cohabiting-couple households. We do have abuse-prevalence studies that look at stepparent families (both married and unmarried) and mother's boyfriends (both cohabiting and dating). Both show for higher levels of child abuse than is found in intact families.[29] In general, the evidence suggests that the most unsafe of all family environments for children is that in which the mother is living with someone other than the child's biological father. This is the environment for the majority of children in cohabiting couple households.[30]

Part of the differences indicated above are due to differing income levels of the families involved. But this points up one of the other problems of cohabiting couples—their lower incomes. It is well known that children of single parents fare poorly economically when compared to the children of married parents. Not so well known is that cohabiting couples are economically more like single parents than like married couples. While the 1996 poverty rate for children living in married couple households was about 6%, it was 31% for children living in cohabiting households, much closer to the rate of 45% for children living in families headed by single mothers.[31]

One of the most important social science findings of recent years is that marriage is a wealth enhancing institution. According to one study, childrearing, cohabiting couples have only about two-thirds of the income of married couples with children, mainly due to the fact that the average income of male cohabiting partners is only about half that of male married partners.[32] The selection effect is surely at work here, with less well-off men and their partners choosing cohabitation over marriage. But it also is the case that men when they marry, especially those who then go on to have children, tend to become more responsible and productive.[33] They earn more than their unmarried counter-parts. An additional factor not to be overlooked is the private transfer of wealth among extended family members, which is considerably lower for cohabiting couples than for married couples.[34] It is clear that family members are more willing to transfer wealth to "in-laws" than to mere boyfriends or girlfriends.

Notes

1. U.S. Census Bureau. *Statistical Abstract of the United States: 2000* (Washington, DC: GPO, 20010): 52.

2. Larry Bumpass and Hsien-Hen Lu. "Trends in Cohabitation and Implications for Children's Family Contexts in the U.S.," *Population Studies* 54 (2000) 29–41. The most likely to cohabit are people aged 20 to 24.

3. The state statues prohibiting "adultery" and "fornication," which included cohabitation, were not often enforced.

4. Alfred DeMaris and K. Vaninadha Rao, "Premarital Cohabitation and Subsequent Marital Stability in the United States: A Reassessment," *Journal of Marriage and Family* 54 (1992): 178–190. A Canadian study found that premarital cohabitation may double the risk of subsequent marital disruption. Zheng Wu, *Cohabitation* (New York: Oxford University Press, 2000), 149.

5. The relationship between cohabitation and marital instability is discussed in the following articles: Alfred DeMaris and William MacDonald, "Premarital Cohabitation and Marital Instability: A Test of the Unconventional Hypothesis," *Journal of Marriage and the Family* 55 (1993): 399–407; William J. Axinn and Arland Thornton, "The Relationship Between Cohabitation and Divorce: Selectivity or Causal Influence," *Demography* 29–3 (1992): 357–374; Robert Schoen "First Unions and the Stability of First Marriages," *Journal of Marriage and the Family* 54 (1992): 281–284; Elizabeth Thomson and Ugo Colella, "Cohabitation and Marital Stability: Quality or Commitment?" *Journal of Marriage and the Family* 54 9 (1992): 259–267; Lee A. Lillard, Michael J. Brien, and Linda J. Waite, "Premarital Cohabitation and Subsequent Marital Dissolution: A Matter of Self-Selection?" *Demography* 32–3 (1995): 437–457; David R. Hall and John Z. Zhao, "Cohabitation and Divorce in Canada: Testing the Selectivity Hypothesis," *Journal of Marriage and the Family* 57 (1995): 421–427; Martin Clarkberg, Ross M. Stolzenberg, and Linda Waite, "Attitudes, Values, and Entrance into Cohabitational versus Marital Unions," *Social Forces* 74-2 (1995): 609–634; Stephen L. Nock, "Spouse Preferences of Never-Married, Divorced, and Cohabiting Americans," *Journal of Divorce and Remarriage* 24-3/4 (1995): 91–108.

6. Stephen L. Nock, "A Comparison of Marriages and Cohabiting Relationships," *Journal of Family Issues* 16–1 (1995): 53–76. See also: Robert Schoen and Robin M. Weinick, "Partner Choice in Marriages and Cohabitations," *Journal of Marriage and the Family* 55 (1993): 408–414; and Scott M. Stanley, Sarah W. Whitton and Howard Markman, "Maybe I Do: Interpersonal Commitment and Premarital and Non-Marital Cohabitation," unpublished manuscript, University of Denver, 2000.

7. William G. Axinn and Jennifer S. Barber, "Living Arrangements and Family Formation Attitudes in Early Adulthood," *Journal of Marriage and the Family* 59 (1997): 595-611. See also Marin Clarkberg, "Family Formation Experiences and Changing Values: The Effects of Cohabitation and Marriage on the Important Things in Life," in Ron Lesthaeghe, ed., *Meaning and Choice: Value Orientations and Life Course Decisions*, NIDI Monograph 38 (The Hague: Netherlands, Netherlands Interdisciplinary Demographic Institute, forthcoming). Axinn and Thornton, 1992, op. cit. and Elizabeth Thomson and Ugo Colella, 1992, op. cit.

8. DeMaris and McDonald, 1993, op. cit.; Jan E. Stets, "The Link Between Past and Present Intimate Relationships," *Journal of Family Issues* 14-2 (1993): 236-260.

9. Susan L. Brown and Alan Booth, "Cohabitation Versus Marriage: A Comparison of Relationship Quality," *Journal of Marriage and the Family* 58 (1996): 668-678.

10. Lynne N. Casper and Suzanne M. Bianchi, *Continuity and Change in the American Family* (Thousand Oaks, CA: Sage Publications, 2002) Ch. 2. Suprisingly, only 52% of those classified as "precursors to marriage" had actually married after five to seven years and 31% had split up!

11. Albert Chevan, "As Cheaply as One: Cohabitation in the Older Population," *Journal of Marriage and the Family* 58 (1996): 656-666. According to calculations by Chevan, the percentage of noninstituionalized, unmarried cohabiting persons 60 years of age and over increased from virtually zero in 1960 to 2.4 in 1990, p. 659. See also R. G. Hatch, *Aging and Cohabitation* (New York: Garland, 1995).

12. Nock, 1995; Brown and Booth, 1996; Linda J. Waite and Kara Joyner, "Emotional and Physical Satisfaction with Sex in Married, Cohabiting, and Dating Sexual Unions: Do Men and Women Differ?" Edward O. Laumann and Robert T. Michaels, eds., *Sex, Love, and Health in America* (Chicago: University of Chicago Press, 2001) 239-269; Judith Treas and Deirdre Giesen, "Sexuality Infidelity Among Married and Cohabiting Americans," *Journal of Marriage and the Family* 62 (2000): 48-60; Renate Forste and Koray Tanfer, "Sexual Exclusivity Among Dating, Cohabiting, and Married Women," *Journal of Marriage the Family* 58 (1996): 33-47; Paul R. Amato and Alan Booth, *A Generation at Risk* (Cambridge, MA: Harvard University Press, 1997) Table 4-2, p. 258.

13. Larry L. Bumpass, James A. Sweet, and Andrew Cherlin, "The Role of Cohabitation in Declining Rate of Marriage," *Journal of Marriage the Family* 53 (1991): 913-927.

14. Lee A. Lillard and Linda J. Waite, "Till Death Do Us Part: Marital Disruption and Mortality," *American Journal of Sociology* 100 (1995): 1131-1156; R. Jay Turner and Franco Marino, "Social Support and Social Structure: A Descriptive Epidemiology," *Journal of Health and Social Behavior* 35 (1994): 193-212; Linda J. Waite, "Does Marriage Matter?" *Demography* 32-4 (1995): 483-507; Sanders Korenman and David Neumark "Does Marriage Really Make Men More Productive?" *The Journal of Human Resources* 26-2 (1990): 282-307; George A. Akerlmof "Men Without Children," *The Economic Journal* 108 (1998): 287-309.

15. Allan V. Horwitz and Helene Raskin White, "The Relationship of Cohabitation and Mental Health: A Study of a Young Adult Cohort," *Journal of Marriage and the Family* 60 (1998): 505-514; Waite, 1995.

16. Linda J. Waite, "Social Science Finds: 'Marriage Matters,'" *The Responsive Community* (Summer 1996): 26-35. See also: Linda J. Waite and Maggie Gallagher, *The Case for Marriage* (New York: Doubleday, 2000).

17. Lee Robins and Darrel Reiger, *Psychiatric Disorders in America* (New York; Free Press, 1990) 72. See also Susan L. Brown, "The Effect of Union Type on Psychological Well-Being: Depression among Cohabitors versus Marrieds," *Journal of Health and Social Behavior* 41-3 (2000).

18. Jan E. Stets, "Cohabiting and Marital Aggression: The Role of Social Isolation," *Journal of Marriage and the Family* 53 (1991): 669-680. Margo I. Wilson and Martin Daly, "Who Kills Whom in Spouse Killings? On the Exceptional Sex Ratio of Spousal Homicides in the United States," *Crimology* 30-2 (1992): 189-215. One study found that, of the violence toward women that is committed by intimates and relatives, 42% involves a close friend or partner whereas only 29% involves a current spouse. Ronet Bachman, "Violence Against Women," (Washington, DC: Bureau of Justice Statistics, 1994) p.6. A New Zeland study compared violence in dating and cohabiting relationships, finding that cohabitors were twice as likely

to be physically abusive toward their partners after controlling statically for selection factors. Lynn Magdol, T.E. Moffitt, A Caspi, and P.A. Silva: "Hitting Without a License," *Journal of Marriage and the Family* 60-1 (1998): 41–55.

19. Todd K. Shackelford, "Cohabitation, Marriage and Murder," *Aggressive Behavior* 27 (2001): 284–291; Margo Wilson, M. Daly and C. Wright, "Uxoricide in Canada: Demographic Risk Patterns," *Canadian Journal of Criminology* 35 (1993): 263–291.

20. Nicky Ali Jackson, "Observational Experiences of Intrapersonal Conflict and Teenage Victimization: A Comparative Study among Spouses and Cohabitors," *Journal of Family Violence* 11 (1996): 191–203.

21. U.S. Census Bureau. *Current Population Survey,* March 2000.

22. Wendy D. Manning and Daniel T. Lichter, "Parental Cohabation and Children's Economic Well-Being," *Journal of Marriage and the Family* 58 (1996): 998–1010.

23. Bumpass and Lu, 2000, op.cit. Using a different data set, however, Deborah R. Graefe and Daniel T. Lichter conclude that only about one in four children will live in a family headed by a cohabiting couple sometime during childhood. "Life Course Transitions of American Children: Parental Cohabitation, Marriage, and Single Motherhood," *Demography* 36-2 (1999): 205–217.

24. Research on the instability of cohabiting couples with children is discussed in Wendy D. Manning, "The Implications of Cohabitation for Children's Well-Being," in Alan Booth and Ann C. Crouter, eds. *Just Living Together: Implications for Children, Families, and Public Policy* (Hillsdale, NJ: Lawrence Erlbaum Associates, 2002). It seems to be the case, however, that—just as with married couples—cohabiting couples with children are less likely to break up than childless couples. Zheng Wu, "The Stability of Cohabitation Relationships: The Role of Children," *Journal of Marriage and the Family* 57 (1995): 231–236.

25. Bumpass and Lu, 2000, op. cit.

26. Elizabeth Thompson, T.L. Hanson and S.S. McLanahan, "Family Structure and Child Well-Being: Economic Resources versus Parental Behaviors," *Social Forces* 73-1 (1994): 221–242; Rachel Dunifon and Lori Kowaleski-Jones, "Who's in the House? Effects of Family Structure on Children's Home Environments and Cognitive Outcomes," *Child Development,* forthcoming; and Susan L. Brown, "Parental Cohabitation and Child Well-Being," unpublished manuscript, Department of Sociology, Bowling Green State University, Bowling Green, OH.

27. By one estimate, 63%. Deborah R. Graefe and Daniel Lichter, 1999, op. cit.

28. Andrea J. Sedak and Diane Broadhurst, *The Third National Incidence Study of Child Abuse and Neglect* (Washington, DC: HHS-National Center on Child Abuse and Neglect, 1996).

29. See, for example, Margo Wilson and Martin Daly, "Risk of Maltreatment of Children Living with Stepparents," in R. Gelles and J. Lancaster, eds. *Child Abuse and Neglect: Biosocial Dimensions* (New York: Aldine de Gruyter, 1987); Leslie Margolin "Child Abuse by Mothers' Boyfriends: Why the Overrepresentation?" *Child Abuse and Neglect* 16 (1992): 541–551. Martin Daly and Margo Wilson have stated: "stepparenthood per se remains the single most powerful risk factor for child abuse that has yet been identified," *Homicide* (New York: Aldine de Gruyter, 1988) p. 87–88.

30. One study in Great Britain did look at the relationship between child abuse and the family structure and marital background of parents and, although the sample was very small, the results are disturbing. It was found that, compared to children living with married biological parents, children living with cohabiting, but unmarried biological parents are 20 times more likely to be subject to child abuse, and those living with a mother and a cohabiting boyfriend who is not the father face an increased risk of 33 times. In contrast, the rate of abuse is 14 times higher if the child lives with a biological mother who lives alone. Robert Whelan, *Broken Homes and Battered Children: A Study of the Relationship Between Child Abuse*

and Family Type (London: Family Education Trust, 1993).... See also Patrick F. Fagan and Dorothy B. Hanks, *The Child Abuse Crisis: The Disintegration of Marriage, Family and the American Community* (Washington DC: The Heritage Foundation, 1997).

31. Wendy D. Manning and Daniel T. Lichter, "Parental Cohabitation and Children's Economic Well-Being," *Journal of Marriage and the Family* 58 (1996): 998–1010.

32. Wendy D. Manning and Daniel T. Lichter, 1996.

33. Sanders Korenman and David Neumark, "Does Marriage Really Make Men More Productive?" *The Journal of Human Resources* 26-2 (1990): 282–307; George A. Akerlof "Men Without Children," *The Economic Journal* 108 (1998): 287–309; Steven L. Nock, *Marriage in Men's Lives* (New York: Oxford University Press, 1998).

34. Lingxin Hao, "Family Structure, Private Transfers, and the Economic Well-Being of Families with Children," *Social Forces* 75-1 (1996): 269–292.

Dorian Solot and Marshall Miller

 **NO**

What the Research Really Says About Cohabitation

In the United States today, most brides and grooms are already living together before they make their trip down the aisle.[1] Eleven million people currently live with an unmarried partner in this country, a 72 percent increase in the last decade alone, and nearly a 1,000 percent increase since 1960.[2] All the evidence suggests these trends will continue.

People choose to live together for many reasons. For most, it's an intermediate step between dating and marriage, a way to bring the relationship to the next level of commitment. Others live together for the long-term instead of marrying, often in relationships that are extremely committed. Still others, like gay, lesbian, and bisexual people in same-sex relationships, don't have the option of marrying.

While cohabitation is a societal norm, that doesn't mean it's right for everyone. Some people choose not to live with an unmarried partner. They might want to wait until they're married to share a home, or prefer a long-term relationship where they "live close by, visit often," as one song title describes it. These preferences are perfectly acceptable. This article is not an argument in favor of cohabitation, which is [a] matter of personal choice, but simply a response to many of the common social-science-based arguments against unmarried partnerships. Cohabitation has always had skeptics, critics, and objectors. Historically, opponents of cohabitation used moral judgments ("living in sin") as a way to express their disapproval. A newer trend has been the use of social science research to attempt to prove that cohabitation is bad for you. Yet the research is frequently misrepresented, or used to tell the truth but not the whole truth. The fact is, unmarried partnerships are part of the thriving diversity of family life in America today, and have the ability to be as happy, healthy, and stable as marriages.

Many Types of Cohabitors

Opponents of cohabitation often portray cohabitors as young couples who casually live with their partners, break up, and move on to the next live-in relationship. While this is true for a fraction of cohabitors, cohabitors also include:

- *People who plan to marry their partner.* Most studies find that between 75–80 percent of cohabitors plan to marry their current partner. Research has also shown that cohabitors who plan to marry their partners are no different than married people in terms of the quality of their relationships.[3]
- *Senior citizens and disabled people.* While the proportion of senior citizens living with an unmarried partner is small, their numbers increased faster than the overall average in the last decade.[4] Some seniors and disabled people on a limited income would lose pension, disability, or other essential benefits if they were to marry. Some live together instead of marrying in order not to complicate their wills or inheritance plans for their children. Some see no reason to marry since their childbearing years are complete or they have no plans for children. Others live together for the same reasons couples of all ages do.
- *People who have been divorced.* The majority of different-sex cohabiting couples include at least one partner who was previously married.[5] In our interviews with divorced people who now live with an unmarried partner, many told us, "Been there, done that." Those who had a negative experience with marriage or were surprised by the pain, time, and expense involved in getting a divorce often want to make an extra effort to be certain before risking marriage again—or at all.
- *People who plan to live together indefinitely and not marry.* About 20 percent of all male-female cohabitors, or 1.9 million people, have been living together for more than five years.[6] No research has ever examined these long-term cohabitors as a group. Based on our interviews and conversations with hundreds of people who fit this description, we know that they either have no plans to marry or are in no rush to do so. Many have said, "If it ain't broke, don't fix it." Their relationships are often extremely stable and committed, and they usually have a great deal in common with married couples.
- *Gay, lesbian, bisexual, and transgender (GLBT) people.* Same-sex couples are not allowed to get legally married anywhere in the United States. Research and articles that assume all unmarried partners have the option of marrying too often ignore all this group. Some different-sex couples —heterosexual and bisexual people—choose not to marry in solidarity with their GLBT friends and relatives who cannot.
- *Poor people.* The poor are much less likely to marry than middle or upper-class Americans. Statistically, they represent a sizable percentage of cohabiting couples. They also experience the negative effects that poverty has on families, such as lower quality health care and housing and fewer educational and employment opportunities. Some poor people would become ineligible for essential benefits if they got married, and others feel that marrying a poor partner would eliminate any

chance of their climbing the economic ladder. Regardless of their reasons for not marrying, the size of this group decreases the statistical averages for all cohabitors on measures like health, income, and child well-being.[7]

- *People who just moved in together.* The pool of cohabitors includes couples who began cohabiting very recently and are in an early phase of figuring out the seriousness of their relationship. While some cohabitors move in together as part of a long, thoughtful process, others move in because one was evicted, to escape from a parental home, to save money on rent, or for other reasons unrelated to the quality of their romantic relationship.[8] This group's relationships are at a very different stage than married people, for whom all (or nearly all) have made a definite decision about the seriousness of their relationship. For this reason, comparisons between random samples of cohabiting couples and married ones can lead to misleading conclusions.

Understanding the diversity within the category "cohabitors" is essential to understanding the research about us. One can think of each type as a different color of paint—red for the cohabitors who plan to get married, blue for the senior citizens, yellow for the long-term cohabitors, and so on. When researchers study a sample of cohabiting couples and arrive at a statistical average, in essence they have mixed all the colors together and come up with an average color: brown. The muddy brown color may be scientifically accurate. But brown doesn't accurately represent the facts about red, blue, yellow or any other kind of cohabitor. In addition, the color of larger cohabiting types (like poor people) "tint" the color of the overall average, while the splash of color of smaller cohabiting types (like committed long-term couples) becomes so diluted it is lost in the average.

Responses to Common Research-Based Arguments Against Cohabitation

Argument: "Living together before marriage increases the risk of divorce."

Response:

This claim has been reported widely in the media, yet there's little evidence to support all the attention. While it's true that on average, cohabitors who later marry have a higher divorce rate than those who marry without living together (correlation), it is a misrepresentation of the research to say that cohabitation *causes* divorce (causation). As people who marry *without* living together have become a shrinking minority, as a group they show some distinct characteristics. Several studies have found that non-cohabitors' religious values and strongly anti-divorce beliefs give them a lower divorce rate, not that the act of living together itself makes a difference.[9] People who cohabit and those who don't are two very different groups of people—an apples and oranges comparison. As Sociologist Judith Seltzer writes, "Claims that individuals who cohabit before marriage hurt their chances of a good marriage pay too little attention to this evidence."[10] The divorce rate in the United States has been stable or falling for two decades, a period with skyrocketing rates of cohabitation. Some cohabitors live together and then separate when they realize they're not a good match for a lifetime commitment. Because of this, it's likely some of these couples successfully avoided a bad marriage that may have ended in divorce. Many experts say the divorce rate would likely be far higher if not for cohabitation.[11]

Argument: "Cohabitators are not committed to each other."

Response:

Of course some cohabitors are not committed to each other, just as we've all known married couples who were not very committed and soon got divorced. Other cohabitors' level of commitment easily matches the most loving, stable married couples. Some have plans to marry and just haven't done so yet, while others stay together for decades without tying the knot. Most studies find that cohabiting couples' average level of commitment lies somewhere between dating couples and married couples, exactly what one would expect.[12] But because some cohabitors have shared their lives for decades while others just moved in together last week, an "average" level of commitment among cohabitors doesn't tell you much.

Also, keep in mind that commitment is a difficult concept to pin down using a survey. Those researchers that try have found the differences between married and cohabiting couples to be small. One oft-cited study asserting that married people are more committed than cohabitors found a 1.3 point difference on a twenty point scale of "commitment."[13] In short, understanding commitment requires an understanding of an individual person and relationship. Conclusions based on marital status alone are merely guesses.

Argument: "Cohabitation harms children."

Response:

Research supports what most of us already know in our hearts and from our own lives: the things children need in order to thrive are a family that has enough money to meet their basic needs, stable relationships with nurturing caretakers who are actively involved in their lives, and a low level of conflict in the household.[14] Studies that emphasize the differences between family types ignore the basic fact that most children do well regardless of family structure. All the research agrees that 70 to 90 percent of children in cohabiting families are not having problems.[15]

Studies show that children with cohabiting biological parents are no more likely to have behavior or emotional problems, and do as well in school, as those with married biological parents.[16] Leading cohabitation researchers question claims that children in cohabiting families are at greater risk for abuse, pointing to the small samples and poor methodology of the studies on which these claims are based.[17]

When differences are found between children of cohabiting and married parents, these result largely from other factors, not whether the parents are wearing wedding rings. For instance, family income is one of the most accurate ways to predict children's well-being. Since cohabiting families are disproportionately likely to be poor, the kids in these families show the effects of poverty: inferior schools, unsafe neighborhoods, second-rate health care, and stressed parents. Almost three-quarters of different-sex cohabitors with biological children have a household income of less than $28,000 for a family of three.[18] Yet many studies of family structure don't take socioeconomic factors into account. Any conclusion about "average" children of cohabitors that doesn't consider economics is primarily a conclusion about poor children.

About three in five children in cohabiting families are part of unmarried stepfamilies, living with one biological parent and that parent's partner. As in two biological parent families, most of these kids do fine, and cohabiting stepfamilies are as stable as married ones.[19] Teenagers in unmarried stepfamilies have been found to have a more difficult time than younger children, possibly because the teen years are a challenging time for major family changes.[20] Other changes often accompany the addition of a new authority figure in the home: children change schools, stepsiblings join the household, sometimes families move. Children may not be clear about how to understand their relationship to their parent's partner. It is certainly a transition that warrants careful attention to children to ensure their well-being.

Today one in three babies in the U.S. is born to parents who are not married, and about two-fifths of children are expected to live in a cohabiting household at some point.[21] Regardless of what one believes about cohabitation, it is critical that we end marital status discrimination because this *does* harm children. It is unwise and unrealistic to try to solve any married-cohabitation differences by adopting policies that pressure people to get married. A smarter approach would focus attention on the needs of all families, both married and cohabiting, to ensure they have equal opportunities, information about how to create a stable, nurturing home for children, and access to the support and recognition they need to thrive.

Argument: "Married women are less likely to experience domestic violence than cohabiting women."

Response:

Thank goodness! One would hope that women would not marry their abusive partners.

It's true that there's a correlation between marital status and domestic violence. However, among both married and cohabiting women the rates are very low, and the difference between the two groups is tiny: one British study that's often cited found that 2 percent of married women had experienced domestic assault in the last year, compared with 3 percent of cohabiting women.[22]

Although some argue that marriage keeps women safer, what's more accurate is that safer women are more likely to get and stay married. A recent study found that the reason for the appearance of slightly higher levels of violence among cohabitors is that non-violent couples are more likely to marry.[23] The group of couples "left over" in the cohabitor pool after the non-violent couples marry are likely using excellent judgement by choosing not to make a lifetime commitment to a dangerous partner.

Marriage is not a shield that protects women from abuse. A non-violent partner is unlikely to turn violent because a couple cohabited too long. Likewise, an abusive partner is unlikely to be transformed if you get married, and in fact, marrying him would probably be an unwise decision. Advising women or trying to legislate based on these kinds of averages is dangerous, because an average doesn't tell any individual woman what will be safest for her.

Argument: "Marriages last longer than cohabitations."

Response:

Of course the average marriage lasts longer than the average cohabitation. The vast majority of married couples have made a definite decision that they intend their relationship to be a long-term one. While some cohabitors have also made this decision and will have very long, stable relationships, the cohabitation group also includes many couples who are still "testing the waters" and deciding whether this partner is right for a long-term commitment. Some of these couples decide they're not right for each other and break up, decreasing the length of the "average" cohabitation.

Don't be misled, either, by articles that claim the average cohabitation lasts only a year or two—that's because after this amount of time, most cohabitors get married![24] The *cohabitation* ends, but the *relationship* continues.

Argument: "Single people aren't as healthy as married people."

Response:

While cohabitors are "single" in a legal sense, when it comes to health, they receive most, if not all of the health advantages that married people enjoy. Many studies find that it is living with a partner in a positive, mutually supportive relationship—not necessarily being married to that person—that correlates with healthier outcomes on average.[25] Most of the reasons why are common sense. Healthier people are probably more likely to form relationships (chronically ill people, for instance, may find it more difficult to find relationships and affect the "average" health for the single category). Married people are more likely to have access to health care; unlike all other industrialized countries, the United States does not guarantee health care to all its citizens, and insurance policies routinely discriminate against unmarried partners.[26] Partners tend to look out for each other, remind each other to wear seatbelts, make sure they make and keep doctor's appointments, take care of each other when they're sick, and spend less time than single people in unhealthy pursuits like drinking and smoking. Most studies about health that are cited to support the "married people are healthiest" assertion don't even include a cohabiting category in the groups they compare, looking instead at married versus single people.

Argument: "Marriage makes people wealthier."

Response:

Abundant evidence shows that wealthy people are more likely to get and stay married than poor people. Unfortunately, getting married won't magically make you wealthy—if it would, marriage alone would be the greatest solution to end poverty ever discovered.[27]

Because of the cultural belief that married men should be able to support their family, men—and in some studies, women, too—are more likely to get married if they are well-educated, if they have a job, and as their salary increases.[28] Poor women may choose to live with but not marry a man who is unemployed or otherwise a risky long-term proposition, preferring instead to hold out hope for the possibility of finding a partner who can help lift them out of poverty.[29] Researchers using focus groups of unmarried non-college educated twentysomethings find that most believe you should be "economically independent" and own a home *before* getting married.[30] Because the average price of a wedding today is nearly $20,000,[31] many couples must wait and save money if they wish to afford the celebration of their dreams. And on average, cohabitors are younger than married people, which partially explains the wage gap between the two groups.

All in all, couples who get married tend to be older, more educated, and more established in their careers: those who feel they can afford a wedding and married life. Many marrying couples have waited years until the right financial moment to tie the knot. Once they're married, it's no surprise that they are wealthier, on average, than couples with a very different set of characteristics.

Argument: "Marriage makes people happier than cohabitation does."

Response:

Most cohabitors describe themselves as happy. According to the National Survey of Families and Households, 83% of cohabitors say they are 5s, 6s, or 7s on a happiness scale of 1 to 7—heavily on the happy end. Only 7% put themselves on the "unhappy" side of the scale (1s, 2s, or 3s). Anti-cohabitation advocates like to talk about how much happier married people are, implying that cohabitors are unhappy. In reality, the difference between the two is minimal, with both groups saying they are quite happy.[32]

Even when careful research finds differences in happiness or other kinds of emotional and psychological well-being between married couples and cohabitors, the differences are often so small as to be meaningless in the real world. For instance, one study on depression found that on average, cohabitors were a mere 3% more depressed than married people, after controlling for age, sex, and race. Cohabitors without children and those with children who had been together several years had equivalent scores to married people.[33] Similarly, studies of loneliness and well-being among senior citizens and divorced people find that having a partner (inside or outside the household), not necessarily being married, is what makes the greatest difference.[34]

Finally, even if it were true that there were small average differences between married and cohabiting couples, there are many possible explanations for this. One is the social support and benefits married people receive. Another is the fact that on average, married people are a wealthier, more privileged group than unmarried people, and that the unmarried group average includes a variety of people who have problems that make them both less likely to marry *and* less likely to be happy. People who lack social skills, have poor personal hygiene, struggle with alcohol or drug addictions, or have mental illness, for example, might affect the group's average.

Finally, averages don't tell us anything about individual lives. On average pet-owners may be happier than non-pet-owners, but that doesn't mean that animal-haters or those with severe allergies would be happier if they got a pet.[35] Even if it were true that some married people are happier than some unmarried ones, it is not necessarily true getting married will make any individual happier.

Argument: "In cohabitation, men get to have sex without having to make a commitment."

Response:

Indeed, we've come far from the days in which one of the motivating reasons to get married was to have sex. Most men and women today have sex before they marry (as they have for the last century).[36] But cohabitation is not primarily an issue of sex without commitment. Casual sex is freely available in the form of one-night-stands and commitment-free hook-ups, without the hassle of joint utility bills and bathtubs that need to be cleaned. Most cohabitors move in together to *increase* the level of commitment in their relationship.

But there's a larger issue that's being missed here: women's feelings about sexuality and relationships. In another era, parents warned daughters that "he won't buy the cow if you give away the milk for free." But many women today recognize themselves as sexual beings with their own desires, who are empowered to seek sexual relationships or choose not to have sex based on their own situation and values. In fact, several young women we know misunderstood the old saying, thinking that they, not their male partners, were getting "free milk" by being able to live together without having to be married. Indeed, there is ample evidence that today, women question the desirability of marriage more than men do.[37] It is a mistake to assume that women suffer while men benefit from cohabitation.

Argument: "The United States needs to restore family values by promoting marriage."

Response:

Some advocates would like to enact laws and policies and intensify social stigma in an attempt to promote marriage, and to strengthen existing policies that put married couples on a pedestal above all other families. But the United States already has one of the highest marriage rates among industrialized countries—and also extremely high levels of poverty and violence.[38] When viewed in an international context, there is clearly no correlation between marriage and the kinds of well-being we associate with "family values." For example in Sweden the majority of births are to unmarried parents, yet Sweden's child poverty rate is one-seventh that of the U.S.[39] At least partly because Sweden makes supporting all children and families a priority, it has lower rates of rape and robbery, lower child mortality rates, and overall better health and longer life expectancies than the U.S.[40] Clearly, promoting marriage is not the solution to the many social issues that concern Americans.

It is not only possible, but also essential to support both married *and* cohabiting couples. It can't be an either-or question, since most people fit in both categories: most cohabitors get married later and most people marrying today have cohabited first.[41]

Cohabitors Are Family, Too

Cohabitation has become a mainstream part of American family life, and every indication suggests it is likely to continue to increase. As it does, the gap widens between real families and our social and legal definitions of "family," based on relationships of blood, marriage, or adoption. Ninety percent of people agree that society "should value all types of families,"[42] and most are glad that cohabitation is no longer the source of neighborhood gossip. People think it's a good thing that children receive the same rights regardless of whether their parents are married, and believe that unmarried people shouldn't be discriminated against at work or when buying or renting a home.

Yet people in unmarried relationships and families continue to face discrimination in insurance, housing, taxes, immigration, inheritance, hospital visitation, medical decisionmaking, and other areas. The Census counts those who check the "unmarried partner" box as "non-family households," and on other forms, cohabitors often feel that neither the "single" nor "married" checkbox describes their situation. Unmarried partners are still shut out of faith communities and excluded from family gatherings. Both adults and children in unmarried families are harmed when people are treated differently based on their marital status.

Regardless of one's personal decisions about cohabitation, it is time for the United States to recognize the danger involved when a growing portion of our nation's families are ignored by the legal system. Countries around the world, including Canada, France, Hungary, the Netherlands, Portugal, and Sweden, have created forward-thinking systems that make broad family rights available to both same-sex and different-sex unmarried couples, along with married ones, and many others are considering similar revisions to their policies. The task before us in this country is to stop pretending that our neighborhoods contain cookie cutter families, each identical to the one next door, and join the rest of the world in embracing the diversity of family life.

Notes

1. Bumpass, Larry and Lu, Hsien-Hen. "Trends in Cohabitation and Implications for Children's Family Contexts in the United States." *Population Studies,* 54: 29–41, 2000.

2. This includes both same-sex and different-sex couples. This number is often given as 5.5 million households. Each household contains a pair of partners, thus, eleven million individual people who live with a partner. U.S. Census Bureau. "Profile of General Demographic Characteristics for the United States: 2000." Table DP-1, 2000 and equivalent data for 1990. U.S. Census Bureau. "UC-1. Unmarried-Couple Households, by Presence of Children: 1960 to Present." Washington, D.C., 2001a.

3. Sweet, James and Bumpass, Larry. "Young Adults' View of Marriage, Cohabitation, and Family." In South, Scott and Tolnay, Stewart, eds. *The Changing American Family: Sociological and Demographic Perspectives.* Boulder: Westview Press, 1992, pp. 143–170. Brown, Susan and Booth, Alan. "Cohabitation Versus Marriage: A Comparison of Relationship Quality." *Journal of Marriage and the Family.* 58: 668–78, 1996.

4. U.S. Census Bureau. "H3. Households with Two Unrelated Adults of the Opposite Sex, by Presence of Children Under 15 and Age, Marital Status, and Race and Hispanic Origin/1 of Householder and Partner: March 1999." Washington, D.C., 2001b. U.S. Bureau of the Census. No. 61. *Statistical Abstract of the United States: 1997.* 117th edition. Washington, D.C., 1997. In Chadwick, Bruce and Heaton, Tim. *Statistical Handbook on the American Family.* Phoenix: The Oryx Press, 1999.

5. U.S. Census Bureau. Unpublished Tables B Marital Status and Living Arrangements: March 1998 (Update). *Current Population Reports,* P20-514. Washington, D.C., 1998. As cited in Smock, Pamela and Gupta, Sanjiv. "Cohabitation in Contemporary North America." In Booth, Alan and Crouter, Ann, eds. *Just Living Together: Implications of Cohabitation on Families, Children, and Social Policy.* Mahwah, NJ: Lawrence Erlbaum Associates, 2002, pp. 53–84.

6. Bumpass and Lu, 2000. Bumpass, Larry; Sweet, James; and Cherlin, Andrew. "The Role of Cohabitation in Declining Rates of Marriage." *Journal of Marriage and the Family.* 53: 913, 1991. Calculation by Dorian Solot.

7. To read more on marriage decision-making among the poor, see Edin, Kathryn. "What Do Low-Income Single Mothers Say About Marriage?" *Social Problems,* 47: 112–133, 2000.

8. Cohabitation rates increase when rental and real estate prices rise. Lillard, Lee; Brien, Michael, and Waite, Linda. "Premarital Cohabitation and Subsequent Marital Dissolution: A Matter of Self-Selection?" *Demography,* 32: 437–57, 1995.

9. Clarkberg, Marin; Stolzenberg, Ross; and Waite, Linda. "Attitudes, Values, and Entrance into Cohabitational Versus Marital Unions." *Social Forces,* 74: 609–34, 1995. Thomson, Elizabeth and Colella, Ugo. "Cohabitation and Marital Stability: Quality or Commitment?" *Journal of Marriage and the Family,* 54: 259–67, 1992. Lillard, Brien, and Waite, 1995. Schoen, Robert. "First Unions and the Stability of First Marriages." *Journal of Marriage and the Family.* 54: 281–4, 1992. Seltzer, Judith.

"Families Formed Outside of Marriage." *Journal of Marriage and the Family.* 62: 1247–68, 2000.

10. Seltzer, 2000.

11. Cherlin, Andrew. *Marriage, Divorce, Remarriage.* 2nd ed. Cambridge, MA: Harvard University Press, 1992, p. 15. DeMaris, Alfred and Rao, Vaninadha. "Premarital Cohabitation and Subsequent Marital Stability in the United States: A Reassessment." *Journal of Marriage and the Family,* 54, 178–90, 1992. Teachman, Jay; Thomas, Jeffrey; and Paasch, Kathleen. "Legal Status and the Stability of Coresidential Unions." *Demography,* 28: 571–86, 1991. Wu, Zheng. *Cohabitation: An Alternative Form of Family Living.* New York: Oxford University Press, 2000, p. 144.

12. Forste, Renata and Tanfer, Koray. "Sexual Exclusivity Among Dating, Cohabiting, and Married Women." *Journal of Marriage and the Family.* 58: 33–47. Laumann, Edward, et al. *Social Organization of Sexuality: Sexual Practices In The United States;* Chicago: University of Chicago Press, 1994, pp. 124–6.

13. Nock, Steven. "A Comparison of Marriages and Cohabiting Relationships." *Journal of Family Issues,* 16: 53–76, 1995.

14. Amato, Paul; Loomis, Laura; and Booth, Alan. "Parental Divorce, Marital Conflict, and Offspring Well-Being During Early Adulthood." *Social Forces.* 73: 895–915, 1995. Cherlin, Andrew. "Going to Extremes: Family Structure, Children's Well-Being, and Social Science." *Demography* 36: 21–28, 1999. Jekielek, Susan. "Parental Conflict, Marital Disruption, and Children's Emotional Well-Being." *Social Forces.* 76: 905–36, 1998. Vandewater, Elizabeth and Lansford, Jennifer. "Influences of Family Structure and Parental Conflict on Children's Well-Being." *Family Relations.*47: 323–30, 1998.

15. Brown, Susan. "Child Well-Being in Cohabiting Families." In Booth and Crouter, 2002, pp. 173–87. Manning, Wendy. "The Implications of Cohabitation for Children's Well-Being." In Booth and Crouter, 2002a, pp. 121–52.

16. Brown, 2002. Manning, 2002a.

17. Manning, 2002a.

18. Brown, 2002, p. 179.

19. Bumpass, Larry; Raley, R. Kelly; Sweet, James. "The Changing Character of Stepfamilies: Implications of Cohabitation and Nonmarital Childbearing." *Demography,* 32: 425–36, 1995.

20. Brown, Susan. "Child Well-Being in Cohabiting Families." In Booth and Crouter, 2002, pp. 173–87. Manning, Wendy. "The Implications of Cohabitation for Children's Well-Being." In Booth and Crouter, 2002a, 121–52. Manning, Wendy and Lamb, Kathleen. "Parental Cohabitation and Adolescent Well-Being." Center for Family and Demographic Research Working Paper 02-03. Bowling Green, OH: Bowling Green State University, 2002b. Thomson et al., 1994.

21. Martin, Joyce, et al. "Births: Final Data for 2000." *National Vital Statistics Reports,* Vol. 50 No. 5. Hyattsville, MD: National Center for Health Statistics, 2002. p. 2. U.S. Census Bureau, 2000b.

22. Mirrlees-Black, Catriona. "Domestic Violence: Findings from a New British Crime Survey Self-Completion Questionnaire." London: Home Office Research Study 191, 1999.

23. McLanahan, Sara and Carlson, Marcia. "Welfare Reform, Fertility and Father Involvement." Working Paper #01-13-FF. Princeton: Center for Research on Child Wellbeing, Princeton University, 2001.

24. Bumpass and Lu, 2000.

25. Anson, Ofra. "Marital Status and Women's Health Revisited: The Importance of a Proximate Adult. *Journal of Marriage and the Family.* 51: 185–94, 1989. Graff, E.J. *What Is Marriage For?* Boston: Beacon Press, pp. 46–7, 1999. Joung, I. M. A. et al. "Differences in Self-Reported Morbidity by Marital Status and by Living Arrangement." *International Journal of Epidemiology.* 23: 91–7, 1994. Peters, Arnold and Liefbroer, Aart. "Beyond Marital Status: Partner History and Well-Being in Old Age." *Journal of Marriage and the Family,* 59: 687–99, 1998.

26. Committee on the Consequences of Uninsurance, Institute of Medicine. *Coverage Matters: Insurance and Health Care.* Washington, D.C.: National Academy Press, 2001. Health Care for All—California. http://www.healthcareforall.org. 25 May 2002.(6 June 2002).

27. McLanahan, Sara and Carlson, Marcia. "Welfare Reform, Fertility and Father Involvement." Working Paper #01-13-FF. Princeton: Center for Research on Child Wellbeing, Princeton University, 2001.

28. Manning, Wendy and Smock, Pamela. "Why Marry? Race and the Transition to Marriage Among Cohabitors." *Demography,* 32: 509–520, 1995. Oppenheimer, Valerie Kincade; Kalmiju, Malthijs; and Lim, Nelson. "Men's Career Development and Marriage Timing During a Period of Rising Inequality." *Demography,* 34: 311–330, 1997. Smock, Pamela and Manning, Wendy. "Cohabiting Partners' Economic Circumstances and Marriage." *Demography,* 34: 331–341, 1997.

29. Edin, 2000.

30. Whitehead, Barbara Dafoe and Popenoe, David. *Why Wed? Young Adults Talk About Sex, Love, and First Unions.* New Brunswick, NJ: National Marriage Project, 1999.

31. Ingraham, Chrys. *White Weddings: Romancing Heterosexuality in Popular Culture.* New York: Routledge, 1999, pp. 28–9.

32. National Survey of Families and Households, 1987. In Chadwick, Bruce and Heaton, Tim. *Statistical Handbook on the American Family.* Phoenix, AZ: Oryx Press, 1992.

33. Brown, Susan. "The Effect of Union Type on Psychological Well-Being: Depression Among Cohabitors Versus Marrieds." *Journal of Health and Social Behavior.* 41: 241–55, 2000.

34. Mastekaasa, Arne. "The Subjective Well-Being of the Previously Married: The Importance of Unmarried Cohabitation and Time Since Widowhood or Divorce." *Social Forces,* 73: 665–92, 1994. Peters, Arnold and Liefbroer, Aart. "Beyond Marital Status: Partner History and Well-Being in Old Age." *Journal of Marriage and the Family.* 59: 687–99, 1997.

35. Vom Saal, Walter, Personal communication, 1999.

36. Laumann, Edward, et. al. *Social Organization of Sexuality; Sexual Practices In The United States;* Chicago: University of Chicago Press, 1994, pp. 502–3. Mintz, Steven and Kellogg, Susan. *Domestic Revolutions: A Social History of American Family Life.* New York: The Free Press, 1988, 177–201.

37. Gallup, George, Jr. *The Gallup Poll: Public Opinion 1996.* Wilmington, DE: Scholarly Resources, Inc., 1997, p. 211. National Survey of Families and Households. "Feelings About Marriage, Dating, and Cohabitation: Unmarried Respondents Aged 18–35 Who Are Not Cohabiting, by Sex." Madison, WI: Center for Demography and Ecology, University of Wisconsin-Madison, 1994. In Chadwick, Bruce and Heaton, Tim. *Statistical Handbook on the American Family.* Phoenix: The Oryx Press, 1999, p. 195. Ropert Starch Worldwide Inc. "The 1995 Virginia Slims Opinion Poll: A 25-Year Perspective on Women's Issues." *Tobacco Documents Online.* 1995. http://tobaccodocuments.org/pm/2070648486-8599.html. (29 June 2002).

38. Eurostat. "First Results of the Demographic Data Collection for 1999 in Europe." *Statistics in Focus,* 2000. Eurostat. "100 Basic Indicators from Eurostate Yearbook

2000." Eurostat Yearbook 2001, 2001. Bruce Bradbury and Markus Jantti. "Child Poverty Across Industrialized Nations." Innocenti Occasional Papers: Economic and Social Policy Series No. 71. 1999.

39. Bradbury and Jantti, 1999.

40. Prescott-Allen, Robert. *The Wellbeing of Nations: A Country-by-Country Index of Quality of Life and the Environment.* Washington, D.C.: Island Press, 2001.

41. Bumpass and Lu, 2000.

42. Coontz, Stephanie. *The Way We Really Are: Coming To Terms With America's Changing Families.* New York: Basic Books, 1997, p. 94.

POSTSCRIPT

Should People Not Cohabit Before Getting Married?

In any relationship, the people involved need to be committed to the process. This includes friendships as well as family and business relationships. If one friend talks incessantly about her problems without reciprocating, the friendship will not survive. If a professional never returns her colleague's phone calls, the business relationship will suffer. If two people make a lifelong commitment to each other expecting no work and all play, they may likely find the task of maintaining a relationship too daunting, and the relationship will not endure.

The United States has seen a significant rise in divorce rates. Some people will hear this news, wag a finger authoritatively, and say, "See? If they had gotten to know each other better and spent some time living together before getting married, they would have known in advance they were incompatible." Others will wave the same authoritative finger and say, "See? All these people are living together before marriage. Of course they don't feel that marriage is a special commitment—they've been living and sleeping together already!"

Should society become more open and extend the legal and social benefits it has for married couples to people who have demonstrated a long-term commitment to each other? If so, should this include same-sex relationships? Does a line need to be drawn somewhere—and if so, where?

Suggested Readings

Alan Booth and Ann C. Crouter, eds., *Just Living Together: Implications of Cohabitation for Children, Families, and Social Policy* (Lawrence Erlbaum Associates, 2002).

E. J. Graff, *What Is Marriage For?* (Beacon Press, 2000).

Patricia Morgan, *Marriage-Lite: The Rise of Cohabitation and Its Consequences* (Institute for the Study of Civil Society, 2000).

Michelle Hindin, Elizabeth Thomson, and Arland Thornton in Linda J. Waite and Christine Bachrach, eds., *The Ties That Bind: Perspectives on Marriage and Cohabitation (Social Institutions and Social Change)* (Aldine de Gruyter, 2000).

James Q. Wilson, *The Marriage Problem: How Our Culture Has Weakened Families* (HarperCollins, 2002).

Do Women and Men
Communicate Differently?

YES: Philip Yancey, from "Do Men and Women Speak the Same Language?" *Marriage Partnership* (Fall 1993)

NO: Mary Crawford, from *Talking Difference: On Gender and Language* (Sage, 1995)

ISSUE SUMMARY

YES: Philip Yancey, editor at large of *Christianity Today,* asserts that communication styles are different between men and women. He argues that in heterosexual relationships, partners are likely to fulfill stereotypical expectations of how men and women are supposed to communicate due to their upbringing and culture.

NO: Mary Crawford, director of the Women's Studies Program at the University of Connecticut, also states that communication styles are learned. However, she discusses the idea that young people are aware of these lessons and that fulfilling the expected communication stereotypes within heterosexual couples can lead to unsatisfying relationships, for women in particular.

Differences between men and women have been discussed, debated, researched, and agonized over for quite some time. More recently, popular culture has depicted these differences in the media for entertainment purposes and in the form of "self-help" books designed to enable heterosexual couples to communicate more effectively. The thought behind many of these books is that men communicate in one manner and women in another. Unless the genders are willing to understand and work with these differences, authors say, a heterosexual relationship will face additional trials and tribulations.

Some people believe that boys and men are socialized to be more assertive and direct, in both verbal and nonverbal communication. Much like the rest of the animal kingdom, eye contact, physical size, body placement, and rough physical contact by males communicate such things as intention, superiority, and territoriality. A nonmale—translated, "female"—interaction is thus seen as weaker. Historically, women have generally been socialized to have a less pronounced presence. For example, while men are more likely to keep a stranger's gaze as they walk down the street, women are much more likely to look away. Stereotypically, women tend to listen empathetically, communicate and elicit emotions, process conflict, and more. As a result, the familiar complaint from women in heterosexual relationships is that their male partners "never want to talk about things," "aren't sensitive to their needs," and, as author and professor Deborah Tannen writes, "just don't understand." Conversely, men often feel like the proverbial deer in the headlights, wondering how a seemingly innocuous comment could result in their female partners' sudden silence or an expressed desire to talk about where the relationship is going.

Clearly, these are stereotypical interactions—but stereotypes are often based in truth. Are the differences in communication based on being male or female? If so, is one communication style superior or preferable to the other? And what happens if a man or woman does not communicate in the style that has been designated for a specific gender?

Some people will maintain that the differences in gendered communication are inevitable, and that if men and women focused less on trying to change the other gender's communication style and focused more on understanding the differences and working within the nuances of each, relationships would be much more successful. Others believe that gendered communication maintains male superiority—that in a conversation between people of different genders, the male norm will prevail. For some, therefore, maintaining differences in communication based on gender is quite important to preserving the "pecking order." For others, these differences sustain oppression.

As you read the following selections, consider the men and women in your own life who are in romantic relationships with someone of another gender. How do the partners communicate with each other—and how much do you think that has to do with being female or male? Think about anyone in your life who may be in a romantic relationship with someone of the same gender. How do these stereotypes around gendered communication affect their relationships, if at all? Are there any differences?

In the following selections, Philip Yancey, discussing Tannen's *You Just Don't Understand: Women and Men in Conversation* (Quill, 2001), describes gendered interactions that start in childhood and continue into adulthood. He maintains that people internalize the values attached to gendered communication to the point that men become used to living within conflict and women prefer and take on the role of peacemaker and relationship-builder. Mary Crawford, pointing to Tannen's book, as well as John Gray's *Men Are From Mars, Women Are From Venus: A Practical Guide for Improving Communication and Getting What You Want in Your Relationships* (HarperCollins, 1992), focuses on the effects gendered communication has on boys and girls, men and women. She illustrates that looking at gender exclusively as the source of different communication styles is a mistake and that such elements as upbringing, socioeconomic status, culture and ethnicity, and more must be considered within this context.

Philip Yancey

 **YES**

Do Men and Women Speak the Same Language?

For five years my wife, Janet, and I met in a small group with three other couples. Sometimes we studied the Bible, sometimes we read books together, sometimes we spontaneously discussed topics like money and sex. Almost always we ended up talking about our marriages. Finally we decided the time had come to investigate an explosive topic we had always avoided: the differences between men and women. We used the book *You Just Don't Understand* [William Morrow & Company, 1990], by Deborah Tannen, as the springboard for our discussions. That study of the different communication styles of men and women had risen to the top of The New York Times bestseller list. Books on gender differences tend to portray one party as the "right" party. Women are sensitive, compassionate, peace-loving, responsible, nurturing; men are boorish slobs whose idea of "bonding" is to slouch in front of a TV with their buddies watching other men chase little round balls. Or, men are rational, organizational geniuses who run the world because they are "hardwired" with leadership skills that women can never hope to master. But in her book, Tannen strives to avoid such bias, focusing instead on what it takes for men and women to understand each other.

She sees males as more competitive, aggressive, hierarchical and emotionally withdrawn. Females, she concludes, are quieter, more relational and mutually supportive. Naturally, any generalities about gender differences do not apply to all men or all women. Yet we found one point of commonality that helped us all: Male/female relationships represent a classic case of cross-cultural communication. The key to effective relationships is to understand the vast "cultural" gap between male and female.

Anyone who has traveled overseas knows that barriers exist between cultures, language being the most obvious. The barriers between men and women can be just as real, and just as frustrating. Typically, says Tannen, men and women don't recognize these differences; they tend to repeat the same patterns of miscommunication, only more forcefully. As a result, marriages often resemble the stereotypical tourist encounter: One party speaks loudly and slowly in a language the other does not comprehend.

The Male/Female Culture Gap

"Shared meaning" is a good, concise definition of culture. By virtue of growing up in the United States, I share the meaning of things like Bart Simpson, baseball and the Fourth of July with 250 million other people, and no one else in the world. Our couples group found that some problems come about because one spouse enters marriage with a different set of "shared meanings" than the other. Consider routine dinner conversation. For some of us, interrupting another's conversation seems an act of impoliteness or hostility; for others, it expresses friendly engagement. Angie, one of the women in our group, said, "When Greg first came to my Italian family's get-togethers he would hardly speak. We usually had a fight on the way home. We later figured out he felt shut down whenever someone interrupted him in the middle of a story or a comment. Well, in my family interrupting is a sign of involvement. It means we're listening to you, egging you on.

"Greg comes from a German family where everyone politely takes turns responding to the previous comment. I go crazy—their conversation seems so boring and stilted. It helped us both to realize there is no 'right' or 'wrong' style of conversation—we were simply acting out of different cultural styles."

Everyone grows up with "rules" or assumptions about how life is supposed to operate. Marriage forces into close contact two people with different sets of shared meanings and then requires them to negotiate a common ground. Bill and Holly told of a disagreement that nearly ruined their Christmas vacation. Bill said, "We visited Holly's family, which is huge and intimidating. That Christmas, one of the sisters bought a VCR and television to present to the parents, without consulting the rest of the family. 'You guys can chip in anything you want,' she told her siblings and in-laws. 'I'll sign the card and present the gift as being from all of us.'

"To me this looked like a set-up job," Bill continued. "I felt pressure to come up with our fair share, which was a lot more than we would have spent on our own. I felt manipulated and angry, and Holly couldn't understand my feelings. She said her sister was absolutely sincere. 'Our family doesn't keep score,' she said. 'Ellen spontaneously felt like buying a present, and she'll be content whether everyone chips in one-eighth or if no one contributes anything. It's not 'tit-for-tat' like your family.'

"Holly was probably right. My family does keep score. You send a letter, you expect one in return. You give a gift, you expect one of equal value. I'm finally coming to grasp that Holly's family doesn't operate like mine."

Another couple, Gayle and Don, identified on-timeness as their major cross-cultural disagreement. Gayle grew up in a family that didn't notice if they were 10 or 15 minutes late, but Don wears a digital watch and follows it punctually. Several times a week they clash over this common cross-cultural difference. In Germany the trains run on time; in Mexico they get there— eventually.

Cross-cultural differences may seem trivial but, as many couples learn, on small rocks great ships wreck. It helps to know in advance where the rocks are.

Cross-Gender Communication

Communication can either span—or widen—the gender gap. Research shows that boys and girls grow up learning different styles of communicating. Boys tend to play in large groups that are hierarchically structured, with a leader who tells the others what to do and how to do it. Boys reinforce status by giving orders and enforcing them; their games have winners and losers and are run by elaborate rules. In contrast, girls play in small groups or in pairs, with "best friends." They strive for intimacy, not status.

These gender patterns continue into adulthood. A man relates to the world as an individual within a hierarchy; he measures himself against others and judges success or failure by his movement up or down the ladder. A woman approaches the world as a network of many social connections. For women, writes Deborah Tannen, "conversations are negotiations for closeness in which people try to seek and give confirmation and support, and to reach consensus."

Tannen's studies of the corporate world show it to be a male-dominated culture where men tend to make pronouncements, to surround themselves with symbols of status, to position themselves against one another, and to improve their standing by opposition. Women, though, tend to seek approval from others and thereby gain their sense of worth. Women are more inclined to be givers of praise than givers of information.

Our couples group agreed that Tannen's observations about the corporate world ring true. "I feel trapped," said Gayle, a management consultant. "At work I find myself changing in order to meet male expectations. I can't be tentative or solicit other people's reactions. I have to appear strong and confident whether I genuinely feel that way or not. I feel I'm losing my femininity."

Because women rely so strongly on feedback from others, they may hesitate to express themselves in a forthright, direct manner. As one psychologist says, "A man might ask a woman, 'Will you please go the store?' where a woman might say, 'I really need a few things from the store, but I'm so tired.'" A man might judge such behavior sneaky or underhanded, but such indirectness is actually the norm in many cultures.

For example, a direct approach such as, "I want to buy that cabbage for 50 cents" will get you nowhere in a Middle Eastern or African market. Both parties expect an elaborate social dance of bluff and innuendo. "If indirectness is understood by both parties, then there is nothing covert about it," Tannen concludes. The challenge in marriage is for both parties to recognize a communication style and learn to work within it.

Battle of the Sexes

We discovered that each couple in our group had what we called a Blamer and a Blamee; two of the Blamers were husbands, two were wives. The Blamer was usually a perfectionist, very detail- and task-oriented, who expected unrealistically high standards of the spouse. "No matter what I do," said one Blamee, "I can never measure up to my husband's standard of cooking or housekeeping or reading or sex, or anything. It's like I'm constantly being graded on my performance. And it doesn't motivate me to improve. I figure I'm not going to satisfy him anyway, so why try?"

All of us would like to make a few changes in the person we live with, but attempts to coax those changes often lead to conflict. And in conflict, gender differences rise quickly to the surface. Men, who grow up in a hierarchical environment, are accustomed to conflict. Women, concerned more with relationship and connection, prefer the role of peacemaker.

In my own marriage, for example, Janet and I view conflict through different eyes. As a writer, I thrive on criticism. I exchange manuscripts with other writers, and I've learned the best editors are the least diplomatic ones. I have two friends who pepper my manuscripts with words like "Ugh!" and "Awk!", and I would hesitate to publish any book without first running it through their gauntlet. In addition, I've gotten used to receiving heated letters from readers. Complimentary letters sound alike; angry letters fascinate me.

Janet, though, tends to feel criticism as a personal attack. I have learned much by watching her manage other people. Sensitive to criticism herself, she has become masterful at communicating criticism to others. When I managed employees in an office setting I would tend to blunder in with a straightforward approach: "There are five things you're doing right and five things you're doing wrong." After numerous failures, I began to see that the goal in criticism is to help the other person see the problem and desire to change. I have learned the necessity of communicating cross-culturally in my conflicts. When dealing with gluttons for punishment like me, I can be as direct as I want. For more sensitive persons, I need to exercise the skills I've gleaned from diplomats like my wife.

As our small group discussed various styles, we arrived at the following "guidelines" for conflict:

First, identify your fighting style. We tend to learn fighting styles from the family we grow up in. In Angie's Italian family, the fighting style was obvious: yell, argue and, if necessary, punch your brother in the nose. She approached marriage much the same way, only without the punches. Meanwhile, her husband would clam up and walk away from an argument. Angie thought Greg was deliberately ignoring her, and their conflicts never got resolved until they sought counseling. There, they realized that Greg was walking away because he knew he had no chance against Angie's well-honed fighting skills. Once both of them realized the dynamics behind their dead-end conflicts, they were able to make appropriate adjustments and change the "rules of engagement."

Second, agree on rules of engagement. Every couple needs to negotiate what constitutes "fighting fair." The couples in our group agreed to avoid these things: fighting in public, straying from the topic at hand, bringing up old history, threatening divorce and using sex as a way to paper over conflict. It's also helpful to consider additional rules, such as "Don't pretend to go along with a decision and then bring it up later as a matter of blame;" and "Don't resort to 'guerrilla warfare'—getting revenge by taking cheap shots after an argument is over."

Third, identify the real issue behind the conflict. A hidden message often underlies conflict. For example, women are sometimes accused of "nagging." On the surface, their message is the specific complaint at hand: not spending enough time with the kids, not helping with housework, coming home late from work. Actually, Deborah Tannen writes, there is another message at work:

"That women have been labeled 'nags' may result from the interplay of men's and women's styles, whereby many women are inclined to do what is asked of them and many men are inclined to resist even the slightest hint that anyone, especially a woman, is telling them what to do. A woman will be inclined to repeat a request that doesn't get a response because she is convinced that her husband would do what she asks if he only understood that she really wants him to do it. But a man who wants to avoid feeling that he is following orders may instinctively wait before doing what she asked in order to imagine that he is doing it of his own free will. Nagging is the result, because each time she repeats the request, he again puts off fulfilling it."

Spouses need to ask themselves questions like, "Is taking out the garbage really the issue, or is it a husband's crusty resistance to anything that infringes on his independence?"

Man Talk, and Woman Talk

In conversation, men and women appear to be doing the same thing—they open their mouths and produce noise. However, they actually use conversation for quite different purposes. Women use conversation primarily to form and solidify connections with other people. Men, on the other hand, tend to use words to navigate their way within the hierarchy. They do so by communicating their knowledge and skill, imparting information to others.

Women excel at what Tannen calls "private speaking" or "rapport-talk." Men feel most comfortable in "public speaking" or "report talk." Even though women may have more confidence in verbal ability (aptitude tests prove their superior skill), they are less likely to use that ability in a public context. Men feel comfortable giving reports to groups or interrupting a speaker with an objection—these are skills learned in the male hierarchy. Many women might perceive the same behavior as putting themselves on display. For example, at a party the men tell stories, share their expertise and tell jokes while the women usually converse in smaller groups about more personal subjects. They are busy connecting while the men are positioning themselves.

Our couples' group discussion became heated when we brought up another female trait that commonly goes by the name "bitching" (Tannen substituted the much more respectable term "ritual lament"). "Yeah, let's talk about this!" Greg said. "I remember one ski trip when I met some of my buddies in Colorado. We spent three days together before our wives joined us. We guys were having a great time, but when the women showed up everything changed. Nothing was right: The weather was too cold and the snow too crusty, the condo was drafty, the grocery store understocked, the hot tub dirty. Every night we heard them complain about sore muscles and raw places where the ski boots rubbed.

"The guys would listen to the griping, then just look at each other and say, 'The women are here!' It was incredible. We were living and skiing in exactly the same conditions. But before the women arrived, we had peace. Afterward, we heard nothing but gripes."

Tannen's explanation is that women tend to bond in pain. Through griping, they reaffirm connections with each other. For men, the immediate response to a complaint is to fix the problem. Otherwise, why complain? Women don't necessarily want the problem solved—who can "fix" the weather, for example? They merely want to feel understood and sympathized with.

Coming Together

Over several months our couples group gained an appreciation for the profound differences between male and female, but also a respect for how difficult it can be to pin down those differences.

Mary Crawford

 **NO**

Two Sexes, Two Cultures

Cross-Cultural Talk

Consider the difficulties of talk between, say, a person of Italian background and one from Japan. Even if the two share a common language, they may have trouble communicating because they are likely to have different ways of expressing politeness, conversational involvement, and so forth. The 'two-cultures' approach proposes that talk between women and men is fraught with potential misunderstanding for much the same reasons that communication across ethnic groups is.

... Talk shows and best-sellers proclaim the frustrations of cross-sex talk (*You just don't Understand*) and describe a gender gap so great that the two sexes might as well be from different planets (*Men are from Mars, Women are from Venus*)....

Talking Across the Gender Divide

... When we think of distinct female and male subcultures we tend to think of societies in which women and men spend virtually their entire lives spatially and interactionally segregated.... In Western societies, however, girls and boys are brought up together. They share the use of common space in their homes; eat, work, and play with their siblings of both sexes; generally attend coeducational schools in which they are aggregated in many classes and activities; and usually participate in religious meetings and activities together. Both sexes are supervised, cared for, and taught largely by women in infancy and early childhood, with male teachers and other authority figures becoming more visible as children grow older. Moreover, they see these social patterns mirrored and even exaggerated in the mass media. How can the talk of Western women and men be seen as talk across cultures?

The two-cultures model was first applied to the speech of North American women and men by Daniel Maltz and Ruth Borker, who proposed that difficulties in cross-sex and cross-ethnic communication are 'two examples of the same larger phenomenon: cultural difference and miscommunication' (1982: 196). Maltz and Borker acknowledge the argument that American women and men interact with each other far too much to be characterized as living in different subcultures. However, they maintain that the social rules for friendly conversation are learned between the ages of approximately 5 and 15, precisely the time when children's play groups are maximally segregated by sex. Not only do children voluntarily choose to play in same-sex groups, they consciously exaggerate differences as they differentiate themselves from the other sex. Because of the very different social contexts in which they learn the meanings and goals of conversational interaction, boys and girls learn to use language in different ways.

Citing research on children's play, Maltz and Borker (1982) argue that girls learn to do three things with words:

1. to create and maintain relationships of closeness and equality;
2. to criticize others in acceptable (indirect) ways;
3. to interpret accurately and sensitively the speech of other girls.

In contrast, boys learn to do three very different things with words:

1. to assert one's position of dominance;
2. to attract and maintain an audience;
3. to assert oneself when another person has the floor.

The Two-Cultures Approach as Bandwagon

... The new twist in the two-cultures model of communication is to conceive relationship difficulties not as women's deficiencies but as an inevitable result of deeply ingrained male–female differences. The self-help books that encode a two-cultures model make the paradoxical claim that difference between the sexes is deeply socialized and/or fundamental to masculine and feminine natures, and at the same time subject to change and manipulation if the reader only follows prescribed ways of talking. . . .

A best-selling exemplar of the genre is *Men are from Mars, Women are from Venus* (Gray, 1992). As its title proclaims, this book dichotomizes and stereotypes women and men to extremes. . . .

Every aspect of personality, motivation, and language is polarized. Women's speech is indirect, men's is direct. Women respond to stress by becoming overwhelmed and emotionally involved, men by becoming focused and withdrawn. Women and men even lunch in restaurants for different reasons: for men, it is an efficient way to approach the task of eating; for women, it is an opportunity to build a relationship.

Women and men are so irredeemably and fundamentally different that they need translators to help them communicate. . . . They also need rules and routines to bridge the gender gap. (Oddly, some of these rules and routines are opposite to those endorsed in assertiveness training books. Instead of 'I would like you to take out the trash,' a wife is exhorted to ask, 'Would you take out the trash?' Like assertiveness prescriptions, however, they are promulgated with detailed specificity and total conviction. If she unthinkingly asks '*Could* you take out the trash?' the wife has doomed her relationship to a period of resistance and resentment.) . . .

Although the book makes prescriptions for both sexes, it leaves little doubt about its intended readership: women in middle-class heterosexual marriages. In this book, Martians come home after a long day at the office to waiting Venusians. Martians are obsessed with paid work and money, Venusians with home and feelings. Venusians seem to do almost all the domestic work, from taking children to the dentist to cooking, cleaning, and calling elderly relatives. Martians may be asked to help, but only if Venusians use carefully circumscribed request forms and recognize that Martians have every right to refuse. Helpful tips are provided for 'Programming a Man to Say Yes' and 'The Art of Empowering a Man.' If all else fails, one can read the section on 'How to Give up Trying to Change a Man.'

. . . Despite the endless lists of how to change each other, the ultimate promise is that women can earn love through acceptance of the status quo. Individual change is not really necessary, much less the restructuring of masculinity and femininity. 'Through understanding the hidden differences of the opposite [sic] sex we can . . . give and receive . . . love. Love is magical, and it can last, if we remember our differences' (Gray, 1992: 14).

Academic psychologists and linguists have tended to ignore self-help materials. The path along the journey to enlightenment and communication heaven in these books is not likely to be cluttered with any actual references to research. . . .

The situation would be different if a prominent and well-respected academic were to claim expertise in male–female communication and write about it for the general public. And that is just what has happened with Deborah Tannen's *You just don't Understand: Women and Men in Conversation* (1990). . . . *You just don't Understand* has been on the *New York Times* bestseller list for over three years and claims over one million copies in print. . . . It seems that the state of gender relations among the middle-class book-buying public demanded an explanation of communication difficulties and frustrations, an explanation that books like *Men are from Mars, Women are from Venus* and *You just don't Understand* promised to provide.

Although Tannen is a much-published and respected linguist, this particular work has been quite controversial among her peers. Scholarly review and commentary have been mixed. . . .

Tannen claims that childhood play has shaped world views so that, when adult women and men are in relationships 'women speak and hear a language of connection and intimacy, while men speak and hear a language of status and independence' (1990: 42). The contrasting conversational goals of intimacy and independence lead to contrasting conversational styles. Women tell each other of their troubles, freely ask for information and help, and show appreciation of others' helping efforts. Men prefer to solve problems rather than talk about them, are reluctant to ask for help or advice, and are more comfortable in the roles of expert, lecturer, and teacher than learner or listener. Men are more talkative in public, women in private. These different styles are labelled 'report talk' (men's) and 'rapport talk' (women's).

Given the stylistic dichotomy between the sexes, miscommunication is almost inevitable; however, no one is to blame. Rather, another banner proclaims, 'The Key is Understanding:' 'Although each style is valid on its own terms, misunderstandings arise because the styles are different. Taking a cross-cultural approach to male–female conversations makes it possible to explain why dissatisfactions are justified without accusing anyone of being wrong or crazy' (1990: 47).

You just don't Understand makes its case for the two-cultures model skillfully and well using techniques that have become standard in popular writing about behavior: characterizations of 'most' women and men, entertaining anecdotes, and the presentation of research findings as fact. However, it is better written than most. . . .

The Two-Cultures Approach: An Evaluation

Beyond Deficiencies and Blame

Proponents of the two-cultures model maintain that it is an advance over approaches that blame particular groups for miscommunication. . . .

Unlike earlier approaches, the two-cultures model does not characterize women's talk as deficient in comparison to a male norm. . . . To John Gray, neither Mars nor Venus is a superior home. To Deborah Tannen, 'report talk,' and 'rapport talk' are equally limiting for their users in cross-sex communication. The speech style attributed to men is no longer 'standard' speech or 'the language,' but merely one way of negotiating the social landscape.

. . . Although *Men are from Mars, Women are from Venus* prescribes rigid rules for talk, the much more sophisticated *You just don't Understand* presents a view of language that stresses its flexibility. . . .

Doing Gender, Doing Power

The two-cultures approach fails to theorize how power relations at the structural level are recreated and maintained at the interactional level. . . .

This failure to recognize structural power and connect it with interactional power has provoked the strongest criticisms of the two-cultures approach. In a review of *You just don't Understand,* Senta Troemel-Ploetz (1991) pointed out that if the majority of relationships between women and men in our society were not fundamentally asymmetrical to the advantage of men,

> we would not need a women's liberation movement, women's commissions, houses for battered women, legislation for equal opportunity, antidiscrimination laws, family therapy, couple therapy, divorce. . . . If you leave out power, you do not understand any talk, be it the discussion after your speech, the conversation at your own dinner-table, in a doctor's office, in the back yards of West Philadelphia, in an Italian village, on a street in Turkey, in a court room or in a day-care center, in a women's group or at a UN conference. . . .

No one involved in debating the two-cultures approach denies that men have more social and political power than women. Maltz and Borker (1982: 199) acknowledge that power differentials 'may make some contribution' to communication patterns. However, they do not theorize the workings of power in interaction or advocate structural changes to reduce inequity.

The Bandwagon Revisited

... Deborah Tannen's critics have charged that, despite the absence of overt woman-blaming and the positive evaluation of 'feminine' modes of talk, the interpretations she offers often disguise or gloss over inequity, and privilege men's interpretations. They have accused her of being an apologist for men, excusing their insensitivity, rudeness, and dominance as mere stylistic quirks, and encouraging women to make the adjustments when needs conflict....

Differences and Dichotomies

In both *You just don't Understand* and *Men are from Mars, Women are from Venus,* women and men are presented as having non-overlapping and inherently conflictual conversational goals and styles....

Both books position cross-sex communication as fundamental. They do not set out to deal with communication across other categories that separate people: class, 'race,' ethnicity, age, sexual orientation, and so on.... With their erasure, the complexities of social position and situation are backgrounded; women become a global category and sex can take center stage....

When sex is the only conceptual category, differences attributable to situations and power relationships are made invisible....

The language of both books further constructs gender as difference. Gray repeatedly characterizes men and women as 'opposite sexes,' describes gender-differentiated behavior as 'instinctive,' and indulges in classic gender polarities: Martians are hard, Venusians soft; Martians are angular, Venusians round; Martians are cool, Venusians warm. 'In a magical and perfect way their differences seemed to complement each other' (1992: 44). Tannen's much more responsible and scholarly work is guilty of none of these excesses; it constructs gender as difference more subtly. The overlap between women and men is obscured by chapter titles ('Different Words, Different Worlds') and banner headings ('Male–Female Conversation is Cross-Cultural Communication') that suggest categorically different speech styles. The demands of mass-market writing preclude the use of numbers, tables, statistical analyses, graphs of distributions of results, or discussions of how persons and situations interact. Without these aids to conceptualizing *degrees* of differences and fluctuation, difference cannot readily be described except in terms of most/many women/men. This contributes to the fundamental attribution error. Instead of a flexible, situation-specific behavior, speech style becomes a static personality trait.

... Although Tannen notes that some women fear *with justification* that 'different' will be heard in reference to an implicit male norm, and that the conceptual step between 'different' and 'worse' is a short and perhaps inevitable one (1990: 14–15), she never develops these insights. Like the acknowledgment of status and power disparities, acknowledgement that difference may be read as women's deficiency appears, then disappears, without becoming a vehicle for further analysis.

... Tannen defends her choice not to write about dominance, control, and the politics of gender.

Asymmetries of Power

... In a chapter titled 'Damned if You Do,' Tannen reviews some of the research showing that the same behavior may be interpreted differently depending on whether it is done by a woman or a man, and that such interpretation is usually to women's disadvantage. The styles more typical of men, she acknowledges, are taken as the norm. Moreover, when women and men interact in mixed-sex groups, men's norms prevail. Women adjust to them, and it is this that gives the *appearance* of male dominance. Women who attempt to emulate the male norms may be disliked and disparaged as unfeminine and aggressive. Although Tannen makes the poignant observation that 'The road to authority is tough for women, and once they get there it's a bed of thorns,' this observation *ends* her chapter on the double bind rather than providing a starting point for further analysis.

> These are important areas of research, and many books have been written about them; they are not new, and they are not the field in which I work. I wrote a book about the role of what I call 'conversational style' in everyday conversation, especially in the context of close relationships, because that has been the subject of my research throughout my academic career. (Tannen, 1992: 249)

... Thirty years of social science research has shown that men have more power in heterosexual marriage and dating relationships due to their ability to access external resources and their higher social status generally.... Though Tannen briefly and belatedly... acknowledges research showing that earning more money is probably the greatest source of marital power, she does not appear to recognize that the actual result of this phenomenon, which she presents as a gender-neutral fact, is greater *male* power....

A Rhetoric of Reassurance

The rhetoric of difference makes everyone—and no one—responsible for interpersonal problems. Men are not to blame for communication difficulties; neither is a social system in which gender governs access to resources. Instead, difference is reified: 'The culprit, then, is not an individual man or even men's styles alone, but the difference between women and men's styles' (Tannen, 1990: 95).

One of the most striking effects achieved in these books is to reassure women that their lot in heterosexual relationships is normal. Again and again, it is stressed that no one is to blame, that miscommunication is inevitable, that unsatisfactory results may stem from the best of intentions....

Tannen explains that when men do most of the talking in a group, it is not because they intend to prevent women from speaking or believe that women have nothing important to say. Rather, they see the women as *equals,* and expect them to compete in the same style they themselves use. Thus, an inequity that feminists have conceptualized in terms of power differentials is acknowledged, but explained as an accidental imbalance created by style and having little to do with a gendered social order.

... In the separate worlds of 'report talk' and 'rapport talk', the goal may be sex-specific but the desire is the same: to be understood and responded to in kind. In *You just don't Understand,* each anecdote is followed by an analysis of the intentions of *both* speakers, a practice that Tannen (1992) feels reflects her fairness to both sexes. But this symmetry is false, because the one kind of intention that is never imputed to any speaker is the intent to dominate. Yet people are aware of such intentions in their talk, and, when asked, can readily describe the verbal tactics they use to 'get their own way' in heterosexual interactions....

Many of the most compelling anecdotes describe situations in which a woman is hurt, frustrated or angered by a man's apparently selfish or dominating behavior, only to find that her feelings were unwarranted because the man's intentions were good. This is psychologically naive. There is no reason to believe that *post hoc* stated intentions are a complete and sufficient description of conversational motives. Accounts of one's intentions are a socially constructed product in which face-saving and self-justification surely play a part. And even if intentions are innocent, language is a form of social action. Speech acts do things, and these things cannot be undone by declaring good intentions.

The emphasis on interpreting a partner's intentions is problematic in other ways as well. As Nancy Henley and Cheris Kramarae (1991: 42) point out, '[F]emales are required to develop special sensitivity to interpret males' silence, lack of emotional expressiveness, or brutality, and to help men express themselves, while men often seem to be trained deliberately to misinterpret much of women's meaning.' Young girls are told that hitting, teasing, and insults are to be read as signs of boys' 'liking.' Adolescent girls are taught to take responsibility for boys' inexpressiveness by drawing them out in conversation, steering talk to topics that will make them feel comfortable, and being a good listener. Girls and women learn from the discourse of popular fiction to reinterpret men's verbal and physical abuse. Indeed, a central theme in the romance novel is that cold, insensitive and rejecting behavior by men is to be read as evidence of their love (Unger and Crawford, 1992). Interpreting their partners' behavior in these ways may function to keep women in unrewarding relationships by making them more bearable.

Analyzing conversation in terms of intentions has a very important implication: it deflects attention from *effects,* including the ways that everyday action and talk serve to recreate and maintain current gender arrangements. Instead, readers are left to analyze what goes on in people's heads—what they say they intend to accomplish, not what they do accomplish, when they are engaged in 'doing gender.' Entering a larger discourse in which women are blamed for the consequences of societal sexism and for their own powerlessness, popularizations of the two-cultures model may be used to deflect responsibility from men.

References

Gray, J. (1992) *Men are from Mars, women are from Venus.* New York: HarperCollins.

Henley, N. M. and Kramarae, C. (1991) Gender, power, and miscommunication. In N. Coupland, H. Giles, and J. M. Wiemann (eds.), *Miscommunication and problematic talk* (pp. 18–43). Newbury Park, CA: Sage.

Maltz, D. N. and Borker, R. A. (1982) A cultural approach to male–female miscommunication. In J. Gumperz (ed.), *Language and social identity.* Cambridge: Cambridge University Press.

Tannen, D. (1990) *You just don't understand: women and men in conversation.* New York: Ballantine.

Tannen, D. (1992) Response to Senta Troemel-Ploetz's 'Selling the apolitical' (1991). *Discourse and Society,* 3, 249–254.

Troemel-Ploetz, S. (1991) Review essay: selling the apolitical. *Discourse and Society,* 2, 489–502.

Unger, R. and Crawford, M. (1992) *Women and gender: a feminist psychology.* New York and Philadelphia: McGraw-Hill and Temple University Press. [2nd edn in press]

POSTSCRIPT

Do Women and Men
Communicate Differently?

No one will likely debate that differences exist in the ways in which different people communicate. However, how many of these differences can be attributed to gender and how many to other factors? Clearly, our society accepts the role of gender, or the ascription of gender, to communication in different environments and under specific circumstances. For example, a woman who speaks assertively and clearly is considered to communicate "like a man"; a man who processes feelings is considered to be effeminate or less of a man. Beyond romantic relationships, it is interesting to look at the differences in the ways women and men communicate within family relationships, friendships, and at work. Our experiences with people of different genders in these different settings inform our feelings about what it is like to communicate as a man or woman, and about what we interpret from the communications from people of the same or different gender. One might hear a coworker complain that she or he "can't stand working for a male/female boss." Based on that complaint alone, the listener will likely jump to her or his own conclusions based on her or his own stereotypes. The listener might wonder whether the person does not care for a male boss because he is too direct, because he is sexually inappropriate, or otherwise. The listener might wonder whether the person does not care for a female boss because she does not make decisions quickly and without consensus of a group, because she cares more about whether or not her staff likes her than about the goals of the company, whether she uses her sexuality to get what she wants, etc.

These examples of stereotypical reactions are not intended to generalize for all men and women but to illustrate the point that the stereotypes exist—in our lives and in our popular culture. The question remains, however, of what value we attach to an interaction we see and interpret to be stereotypically male or female.

As mentioned in the introduction to this issue, it is interesting to consider the ways in which these issues affect same-gender interactions, whether in a friendship, family relationship, or romantic relationship. Tie this into race, culture, ethnicity, and age, and the similarities and differences form an interesting mosaic of communication. Moving through a city or through your school environment, look around you. How do boys and men greet each other? A nod in the air? A mumbled, "What's up?" A handshake and half-hug? Look at the girls and women. How do they approach each other? Who throws her arms around her girlfriends, and who walks up and simply makes her presence known? How much distance is there between people of the same gender when they greet or part from each other? In romantic relationships between people of the same genders, are gendered communication stereotypes irrelevant? Or are people freer to communicate as they will without worrying that one style will be considered "male" or "female"?

With such averred differences between gendered communication, one wonders how there can be any commonality between men and women at all. Yet there is—we all live together in societies, work together, and form friendships, family relationships, and romantic connections. There are differences in the ways in which people interact for a variety of reasons. The challenge comes in accepting these differences without attaching a value that one group of people is superior to another because of the ways in which they communicate.

Suggested Readings

Elizabeth Aries, *Men and Women in Interaction: Reconsidering the Differences* (Oxford University Press, 1997).

John Gray, *Men Are From Mars, Women Are From Venus: A Practical Guide for Improving Communication and Getting What You Want in Your Relationships* (HarperCollins, 1992).

Diana K. Ivy and Phil Backlund, *Exploring GenderSpeak: Personal Effectiveness in Gender Communication* (McGraw-Hill, 1999).

Deborah Tannen, *Gender and Discourse* (Oxford University Press, 1996).

Deborah Tannen, *You Just Don't Understand: Women and Men in Conversation* (Quill, 2001).

Deborah Tannen, *Talking From 9 to 5: Women and Men in the Workplace: Language, Sex, and Power* (Quill, 2001).

The American Civil Liberties Union (ACLU)

The American Civil Liberties Union (ACLU) was founded in 1920. It is a non-profit, nonpartisan organization of nearly 300,000 members and supporters, with offices in almost every state. The mission of the ACLU is to protect the Constitution's Bill of Rights.

`http://www.aclu.org`

The Cato Institute

The Cato Institute seeks to broaden the parameters of public policy debate to allow consideration of the traditional American principles of limited government, individual liberty, free markets, and peace.

`http://www.cato.org`

The Heritage Foundation

Founded in 1973, the Heritage Foundation is a research and educational institute—a think tank—whose mission is to formulate and promote conservative public policies based on the principles of free enterprise, limited government, individual freedom, traditional American values, and a strong national defense.

`http://www.heritage.org`

PART 6

Public Policy Issues

*T*he laws that are passed in any society are created, one hopes, with the best interests of the members of that society in mind. What happens, then, when members of that society disagree on what should and should not be legal? What should a society or community do when one group believes that common funds should support something with which another group disagrees? This part examines these and other questions within the context of five topics.

- Should Prostitution Be Legal?

- Is Court-Ordered Child Support Doing More Harm Than Good?

- Should Health Insurers Be Required to Pay for Infertility Treatments?

- Should Male Prison Inmates Be Allowed to Father Children?

- Should Congress Facilitate Transracial Adoptions?

ISSUE 15

Should Prostitution Be Legal?

YES: James Bovard, from "Safeguard Public Health: Legalize Contractual Sex," *Insight on the News* (February 27, 1995)

NO: Anastasia Volkonsky, from "Legalizing the 'Profession' Would Sanction the Abuse," *Insight on the News* (February 27, 1995)

ISSUE SUMMARY

YES: Author James Bovard writes about the potential benefits of legalizing prostitution, such as increased human rights protections and health precautions. He argues that legalizing prostitution would decriminalize it, thereby reducing the criminal practices of rape and other abuses.

NO: Author and researcher Anastasia Volkonsky writes that prostitution itself is a human rights violation for every person who sells her or his body and sexual behaviors for money. She does not believe that legalization will reduce the incidences of abuse or other illegal activities, nor will it guarantee that either prostitute or customer would comply with laws pertaining to commercial sex work.

Debates surrounding the legalization of prostitution have been around probably since prostitution first existed. At the base of some arguments are morals, of others are financial and law enforcement issues, and of others, human rights.

Proponents of legalization argue that prostitution always has been and always will be. Following a harm-reduction model, they argue that legalization would increase condom use and in turn lead to a reduction of HIV and other sexually transmitted diseases. Regulation of prostitution, they say, would reduce the hazards currently faced by commercial sex workers, such as rape and other physical abuses. Some believe that legalizing commercial sex work could benefit the national economy, since income could be tracked and taxes paid as a result.

Still other supporters of legalization believe that prostitutes have the right to choose how they earn their income. Since commercial sex work—whether prostitution, exotic dancing, or appearing in porn films—often pays well, how can society stand in the way of someone earning a good living? Young adults and teens have put themselves through college and supported families thanks to the money they have earned while doing sex work. Without such a high-paying job, they may not have been able to improve their lives.

Opponents of prostitution legalization point to literature showing that the vast majority of prostitutes are forced into sexual slavery—kidnapped, lured from their homes with promises of a better life, or purchased from their parents or partners. They argue that legalization would give rise to a black market that would continue to be as frightening and abusive as the sex industry is today. For example, the desire for child prostitutes would remain, so the illegal activities for procuring them would as well. Even prostitutes who would be required by law to use condoms might be tempted to break this law if it meant earning a higher fee for a particular sex act if they did not use protection. This would put their health, as well as the health of their customers, at risk.

For some opponents to legalizing prostitution, the issue is a moral one. This is not because of the sexual nature of prostitution, although that is certainly the case for some who simply believe that prostitution is wrong. Some opponents believe it is a moral issue because prostitution gives rise to dehumanizing, unsafe, illegal activities. It is morally reprehensible, they say, for the people who end up as prostitutes to be treated as too many are treated. They conclude that the abuses and potential threat for ongoing abuse far outweigh the potential benefits of legalization.

What do you think of these arguments? If society accepts that prostitution will always be here, shouldn't we do all we can to protect the individuals involved? Or would doing that give society's implicit approval of prostitution? Should we instead be looking for viable alternatives for people seeking sexual intimacy in a way that neither coerces nor hurts anyone?

In the following selections, James Bovard argues that legalization of prostitution would serve public health interests by mandating healthcare and sexually transmitted disease (STD) testing. Further, he asserts that legalizing prostitution would improve public safety by limiting the practice to remote areas and freeing up law enforcement officials, the judicial system, and jails for more serious offenses. Anastasia Volkonsky believes that current laws relating to prostitution are designed to protect the customers, not the prostitutes. Therefore, creating more laws would only serve the customers better rather than improving safety for sex workers. She cites statistics demonstrating that most prostitutes become prostitutes because they feel they have no other choice or because they are forced into it against their will. Legalizing prostitution, she believes, will do nothing to prevent these ongoing abuses.

James Bovard

 **YES**

Safeguard Public Health: Legalize Contractual Sex

T he call to legalize prostitution once again is becoming a hot issue. Columnists have been complaining about the conviction of Heidi Fleiss, the "Hollywood madam," saying it is unfair that the law punishes her but not her clients. San Francisco has appointed a task force to analyze the issue of legalizing prostitution. (A similar task force in Atlanta recommended legalization in 1986, but the city has not changed its policies.)

As more people fear the spread of AIDS, the legalization of prostitution offers one of the easiest means of limiting the spread of the disease and of improving the quality of law enforcement in this country.

Prostitution long has been illegal in all but one state. Unfortunately, laws against it often bring out the worst among the nation's law-enforcement agencies. Since neither prostitutes nor their customers routinely run to the police to complain about the other's conduct, police rely on trickery and deceit to arrest people.

In 1983, for example, police in Albuquerque, N.M., placed a classified advertisement in a local paper for men to work as paid escorts—and then arrested 50 men who responded for violating laws against prostitution. In 1985, Honolulu police paid private citizens to pick up prostitutes in their cars, have sex with them and then drive them to nearby police cars for arrest. (One convicted prostitute's lawyer complained: "You can now serve your community by fornicating. Once the word gets out there will be no shortage of volunteers.") In San Francisco, the police have wired rooms in the city's leading hotels to make videotapes of prostitutes servicing their customers. But given the minimal control over the videotaping operation, there was little to stop local police from watching and videotaping other hotel guests in bed.

Many prostitution-related entrapment operations make doubtful contributions to preserving public safety. In 1985, eight Fairfax County, Va., police officers rented two $88-a-night Holiday Inn rooms, purchased an ample supply of liquor and then phoned across the Potomac River to Washington to hire a professional stripper for a bachelor party. The stripper came, stripped and was busted for indecent exposure. She faced fines of up to $1,000 and 12 months in jail. Fairfax County police justified the sting operation by claiming it was necessary to fight prostitution. But the department had made only 11 arrests on prostitution charges in the previous year—all with similar sting operations.

In 1992, police in Des Moines, Wash., hired a convicted rapist to have sex with masseuses. The local police explained that they hired the felon after plain-clothes police officers could not persuade women at the local Body Care Center to have intercourse. Martin Pratt, police chief in the Seattle suburb, claimed that the ex-rapist was uniquely qualified for the job and, when asked why the police instructed the felon to consummate the acts with the alleged prostitutes, Pratt explained that stopping short "wouldn't have been appropriate."

A New York sting operation [in 1994] indirectly could have helped out the New York Mets: Two San Diego Padres baseball players were arrested after speaking to a female undercover officer. A Seattle journalist who also was busted described the police procedure to *Newsday:* "He said that he was stuck in traffic when he discovered that a miniskirted woman in a low-cut blouse was causing the jam, approaching the cars that were stopped. 'She came up to the windows, kind of swaggering,' he said. He said that she offered him sex, he made a suggestive reply, and the next thing he knew he was surrounded by police officers who dragged him out of his car and arrested him."

Many police appear to prefer chasing naked women than pursuing dangerous felons. As Lt. Bill Young of the Las Vegas Metro Police told Canada's *Vancouver Sun,* "You get up in a penthouse at Caesar's Palace with six naked women frolicking in the room and then say: 'Hey, baby, you're busted!' That's fun." (Las Vegas arrests between 300 to 400 prostitutes a month.) In August 1993, Charles County, Md., police were embarrassed by reports that an undercover officer visiting a strip joint had had intercourse while receiving a "personal lap dance."

In some cities, laws against prostitution are transforming local police officers into de facto car thieves. Female officers masquerade as prostitutes; when a customer stops to negotiate, other police rush out and confiscate the person's car under local asset-forfeiture laws. Such programs are operating in Detroit, Washington, New York and Portland, Ore. The female officers who masquerade as prostitutes are, in some ways, worse than the prostitutes—since, at least, the hookers will exchange services for payment, while the police simply intend to shake down would-be customers.

Shortly after the Washington police began their car-grabbing program in 1992, one driver sped off after a plainclothes officer tried to force his way into the car after the driver spoke to an undercover female officer. One officer's foot was slightly injured, and police fired six shots into the rear of the car. The police volley could have killed two or three people—but apparently the Washington police consider the possibility of killing citizens a small price to pay for slightly and temporarily decreasing the rate of prostitution in one selected neighborhood.

The same tired, failed antiprostitution tactics tend to be repeated ad nauseam around the country. Aurora, Colo., recently announced plans to buy newspaper ads showing pictures of accused johns. The plan hit a rough spot when the *Denver Post* refused to publish the ads, choosing not to be an arm of the criminal-justice system. One Aurora councilman told local radio host Mike Rosen that the city wanted to publish the pictures of the accused (and not wait until after convictions) because some of them might be found not guilty "because of some legal technicality."

In recent years, the Washington police force has tried one trick after another to suppress prostitution—including passing out tens of thousands of tickets to drivers for making right turns onto selected streets known to be venues of solicitation. (Didn't they see the tiny print on the street sign saying that right turns are illegal between 5 p.m. and 2 a.m.?) Yet, at the same time, the murder rate in Washington has skyrocketed and the city's arrest and conviction rates for murders have fallen by more than 50 percent.

The futile fight against prostitution is a major drain on local law-enforcement resources. A study published in the *Hastings Law Journal* in 1987 is perhaps the most reliable estimate of the cost to major cities. Author Julie Pearl observed: "This study focuses on sixteen of the nation's largest cities, in which only 28 percent of reported violent crimes result in arrest. On average, police in these cities made as many arrests for prostitution as for all violent offenses.

Last year, police in Boston, Cleveland, and Houston arrested twice as many people for prostitution as they did for all homicides, rapes, robberies, and assaults combined, while perpetrators evaded arrest for 90 percent of these violent crimes. Cleveland officers spent eighteen hours—the equivalent of two workdays—on prostitution duty for every violent offense failing to yield an arrest." The average cost per bust was almost $2,000 and "the average big-city police department spent 213 man-hours a day enforcing prostitution laws." Pearl estimated that 16 large American cities spent more than $120 million to suppress prostitution in 1985. In 1993, one Los Angeles official estimated that prostitution enforcement was costing the city more than $100 million a year.

Locking up prostitutes and their customers is especially irrational at a time when more than 35 states are under court orders to reduce prison overcrowding. Gerald Arenberg, executive director of the National Association of the Chiefs of Police, has come out in favor of legalizing prostitution. Dennis Martin, president of the same association, declared that prostitution law enforcement is "much too time-consuming, and police forces are short-staffed." Maryland Judge Darryl Russell observed: "We have to explore other alternatives to solving this problem because this eats up a lot of manpower of the police. We're just putting out brush fires while the forest is blazing." National surveys have shown that 94 percent of citizens believe that police do not respond quickly enough to calls for help, and the endless pursuit of prostitution is one factor that slows down many police departments from responding to other crimes.

Another good reason for reforming prostitution laws is to safeguard public health: Regulated prostitutes tend to be cleaner prostitutes. HIV-infection rates tend to be stratospheric among the nation's streetwalkers. In Newark, 57 percent of prostitutes were found to be HIV positive, according to a *Congressional Quarterly* report. In New York City, 35 percent of prostitutes were HIV-positive; in Washington, almost half.

In contrast, brothels, which are legal in 12 rural Nevada counties, tend to be comparative paragons of public safety. The University of California at Berkeley School of Public Health studied the health of legal Nevada brothel workers compared with that of jailed Nevada streetwalkers. None of the brothel workers had AIDS, while 6 percent of the unregulated streetwalkers did. Brothel owners had a strong incentive to police the health of their employees, since they could face liability if an infection were passed to a customer.

Prostitution is legal in several countries in Western Europe. In Hamburg, Germany, which some believe has a model program of legalized prostitution, streetwalkers are sanctioned in certain well-defined areas and prostitutes must undergo frequent health checks. Women with contagious diseases are strictly prohibited from plying their trade. (While some consider Amsterdam a model for legalization, the system there actually has serious problems. A spokesman for the association of Dutch brothels recently told the Associated Press: "The prostitutes these days are not so professional any more. In the past, prostitutes had more skills and they offered better services. Most of them now work only one or two evenings per week, and that's not enough time for them to become good.")

Bans on prostitution actually generate public disorder—streetwalkers, police chases, pervasive disrespect for the law and condoms littering lawns. As long as people have both money and sexual frustration, some will continue paying others to gratify their desires. The issue is not whether prostitution is immoral, but whether police suppression of prostitution will make society a safer place. The ultimate question to ask about a crackdown on prostitution is: How many murders are occurring while police are chasing after people who only want to spend a few bucks for pleasure?

In 1858, San Francisco Police Chief Martin Burke complained: "It is impossible to suppress prostitution altogether, yet it can, and ought to be regulated so as to limit the injury done to society, as much as possible." Vices are not crimes. Despite centuries of attempts to suppress prostitution, the profession continues to flourish. Simply because prostitution may be immoral is no reason for police to waste their time in a futile effort to suppress the oldest profession.

Anastasia Volkonsky

 **NO**

Legalizing the "Profession"
Would Sanction the Abuse

Prostitution commonly is referred to as "the world's oldest profession." It's an emblematic statement about the status of women, for whom being sexually available and submissive to men is the oldest form of survival.

As the "world's oldest," prostitution is presented as an accepted fact of history, something that will always be with us that we cannot eradicate. As a "profession," selling access to one's body is being promoted as a viable choice for women. In an era in which the human-rights movement is taking on some of history's most deeply rooted oppressions and an era in which women have made unprecedented strides in politics and the professions, this soft-selling of prostitution is especially intolerable.

Calls for legalization and decriminalization of prostitution put forth by civil libertarians are not forward-thinking reforms. They represent acceptance and normalization of the traffic in human beings. Moreover, the civil-libertarian portrayal of the prostitute as a sexually free, consenting adult hides the vast network of traffickers, organized-crime syndicates, pimps, procurers and brothel keepers, as well as the customer demand that ultimately controls the trade.

In studies replicated in major cities throughout the United States, the conditions of this "profession" are revealed to be extreme sexual, physical and psychological abuse. Approximately 70 percent of prostitutes are raped repeatedly by their customers—an average of 31 times per year, according to a study in a 1993 issue of the *Cardozo Women's Law Journal*. In addition, 65 percent are physically assaulted repeatedly by customers and more by pimps. A majority (65 percent and higher) are drug addicts. Increasingly, prostituted women are HIV positive. Survivors testify to severe violence, torture and attempted murders. The mortality rate for prostitutes, according to Justice Department statistics from 1982, is 40 times the national average.

What can be said of a "profession" with such a job description? How can it be said that women freely choose sexual assault, harassment, abuse and the risk of death as a profession? Such a term might be appealing for women who are trapped in the life, as a last-ditch effort to regain some self-respect and identify with the promises of excitement and glamor that may have lured them into prostitution in the first place. A substantial portion of street-walkers are homeless or living below the poverty line. Even most women who work in outcall or escort services have no control over their income because they are at the mercy of a pimp or pusher. Most will leave prostitution without savings.

Prostitution is not a profession selected from among other options by today's career women. It comes as no surprise that the ranks of prostitutes both in the United States and globally are filled with society's most vulnerable members, those least able to resist recruitment. They are those most displaced and disadvantaged in the job market: women, especially the poor; the working class; racial and ethnic minorities; mothers with young children to support; battered women fleeing abuse; refugees; and illegal immigrants. Women are brought to the United States from Asia and Eastern Europe for prostitution. In a foreign country, with no contacts or language skills and fearing arrest or deportation, they are at the mercy of pimps and crime syndicates.

Most tellingly, the largest group of recruits to prostitution are children. The average age of entry into prostitution in the United States is approximately 14, sociologists Mimi Silbert and Ayala Pines found in a study performed for the Delancey Foundation in San Francisco. More than 65 percent of these child prostitutes are runaways. Most have experienced a major trauma: incest, domestic violence, rape or parental abandonment. At an age widely considered too young to handle activities such as voting, drinking alcohol, driving or holding down a job, these children survive by selling their bodies to strangers. These formative years will leave them with deep scars—should they survive to adulthood.

❧

Sensing this contradiction between the reality of prostitution and the rhetoric of sexual freedom and consensual crime, some proposals to decriminalize prostitution attempt to draw a distinction between "forced" prostitution and "free" prostitution. A June 1993 *Time* article about the international sex industry notes that "faced with the difficulty of sorting out which women are prostitutes by choice and which are coerced, many officials shrug off the problem," implying that when one enters prostitution, it is a free choice. The distinction between force and freedom ends in assigning blame to an already victimized woman for "choosing" to accept prostitution in her circumstances.

"People take acceptance of the money as her consent to be violated," says Susan Hunter, executive director of the Council for Prostitution Alternatives, a Portland, Ore.-based social-service agency that has helped hundreds of women from around the country recover from the effects of prostitution. She likens prostituted women to battered women. When battered women live with their batterer or repeatedly go back to the batterer, we do not take this as a legal consent to battering. A woman's acceptance of money in prostitution should not be taken as her agreement to prostitution. She may take the money because she must survive, because it is the only recompense she will get for the harm that has been done to her and because she has been socialized to believe that this is her role in life. Just as battered women's actions now are understood in light of the effects of trauma and battered woman syndrome, prostituted women suffer psychologically in the aftermath of repeated physical and sexual assaults.

To make an informed choice about prostitution, says Hunter, women need to recover their safety, sobriety and self-esteem and learn about their options. The women in her program leave prostitution, she asserts, "not because we offer them high salaries, but because we offer them hope.... Women are not voluntarily returning to prostitution."

Proponents of a "consensual crime" approach hold that the dangers associated with prostitution are a result of its illegality. Legal prostitution will be safe, clean and professional, they argue; the related crimes will disappear.

Yet wherever there is regulated prostitution, it is matched by a flourishing black market. Despite the fact that prostitution is legal in 12 Nevada counties, prostitutes continue to work illegally in casinos to avoid the isolation and control of the legal brothels. Even the legal brothels maintain a business link with the illegal pimping circuit by paying a finder's fee to pimps for bringing in new women.

Ironically, legalization, which frequently is touted as an alternative to spending money on police vice squads, creates its own set of regulations to be monitored. To get prostitutes and pimps to comply with licensing rules, the penalties must be heightened and policing increased—adding to law-enforcement costs.

Behind the facade of a regulated industry, brothel prostitutes in Nevada are captive in conditions analogous to slavery. Women often are procured for the brothels from other areas by pimps who dump them at the house in order to collect the referral fee. Women report working in shifts commonly as long as 12 hours, even when ill, menstruating or pregnant, with no right to refuse a customer who has requested them or to refuse the sexual act for which he has paid. The dozen or so prostitutes I interviewed said they are expected to pay the brothel room and board and a percentage of their earnings—sometimes up to 50 percent. They also must pay for mandatory extras such as medical exams, assigned clothing and fines incurred for breaking house rules. And, contrary to the common claim that the brothel will protect women from the dangerous, crazy clients on the streets, rapes and assaults by customers are covered up by the management.

Local ordinances of questionable constitutionality restrict the women's activities even outside the brothel. They may be confined to certain sections of town and permitted out only on certain days, according to Barbara Hobson, author of *Uneasy Virtue*. Ordinances require that brothels must be located in uninhabited areas at least five miles from any city, town, mobile-home park or residential area. Physically isolated in remote areas, their behavior monitored by brothel managers, without ties to the community and with little money or resources of their own, the Nevada prostitutes often are virtual prisoners. Local legal codes describe the women as "inmates."

Merely decriminalizing prostitution would not remove its stigma and liberate women in the trade. Rather, the fiction that prostitution is freely chosen would become encoded into the law's approach to prostitution. Decriminalization would render prostitution an invisible crime without a name. "The exchange of money [in prostitution] somehow makes the crime of rape invisible" to society, says Hunter.

Amy Fries, director of the National Organization For Women's International Women's Rights Task Force, speaks from experience in studying and combating the sex trade both internationally and in the Washington area. Decriminalization, she says, does not address the market forces at work in prostitution: "[Prostitution] is based on supply and demand. As the demand goes way up, [the pimps] have to meet it with a supply by bringing in more girls."

Ultimately, changing the laws will benefit the customer, not the prostitute. Legalization advocates identify the arrest as the most obvious example of the abuse of prostitutes. But, surprisingly, former prostitutes and prostitutes' advocates say the threat of jail is not a top concern. Considering the absence of any other refuge or shelter, jail provides a temporary safe haven, at the very least providing a bunk, a square meal and a brief respite from johns, pimps and drugs. This is not to make light of abuses of state and police power or the seriousness of jail—the fact that for many women jail is an improvement speaks volumes about their lives on the streets.

It is the customers who have the most to lose from arrest, who fear jail, the stigma of the arrest record and the loss of their anonymity. The argument that prostitution laws invade the privacy of consenting adults is geared toward protecting customers. Prostitutes, working on the streets or in brothels controlled by pimps, have little to no privacy. Furthermore, decriminalization of prostitution is a gateway to decriminalizing pandering, pimping and patronizing—together, decriminalizing many forms of sexual and economic exploitation of women. A 1986 proposal advocated by the New York Bar Association included repeal of such associated laws and the lowering of the age of consent for "voluntary" prostitution. Despite the assertion that prostitutes actively support decriminalization, many women who have escaped prostitution testify that their pimps coerced them into signing such petitions.

Of the many interests contributing to the power of the sex industry—the pimps, the panderers and the patrons—the acts of individual prostitutes are the least influential. Yet, unfortunately, there are incentives for law enforcement to target prostitutes for arrest, rather than aggressively enforcing laws against pimps, johns and traffickers. It is quicker and less costly to round up the women than to pursue pimps and traffickers in elaborate sting operations. The prostitutes are relatively powerless to fight arrest; it is the pimps and johns who can afford private attorneys. And, sadly, it is easier to get a public outcry and convictions against prostitutes, who are marginalized women, than against the wealthier males who are the majority of pimps and johns.

Prostitution is big business. Right now, economics provide an incentive for procuring and pimping women. In all the debates about prostitution, the factor most ignored is the demand. But it is the customers—who have jobs, money, status in the community, clean arrest records and anonymity—who have the most to lose. New legal reforms are beginning to recognize that. An increasing number of communities across the country, from Portland to Baltimore, are adopting car-seizure laws, which allow police to impound the automobiles of those who drive around soliciting prostitutes. This approach recognizes that johns degrade not only women who are prostitutes, but also others by assuming that any females in a given area are for sale. Other towns have instituted, legally or as community efforts, measures designed to publicize and shame would-be johns by publishing their names or pictures and stepping up arrests.

Globally, a pending U.N. Convention Against All Forms of Sexual Exploitation would address the modern forms of prostitution with mechanisms that target pimps and johns and that hold governments accountable for their policies.

Hunter supports the use of civil as well as criminal sanctions against johns, modeled after sexual harassment lawsuits. "People will change their behavior because of economics," she points out, using recent changes in governmental and corporate policy toward sexual harassment as an example of how the fear of lawsuits and financial loss can create social change.

At the heart of the matter, prostitution is buying the right to use a woman's body. The "profession" of prostitution means bearing the infliction of repeated, unwanted sexual acts in order to keep one's "job." It is forced sex as a condition of employment, the very definition of rape and sexual harassment. Cecilie Hoigard and Liv Finstad, who authored the 1992 book *Backstreets*, chronicling 15 years of research on prostitution survivors, stress that it is not any individual act, but the buildup of sexual and emotional violation as a daily occurrence, that determines the trauma of prostitution.

Cleaning up the surrounding conditions won't mask the ugliness of a trade in human beings.

POSTSCRIPT

Should Prostitution Be Legal?

Laws are created, one hopes, in order to improve the lives of members living in a society. However, when a bill is introduced that can potentially improve the lives of one group while potentially decreasing the quality of life for another, how should we make our decisions? Lots of laws have been found to be unconstitutional in the past because they have attempted to regulate our private behaviors. For example, a landmark Supreme Court decision in *Griswold v. Connecticut* in 1965 argued that Connecticut's law prohibiting the use of birth control by married couples was unconstitutional because it infringed upon an adult couple's right to make a private decision.

Do you think we can attach the tenets of Griswold to the issue of prostitution? If the two people involved are consenting adults, neither of whom is hurt physically, emotionally, or psychologically as a result of the sex act, then can we not say that they are simply entering into a private business agreement? Or is there something inherently different about exchanging sex acts for money that cannot be compared to other business transactions, such as selling a car or contracting with an attorney or therapist in private practice?

As you read the following selections, you may have noticed that both sides of the argument focus exclusively on female prostitutes. We know that there are many adult and teen male prostitutes who have both female and male customers. Why do you think male prostitution was left out of this discussion? What kinds of values do you think this omission makes relating to women and men? Would considering male prostitution change your opinions at all? Regardless of whether or not it would change your views, it is important to keep in mind that this is a significant population within commercial sex work.

Suggested Readings

Belinda J. Carpenter, *Re-Thinking Prostitution: Feminism, Sex, and the Self* (Peter Lang Publishing, 2000).

Ronald B. Flowers, *Sex Crimes, Predators, Perpetrators, Prostitutes, and Victims: An Examination of Sexual Criminality and Victimization* (Charles C. Thomas Publishing, Ltd., 2000).

William W. Sanger, *The History of Prostitution: Its Extent, Causes and Effects Throughout the World* (Fredonia Books, 2002).

ISSUE 16

Is Court-Ordered Child Support Doing More Harm Than Good?

YES: Stephen Baskerville, from "This Engine of the Divorce Industry Is Destroying Families and the Constitution," *Insight on the News* (August 2, 1999)

NO: Geraldine Jensen, from "Child Support Fights Poverty for Millions of Kids and Helps Families Get Off Welfare," *Insight on the News* (August 2, 1999)

ISSUE SUMMARY

YES: Stephen Baskerville, teacher and spokesperson for Men, Fathers, and Children International, contends that the current state of the divorce "industry" discriminates against fathers, punishing those who have done nothing wrong along with those who have abused their children or broken other laws. He argues that the system relating to child support enforcement is corrupt and that it is fueled by individuals who make money by the fees they charge for their services.

NO: Geraldine Jensen, president of the Association for Children for Enforcement of Support, maintains that without court-ordered child support, children and families would remain dependent on welfare payments. She asserts that fathers deserve support as well but that collection of child support belongs with the federal government through the IRS to avoid overburdening child welfare agencies and the judicial system.

$\mathbf{T}$he Child Support Enforcement Program (CSE) was established in 1975 as part of the Social Security Act. The goal of this program was to ensure that parents provide financial support to their children. In 1996, the welfare reform law that was signed by then-President Bill Clinton included provisions that, among other things, enable officials to collect child support across state lines and that provide tough new penalties for parents who do not fulfill their obligations for child support (including driver's license revocation, seizure of assets, and denial of passports). CSE also locates noncustodial parents, establishes paternity and child support obligations, and enforces child support orders.

Child support payments are most commonly made through income withholding, withholding of unemployment compensation, and state and federal income tax refund offsets (thanks to the Uniform Child Support Enforcement Act of 1997). However, wage withholding is by far the most effective, and this accounted for 62 percent of all collections in 2000. At the same time, however, billions of dollars in current and prior years' support remain due.

While the language of CSE is gender-neutral, more often than not, the focus is on collecting support from fathers. Regardless of whether a father reneges on his financial obligation or is unable to pay due to financial hardship, the stigmatized term "deadbeat dad" is often applied. However, in a relationship where a man chooses to stay home and raise the children while his female partner earns the family income (there is limited information relating to how child support laws apply to same-sex couples), he would have recourse as well were the relationship to break up and he retained custody of the children. "Deadbeat moms," therefore, also exist.

Supporters of government involvement in child support collection point to cases indicating that children would not receive these funds without this intervention. In the end, supporters say, it is the children who suffer. Opponents of court-ordered child support express a range of beliefs relating to the system. Some oppose it because it demonizes fathers and encourages female partners to make up charges of child abuse in order to receive additional restitution. These programs, they say, ignore the possible reasons behind delayed or unfulfilled payments. If a man is barely able to pay his own expenses, how can he be expected to help support one or more children at the same time?

Do you think that a parent should have to continue to pay child support once the marriage or relationship has broken up? If not, why not? If so, on what does this depend? Gender? Income? Circumstances of the divorce or breakup?

In the following selections, Stephen Baskerville argues that corruption and fabrication of information abound in the child support enforcement system and that the officials of this system end up benefiting at the cost of these fathers' constitutional rights. Geraldine Jensen maintains that child support plays a key role in keeping children and their families out of the welfare system and that the most effective way of collecting this support is through state, local, and federal government intervention.

Stephen Baskerville

 **YES**

This Engine of the Divorce Industry Is Destroying Families and the Constitution

Geoff came home one day to find a note on the kitchen table saying his wife had taken their two children to live with their grandparents. He quit his job as head of his department in a university and followed. He was summoned to court on eight-hours' notice and, without a lawyer and without being permitted to speak, was stripped of custody rights and ordered to stay away from his wife and children most of the time. Because he had no job, no car and no place to live, his mother cancelled a pending sale of her house, and he moved in with her. Geoff and his mother now pay about $1,200 a month to his wife and her wealthy parents, and he is left to live and care for his two children on about $700 a month. A judge also threatened him with jail if he did not pay a lawyer he had not hired. When his temporary job ends, the payments must continue, and he is not permitted to care for the children while unemployed. He also expects to be coerced into paying more legal fees. He has never been charged with any wrongdoing, either criminal or civil.

Geoff's experience increasingly is common. In fact, it is epidemic. Massive numbers of fathers who are accused of no wrongdoing now are separated from their children, plundered for everything they have, publicly vilified and incarcerated without trial.

About 24 million American children live in homes where the father is not present, with devastating consequences for both the children and society. Crime, drug and alcohol abuse, truancy, teenage pregnancy, suicide and psychological disorders are a few of the tragic consequences. Conventional wisdom assumes that the fathers of these children have abandoned them. In this case the conventional wisdom is dangerously wrong. It is far more likely that an "absent" father is forced away rather than leaving voluntarily.

In his new study, *Divorced Dads: Shattering the Myths,* Sanford Braver of Arizona State University has shown conclusively that the so-called "deadbeat dad," one who deserts his children and evades child support, "does not exist in significant numbers." Braver confirms that, contrary to popular belief, at least two-thirds of divorces are filed by mothers, who have virtual certainty of getting the children and a huge portion of the fathers' incomes, regardless of any fault on their part. The title of Ashton Applewhite's 1997 book says it succinctly: *Cutting Loose: Why Women Who End Their Marriages Do So Well.*

Other studies have found even higher percentages of divorces filed by mothers, and lawyers report that, when children are involved, divorce is the initiative of the mother in virtually all instances. Moreover, few of these divorces involve grounds such as desertion, adultery or violence. The most frequent reasons given are "growing apart" or "not feeling loved or appreciated." (Surveys consistently show that fathers are much more likely than mothers to believe parents should remain married.) Yet, as Braver reports, despite this involuntary loss of their children, 90 percent of these deserted fathers regularly pay court-ordered child support (unemployment being the main reason for nonpayment), often at exorbitant levels and many without any rights to see their children. Most make heroic efforts to stay in contact with the children from whom they are forcibly separated.

The plight of unmarried inner-city fathers is harder to quantify, but there is no reason to assume they love their children any less. A recent study conducted in Washington with low-income fathers ages 16 to 25 found that 63 percent had only one child; 82 percent had children by only one mother; 50 percent had been in a serious relationship with the mother at the time of pregnancy; only 3 percent knew the mother of their child only a little; 75 percent visited their child in the hospital; 70 percent saw their children at least once a week; 50 percent took their child to the doctor; large percentages reported bathing, feeding, dressing and playing with their children; and 85 percent provided informal child support in the form of cash or purchased goods such as diapers, clothing and toys. University of Texas anthropologist Laura Lein and Rutgers University professor Kathryn Edin recently found that low-income fathers often are far worse off than their government-assisted families, "but economically and emotionally marginal as many of these fathers are, they still represent a large proportion of low-income fathers who continue to make contributions to their children's households and to maintain at least some level of relationship with those children."

Yet the voices of these fathers rarely are heard in the public arena. Instead we hear the imprecations of a government conducting what may be the most massive witch-hunt in this country's history. Never before have we seen the spectacle of the highest officials in the land—including the president, the attorney general and other Cabinet secretaries, and leading members of Congress from both parties—using their offices as platforms from which publicly to vilify private citizens who have been convicted of nothing and who have no opportunity to reply.

Under the guise of pursuing deadbeat dads, we now are seeing mass incarcerations without trial, without charge and without counsel, while the media and civil libertarians look the other way. We also have government officials freely entering the homes and raiding the bank accounts of citizens who are accused of nothing and simply helping themselves to whatever they want— including their children, their life savings and their private papers and effects, all with hardly a word of protest noted.

And these are fathers who are accused of nothing. Those who face trumped-up accusations of child abuse also must prove their innocence before they can hope to see their children. Yet now it is well established that most child abuse takes place in the homes of single mothers. A recent study from the Department of Health and Human Services, or HHS, found that "almost two-thirds [of child abusers] were females." Given that male perpetrators are not necessarily fathers but much more likely to be boyfriends and stepfathers, fathers emerge as the least likely child abusers. A British study by Robert Whelan in 1993 titled *Broken Homes and Battered Children* concluded that a child living with a single mother is up to 33 times more likely to be abused than a child living in an intact family. The argument of many men legally separated from their families is that the real abusers have thrown the father out of the family so they can abuse his children with impunity.

In Virginia alone the state Division of Child Support Enforcement now is "pursuing" 428,000 parents for up to $1.6 billion, according to its director, Nick Young. In a state of fewer than 7 million people, the parents of 552,000 children are being "pursued." That is the parents of roughly half the state's minor dependent children. HHS claims that almost 20 million fathers in the nation are being pursued for something close to $50 billion. We are being asked to believe that half the fathers in America have abandoned their children willfully.

These figures essentially are meaningless. If they indicate anything it is the scale on which families are being taken over by a destructive and dangerous machine consisting of judges, lawyers, psychotherapists, social workers, bureaucrats and women's groups—all of whom have a direct financial interest in separating as many children from their fathers as possible, vilifying and plundering the fathers and turning them into criminals. The machine is so riddled with conflicts of interest that it is little less than a system of organized crime. Here is how it works: Judges are appointed and promoted by the lawyers and "custody evaluators," into whose pockets they funnel fees; the judges also are influenced with payments of federal funds from child-support enforcement bureaucracies that depend on a constant supply of ejected fathers; child-support guidelines are written by the bureaucracies that enforce them and by private collection companies that have a financial stake in creating as many arrearages and "deadbeat dads" as possible. These guidelines are then enacted by legislators, some of whom divert the enforcement contracts to their own firms, sometimes even taking personal kickbacks (as charged in a recent federal indictment in Arkansas). Legislators who control judicial appointments also get contracts (and kickbacks, again the case in Arkansas) for providing legal services at government expense in the courts of their appointees. And, of course, custody decisions and child-support awards must be generous enough to entice more mothers to take the children and run, thus bringing a fresh supply of fathers into the system. In short, child support is the financial fuel of the divorce industry. It has very little to do with the needs of children and everything to do with the power and profit of large numbers of adults.

For their part, politicians can register their concern for fatherless children relatively cheaply by endlessly (and futilely) stepping up "child-support" collection while creating programs ostensibly designed to "reunite" fathers with their children. Even some fatherhood advocates jump on the bandwagon, attacking "absent" fathers while holding their tongues about the judicial kidnapping of their children. Though almost everyone now acknowledges the importance of fathers, for too many there are more political and financial rewards in targeting them as scapegoats than in the more costly task of upholding the constitutional rights of fathers and their children not to be ripped apart.

There is no evidence that endless "crackdowns" on evicted fathers serve any purpose other than enriching those in the cracking-down business. With child-support enforcement now a $3 billion national industry, the pursuit of the elusive deadbeat yields substantial profits, mostly at public expense. "In Florida last year," writes Kathleen Parker in the *Orlando Sentinel,* "taxpayers paid $4.5 million for the state to collect $162,000 from fathers"; and the story is the same elsewhere.

Instead of the easy fiction that massive numbers of fathers are suddenly and inexplicably abandoning their children, perhaps what we should believe instead is that a lucrative racket now is cynically using our children as weapons and tools to enrich lawyers and provide employment for judges and bureaucrats. Rather than pursuing ever greater numbers of fathers with ever more Draconian punishments, the Justice Department should be investigating the kind of crimes it was created to pursue—such as kidnapping, extortion and racketeering—in the nation's family courts.

Geraldine Jensen

← **NO**

Child Support Fights Poverty for Millions of Kids and Helps Families Get Off Welfare

How important is child support to American mothers? Consider the testimony of a single parent who wrote to me: "After the divorce, my minimum-wage job wasn't enough to support my children. I got behind on the house payments and the bank began foreclosure proceedings. The utilities were shut off. We ended up on welfare, reliant on the government to collect child support. The bureaucracy was slow to act and difficult to work with. It took two years to get my case to court. We collected $250 a month in current support and $50 a month in back support as payments on the $12,000 in arrears. I thought these payments were too low, but I was told that the average child-support payment in the U.S. is about $3,700 year. Even though the payments were not a large amount of money, when added to my wages, it was possible to get off welfare. Now my sons see that you work for a living rather than rely on welfare. Also, enforcing the child support got the father's attention. Finally, he is spending time with his sons."

In 1995, the U.S. Census study of children growing up in single-parent households showed that 2.7 million children received full payments, 2 million received partial payments and 2.2 million who had support orders received no payments. About 6.8 million children received no payments because they needed paternity or an order established. About 32 percent of the families who do not receive child support live in poverty. In single-parent households, 28 percent are white children, 40 percent are black children and 48 percent are Hispanic children.

There are now millions of children owed more than $41 billion in unpaid child support, according to the federal Office of Child Support Enforcement's 21st Annual Report to Congress. If we truly are serious about strengthening families and promoting self-sufficiency rather than welfare-dependency by making parents responsible for supporting their children, it is time to get serious about setting up an effective national child-support enforcement system. Taking care of the children one brings into the world is a basic, personal responsibility and a true family value.

From Geraldine Jensen, "Child Support Fights Poverty for Millions of Kids and Helps Families Get Off Welfare," *Insight on the News* (August 2, 1999). Copyright © 1999 by News World Communications, Inc. Reprinted by permission of *Insight on the News*.

Due to the nation's 50 percent divorce rate and the fact that 25 percent of all births are to parents who are not married, 60 percent of the children born in the nineties will spend part of their lives in a single-parent household. As far as the impact on children is concerned, the child-support collection system is second only to the public-school system. We need a national enforcement system where support payments are collected just like taxes, instead of a 50-state bureaucracy full of loopholes and red tape.

Republican Rep. Henry Hyde of Illinois and Democratic Rep. Lynn Woolsey of California have proposed HR1488, legislation designed to set up a federal/state partnership to collect child support throughout the nation, even when parents move across state lines. These interstate cases make up almost 40 percent of the caseload and are the most difficult to enforce. State courts or government agencies through administrative hearings would establish orders within the divorce process or through establishment of paternity and would determine the amount to be paid based on parental income, modifying orders as needed. Enforcement would be carried out at the federal level by building on the current system in which employers deduct child-support payments from their payrolls. Instead of the state-government agencies in each state having their own system to enforce child-support payments, the new law would withhold payments in a manner similar to federal income taxes. Withholding would be triggered by completion of a W-4 form and a verification process. Self-employed parents would pay child support quarterly, just like Social Security taxes. At the end of the year, if all child support due was not paid, the obligated parent would be required to pay it just like unpaid federal taxes or collection would be initiated by the IRS.

For low-income and unemployed fathers, states could continue to operate fatherhood programs. Such programs offer fathers, many of whom are young, an opportunity to develop parenting and job skills that will allow them to support their children financially. Approximately 40 percent of the children who live in fatherless households haven't seen their fathers in at least a year. Census Bureau data show that fathers who have visitation and custody arrangements are three times as likely to meet their child-support obligations as those who do not. If collection of child support were done through the tax-collection system, local domestic-relations courts would have more time and resources to focus on visitation and custody issues.

The child-support system was established in 1975 as part of the Social Security Act. Although challenged in court, the Supreme Court ruled it constitutional. In 1984—when the first group of eligible children was nine years old—Congress deemed it necessary to enact child-support amendments because the collection rate for children with cases open at the state-government level was only about 20 percent, and 50 percent of the children still needed orders established. When these children were age 13 in 1988, Congress acted again and passed the Family Support Act. This law promised collection of child support via payroll deduction from the time the order was entered in the divorce of paternity decree. It required states to place a lien on the property of those who failed to pay support and set up mathematical guidelines to determine a fair amount of support to be paid. In 1996, with the child-support system's first beneficiaries grown (age 21), only 20 percent of them received child support and 50 percent never did get an order established to collect support. Congress acted again through the welfare-reform laws. Unfortunately, this didn't solve the problem because the infrastructure for an effective state-based, child-support enforcement system does not exist.

State child-support caseloads grow yearly and the amount of support collected increases, but the percentage of families receiving support remains at about 25 percent. Studies cited in the book *Small Change* by Andrea Beller and John Graham show that income withholding is one of the most effective ways to collect child support. The only more effective method was nonpayment-of-support prosecution, which increased collection 10 percent more than income withholding. However, states rarely use criminal nonpayment-of-support actions, more often using civil contempt proceedings.

Nonpayment of support is a crime against children, a crime that causes poverty and in all states can be punished by jail time. The criminal sanction ensures payment from some negligent fathers. In a court-monitoring project undertaken by the Association for Children for Enforcement of Support, we found that if cases were processed as contempt-of-court charges, the amount collected would be only 10 percent of that collected in criminal nonpayment-of-support cases. For example, in a monitoring project done in Wood County, Ohio, about $20,000 was collected on 20 contempt cases while $200,000 was collected on 20 criminal nonpayment cases. Noncustodial parental rights are protected in contempt- and criminal proceedings due to the Supreme Court having found that anyone who faces possible jail time must be appointed an attorney if they can not afford one.

Some have charged that incarcerating someone for not paying child support creates debtor prisons. This is not true because those who are found in contempt of court are violating the civil-law principle of failing to follow a court order. Those charged with criminal nonpayment are guilty of child abuse and neglect. Terry Adams, author of *Making Fathers Pay,* studied the Michigan child-support enforcement system of arresting those who fail to pay child support and found that nine out of 10 end up paying child support.

We now have lost a whole generation of children because of a "broken system"—one that is state-based and different everywhere and in which judges review cases one at a time in a slow, antiquated process designed for the 19th century, when divorce or having children outside of marriage was unusual. For example, in Ohio 600 judges are tasked with more than 700,000 child-support cases to establish or enforce a child-support order. Even if every judge—from traffic court to the Supreme Court—worked day and night on child-support cases, they could not handle this caseload.

A recent report from the General Accounting Office shows that states have spent $2.6 billion on statewide automated child-support-enforcement tracking systems. The results are dismal: Only 40 percent of the caseload is accounted for by the computer systems. Most states have experienced numerous hardware and software problems. Some states' systems have crashed as soon as they have gone online. Others have not been capable of handling the current child-support caseload. Still others have not performed according to the requirements outlined by the federal government. For example, California paid a private contractor more than $200 million for a system whose design was so flawed it was unable to perform even basic required functions. With all of these problems experienced within the states, how can we expect these systems to be successfully linked nationwide?

Further, privacy issues associated with passing sensitive Social Security and financial information between many agencies and private contractors hired by government is worrisome. It almost is impossible to ensure confidentiality when states have county child-support agencies and contracts with private collection companies. Any child-support workers in the country could gain access to sensitive financial information that is essential for successful child-support enforcement. The IRS already has information listing place of employment and income and has a proven track record of maintaining confidentiality.

The child-support agencies and courts throughout the country already are overburdened and backlogged. They will not be capable of handling the new tools provided to them by the child-support provisions in welfare-reform legislation. It is time to make children as important as taxes. Congress should act expeditiously to pass HR1488 for the children's sake.

POSTSCRIPT

Is Court-Ordered Child Support Doing More Harm Than Good?

Many people who enter into a committed relationship or marriage intend for the relationship to last forever—especially when children are involved. However, this is far from an ideal world. Relationships do not last, and when they end, many end negatively. Partners cheat, partners change, and partners make decisions without consulting the other partners. When these decisions involve larger family issues, such as whether or when to have a child, the outcome can be devastating.

Many couples are able to break up civilly and agree upon child support themselves or through a mediator. In the end, however, there is a good number of parents who refuse to pay child support to spite their former partners or spouses. Some did not want to become parents in the first place, others are bitter due to the nature of the breakup or divorce. Unfortunately, children often get caught in the cross fire.

Should government remain involved in ensuring that child support payments are met? Some may argue that once government involvement starts it becomes challenging to draw a line as to where it should stop. Do you see any limits on government involvement in this process—and if so, how do you think these limits could be put into place?

The issues of custody and intentionality in the pregnancy should both be reviewed as well. If a woman earns more than her male partner and retains custody of the children, should her former partner still have to pay some money toward child support? Should a woman who becomes pregnant accidentally and chooses to become a mother be able to secure financial support from the baby's father—even if he expresses no interest in parenting and would have wanted her to terminate the pregnancy? What about a situation where a man and a woman have a "one-night stand" and a pregnancy results? If a pregnancy happens as a result, and a woman chooses to carry the baby to term and become a parent, should the man she met one time be responsible to help her financially to raise her child? What if he is in a relationship with another person and already has children to help support?

This topic raises question upon question. In the end, however, we have to reflect on our own values relating to parental rights and responsibilities and our beliefs in the appropriateness or inappropriateness of government intervention when it comes to family issues to determine how we truly feel about this issue.

Suggested Readings

Ashton Applewhite, *Cutting Loose: Why Women Who End Their Marriages Do So Well* (HarperCollins, 1998).

Sanford L. Braver and Diane O'Connell, *Divorced Dads: Shattering the Myths* (J. P. Tarcher, 1998).

Irwin Garfinkel, Sara McLanahan, and Daniel Meyer, eds., *Fathers Under Fire: The Revolution in Child Support Enforcement* (Russell Sage Foundation, 2001).

J. Thomas Oldham and Marygold S. Melli, eds., *Child Support: The Next Frontier* (University of Michigan Press, 2000).

U.S. Government Printing Office, *Green Book, 2000: Background Material and Data on Programs Within the Jurisdiction of the Committee on Ways and Means* (U.S. Government Printing Office, 2000).

ISSUE 17

Should Health Insurers Be Required to Pay for Infertility Treatments?

YES: Diane D. Aronson, from "Should Health Insurers Be Forced to Pay for Infertility Treatments? Yes," *Insight on the News* (February 8, 1999)

NO: Merrill Matthews, Jr., from "Should Health Insurers Be Forced to Pay for Infertility Treatments? No," *Insight on the News* (February 8, 1999)

ISSUE SUMMARY

YES: Diane D. Aronson, executive director of RESOLVE, the National Infertility Association, argues that reproduction is an inherent right, and therefore the inability to become or cause a pregnancy should be covered by health insurance just as any other physical or mental challenge that inhibits a major life activity.

NO: Merrill Matthews, Jr., vice president of domestic policy at the National Center for Policy Analysis, asserts that mandating coverage of infertility treatment, a costly process, would unfairly burden subscribers whose rates would go up to help offset these costs, as well as small businesses that are not insured under the Employee Retirement Income Security Act (ERISA) as are large businesses.

If a woman attempts for one year unsuccessfully to become pregnant, concern over possible infertility arises. She may be tested to ensure that the follicles in her ovaries are maturing and her ovaries are releasing eggs regularly. Her male partner may be tested to review the number of sperm in his semen. These tests may reveal that one or both partners are either unable or less likely to cause a pregnancy or become pregnant.

According to one source, infertility affects approximately 10 percent of women in the United States who are of reproductive age and their partners. One in 10 of these women needs medical intervention in order to become pregnant. Of these who obtain medical treatment, 65 percent succeed in having a baby.

The treatments can involve a range of efforts. This might include having a medical professional "spin" a male partner's or donor's semen to eliminate dead or slow-moving sperm. It might include having the sperm inserted intra-uterinely, by dilating a woman's cervix and inserting the sperm higher up than intercourse or standard fertilization would do.

With in vitro fertilization, a woman's mature ovum is removed from her ovary and fertilized in a laboratory. Once fertilized, the blastocyst or embryo is reintroduced into the woman's uterus where it will hopefully implant on the uterine wall and become a pregnancy. This process takes time—and money. One estimate made by the University of Rochester Medical Center puts the costs for in vitro fertilization (depending upon the amount of medication, lab tests, and services required) between $8,000 and $10,000 per cycle.

While there are currently no federal laws that require insurance coverage for infertility treatment, 15 states have enacted some type of infertility insurance coverage law. In some states, there is a mandate to cover, and in others, a mandate to offer. With a mandate to cover, health insurance companies must provide coverage for infertility treatment in every policy, with a premium that reflects this coverage. With a mandate to offer, health insurance companies must make a policy available that offers coverage of infertility treatment—but the employers are not required to pay for the infertility treatment coverage. The vast majority of health insurance companies in the United States do not cover these costs; many of those that do put a cap on the payments they will make.

Supporters of mandated infertility coverage maintain that infertility is a physical issue, and therefore it should be treated as any other physical issue. They point to the fact that individuals and couples pay premiums that reflect coverage for health services they will never be able to use themselves, such as prenatal and well-mother care. Therefore, infertility benefits should be included and all subscribers be required to pay a premium that includes these services as well.

Opponents often say that the needs of the many outweigh the needs of the few—that the number of people who require infertility treatment is not large enough to place the burden of financial contribution on general subscribers. As insurance premiums go up, the chances that lower-income individuals will be unable to cover the costs rise as well. Opponents also argue that since there is no guarantee that fertility treatments will work, the often exorbitant payments are often wasted in this process.

Should health insurance companies be mandated nationwide to cover infertility treatment? Does doing so place an undue burden on people who are past their reproductive years or on those who do not intend to have children themselves biologically?

In the following selections, Diane D. Aronson asserts that infertility is and should be seen as "a disease of the reproductive system" and as such, should be treated as any other disease by health insurance companies and covered accordingly. Merrill Matthews, Jr., provides a cost-benefit analysis of this type of health coverage and maintains that coverage of infertility procedures places an undue financial burden on the general population.

Diane D. Aronson  **YES**

Should Health Insurers Be Forced to Pay for Infertility Treatments? Yes

W hat is the most important concern in your life? For many people, the answer would be family. If you are a couple with a vision of building a family, the condition of infertility can interrupt this basic human desire. Infertility is a life-changing crisis that affects more than 10 percent of the reproductive-age population in the United States. Having children and raising a family, which comes easily to many couples, can be a heartbreaking challenge for those afflicted with infertility.

Infertility is a disease of the reproductive system which affects both men and women; it is not elective or selective. It strikes people in all walks of life, and it crosses racial, ethnic, religious and socioeconomic boundaries. Couples who experience infertility most often have to pay out of pocket for their diagnoses and treatments. Health-insurance coverage usually either is nonexistent or minimal.

For many couples, only medical treatment can enable them to become pregnant and have children. While adoption is an option for many, the costs can reach $30,000, and there are not enough babies available in the United States to meet the need. Proven medical treatments are available, and insurance coverage should be provided as it is for other diseases. Insurance covers the maternal and neonatal costs for fertile couples who are able to have children. Individuals with infertility pay into the insurance plans that cover those costs, even though they often cannot access care to bear children. Couples who need medical assistance should not be denied the opportunity to become pregnant and have children.

In any given month, a normally fertile couple has a 22 percent chance of becoming pregnant. Nearly two-thirds of couples receiving infertility treatments have successful pregnancies. Most who successfully obtain medical assistance for infertility are able to do so through relatively low-cost ($500 to $2,000) and noninvasive treatments such as medication or intrauterine insemination.

Approximately 5 percent of couples who seek treatment undergo assisted reproductive technology, or ART, such as in vitro fertilization, which costs approximately $12,000 per attempt. When the woman has blocked fallopian tubes or the man has a low sperm count, ART treatment may be the only method by which a couple can become pregnant. Another treatment option is surgery, which usually costs more than ART but often is covered by insurance plans. Because of this coverage, couples may undergo multiple surgical procedures, even if ART would be the best and most cost-effective option. Such partial coverage encourages inefficiency and, at times, incorrect treatment choices. Insurance coverage of the range of treatments would allow for better management of care, as physicians and patients could then better determine the most effective treatment path.

Infertility insurance coverage also would help to manage the rate of multiple births that result from some treatments. The multiple-birth rate among those who obtain infertility treatments is higher than among the general population. The neonatal costs following multiple births are high, as are the health risks to the mother and the babies. (The neonatal costs of the Chukwu octuplet births in Houston on Dec. 20, 1998, are estimated to be more than $2 million.)

When couples are struggling to have a child and do not have insurance coverage, they may be more willing to take risks in treatment that increase their chances of having a pregnancy but also could increase the chances of having a multiple birth. When paying out of pocket, knowing that they will not be able to afford more than a certain number of treatments affects their decisions and their willingness to take risks. Insurance coverage would remove that incentive. Further, insurance coverage would bring about additional oversight and management of care from the insurance company, which could in turn reduce the rate of multiple births. A 1998 study, led by physician David Frankfurter of Beth Israel Deaconess Medical Center in Boston, found that in states with mandated infertility-insurance coverage the average number of embryos transferred in an in vitro fertilization attempt was lower and the multiple-birth rate per attempt was lower than in states without mandates. The study's authors concluded that this lower rate of multiple births may be a result of less pressure from patients to maximize the chance of pregnancy and increased pressure from insurers to minimize the likelihood of multiple births.

Couples who experience infertility ride an emotional roller coaster—from diagnosis through treatment—a very difficult experience. The physical and emotional struggles are further exacerbated when couples face financial hurdles because of a lack of insurance coverage. Alice D. Domar of the Mind/Body Institute at Beth Israel Deaconess Medical Center led a study of women with chronic diseases which found that the psychological effect of experiencing infertility was similar to that of cancer and heart disease. Compounding the emotional distress is the stigma of infertility and the difficulty that many couples have in telling their family and friends.

What is fair when it comes to insurance coverage? The Supreme Court strengthened the arguments in favor of infertility-insurance coverage when it issued a ruling in June 1998 that demonstrated the importance of reproduction and the ability to have children. In *Bragdon vs. Abbott* the high court ruled that reproduction is a major life activity under the Americans with Disabilities Act, or ADA. According to the ADA, an individual is disabled if he or she has a mental or physical impairment that substantially limits one or more major life activities. Therefore, those who are impaired in their ability to reproduce may qualify for protection from discrimination based on that disability. This ruling allows those experiencing infertility to make claims of discrimination when employers specifically exclude infertility treatment from insurance plans. A number of lawsuits have arisen in the wake of that decision.

While Bragdon was not a case involving infertility (the plaintiff was an HIV-positive woman who was denied dental care), lower courts have ruled in cases specific to infertility that it qualifies as a disability under the ADA. In *Bielicki vs. The City of Chicago,* police officers Anita and Vince Bielicki sued the city of Chicago for excluding infertility treatment from their health plans. After the U.S. District Court for the Northern District of Illinois ruled that reproduction is a major life activity and that the Bielickis' lawsuit could go forward, the city decided to settle. Most infertility-treatment costs incurred by employees in the previous 10 years were reimbursed, and city health-insurance plans now include infertility coverage. The precedents set by this case and the Supreme Court ruling, and the prospect of further lawsuits, have brought infertility-insurance coverage to the attention of a growing number of employers and legislators.

William M. Mercer, a benefits consulting firm, published a report in 1997 which disclosed that approximately 25 percent of employers provide some infertility insurance coverage. Another consulting firm, the Segal Co., issued an August 1998 report which found that only 7 percent of employer plans cover infertility treatment, and about 14 percent of plans cover the costs of infertility diagnosis. Most of those plans that cover treatment do not cover all infertility services.

The costs of including infertility coverage in an insurance plan are low. Studies cited by the Mercer report found that the cost of in vitro fertilization coverage is approximately $2.50 per member per year. Another study, by Martha Griffin and William F Panak, published in the July 1998 issue of *Fertility and Sterility,* found that the cost of comprehensive infertility coverage is $1.71 per family plan per month. Isn't it worth the cost of a monthly cup of coffee to ensure that couples who are struggling to build much-wanted families are afforded the option?

Several state legislatures have responded to the needs of their constituents and recognized the importance of supporting couples who are striving to build their families. Thirteen states enacted infertility insurance laws after they determined that such financial assistance is in the best interest of their residents. The mandates are quite different in scope and substance. Ten states have a mandate to provide some level of infertility insurance. Three states have a mandate to offer under which insurance companies must have infertility insurance available for purchase, but employers do not have to choose to provide that coverage to their employees.

A number of state legislatures considered infertility-insurance laws in the 1997–98 legislative session, and new legislation is being drafted for introduction in 1999. Mandates may be introduced in Florida, Indiana, Michigan, Nevada, New Hampshire, New Jersey, New York, Pennsylvania, Tennessee and Texas. Infertility patients, providers and others who understand the need for insurance coverage are working to gather support for mandates, and a number of legislators have committed to assist.

The existing infertility-insurance mandates have allowed many couples to obtain needed medical treatments and to build their families. However, even in states with mandates, many employees still do not have insurance coverage because of the Employee Retirement Income Security Act, or ERISA. Employers who self-insure are exempt from any state health-insurance mandates, including infertility mandates. In some states, more than 50 percent of employees work for exempted employers. Self-insured employers sometimes do choose to follow the state's policy lead and provide infertility coverage to their employees. A federal infertility insurance mandate, a long-term goal of infertility community, would cover all employers and make coverage consistent across states.

Legislators and employers are beginning to recognize that helping couples who are struggling to build much-wanted families is the right thing to do. In a country that places great value in family, it is salutary that insurance coverage for couples with infertility is just around the corner.

Merrill Matthews, Jr.

 **NO**

Should Health Insurers Be Forced to Pay for Infertility Treatments? No

When miracles happen on a regular basis, they no longer are miracles—and they may even be seen as problems. That's what has happened with the miracle of multiple births.

Geraldine Brodrick, 29, of Sydney, Australia, performed a miracle in 1971 when she gave birth to nine babies. All died. But 30 years of advances in infertility treatments and neonatology have made multiple births almost common and fairly safe. Bobbi McCaughey of Carlisle, Iowa, also 29, gave birth to septuplets in 1997, all of whom survived. And now Nkem Chukwu of Houston has given birth to octuplets, one of whom died. There also are nonscientific reasons for the increase in the frequency of multiple births. One is that health insurers often are willing or required to pay for infertility treatments. As a result, an increasing number of infertile couples seeks counseling and medical help in having a baby.

According to the Centers for Disease Control and Prevention, 1.2 million women (about 2 percent) of reproductive age visited a medical professional about infertility in 1995. And 9.3 million women (15 percent) had used some kind of fertility service at one time in their lives, compared with 6.8 million (12 percent) who had done so in 1988.

Most women who pursue treatment need only moderate medical intervention, such as counseling or drug therapy. Others need more aggressive or invasive care, such as surgery or assisted reproductive technology, or ART. ART includes such procedures as in vitro fertilization, in which eggs and sperm are taken from the couple, fertilized outside the womb and then implanted in the uterus.

While moderate medical intervention for infertility can be relatively affordable for most couples—$500 to $2,000—more aggressive therapy can cost as much as $12,000. And in vitro fertilization can be expensive—$10,000 to $15,000 per attempt. It often takes several attempts before a prospective mother is successfully impregnated—which can drive up the cost significantly.

According to a 1994 *New England Journal of Medicine* study by Peter J. Neumann et al., the estimated cost per live delivery for in vitro fertilization ranged between $66,667 in the first cycle to $114,286 by the sixth cycle. A July 1998 study by Martha Griffin and William F. Panak, published in *Fertility and Sterility,* found the cost of ART per live delivery in 1993 was $59,484.

Because some infertility treatments can be prohibitively expensive for middle- and lower-income families, advocacy groups have lobbied legislators to require insurance to cover the treatments—and many have listened. For years state legislatures have passed laws—"mandates"—that require insurers to cover providers such as chiropractors and podiatrists or for services such as drug and alcohol-abuse treatments. In 1965 there were only eight mandates nationwide. Today there are more than 1,000. And one mandate that has been gaining popularity—especially among politicians who want to be perceived as sympathetic to women's needs —requires health insurers to cover infertility treatments.

While these mandates make insurance coverage more comprehensive, they also make it more expensive because people use insurance for services they previously paid for out of pocket. For example, consider a patient who was spending $50 a month out of pocket to visit a chiropractor. If the government requires insurers to cover 80 percent of his cost, the patient then is out only $10 a month. If he believes he benefits from the chiropractic care, he may double the frequency of his visits and still spend less than he spent before the mandate was passed. While the patient's personal health-care costs have gone down, total costs to the system have doubled—from $50 to $100 a month. If many patients do the same, insurers eventually will have to increase their rates to make up for the additional costs.

So while it may be true that chiropractors charge less per service than medical doctors and may in certain circumstances provide better care, the additional utilization increases overall health-care costs. Of course, special interests who push for insurance coverage of their particular specialty may believe that such action will improve the quality of care. But they also know that providers will get more visits and therefore more money. That's one of the reasons they work so hard to get legislators to mandate coverage of their specialty. And that's also why they search for data and justifications that will "prove" their assertions.

For example, Griffin, a doctoral candidate in the College of Nursing at the University of Rhode Island, and Panak, a psychologist at the University of Northern Iowa, believe that insurance should cover infertility treatments and produced a study to justify their beliefs. Their examination of the Massachusetts infertility mandate led them to claim that "limiting the number of ART attempts could motivate clinics to maintain policies of transferring numerous embryos as a way of increasing success rates for couples who cannot afford numerous ART attempts. Thus, limits on ART cycles inadvertently could maintain high rates of multiple births and the associated medical complications and economic costs of these births."

In other words, if cost were not a factor, infertility clinics and patients might be less aggressive in their attempts to ensure pregnancy on the first attempt by implanting numerous embryos. If true, that could decrease the number of multiple births and costs would go down.

The problem is that mandates also increase total utilization of health care. If insurance is required to cover infertility treatments, more women will get the treatments. The attempt to remove or destroy some of the fertilized embryos, a process known as selective reduction, is seen by many couples as abortion, a broader social issue that many people oppose. Chukwu was offered selective reduction and declined for religious reasons. Indeed, because some women are reluctant to have embryos removed, there is a debate within the medical community about whether such women should even be offered fertility drugs. Thus, multiple births will not go down as the authors suggest.

Proponents of infertility mandates also assert that the cost of adding the coverage is minimal and would have little impact on premiums. In support, they cite various studies that project a premium increase of between $0.40 and $2.50 per family per month.

There are several problems with these projections. First, they seldom take into consideration other factors. For example, Chukwu's medical bills for her octuplets will reach an estimated $2 million. She is covered by insurance, so the family will not have to bear most of the cost; the insurer will. But insurance is just a pass-through mechanism. That is, insurers pass expenses on to all the people who pay the premiums. Thus policyholders pay higher premiums for the infertility treatments of others and eventually bear the costs of postnatal care.

Actuaries take these collateral effects into consideration when calculating the costs of mandates. For example, when Milliman & Robertson, one of the leading actuarial firms in the country, did a cost analysis of a typical infertility mandate adopted by state legislatures, it estimated the mandate would increase the cost of a health-insurance policy 3 to 5 percent per year, or $105 to $175 a year for a basic health-insurance policy that had no other mandates included.

Which brings us to a second problem. Even if proponents of insurance coverage for infertility were correct in asserting that a mandate would be relatively inexpensive, the larger problem is the total number of mandates. Most states have adopted 30 to 40 health-insurance mandates. While the Milliman & Robertson study makes it clear that most of these mandates are inexpensive—adding less than 1 percent to the cost of a policy—the sum of their costs can make a health-insurance policy prohibitively expensive, boosting premiums by 40 percent to 50 percent in most states.

A third problem is fairness. Thirteen states have adopted some form of infertility mandate. In some cases the legislation requires insurers to cover infertility treatments; in other cases it requires only that coverage be offered. Some states limit how much money insurers are required to spend on treatments (say, to $15,000), while other states exempt very small employers (those with, say, fewer than 25 employees).

However, state-insurance laws primarily affect only small employers and individuals such as the self-employed who purchase private insurance for themselves and their families. That's because most large employers self-insure under the Employee Retirement Income Security Act, or ERISA, a federal law that supersedes state laws. Companies that insure their employees under ERISA avoid state mandates completely.

Thus state mandates affect only a small segment of those with private insurance, and the costs of those mandates fall on a relatively small number of people. As a result, premium increases in the small group and individual health-insurance markets grow much faster than in the large group market. Ironically, it is in the small group and individual markets where people are least able to afford the premium increases.

Of course, many large companies that self-insure voluntarily cover infertility treatments. But that's a choice the companies have made, not one imposed by government. It's those governmental impositions that can lead a business or a family to decide to cancel coverage. Which leads us to the real question: Do we want to put an increasing number of low-income families at risk of lacking basic health insurance so that infertile couples can have their treatments paid for by somebody else?

At a time when health-insurance premiums are projected to increase significantly during the next few years and demographers are worried about world population growth, it simply makes no sense for the government to force insurers to subsidize infertility treatments. Those who have the income to pay for the treatments or who are disciplined enough to save the money to pay for them should have that option. But since it is their choice, it should be their responsibility, not a financial burden that others must bear.

POSTSCRIPT

Should Health Insurers Be Required to Pay for Infertility Treatments?

Debates continue to rage around what should and should not be covered under health insurance plans. Some reproductive health advocates shake their heads in amazement that Viagra, a medication to treat erectile dysfunction in men, is covered, yet many hormonal contraceptive methods are not. In 2001, a bill was introduced specific to the federal employees' health benefits program to ensure "equitable treatment of fertility and impotence in health care coverage under group health plans, health insurance coverage, and health plans." Basically, this act said that if a medication created to treat impotence is covered (like Viagra), then fertility-related medications and treatments must be covered as well.

We are also seeing movement on the constitutional level relating to the rights of individuals to have their reproductive decisions supported by their health insurance companies. In 1998, the Supreme Court decided in *Bragdon v. Abbott* that reproduction is a "major life activity" under the Americans with Disabilities Act (ADA). While the case was decided within the context of HIV, it has strong implications for people who are infertile. We may be seeing future challenges to health insurance companies and lawsuits asserting that insurance policies excluding infertility treatments are in violation of the ADA.

How should decisions be made about what is and is not covered by health insurance companies? On the one hand, a health insurance company is a business like any other business. While there are laws governing legal activities of major businesses, can and should the government become involved on more minute details? Should the government be able to tell toy manufacturers, for example, that they can no longer make toy guns or action figures for fear that such toys will cause excessive aggression in children? Similarly, should the government go through the entire list of what a health insurance company does or does not offer its subscribers and make similar judgments?

At the heart of this debate, of course, is the issue of discrimination. When discrimination is about a person's ability and right to access a major life event that others can without medical intervention, that is one thing. When the discrimination is based in dollars and cents, that is another thing altogether—or is it? Where do we draw this proverbial line in the sand? Will people who have no family history of cancer and who are healthy suddenly decide they no longer wish to contribute to premiums that include coverage for cancer treatment? How about other rare diseases?

The issue of how an increase in premiums could affect lower-income individuals cannot be ignored, keeping in mind that the vast majority of low-income individuals in the United States are people of color. Therefore, such efforts could arguably be seen as discriminatory based on more than income.

Clearly, this is only the beginning of what is sure to be an ongoing discussion and debate. It will be interesting to see how successfully or unsuccessfully legal and public policy professionals are able to apply constitutional as well as legal precedents to the issue of health insurance coverage, and the responses of companies and subscribers alike.

Suggested Readings

Insure.com, *The Insurance Guide, Paying the Price for Infertility* (May 8, 2001). Accessible online at `http://www.insure.com/health/infertility.html`.

Geoffrey Sher, "In Vitro Fertilization and Universal Insurance Coverage: The Need Is Great and the Time Is NOW!!" *Las Vegas Health Guide* (vol. 1, no. 1, January 2001). Accessible online at `http://haveababy.com/news/lvhg.asp`.

ISSUE 18

Should Male Prison Inmates Be Allowed to Father Children?

YES: Myron H. Bright, from Majority Opinion, *William Gerber v. Roderick Hickman,* U.S. Court of Appeals for the Ninth Circuit (September 5, 2001)

NO: Barry G. Silverman, from Dissenting Opinion, *William Gerber v. Roderick Hickman,* U.S. Court of Appeals for the Ninth Circuit (September 5, 2001)

ISSUE SUMMARY

YES: Federal Court of Appeals judge Myron H. Bright cites past Supreme Court decisions to demonstrate that prison inmates retain certain constitutional rights even though they have broken the law. This includes, he asserts, the right to procreate.

NO: Federal Court of Appeals judge Barry G. Silverman cites constitutional precedence to argue that while inmates have a right to marriage, the Constitution does not guarantee the right to conjugal visits. As a result, the right to procreate is reserved as a future right that can be fulfilled once an inmate has served his or her time for crimes committed.

T here are extensive laws governing the rights of prison inmates throughout the United States. Some are created and maintained on a federal level, and others are done state by state. Visitation regulations, including regulations about conjugal visits, fall under state regulation. Some states allow conjugal visits, such as California and New York. Others, like Arkansas, do not. Some state laws are specific about the types of physical contact an inmate can have with a visitor, regardless of their relationship to this visitor. For example, while hugging and kissing may be considered permissible under some state laws, it can only be done to a "reasonable" extent and only upon the visitor's arrival and departure.

The court case described in this issue involves a prison inmate named William Gerber who is serving a 100-year-to-life sentence. While California state law does permit conjugal visits, it does not permit it for inmates who are serving life sentences without chance of parole or specific parole date set. However, before he went to prison, Gerber and his wife had decided they wanted to have a baby together. He was incarcerated before this could happen. Since he is not permitted to inseminate his wife through intercourse, he asked to provide a semen sample so that his wife could be inseminated medically. The prison denied his request, even though he and his wife agreed to pay all financial costs involved, because the procedure was not "medically necessary." Gerber maintains that in doing so, the prison is denying his constitutional right to procreate under the due process clause of the Fourteenth Amendment to the U.S. Constitution. The district court concluded, "Whatever right [the] plaintiff has to artificial insemination, it does not survive incarceration." Gerber appealed the decision, and it was reversed by the Ninth Circuit Court of Appeals in San Francisco, California.

What is your feeling about prisoners' rights? As you will read, Gerber's long sentence comes as a result of California's stringent "three strikes" policy. Based on his crimes, do you think he forfeits his right to cause a pregnancy with his wife? Do you think that once a person has broken the law, he or she should no longer have certain rights? If so, at what point do you draw the line with regard to effective incarceration regulations versus human rights?

In the following selections, Myron H. Bright interprets previous court decisions to support Gerber's assertion that he should have the right to impregnate his wife through alternative fertilization methods. In a previous decision, the Court ruled that a prisoner's constitutional rights can only be abridged if doing so would be "reasonably related to penological interests." Bright argues that in this case, the prison cannot deny the inmate's rights. Barry G. Silverman asserts that Bright has incorrectly applied the precedents of other cases to this case. The cases cited, he argues, refer more to the Eighth Amendment guarantee that a prison inmate cannot be surgically sterilized during incarceration. This is, he says, a far cry from enabling an inmate to impregnate his female partner while incarcerated. He uses the cases cited by Bright, while citing other court cases, to demonstrate that inmates do not have the right to procreate while they are serving a prison sentence.

Majority Opinion

Background

This case concerns a life-term prisoner's effort to have a child by artificially inseminating his wife. Artificial insemination is a noncoital process in which semen is collected from a man under laboratory conditions and then introduced into a woman's body with a needleless hypodermic syringe at a favorable time in her ovulation cycle. . . .

Appellant William Gerber desires to artificially inseminate his wife because his particular circumstances disallow the "natural" method of procreation. Gerber was sentenced to 100 years to life imprisonment plus eleven years pursuant to California's three strikes law, Cal. Penal Code § 667, after his 1997 conviction for discharging a firearm, making terrorist threats, and using narcotics. Prior to his conviction, he and his now forty-six-year-old wife wished to conceive a child. However, he is constrained in employing the usual methods for achieving this goal because he is a life-term prisoner incarcerated in California, and, under CDC [Centers for Disease Control] regulations, conjugal visits are prohibited for inmates "sentenced to life without the possibility of parole [or] sentenced to life, without a parole date established by the Board of Prison Terms." CAL. CODE REGS. tit. 15, § 3174(e)(2). Given Gerber's sentence and his wife's age, he alleges that artificial insemination is the only method by which they can conceive a child together.

Gerber requested that prison authorities permit him to provide a semen specimen to a laboratory so that his wife may be artificially inseminated with it. According to Gerber, the University Andrology Laboratory and Sperm Bank at the University of Illinois at Chicago Medical Center would mail him a packet containing a plastic receptacle and a postage-paid return mailer. Then, Gerber would ejaculate into the receptacle, place it into the return mailer, and send it by overnight mail back to the laboratory. Gerber's privately retained lawyer offered to retrieve the return mailer directly from Gerber if prison authorities

From *William Gerber v. Roderick Hickman*, No. 00-16494 (2001). Some notes omitted.

do not want Gerber to place it in the mail himself. Gerber does not object to the inspection of his return package in accordance with the prison's usual procedures. Furthermore, Gerber and his wife are willing to bear all of the costs necessary to facilitate the specimen collection, including paying for a licensed physician to come on the premises to oversee the procedure. The prison denied his request after determining that the procedure was not medically necessary and that Gerber as a prisoner had not shown that the CDC had violated any of his constitutional rights. . . .

On October 7, 1999, Gerber filed the amended complaint, naming Warden Rodney [Roderick] Hickman as the sole defendant and seeking injunctive relief. In the complaint, he alleged that the Warden's policy violated his constitutional right to procreate under the Due Process Clause of the Fourteenth Amendment and his statutory rights as a California prisoner guaranteed by CAL. PENAL CODE §§ 2600 and 2601. The parties consented, under 28 U. S. C. § 636(c), to conduct all proceedings before Magistrate Judge John F. Moulds. On January 5, 2000, the Warden moved to dismiss the complaint pursuant to F ED. R. CIV. P. 12(b)(6), for failure to state a claim upon which relief can be granted, or, alternatively, for summary judgment, on the basis that the right to procreate does not survive incarceration and that, even if it did, the restriction on artificial insemination is reasonably related to the legitimate penological goals of treating male and female inmates equally to the extent possible, conserving prison resources, maintaining institutional security interests, and preserving inmates' rehabilitation.

The magistrate judge heard oral argument on the Warden's motion on March 2, 2000. On March 7, 2000, the magistrate judge filed findings and recommendations, recommending denial of the Warden's motion to dismiss and denial of both parties' motions for summary judgment without prejudice. The magistrate judge found that the Warden failed to establish as a matter of law that the right to procreate does not exist during incarceration, that an inquiry into both the practical aspects of restrictions that arise as a consequence of an individual's status as a prisoner and the legitimate penological objectives of the corrections system is best undertaken on a fully developed factual record and not on a motion to dismiss, and that Gerber made a substantial showing that numerous facts are disputed underlying the determination of legal issues, thus obviating summary judgment dismissal.

Subsequently, the district court rejected the magistrate judge's findings and recommendations and dismissed the complaint for failure to state a claim upon which relief can be granted. The district court made no ruling on the motion for summary judgment. On June 23, 2000, the district court filed an amended memorandum and order and entered judgment that same day. The district court concluded that:

> Whatever right plaintiff has to artificial insemination, it does not survive incarceration.

Gerber v. Hickman, 103 F. Supp. 2d 1214, 1218 (E. D. Cal. 2000). Gerber appealed....

Discussion

A. Section 1983 Claim

... In urging this court to reverse the district court's dismissal, Gerber asserts that he set forth a violation of his substantive due process rights by the CDC and that the district court erred in its determination that the fundamental right to procreate does not survive incarceration.[1]

We must undertake a two-step analysis to determine whether Gerber's substantive due process rights were violated. First, we must determine whether there is a fundamental right involved (in this case, the right to procreate) and whether that fundamental right is not "inconsistent with [Gerber's] status as a prisoner." *Pell v. Procunier,* 417 U. S. 817, 822 (1974). Second, if we decide that the fundamental right at issue survives incarceration, we then ask whether there are legitimate penological interests which justify the prison's restriction of the exercise of that fundamental right. *See Turner v. Safley,* 482 U. S. 78, 96–97 (1987).

[2] The Supreme Court has recognized a fundamental constitutional right to procreate on several occasions. *Carey v. Population Servs. Int'l,* 431 U.S. 678, 684–85 (1977) ("It is clear that among the decisions that an individual may make without unjustified government interference are personal decisions 'relating to marriage... [and] procreation.'") (internal citations omitted); *Stanley v. Illinois,* 405 U.S. 645, 651 (1972) ("The rights to conceive and to raise one's children have been deemed 'essential'... [and] 'basic civil rights of man.'") (internal citations omitted); *Skinner v. Oklahoma,* 316 U.S. 535, 541 (1942) (stating that legislation deprived individuals "of a right which is basic to the perpetuation of a race—the right to have offspring"). The right to procreate has been recognized in a number of other cases outside the prison context.[2] The question raised in this case is whether this fundamental right survives incarceration; that is, whether the fundamental right of procreation exists for prisoners during their term of imprisonment.

We apply a distinct constitutional analysis to cases involving prisoner rights. Because "[n]o iron curtain separates" prisoners from the Constitution, *Hudson v. Palmer,* 468 U.S. 517, 523 (1984) (internal citation omitted), a prisoner "retains those [constitutional] rights that are not inconsistent with his status as a prisoner or with the legitimate penological objectives of the corrections system." *Pell v. Procunier,* 417 U.S. 817, 822 (1974). The Supreme Court has held that some constitutional rights survive incarceration. *See, e.g., O'Lone v. Estate of Shabazz,* 482 U.S. 342 (1987) (affirming free exercise of religion retained during incarceration); *Bounds v. Smith,* 430 U.S. 817 (1977) (affirming access to courts retained); *Estelle v. Gamble,* 429 U.S. 97 (1976) (holding prisoners have right of protection against cruel and unusual punishment); *Wolff v. McDonnell,* 418 U.S. 539 (1974) (holding prisoners have protections of due process clause); *Pell,* 417 U.S. 817 (affirming right of free speech retained).

In this case, the district court determined that "during incarceration a prisoner loses his or her right to access to a means of procreation, be it conjugal visits, artificial insemination, *in vitro* fertilization, etc."*Gerber,* 103 F. Supp. 2d at 1219. The district court cited two other district court opinions in support of this proposition. The cited cases, however, do not serve as binding precedent for our decision, nor do we find them particularly probative. Contrary to the district court's conclusion, we hold that the right to procreate does indeed survive incarceration.

[4] No case has directly addressed whether the right to procreate is a right that prisoners possess during their time in prison. There are a few cases, however, that shed light on the question. In *Turner v. Safley,* 482 U.S. 78 (1978), the Supreme Court established that the right to marry survives incarceration. *Id.* at 96. The Court stated that prisoner marriages are included within the fundamental right to marry and that, although certain aspects of marriage could not exist in a prison setting (e.g., cohabitation), sufficient attributes of marriage remained to conclude that the right to marry continues within the prison walls. *Id.* at 95-96.

Although the Supreme Court has not yet decided whether the right to procreate survives incarceration, in *Skinner v. Oklahoma,* the Supreme Court stated that prisoners have a constitutional right to maintain their procreative abilities for use once released from custody. *Skinner,* 316 U. S. at 536. The Supreme Court struck down Oklahoma's Habitual Criminal Sterilization Act, legislation which authorized the sterilization of persons convicted three times of a felony involving moral turpitude. *Id.* at 541 (invalidating statute on equal protection grounds). The Court stated that

> We are dealing here with legislation which involves one of the basic civil rights of man. Marriage and procreation are fundamental to the very existence and survival of the race. The power to sterilize, if exercised, may have subtle, farreaching and devastating effects. In evil or reckless hands it can cause races or types which are inimical to the dominant group to wither and disappear. There is no redemption for the individual whom the law touches. Any experiment which the State conducts is to his irreparable injury.

...Taken together, *Turner* and *Skinner* suggest that the fundamental right of procreation may exist in some form while a prisoner is incarcerated, despite the fact that a prisoner necessarily will not be able to exercise that right in the same manner or to the same extent as he would if he were not incarcerated. *Turner* stands as an example of how a right related to marriage and family may be exercised in prison despite a prisoner's inability to carry out the "typical" marriage while in prison. *Skinner* states that, at a minimum, a prisoner while in prison cannot be deprived of his ability to procreate upon release, which in turn tends to support the notion that a person's procreative rights survive while he is in prison. The specific question, however, whether the right of procreation is *temporarily* extinguished simply by virtue of the fact of incarceration is a matter of first impression for this circuit. Indeed, no circuit court has yet answered that question.

[6] The issue of procreation while in prison has arisen in the context of prisoners' requests for conjugal visits. In *Hernandez v. Coughlin,* 18 F. 3d 133 (2d 1994), the Second Circuit held that "[t]he Constitution...does not create any protected guarantee to conjugal visitation privileges while incarcerated." *Id.* at 137. However, the language in the opinion suggests that the court intended to reject the narrow right to conjugal visitation without denying the possibility that a broader right to procreate survives incarceration. The court stated that Hernandez argued for "right to marital intimacy...derived from the fundamental rights of marriage and procreation." *Id.* at 136. The court went on to state that "Hernandez's understanding of these two rights is misguided" and subsequently held that there was no protected right to conjugal visitation. *Id.*

It is unclear how much of the *Hernandez* court's determination regarding the existence of the right to conjugal visits was intertwined with its consideration of penological concerns. The court stated: "Rights of marital privacy, like the right to marry and procreate, are necessarily and substantially abridged in a prison setting." *Id.* at 137. This language suggests, contrary to the district court's position, that the right to procreate survives incarceration but that the exercise of that right can be restricted for legitimate penological reasons. We have no quarrel with that proposition....

Other courts have also stated that there is no constitutional right to contact visitation while simultaneously framing the discussion in terms of legitimate restrictions on a prisoner's exercise of his rights. *See, e.g., Bellamy v. Bradley,* 729 F. 2d 416, 420 (6th Cir. 1984)....

The contact visitation and conjugal visit cases to not in any event preclude our finding that the right to procreate survives incarceration. The recognition that a general right to procreate exists during periods of imprisonment is not inconsistent with a holding that there is no specific right to conjugal or contact visits during such times, nor with the idea that a prison can restrict the exercise of the right to procreate in regard to conjugal visitation (a restriction similar to that on the right of association). Procreation that results from the employment of recently developed methods or techniques that bypass physical contact with the prisoner's spouse is not inherently inconsistent with one's status as a prisoner. In fact, even conjugal visits and childbirth are not inherently inconsistent with such status, as the experience in California's prisons demonstrates....

In sum, we conclude that the fundamental right to procreate survives incarceration. The exercise of that right by Gerber is, however, subject to restriction based on legitimate penological interests. The next question, therefore, is whether the existing prison regulation prohibiting artificial insemination is reasonably related to such interests....

In support of his argument for dismissal of Gerber's claim, the Warden cites three governmental interests that he claims are furthered by the policy of denying inmates the right to provide semen to their spouses for artificial insemination: the policy of treating men and women prisoners the same, when possible; safety risks caused by prisoners collecting semen; and concerns about the cost of litigation relating to the procedure.

First, the Warden argues that permitting men to provide semen for artificial insemination would hamper the prison's efforts to treat male and female prisoners similarly. He notes that if men were afforded this opportunity, women would seek to be artificially inseminated, and granting women such an opportunity would lead to "obvious" and "prohibitive" burdens. The Warden's equal protection argument assumes matters not before the court or in the limited record.

Further, Gerber does not seek to *be* artificially inseminated. That right, to be artificially inseminated, which certainly would apply to women, does not apply to Gerber or other male prisoners. The two sexes are not similarly situated here. In this case, we cannot ignore the biological differences between men and women. *Cf. Nguyen v. INS,* 121 S. Ct. 2053, 2066 (2001).... Women cannot avail themselves of the opportunity Gerber narrowly seeks—to provide a semen specimen to his mate so that she can be artificially inseminated—and men cannot do what Mrs. Gerber is likely capable of doing—conceive and give birth to a child after receiving sperm from a marital partners. Therefore, the policy of treating inmates "equally to the extent possible" is not implicated.[3] ...

Next, the Warden argues that the procedure for collecting semen would create an unacceptable risk that prisoners would misuse their semen by either throwing their bodily fluids on others (a process called "gassing"), or sending their semen through the mail to individuals who do not want it. These concerns are argumentative only, in the context of a motion for dismissal under Rule 12(b)(6) and the lack of a full record. Gerber apparently has offered to pay for medical supervision of the procedure for collecting his semen specimen and Gerber's private lawyer has offered to pick up the laboratory mailer from the prison....

Lastly, the Warden asserts that permitting a prisoner to provide a semen specimen would create an unacceptable risk of liability for the prison, either because of mishandling of the specimen by prison authorities or suits by women inmates seeking to be artificially inseminated. The argument that women prisoners would assert their Equal Protection rights to challenge the denial of an opportunity for artificial insemination, thereby imposing on prisons the burden of defending against such suits, cannot justify denying men their constitutional right to procreate. It is simply impermissible to restrict the constitutional rights of one group because of fear that another group will assert its constitutionally protected rights as well. Moreover, it is generally reprehensible to suggest that restricting protected fundamental constitutional rights is justified by fear of increasing a party's liability.[4]

We conclude that, on the basis of the record before us, none of the rationales offered by the Warden falls within *Turner's* proscription—that the prison may only deny a constitutional right if the regulation is "reasonably related to legitimate penological interests." *Turner,* 482 U.S. at 89.... The rationales offered by the Warden in this case fail under the first factor discussed in *Turner:* there is no " 'valid, rational connection' between the prison regulation and the legitimate governmental interest put forward to justify it." *Id.* at 89. Therefore, we reverse the district court's decision dismissing Gerber's § 1983 claim and remand that claim for further consideration....

Conclusion

The district court erred by concluding that the right to procreate does not survive incarceration. Furthermore, consideration of the Warden's arguments requires the development of a record to permit the court to determine whether legitimate penological interests exist that would justify a total ban on Gerber's exercise of his procreative rights during his period of incarceration (presumably for the rest of his natural life).

Accordingly, we **REVERSE** the district court's decision dismissing Gerber's claims and **REMAND** this matter for further proceedings consistent with this opinion.

Notes

1. The district court concludes in part that a prisoner does not have a fundamental right to artificial insemination. *Gerber,* 103 F. Supp. 2d at 1218. The district court erred in its framing of the fundamental right involved in this case. The question of whether a prisoner retains a fundamental right to procreate while in prison is a different question then whether a constitutional right to artificial insemination exists and survives incarceration. The district court goes on to state that "during incarceration a prisoner loses his or her right to access to a means of procreation." *Id.* at 1219. We take this statement to mean that the district court concluded that the fundamental right to procreation is inconsistent with imprisonment and thus, does not survive incarceration.

2. *See Planned Parenthood v. Casey,* 505 U.S. 833, 851 (1992) (concerning right to an abortion); *Carey v. Population Services Int'l,* 431 U.S. 678, 685 (1977) (finding right of minors to have access to birth control); *Cleveland Bd. of Educ. v. Chesterfield County Sch. Bd.,* 414 U.S. 632, 640 (1974) (concerning right of school teacher not to be fired for becoming pregnant); *Eisenstadt v. Baird,* 405 U.S. 438, 453 (1972) (holding right of unmarried individuals to have access to birth control); *Stanley v. Illinois,* 405 U.S. 645, 651–52 (1972) (concerning right of unmarried father to have custody of his child after death of child's mother).

3. A more apt parallel may be the question of whether a woman prisoner has the right to donate an egg to her lesbian partner or to a surrogate mother. The Warden has put forth no evidence that this procedure has been requested by any prisoner, that it would be a burden on the prison, or that these two procedures are similar enough as to raise equal protection concerns.

4. There may be increased administrative costs with allowing the procedure, such as increased safety and security costs. However, the Warden has not, on the limited record before us, shown this to be the case or that there costs would be overly burdensome.

NO ↩

Barry G. Silverman

Dissenting Opinion

SILVERMAN, Circuit Judge, dissenting:

This is a seminal case in more ways than one. Contrary to all precedent, the majority today holds that a prison inmate—in this instance, an inmate serving a life sentence—has a *constitutional* right to mail his semen from prison so that his wife can be artificially inseminated. With the utmost respect, the majority's reading of the Constitution is as unprecedented as it is ill-conceived.

The majority simply does not accept the fact that there are certain downsides to being confined in prison, and that the interference with a normal family life is one of them. *Morrissey v. Brewer,* 408 U.S. 471, 482 (1972). It is true that inmates do not lose all constitutional rights upon incarceration. It is true that they retain the right to marry. *Turner v. Safley,* 482 U.S. 78 (1987). It is true that the Eighth Amendment protects them against forced surgical sterilization. *Skinner v. Oklahoma,* 316 U.S. 535 (1942). All of that, however, is a far cry from holding that inmates retain a constitutional right to procreate from prison via FedEx. The *Turner* Court recognized that even though the right to marry survives incarceration, the right to have the marriage "fully consummated" is but an "expectation" postponed until the inmate is released from custody. 482 U.S. at 96. That is why the Second Circuit held that the Constitution does not guarantee prison inmates a right to conjugal visits. *Hernandez v. Coughlin,* 18 F.3d 133, 136–37 (2d Cir. 1994):

> Although it is clear that prisoners have a fundamental right to marry, this constitutionally protected guarantee is substantially limited as a result of incarceration. Similarly, inmates possess the right to maintain their procreative abilities *for later use* once released from custody, even though this right is restricted. [citing *Skinner v. Oklahoma*]*** Rights of marital privacy, like the right to marry and procreate, are necessarily and substantially abridged in a prison setting.

Citations omitted; emphasis added.

From *William Gerber v. Roderick Hickman,* No. 00-16494 (2001).

In no reported decision concerning a prisoner's claim of a right to procreate from prison by artificial insemination has any court ever upheld such a right. Quite to the contrary:

- *Anderson v. Vasquez,* 827 F. Supp. 617, 620 (N.D. Cal. 1992) ("no constitutional right to have an inmate's sperm preserved for artificial insemination exists") *aff'd in part, rev'd in part on other grounds,* 28 F.3d 104 (9th Cir. 1994) (unpublished mem. disposition).
- *Goodwin v. Turner,* 702 F. Supp. 1452, 1453–54 (W.D. Mo. 1988) ("The Court has approached this novel case fully cognizant of the legal parameters, but with a willingness to stretch those boundaries as necessary to satisfy any fundamental right that petitioner may have in regard to artificial insemination of his wife. There exists, however, an insurmountable obstacle—the fact of incarceration—that necessarily restricts any decision rendered herein. *** Regardless of the marital rights that do survive incarceration, many aspects of marriage that make it a basic civil right, such as cohabitation, sexual intercourse, and the bearing and rearing of children, are superseded by the fact of confinement.").
- *Goodwin v. Turner,* 908 F.2d 1395 (8th Cir. 1990) ("Even assuming, without deciding, that the exercise of Goodwin's right to procreate is not fundamentally inconsistent with his status as a prisoner, the restriction imposed by the Bureau [of Prisons] is reasonably related to achieving its legitimate penological interest.").
- *See also State v. Oakley,* 629 N.W. 2d 200, 209 (Wis. 2001) ("incarceration, by its very nature, deprives a convicted individual of the fundamental right to be free from physical restraint, which in turn encompasses and restricts other fundamental rights, such as the right to procreate.").

Common sense also suggests that procreation is fundamentally inconsistent with incarceration. A lawful prison sentence "constitutionally deprive[s] the criminal defendant of his liberty to the extent that the State may confine him and subject him to the rules of its prison system." *Meachum v. Fano,* 427 U. S. 215, 224 (1975). "[T]hese restrictions or retractions also serve, incidentally, as reminders that, under our system of justice, deterrence and retribution are factors in addition to correction." *Hudson v. Palmer,* 468 U.S. 517, 524 (1983). Because the right to procreate is "fundamentally incompatible with imprisonment itself" (the standard applied in *Hudson*), the majority's analysis of whether there is a legitimate penological reason to abridge that right is all beside the point. There is no such right. Prisoners do not have a right to procreate while in prison.

Charles H. Whitebread, the renowned and witty professor of constitutional law at the University of Southern California, is fond of saying that some people believe that inmates retain only two rights when they go to prison—the right to serve their time and the right not to be exposed to second-hand smoke. That is not my view. I fully recognize that "[p]rison walls do not form a barrier separating prison inmates from the protections of the Constitution." *Turner,*

482 U.S. at 84. However, I do believe that "[c]ertainly most, if not all, reasonable minds would agree that a prohibition against artificial insemination does not subject a federal prisoner to a 'fate forbidden by the principle of civilized treatment guaranteed by the Eighth Amendment,'" *Goodwin,* 702 F. Supp. at 1455, or in this case, by the Fourteenth Amendment. And because prison inmates have no right to procreate while in prison, I would hold, as the district judge did, that the plaintiff's state law claim necessarily fails.

For there reasons, I would affirm the district court's dismissal of the plaintiff's lawsuit, and therefore, respectfully dissent.

POSTSCRIPT

Should Male Prison Inmates Be Allowed to Father Children?

Emotions relating to prison inmates can run high. Some people feel very strongly that once a person has broken the law, that person should no longer have access to certain rights. Others believe that even though someone has broken the law, that person is still a human being. If she or he is serving the sentence imposed by a jury, she or he should still be able to do certain things in order to become a productive member of society upon release.

Up to what point do you think prison inmates should have rights? Some people who have broken the law, in so-called white-collar crimes, which involve crimes like fraud, end up in prisons that are almost more like country clubs than prisons. Others break laws by using weapons or violence and are placed in prisons that are diametrically opposite to a country club.

Should a male prison inmate have the right to procreate? One might argue that while certain crimes come as a result of social factors, there may be a psychological predisposition to antisocial behaviors—including disrespect for the law. Should someone who has such a predisposition be allowed to procreate and possibly pass this predisposition genetically to an offspring? Or, is this a man who simply made some poor decisions and who should still be able to provide his wife with a child, considering that he and his wife will never again have a shared life the way other couples do?

Both judges allude to another issue, which is the issue of gender here. If Gerber has the right to impregnate his wife, would a female prisoner have the right to be inseminated? If she were placed in a safe area of the prison for nine months and provided with prenatal care and support, should she be allowed to have the baby and then let her partner raise it outside of prison during the remainder of her incarceration? Bright seems to believe that there is a difference between the two situations. However, his opinion certainly opens the door for this argument. It will be interesting to see how he and other judges will apply the same court cases to a female inmate looking to have a baby while incarcerated.

Suggested Readings

Amnesty International, *Rights for All: United States of America* (October 1998). Accessible online at http://www.rightsforall-usa.org/info/report/index.htm.

Joanna Grossman, "Do Prisoners Have a Constitutional Right to Procreate Via Fedex? A Recent Appeals Court Ruling Says Yes, but the Supreme Court May Disagree," *Find Law: Corporate Counsel Center* (November 20, 2001). Accessible online at `http://writ.corporate.findlaw.com/grossman/20011120.html`.

Richard S. Jones and Thomas J. Schmid, *Doing Time: Prison Experience and Identity Among First-Time Inmates* (JAI Press, 2000).

National Public Radio, "Right to Procreate," an audiocast of an interview between Robert Siegel and *Los Angeles Times* staff writer Greg Krikorian on *All Things Considered* (September 6, 2001). Accessible online at `http://search.npr.org/cf/cmn/cmnpd01fm.cfm?PrgDate=09%2F06%2F2001&PrgID=2`.

George Will, "An Inmate's Right to Procreate," *Town Hall* (November 8, 2001). Accessible online at `http://www.townhall.com/columnists/georgewill/gw20011108.shtml`.

ISSUE 19

Should Congress Facilitate Transracial Adoptions?

YES: Darlene Addie Kennedy, from "End the Foster-Care Ordeal for Black Children," *Insight on the News* (June 5, 1995)

NO: Ruth G. McRoy, from "Lower Barriers to Black Adoptive Families," *Insight on the News* (June 5, 1995)

ISSUE SUMMARY

YES: Author Darlene Addie Kennedy states that race and ethnicity are less important in foster and adoption decisions than strong parenting skills and the capacity to love and care for a child. She responds to concerns of opponents to transracial adoption with studies indicating positive adjustments by children raised by parents whose race, culture, or ethnicity was different from theirs.

NO: Professor Ruth G. McRoy contends that there are many more adoptive parents of color waiting to adopt children of their same race, ethnicity, or culture but that social service agencies are actively inhibiting the process from taking place. Institutional biases, she argues, as well as personal preconceptions by some social service professionals about race, ethnicity, culture, and parenting issues, impede parents of color from adopting the children they seek.

For nearly 40 years, the issue of transracial and transcultural adoption of children has raised great controversy. Emotions run deep and passion runs high when individuals discuss the potential outcome of any child who is awaiting a permanent home. When it comes to issues of race and ethnicity, debates can be even more sensitive. The selections in this issue focus on the adoption of African American or black children by white families. This is in no way meant to imply that any child deserves adoption more or less, but it is indicative of the plethora of information and opinions relating specifically to this type of family composition.

Figures relating to the number of children in foster care and awaiting adoption vary depending on the source. According to one source, there are approximately 440,000 children in the foster care system in the United States, with the majority being between the ages of 6 and 12. According to 1999 statistics from the United States Department of Health and Human Services (USDHHS), 50 percent of the children waiting to be adopted are African American. The majority of families awaiting an adoptive child, nearly 67 percent, are white. The USDHHS also estimated that 15 percent of the 36,000 adoptions of foster children in 1998 were transracial or transcultural.

Before the 1960s, restrictions were placed on who could adopt whom, based on race. With the civil rights and other social movements of the 1960s, these restrictions were lifted. White families were eligible to adopt so-called minority children, which included primarily African American babies. In the 1970s, a backlash came from a group of professionals within the social work community. The National Association of Black Social Workers (NABSW) published a strong admonishment against transracial adoption, comparing it to "cultural genocide." The group stated that African American children should only be adopted by African American parents.

By the late 1980s, many white parents seeking adoption ended up spending upwards of $10,000 to adopt children from China, South Korea, or Guatemala, and to a lesser extent, black or biracial children from the Caribbean and some countries in Africa. International adoption is thought to be fueled primarily by the desire among adoptive parents for infants. Considering that international adoption costs significantly more than it did in the 1980s, this desire must be strong indeed.

In 1994, the Howard M. Metzenbaum Multiethnic Placement Act (MPA) was passed. It prohibits any federally funded agency from delaying or denying child placement on the basis of the race, color, or national origin of the adoptive or foster parent or the child. In 1996, this act was amended by the Interethnic Adoption Provisions. According to the American Bar Association's Center on Children and the Law, the provisions, among other things, were designed to remove potentially misleading language from the MPA and to strengthen compliance and enforcement procedures. The overall goals were to decrease the length of time that children must wait to be adopted, facilitate the recruitment and retention of foster and adoptive parents, and eliminate discrimination during the placement process.

The federal government has taken some steps in facilitating adoption for children awaiting adoption. However, should the government have done so, and should it do more? In the following selections, Darlene Addie Kennedy, an African American adopted child herself, argues that values and good parenting transcend race and ethnicity. She believes that any parent can facilitate the understanding of a child's racial and ethnic heritage, regardless of the parent's own race or ethnicity. Ruth G. McRoy points to the foster care system itself as leading to dramatic increases in children of color who are removed from their homes and entered into the foster care system, only to be placed with white parents. She points to data indicating that African American parents adopt at much higher rates than white parents. She argues that placement of African American children in white families is based in institutional biases, misperceptions, and cultural insensitivity and ignorance.

Darlene Addie Kennedy  **YES**

End the Foster-Care Ordeal
for Black Children

As an adopted child, I long believed that adoption agencies placed the "best interests of the child" above all other considerations. But you'd be surprised how antiquated this commonsense view really is. Today, black children are sinking in bureaucratic quicksand while many of the families best prepared to adopt them are denied the right because, frankly, they have insufficient amounts of melanin in their skin. Children are pawns in a racially charged, politically correct battle over who is qualified to be a parent. And the list of casualties is growing.

In the racially enlightened 1960s, adoption agencies ended restrictions based on race and whites became eligible to adopt minority children. The enlightenment was short-lived, however. In 1972 the National Association of Black Social Workers, or NABSW, helped discredit transracial adoptions, calling them tantamount to cultural genocide and arguing that, without exception, only black parents should raise black children. That stance was restated in a NABSW position paper in April 1991: "African-American children should not be placed with white parents under any circumstances." A more recent paper allows for transracial adoption only after all efforts to reunite the child's family or to obtain adoption within the same race have been exhausted.

NABSW and other opponents of transracial adoption charge that white parents are less qualified than African-American parents to care for minority children or prepare them for the pressures of growing up in a hostile society. They also claim that the parental eligibility standards for most black applicants are too rigorous and discriminate against low-income families who want to adopt. In many cases, they say, such policies have "destroyed" black families.

Contrary to their claim that less-affluent black families are discouraged by the system from participation in adoptions, eligibility standards in fact have been systematically lowered to increase the pool of qualified black applicants. Public agencies accept applicants from the welfare rolls. Whites of similar means are deemed ineligible. Harvard law professor Elizabeth Bartholet cites a 1986 study showing that half of all minority adoptive families earned below $20,000, compared with only 14 percent of white adoptive families; one-fifth of all minority adoptive families had incomes below $10,000, compared with only 2 percent of adoptive white families. Federally funded agencies offer subsidies to families who adopt minority children by authority of the Adoption Assistance and Child Welfare Act of 1980. The same largess is not available to whites, who must care for their adopted children without a government handout. The NABSW is correct in saying the system is racist. Any program that gives preferential treatment to black families while holding whites to a higher standard is discriminatory.

NABSW would have us believe that transracial adoptions destroy the black family. This claim ignores the bitter reality that a mother or family forced to give up a child already is irreparably damaged. Adoption becomes the child's last hope for a quality life. Relegating the child to years of foster care merely extends the tragedy to another generation. If you don't think the stakes in this debate are high, take a closer look. A New York study in the early 1990s concluded that 70 percent of male prison inmates between the ages of 19 and 23 came from a foster-care system that never placed them with permanent adoptive parents. Families do matter.

Because of absent fathers, drug-addicted mothers and exploding rates of teen pregnancy, nearly 460,000 children are in foster care. CBS News cited a report recently that up to two-thirds of all children needing adoption are black, whereas nearly two-thirds of families applying to adopt are white. There are more minority children than minority families able to take them. Black kids wait more than twice as long as white kids to find parents.

Opponents of transracial adoption resent the idea of whites raising blacks. Yet they usually are silent when the least "desirable" black kids, usually older or emotionally troubled, are adopted by whites. The Packard Foundation of California concluded that, of transracially adopted children in the Midwest, 40 percent are disabled, 23 percent had (or still have) psychological problems and fully one-third were sexually abused by a biological parent. White families accept these children in disproportionately high numbers.

Many well-intentioned skeptics of transracial adoption bring up the black child's culture and heritage and wonder if white adoptive parents are capable of passing along the values important to black children. Such questions merely divert us from the true debate. Culture and heritage are important only if *American* culture and heritage are at issue. As a black American, I am as interested in teaching my 2-year-old about Africa as white Americans are eager to teach their children about Ireland, Italy, Poland, Japan or whatever other nation of origin. As it happens, my parents taught me little about Africa, and I certainly don't have the time to survey even one of the hundreds of cultures that flourish on that continent.

My child will learn American culture, history and traditions, which are the culture, history and traditions of his parents. This is what my black (adoptive) parents taught me; I would expect no less today from white adoptive parents. When the day is done, whatever self-esteem my son has will come from the knowledge that he is loved by his family and, I hope, from having advanced as far as his talents will take him. "Values" aren't race-specific; they apply to any child and white parents are as qualified to impart them as black parents. In short, cultural awareness is nice, but it shrinks to insignificance when compared with the benefits of growing up in a loving family.

These children urgently need parents who will love them. What is the virtue of starving a child of love so that, eventually, he may learn about his "cultural heritage"? What does it say about the African-American value system that it would deny a child the love for which he or she so desperately yearns, or that it would deny parents the child they want to nurture? What kind of morality stands defiantly in the way of their well-being? What is there left to say about the misguided attempts of 15th-generation black Americans whose sole mission seems to be to indoctrinate children in pseudo-African traditions and cautionary psychobabble about the hardships of "growing up black in America." Surely this cannot be the reason countless kids are forced to wait for years in foster care.

Last year, in one of his final acts before leaving the Senate, Howard Metzenbaum of Ohio introduced the Multiethnic Placement Act of 1994. The legislation would have prohibited foster-care agencies from denying otherwise-qualified parents the right to adopt black children solely on the basis of race. This fine idea is a catastrophe in practice. Its final version, drafted by ultra-liberals in the Clinton administration, placed nearly insurmountable obstacles in front of white families seeking to adopt black children. The act authorizes agencies to use the "cultural, ethnic or racial background of [a] child" in determining placement and to "consider the capacity of a prospective adoptive parent to meet the needs of a child of this background." The code words here are easy to decipher. Agencies effectively were given carte blanche authority to hold children hostage in foster care for as long as necessary to find the right "racial match."

And what of the black children who are adopted by whites? In 1972, psychologist Rita Simon of American University in Washington studied 204 middle-class families who transracially adopted. A decade later, she reassessed 96 of these families and reported that 94 percent of the transracial adoptees said they enjoyed their family life and 93 percent felt they had loving and supportive parents. Simon concluded that there was no evidence that transracial adoptions left children incapable of living well-adjusted lives. Other studies report similar findings. Ruth McRoy cowrote a report that the black adoptees she interviewed (30 from same-race, 30 from transracial adoptions) enjoyed high self-esteem regardless of who adopted them. The authors concluded that "positive self-esteem [could] be generated as effectively among black children in white adoptive families as in black adoptive families."

Phoebe Dawson, an African-American and executive director of New Beginnings, a Christian adoption agency in Columbus, Ohio, states that "it is in the best interest of any child to be in a permanent placement as quickly as possible. If it means an African-American or biracial child being placed in a white family, that is all right, and our birth parents are totally in agreement." CBS News polls in 1971 and 1991 of black and white Americans on the issue of transracial adoptions found that support, after 20 years, remained constant among 70 percent of white families and 71 percent of black families. Opponents of transracial adoptions would have you believe otherwise, but they do not speak for all blacks or even for all adoption agencies. Many private agencies support and encourage transracial adoptions. It's ironic that, only a generation since the passing of Martin Luther King Jr., we find state agencies enforcing discriminatory racial preferences while private firms look solely at applicants' individual qualification.

The time for color-blind, race-neutral enforcement of the law has arrived. The Constitution demands it and the children desperately need it. Rep. Jim Bunning, a Kentucky Republican, introduced legislation to repeal the Multiethnic Placement Act of 1994 and return us to the sane, merit-based, character-over-color philosophy of the 1964 Civil Rights Act. Agencies would be barred from delaying a child's placement because of race; parents would be freed from the stranglehold of race-obsessed foster-care administrators; and children, who have been languishing in the system for far too long, would finally see their interests made paramount.

Try reversing the situation: If a "National Association of White Social Workers" sought legislation to place white children solely with white families to ensure that they learned of their "white heritage," is there any doubt they would be labeled racist? The same people who drafted the Multiethnic Placement Act of 1994 would grow hoarse denouncing such a proposal. It is time for those same people to denounce the agenda of the race-obsessed adoption bureaucrats.

Ruth G. McRoy

← **NO**

Lower Barriers to Black Adoptive Families

Congress is debating a bill sponsored by Rep. Jim Bunning, a Kentucky Republican, designed to prohibit any delays in adoptive placements in order to seek a same-race adoptive family. This legislation, as well as the Metzenbaum bill of 1994 and recently passed state statutes that prohibit discrimination on the basis of race, were influenced by the growing number of court cases in which white foster families are seeking to adopt black children for whom they have cared since infancy. The elimination of race-matching policies is touted as a so-called remedy for the many children of color languishing in foster care since white families would be free to adopt these children.

But let's examine the reasons leading to the growing numbers of children of color in need of permanent homes and the proposed solution: transracial adoption. In 1991, child-protection agencies received reports on an estimated 2.7 million children in need of state intervention. Just under 50 percent were reported as cases of neglect, 25 percent physical abuse, 14 percent sexual abuse and 6 percent emotional abuse. Economic stress, substance abuse and inability to fulfill parenting responsibilities were identified as causes of abuse and neglect. Many of these children were removed from their families and placed in foster care.

Neglect often is correlated with poverty; since minority populations are disproportionately poor, minority children are put disproportionately in out-of-home care or placed for adoption. In 1991, about 429,000 children nationwide were in out-of-home care; by 1992, the number had grown to 450,000. Should this trend continue, there may be as many as 900,000 children in out-of-home care by the year 2000. Although accurate statistics on children needing placements are unavailable, experts estimate that there may be as many as 85,000 children who need adoption services. Children of color are overrepresented in these statistics. In New Jersey, Maryland and Louisiana, more than 50 percent of the children in foster care are African-American. More than half of the children waiting for adoption nationwide are children of color, and this population is increasing rapidly in most states.

Since in many states the number of African-American children in foster care far exceeds the number of African-American foster families, African-American children often are placed in transracial foster care. Many of these children will remain with white foster families, often separated from their siblings and with limited contact with their parents or extended families, for several years before they either are returned to their families or freed for adoption. The children and families become attached and in a few cases, the foster parents will seek to adopt a child in their care. Unfortunately, it is after these close bonds have formed that agencies then seek to place the child with a same-race adoptive family.

Although the policy of encouraging same-race placement frequently is cited as the reason black children remain in foster care longer than white children, research data reveal that adoption-agency workers may be less active in seeking permanent homes for minority children. Black children enter care at an average age of 7 and spend an average of almost two years in care. They may experience several caseworkers and school changes and generally move at least twice while in care.

When adoption planning is needed for a child of color, many agencies find that they have a short supply of African-American families seeking to adopt. Some assume that black families are not interested in adopting. The fact is that black families generally adopt at much higher rates than whites. According to J. Mason and C. W. Williams, contributors to the 1985 book *Adoption of Children With Special Needs,* the black inracial adoption rate is 18 per 10,000 families, more than four times the rate for whites. The Urban League's 1980 Black Pulse Survey showed that there were 3 million African-American households interested in adopting. With such a pool of potential parents, why are agencies still indicating that they are having difficulty finding black adoptive families?

The answer lies in the high barriers to prospective minority parents set up by the agencies themselves. According to a 1991 survey by the North American Council on Adoptable Children, barriers to same-race placements include institutional racism, culturally insensitive attitudes of workers, adoption-agency fees, negative perceptions of agencies and their practices, inflexible standards, lack of minority staff and poor recruitment techniques. Other studies have raised the issue of bias linked to the ethnicity of adoption workers and supervisors—more than 75 percent nationwide are white. Little is being done to train current staff in cultural competence or to recruit new minority staff to respond to changing racial demographics and needs of families.

Studies done by the council of the placement patterns of minority children have found that agencies specializing in minority adoption placed 94 percent of black children inracially while agencies without specialized programs in minority adoptions placed 51 percent of black children inracially. Although traditional adoption agencies have been very successful in placing with white adoptive families, many have not adapted their procedures and policies to provide families for the growing numbers of children in care. Clearly, the success of agencies specializing in minorities, such as the Institute for Black Parenting in Los Angeles and Homes for Black Children in Detroit, suggests that African-American families can and do adopt.

Ann Sullivan of the Child Welfare League of America has argued that some agencies perpetuate the myth that African-American families are not available for infants and preschoolers so that such children may be placed with infertile white couples who cannot secure a white infant. Sullivan insists that the majority of African-American school-age children and adolescents can be placed with African-American families. Only after such efforts have failed, she says, should a transracial adoptive family be considered.

Likewise, the positions of several other advocacy groups, including Adoptive Families of America, the North American Council on Adoptable Children and the National Association of Black Social Workers, emphasize the need to give black children an equal opportunity to live in their own families, culture and race, just as white children have the opportunity to live within their own culture and race. However, they do not eliminate transracial adoption as an option if same-race placements cannot be made.

Much of the debate about transracial adoption suggests that race is the only factor that adoption agencies consider in selecting adoptive families. But adoption agencies weigh many factors, including the fit or match between the child and family, the stability of the adoptive family, the ability of the family to deal with the child's special needs, marital relationship, parenting skills and the ability to handle issues associated with the adoption.

The practice of matching the race of children with that of prospective parents is not new. For years agencies have taken the position that the more similar the characteristics of the child are to others in his or her environment, the easier the child can be assimilated into the adoptive family. The fit or compatibility is a joint product of the characteristics of the child, the characteristics of the family and the family's social situation. Until the shortage of white infants and young children, most agencies typically followed the principle of race matching, which was thought to be in the best interest of children and families. Race matching of white children and families still is standard practice, as there are only a few reported accounts of a white child being placed with a black family.

Research findings on outcomes of transracial adoptions suggest that most of the children become relative healthy, emotionally stable young adults. But some other findings suggest that the formation of a positive and unambiguous racial identity may be particularly problematic for minority children in white families growing up in a race-conscious society.

To adopt a race-neutral stance and deny the significance of the child's race in family-placement decisions is to negate a very significant part of the child's background. Transracially adopted children must know more than just their racial background; they must learn to cope with racism, to be in the minority most of the time and to adjust to having very different phenotypic as well as genotypic characteristics from their families.

However, the majority of researchers, like many of the advocacy organizations, have concluded that although same-race placements are preferable, transracial adoption is certainly a far better alternative than remaining in the child-welfare system.

Interestingly, issues of cultural identity are taken for granted through the usual practice of placing white children with white families. Race matching for white children typically is justified by the argument that a great supply of white families is seeking to adopt the very limited supply of available, healthy white infants and young children. Although there are thousands of older white children available for adoption, there is a shortage of families seeking to adopt them, despite an estimated 2 million white couples seeking to adopt. As a result, many white families seek to adopt infants through either intercountry adoptions or transracial adoptions.

Clearly, there are very serious problems that have led to a half-million children in foster care. The majority of such children are school-age; many are in sibling groups and some have experienced abuse and neglect. Many have been moved several times in care. However, legislation aimed primarily at eliminating barriers to white families adopting black children is not the answer to their problem, since transracial adoptions by whites make up a very small percentage of all adoptions and since the majority of families seeking to adopt transracially are seeking only infants and young children.

America needs to focus its efforts on finding permanent homes for both white and minority children available for adoption and reducing the number of children entering the system as a result of child abuse and neglect. We should work toward family preservation, provide effective and efficient services to children and families once they become part of the system, reduce the barriers to African-American families adopting and develop culturally specific approaches to service delivery. Policies pertaining to the adoption rights of African-American families should be examined with the same vigor as those of the right of white families to adopt black children.

POSTSCRIPT

Should Congress Facilitate Transracial Adoptions?

As mentioned in the introduction, issues relating to transracial and transcultural adoption apply to people of all backgrounds. In the United States, this debate has focused most prominently on adoption or foster care of African American children by white families. Resources addressing these issues focus on a wide range of topics, ranging from childhood adjustment, to language and cultural traditions, to manner of dress and hair.

There are other issues within the adoption process that may explain some of the differences between who can and does adopt whom, even today. According to the North American Council for Adoptable Children, many prospective adoptive parents are put off by the procedures involved, especially if they are not explained to the prospective parents. For example, in a country that is still riddled with institutional and social racism, it can be intimidating for a prospective African American adoptive parent or parents from another country who have settled in the United States to be told that the first thing that will happen to them is that they will be fingerprinted. The United States has a history in which people of color have been indiscriminately arrested. People from other countries sometimes come from a history of corrupt government, and they have experienced the same. Misunderstandings can be avoided by training foster care and adoption professionals to describe the processes involved, explaining the universality of the requirement.

According to the Latino Family Institute, "Latinos have an established history of informal adoption—children have long been raised by grandparents, aunts and uncles, and godparents." The Institute believes that lack of knowledge about eligibility requirements, cultural stigma attached to infertility for couples who seek adoption for this reason, and the high number of male Latino children available for adoption (research shows that Latino families tend to prefer male children in a biological birth but female children for adoption) all inhibit higher numbers of adoption by Latino parents. In addition, if foster and/or adoption agencies are not community-friendly—specifically, if they do not have Spanish-speaking staff as well as individuals who understand cultural specificities of the many groups within Latino and Hispanic culture—Latino parents will be less likely to trust these agencies.

While there are many visceral emotions at the heart of this discussion, the issue at hand is whether or not the federal government should play a role in facilitating transracial adoption. Interestingly enough, the term itself is inaccurate. If the issue were transracial adoption, then steps would be taken to facilitate adoption of white children by African American parents. At issue here is the adoption of African American children by white parents, and that should remain clear as you consider your feelings on the topic.

Building on that point, it is striking that the discussion focuses on adoption by white families of children of color. Rarely do we see parents of color who have adopted a white child. This may simply be due to the fact that there is no shortage of children of color awaiting adoption and that most parents of color who are able to adopt a child say they would like to give a home to a child of color because of the lower chances that child has for adoption. It would be interesting to examine, however, the issues that would arise were the situation reversed. What are the cultural traditions of being white in the United States? What kinds of information and training would parents of color need in order to parent a child who is different from them? In this culture, the questions are almost moot—but interesting fodder for discussion all the same.

Suggested Readings

Howard Altstein, Marygold S. Melli, Rita James Simon, and Howard Marygold, *The Case for Transracial Adoption* (American University Press, 1994).

Hawley Fogg-Davis, *The Ethics of Transracial Adoption* (Cornell University Press, 2002).

Madelyn Freundlich, *Adoption and Ethics: The Role of Race, Culture, and National Origin in Adoption* (Child Welfare League of America, 2000).

Sandra Patton, *Birthmarks: Transracial Adoption in Contemporary America* (New York University Press, 2000).

A. R. Sharma, M. K. McGue, and P. L. Benson, "The Emotional and Behavioral Adjustment of United States Adopted Adolescents: Part 1. An Overview," *Children & Youth Services Review* (vol. 18, 1996).

Rita James Simon and Howard Altstein, *Adoption Across Borders* (Rowman & Littlefield Publishing, 2000).

Rita James Simon and Howard Altstein, *Adoption, Race, and Identity: From Infancy to Young Adulthood* (Transaction Publishing, 2002).

Gail Steinberg and Beth Hall, *Inside Transracial Adoption* (Perspectives Press, 2000).

Richard C. Tessler, Gail Gamache, and Liming Liu, *West Meets East: Americans Adopt Chinese Children* (Praeger Publications Text, 1999).

Contributors to This Volume

EDITOR

ELIZABETH SCHROEDER is a professional trainer and consultant in the areas of sexuality, counseling, and nonprofit administration and supervision. She has provided trainings throughout the United States to youth-serving professionals and to teens, presented at national conferences, and written about sexuality issues and training for a range of national newsletters, magazines, and monographs. Most recently, she is the author of a chapter on Nepal for *The International Encyclopedia of Sexuality*, 5th ed., to be published in 2003, and of a chapter on counseling skills for a health counseling textbook to be published in the fall of 2002. Recently moving into the international arena, she has developed adult peer educator and teacher training programs on sexuality and reproductive health in Kathmandu, Nepal. She also serves as a sexuality expert for the Network for Family Life Education's award–winning Web site, Sex, Etc.

Schroeder is the former associate vice president of education and training at Planned Parenthood of New York City, where she established the agency's first professional training institute for social service and school professionals. Before that she was the manager of education and special projects at Planned Parenthood Federation of America, where she coordinated the production of their multiple-award-winning video kit for families with adolescent children entitled, *Talking About Sex: A Guide for Families*.

Schroeder is a recipient of the Apple Blossom Award, which is a national award that recognizes a Planned Parenthood education or training director who has "risen quickly to the forefront with new ideas, energy, and commitment." An adjunct professor of human sexuality and health counseling at Montclair State University, Schroeder earned a master's degree in social work from New York University and is pursuing a doctorate in human sexuality education at Widener University.

STAFF

Theodore Knight   List Manager
David Brackley   Senior Developmental Editor
Juliana Gribbins   Developmental Editor
Rose Gleich   Administrative Assistant
Brenda S. Filley   Director of Production/Design
Juliana Arbo   Typesetting Supervisor
Diane Barker   Proofreader
Richard Tietjen   Publishing Systems Manager
Larry Killian   Copier Coordinator

AUTHORS

ALEXANDER GRAHAM BELL ASSOCIATION FOR THE DEAF AND HARD OF HEARING is an international membership organization and resource center on hearing loss and spoken language approaches and related issues. Founded in 1890 by Alexander Graham Bell, the association offers a wide range of programs, services, and information on a vast array of issues pertaining to hearing loss.

AMERICAN CIVIL LIBERTIES UNION (ACLU), a nonprofit and nonpartisan organization, was founded in 1920 and works to preserve the individual rights and liberties of all Americans.

DIANE D. ARONSON is the former executive director of RESOLVE, the national infertility association, and a member of the National Institutes of Health (NIH) Embryo Research Panel. She is a coauthor and editor of RESOLVE's *Resolving Infertility: Understanding the Options and Choosing Solutions When You Want to Have a Baby* (HarperResource, 2001).

STEPHEN BASKERVILLE teaches political science at Howard University in Washington, D.C. Baskerville taught at the Department of Politics and European Studies at Palacky University in the Czech Republic, from 1992 to 1997. He serves as spokesman for Men, Fathers, and Children International, a coalition of 12 fatherhood organizations from nine countries (including the Czech Republic) and serves on the advisory board of Gendercide Watch, a human rights organization that monitors gender-based killings.

SANDRA LIPSITZ BEM is professor of psychology and women's studies at Cornell University. Her research interests focus on the social construction of gender and sexuality. In 1995 she was selected as an "Eminent Woman in Psychology" by the divisions of General Psychology and the History of Psychology of the American Psychological Association. She is the author of the award-winning book *The Lenses of Gender* (Yale University Press, 1993).

JAMES BOVARD is the 1996 Warren T. Brookes Fellow in Environmental Journalism at the Competitive Enterprise Institute, a free-market, public policy group in Washington, D.C. He is a frequent contributor to the editorial pages of the *Wall Street Journal, Playbook, The American Spectator,* and other publications. He is the author of several books, including *Shakedown: How Government Screws You From A to Z* (Viking Penguin, 1995) and *Lost Rights: The Destruction of American Liberty* (St. Martin's Press, 1994).

MYRON H. BRIGHT is the senior circuit judge for the U.S. Court of Appeals, Eighth Circuit. He is the author and coauthor of numerous publications about national and state-specific objections at trial, and he is the recipient of the 1997 Francis Rawle Award for outstanding achievement in post-admission legal education.

B. CHERTIN is on the faculty of health science at Ben-Gurion University in Jerusalem, Israel.

TERESA STANTON COLLETT is a professor of law at South Texas College of Law, specializing in professional ethics and ethical issues in the law.

Recent publications relating to family issues include "Independence or Interdependence? A Christian Response to Liberal Feminists," in Michael W. McConnell, Robert F. Cochran, Jr., and Angela C. Carmella, eds., *Christian Perspectives on Legal Thought* (Yale University Press, 2001).

STEPHANIE COONTZ teaches history and family studies at the Evergreen State College in Olympia, Washington. She is the national co-chair of the Council on Contemporary Families and the author of *The Way We Never Were: American Families and the Nostalgia Trap* (Basic Books, 2000); *The Way We Really Are: Coming to Terms With America's Changing Families* (Basic Books, 2000); and *The Social Origins of Private Life: A History of American Families, 1600-1900* (W. W. Norton & Company, 1988).

MARY CRAWFORD is the director of the Women's Studies Program and professor in the Department of Psychology at the University of Connecticut. She is the author, with Rhoda K. Unger, of *Women and Gender: A Feminist Psychology*, 3rd ed. (McGraw-Hill, 1999) and editor, with Ellen B. Kimmel, of *Innovations in Feminist Psychological Research*, vols. 1 & 2 of *Psychology of Women Quarterly Series* (Cambridge University Press, 2000).

TIMOTHY J. DAILEY is a senior writer/analyst for cultural studies for the Family Research Council, where he specializes in countering the homosexual agenda and other perceived threats to the institutions of marriage and the family.

ALICE DOMURAT DREGER is an assistant professor of science and technology studies in the Lyman Briggs School, a division of the College of Natural Science at Michigan State University. She is also adjunct assistant professor in the Center for Ethics and Humanities in the Life Sciences. She is the author of *Hermaphrodites and the Medical Invention of Sex* (Harvard University Press, 1998); *Intersex in the Age of Ethics* (University Publishing Group, 1999); and many published articles.

GREG D. ERKEN is executive director for Of the People, a nonprofit, nonpartisan grassroots organization working to enact a proposed parental-rights amendment to state constitutions.

PATRICK FAGAN, a resident scholar in family and culture at The Heritage Foundation, served as deputy assistant secretary of health and human services during the Bush administration. A native of Ireland, he earned his master's degree in psychology at University College Dublin and has pursued doctoral studies at The American University.

AMICUR FARKAS is the director of the Urology Department at Shaare Zedek Medical Center. Farkas is also on the faculty of health science at Ben-Gurion University in Jerusalem, Israel.

BARBARA LOE FISHER is cofounder and president of the National Vaccine Information Center (NVIC). She is the author of *The Consumer's Guide to Childhood Vaccines* (National Vaccine Information Center, 1997) and coauthor, with Harris L. Coulter, of *DPT: A Shot in the Dark* (Warner Books, 1986).

DAVID GATELY was a graduate student of psychology at the Ohio State University in Columbus, Ohio, when he coauthored "Favorable Outcomes in Children After Parental Divorce" for *The Journal of Divorce and Remarriage.*

ROBERT P. GEORGE is a McCormick Professor of Jurisprudence, a professor of politics, and director of the James Madison Program in American Ideals and Institutions. He is the author of *In Defense of Natural Law* (Oxford University Press, 2001) and *Making Men Moral: Civil Liberties and Public Morality* (Oxford University Press, 1995). He is also the editor of *Natural Law Theory: Contemporary Essays* (Oxford University Press, 1992). He is a former presidential appointee to the United States Commission on Civil Rights.

IRITH HADAS-HALPREN is director of the radiology and imaging department at Shaare Zedek Medical Center and is on the faculty of health science at Ben-Gurion University in Jerusalem, Israel.

CATHERINA HURLBURT is a public policy writer for Concerned Women for America in Washington, D.C. Concerned Women for America is the nation's largest public policy women's organization with more than 500,000 members nationwide.

IRWIN A. HYMAN is a professor of school psychology and the director of the National Center for the Study of Corporal Punishment and Alternatives at Temple University. He is the author of numerous books and articles, including *School Discipline and School Violence: The Teacher Variance Approach* (Allyn & Bacon, 1997).

GERALDINE JENSEN is the founder and president of The Association for Children for Enforcement of Support (ACES), a nonprofit, child-support organization.

DARLENE ADDIE KENNEDY is an assistant professor at Regent University School of Law. She is also the author of "Let's Hold Juveniles Responsible for Their Crimes," *National Policy Analysis* (August 1997).

LAMBDA LEGAL DEFENSE AND EDUCATION FUND is a national organization committed to achieving full recognition of the civil rights of lesbian, gay, bisexual, and transgender individuals, as well as people living with HIV or AIDS, through impact litigation, education, and public policy work. The organization pursues litigation in such areas as discrimination in employment, housing, public accommodations, and the military; HIV/AIDS-related discrimination and public policy issues; parenting and relationship issues; equal marriage rights; equal employment and domestic partnership benefits; "sodomy" law challenges; immigration issues; anti-gay initiatives; and free speech and equal protection rights.

MERRILL MATTHEWS, JR., is the vice president for domestic policy and the director of the Center for Health Policy Studies at the National Center for Policy Analysis, a Dallas-based, public policy research institute founded in February 1983.

RUTH G. McROY is associate dean for research and director of the Center for Social Work Research at the School of Social Work at the University of Texas,

Austin. She is also the Ruby Lee Piester Centennial Professor in Services to Children and Families at the university.

MARSHALL MILLER is a speaker, writer, and researcher on unmarried relationships. In 1998 Miller and his partner, Dorian Solot, founded the Alternatives to Marriage Project, a national, nonprofit organization that advocates for equality and fairness for unmarried people. Miller was named a Person to Watch in 2001 by *USA Today* for his work as an advocate for the rights of the unmarried.

NATIONAL ASSOCIATION OF THE DEAF (NAD), established in 1880, is the oldest and largest constituency organization safeguarding the accessibility and civil rights of 28 million deaf and hard of hearing Americans in education, employment, health care, and telecommunications.

JENNIFER L. PIERCE is an associate professor of sociology at the University of Minnesota. Her research interests include gender, feminist theory, race relations, the sociology of work and occupations, sociological theory, qualitative methods, and the sociology of emotions. She is the author of *Gender Trials: Emotional Lives in Contemporary Law Firms* (University of California, 1995) and coeditor of the anthology *Is Academic Feminism Dead? Theory in Practice* (New York University Press, 2000).

PLANNED PARENTHOOD FEDERATION OF AMERICA, INC., is the world's oldest and largest voluntary reproductive health care organization. Founded by Margaret Sanger in 1916 as America's first birth control clinic, Planned Parenthood believes in the fundamental right of each individual, throughout the world, to manage his or her fertility, regardless of the individual's income, marital status, race, ethnicity, sexual orientation, age, national origin, or residence.

DAVID POPENOE is a professor of sociology at Rutgers University in New Brunswick, New Jersey, where he is also codirector of the National Marriage Project and former dean of social and behavioral sciences.

S. DUBOSE RAVENEL is a board-certified pediatrician in private practice in High Point, North Carolina. He served for 11 years on the pediatric faculty of the University of North Carolina School of Medicine prior to entering private practice.

ANDREW I. SCHWEBEL is a professor in the Department of Psychology at the College of Social and Behavioral Sciences at Ohio State University in Columbus, Ohio. He is coauthor, with Mark A. Fine, of *Understanding and Helping Families: A Cognitive-Behavioral Approach* (Lawrence Erlbaum, 1994). He is also coauthor, with Bryce F. Sullivan, of "Birth-Order Position, Gender, and Irrational Relationship Beliefs," *Journal of Individual Psychology* (Spring 1996).

DENISE A. SEGURA is associate professor of sociology and director of the Center for Chicano Studies at the University of California at Santa Barbara. She is the author of *Latinos in Isla Vista: A Report on the Quality of Life Among Latino Immigrants* (UCSB Research Report, 1999). She is coauthor, with Batriz M. Pesquera, of "Chicana Feminisms: Their Political Context and Contemporary Expressions," in Jo Freeman, ed., *Women: A Feminist Perspective*, 5th ed. (Mayfield Publishing Company, 1995).

STEVEN P. SHELOV is chairman of the Department of Pediatrics at Maimonides Medical Center and professor of pediatrics at the State University of New York Health Science Center in Brooklyn. Immediately prior to these appointments, Shelov was professor and vice chairman of pediatrics and director of the Division of Pediatrics Education at the Albert Einstein College of Medicine, Montefiore Medical Center, Bronx, New York.

BARRY G. SILVERMAN is a judge for the U.S. Court of Appeals, Ninth Circuit. He earned his B.A. degree from Arizona State University in 1973 and his J.D. from the same institution in 1976. He was appointed to the Ninth Circuit Court of Appeals by former president William Jefferson Clinton.

DORIAN SOLOT is the executive director and cofounder of the Alternatives to Marriage Project, a national, nonprofit organization that advocates for equality and fairness for unmarried people. Along with partner Marshall Miller, she authored the book, *Unmarried to Each Other: The Essential Guide to Living Together and Staying Together*, to be published in November 2002. A speaker, writer, and researcher, Solot has appeared on CNN, the *NBC Nightly News*, and MSNBC.

DEN A. TRUMBULL is a board-certified pediatrician in private practice in Montgomery, Alabama. He is a member of the Section on Developmental and Behavioral Pediatrics of the American Academy of Pediatrics.

UNITED STATES FUND FOR UNICEF was created to promote the survival, protection, and development of all children worldwide through fundraising, advocacy, and education. The United States Fund for UNICEF is one of 37 national committees set up around the world to raise money for UNICEF, which works in more than 160 countries and territories to provide health care, clean water, improved nutrition, and education to millions of children in Africa, Asia, Central and Eastern Europe, Latin America, and the Middle East.

ANASTASIA VOLKONSKY is a writer and researcher based in San Francisco, California. She is a founding director of PROMISE, an organization dedicated to combating sexual exploitation.

JACK C. WESTMAN is professor emeritus of psychiatry at the University of Wisconsin Medical School in Madison, Wisconsin. His many books include *Born to Belong: Becoming Who I Am* (C. S. S. Publishing Company, 1997) and, with Charles D. Gill, *Licensing Parents: Can We Prevent Child Abuse and Neglect?* (Da Capo Press, 1994).

BARBARA DAFOE WHITEHEAD speaks and writes about family and child well-being. Her work has appeared in many publications, including *The American Enterprise, Commonweal, The Wilson Quarterly, Slate*, the *Times Literary Supplement*, the *New York Times*, the *Wall Street Journal*, the *Washington Post, Reader's Digest*, the *Los Angeles Times*, and the *Boston Globe*. She is the author of *The Divorce Culture* (Alfred A. Knopf, 1997).

PHILIP YANCEY writes articles and a monthly column for *Christianity Today* magazine, for which he also serves as editor at large. He has authored numerous books, including *The Jesus I Never Knew* (Zondervan Publishing House, 1995) and *What's So Amazing About Grace?* (Zondervan Publishing House, 1997).

KARL ZINSMEISTER, editor in chief of *The American Enterprise*, is a J.B. Fuqua Fellow at the American Enterprise Institute, the major Washington, D.C. think tank that is the magazine's publisher. He has been published in many places in addition to *The American Enterprise*, including *The Atlantic Monthly, Reader's Digest, The Wilson Quarterly, The Public Interest, National Review, Reason, Commentary*, the *Wall Street Journal*, the *New York Times*, and the *Washington Post*.

Index